BOTH
OF
ME

BOTH
OF
ME

MARY STUART

Doubleday & Company, Inc., Garden City, New York
1980

For the use of their photographs, grateful acknowledgment is made to Bob Deutsch, Lois Greenfield, Robert Roland, Shelly Smith Studios, CBS, Daytime TV, TV by Day, and the Toronto Globe and Mail.

ISBN 0-385-14494-6
Library of Congress Catalog Card Number 79-8038
Copyright © 1980 by Mary Stuart
All Rights Reserved
Printed in the United States of America
First Edition

To my mother,
my father,
my brother

To my daughter
and my son

And to life that is ending
the day it's begun.

There are many friends whose names do not appear in these pages, but they are here in spirit and will always be with me, especially the ones who have written me so many thousands of beautiful letters over the years.

There is one person whose support and wise counsel made it all possible. For that, and so much more, I thank my friend Carolyn Blakemore.

For extremely sensitive copy editing, I thank Glenn Rounds.

And for months of sharing every page, love and gratitude to Pam Kristian.

AUTHOR'S NOTE

There is no real reason, I can think of, to record the events of a life that has included no major accomplishments unless there is truth between the pages that is recognizable and useful to someone else. I have been as truthful as I am able, but I have discovered that truth is not always an absolute. There is the truth of the words spoken, or the action taken. There is also the effect of the words or the actions, and that seems to vary widely. Circumstances and experience change or color the meaning, sometimes distorting it completely.

I have been looking back down the corridors of my own life for quite a while, shining a light into long-forgotten corners. The dust I have accumulated is certainly mine to examine if I choose, and now it is yours to keep or sweep away, but the light has also caught glimpses of other lives forever tangled with my own and to them I owe a debt of gratitude or apology. The imperfect truth of the moments did not always show them to advantage, and most certainly does not even attempt to show the whole person. It is the effect of each moment passing that tells the story. It is what I felt that was real, and therefore the truth as I see it.

*BOTH
OF
ME*

If you have told three distinctly different, very nice young men that you would love to have lunch on Saturday, and you know very well that it is now Saturday and the clock says it is eleven-thirty and not only have you done nothing to straighten out the mess you have created, you are not even out of bed, the chances are, you are not really dealing with it. When you know in your heart that all three of the gentlemen expect not only to have lunch but also to spend the afternoon and go to dinner, and two of them believe you are going to marry them because you have told them that you would love to, but really the third one is looking very attractive at the moment, there are only two things you can possibly do. You can be honest and straightforward and explain that your feelings have changed, or you can leave immediately for Texas and take a job selling heavy farm equipment.

Actually, what I did was to call the desk of the little hotel where I lived on West Forty-fourth and tell the clerk to tell any callers that I was suddenly very ill, and went back to bed.

I didn't know what to say to Norwell. I hadn't seen him since California and that was two whole months and a lot had happened. I had dearly loved Norwell in California. I loved his mama and papa and the big, noisy mansion where they lived in Beverly Hills with linen sheets on all the beds. I loved the tennis lessons and the riding lessons and the brandy milk punch. However, I was in New York and in my mind Norwell was away, far away, in California and the handsome young dentist who fixed my teeth when the braces came off was here and he was six foot five. I loved his family, too. I loved the warm kitchen in the Bronx and the chopped liver and the chicken soup. He had an apartment on Central Park West with a view of the park. But then I met Richard.

When I told Norwell I loved him and wanted to marry him, I meant it with all my heart. He was going to take me to live in Paris and we would spend our honeymoon at St. Moritz. Now he was in New York with an engagement ring in his pocket and I suddenly realized I didn't know how to speak French and I couldn't ski.

I had truly loved the handsome dentist. He liked to take me tea dancing and I could stand under his arm. I loved to drive all over Central Park on a cool night with the top down. Now his father was ill and he kept saying the "family" should all be with him. I wasn't ready to be family and besides I had met Richard.

Richard was tall too, and slim and handsome. He had gone to Dartmouth, and he wore Brooks Brothers suits and his family lived in a duplex on Park Avenue. Richard was charming and witty. Richard was smooth and Richard was cool.

That was late in September of 1950. I had arrived about a month before with $800 left of the $1,300 I got when I sold my car. I was down to about $500 and there was almost nothing coming in. The rent on my room was only $40 a week, and they didn't have room service, so if I went out to a drugstore to make phone calls there were no extras on the bill. It was the taxi fares that kept mounting up. Every time I had an appointment it would take me so long to get ready I was too late to make the bus or take a chance on getting lost in the subway. The little pad of traveler's checks was dwindling.

I was luckier than most young actresses starting out in New York. I had a few credits and I knew people. I even had an agent. I was also keenly aware that there was absolutely nothing besides a little singing and a little acting that I could do to support myself, except possibly going to Texas to sell tractors. I had never in my life even been close to a tractor. Still, that idiotic fantasy lurked in the back of my mind as a possible means of escape if it became necessary.

I was booked on a couple of TV game shows that first month, but they didn't pay money in those days. One of them gave me a ham, which I gave to the dentist's mother, and the other one gave me a trick golf stick, with interchangeable heads, or feet, whichever it is. I kept that behind my door, since it wasn't such a great hotel.

I didn't do any actual acting until my old buddy Yul Brynner came to town. He called some people and got me a job on "The Web" with Eddie Albert and Margo. They said I was very good, but all I remember is falling desperately in love with Mr. Albert and getting lost trying to find the studio. It was somewhere in Grand Central Station, and if you took the wrong elevator you had to cross a kind of catwalk over the rotunda. I always did.

I spent as little time as possible in the hotel. It was a dreary little room, and besides I hated being alone and used any excuse to avoid it. I knew a few people, and friends moved here from California. Bill Harbach and his wife Dougy had an apartment in an old brownstone on East Fifty-fifth, where they invited me to a couple of parties. Yul used to stand across the street from the hotel and whistle for me to come out and play. Harry Kurnitz came to town for a week and took me to dinner at Sardi's and parties at Leonard Bernstein's, and I was going out with Richard. But the phone company in California had tracked me down and I owed them $250.

I thought maybe I could get back into singing. My total experience as a professional singer consisted of weekends with Bob Wills and his Texas Playboys, when I was a kid, one week at the Ritz Theatre in Tulsa singing "Rose of Washington Square," and a contest I won when I was nine. The winner got to come back on Saturday night and sing with the name band they brought in for weekends, and that Saturday it just happened to be Duke Ellington. Aunt Ruth had taught me to sing "Mood Indigo," so I was, what you might call, a natural. Nobody laughed and they let me sleep on a table in the kitchen between shows. Since I was going for the biggies I didn't mention my debut, but I did stand out when my first grade Sunday School put on a show. They were singing "Jesus Loves Me," and I didn't know the words, so I sang "Ain't Much Sense Sittin' on a Fence All by Yourself in the Moonlight."

I went over to the Brill Building on Broadway and started knocking on doors. I did make a few demo discs for Chappell Music and was glad to get the five dollars and the dinners Micky Addy bought me. Then out of the blue he called and asked if I would sing a new song they were pushing called "Far Away Places" on "The Bob Smith Show." Of course I said yes, and all the way to the Brill Building I replayed one of my favorite fantasies: the true-life version of *A Star Is Born*.

A piano player ran through it a couple of times to make sure I knew the tune, then I asked casually when the show was.

"Eight o'clock, rehearsal is at four."

"Today!" I remember experiencing the first flash of panic, but after all, that is the way Judy Garland had always done it. The leading lady in all those movies swallowed her bubble gum at three in the afternoon and by curtain time she knew all the dances and all the songs. If she could do it, so could I.

With the lyrics clutched in my hand I ran over to the Harbachs' and borrowed a dress from Dougy. Then I went back to the hotel and got into the shower. It was the quickest way to warm up the voice, and, besides, it made me sound good. I wouldn't turn on the radio, or even let the maid into the room. I just kept singing that song over and over. I was afraid to tip my head for fear it would spill out altogether. At four I went to the theatre, and they said Dougy's dress was cut too low so I bought a flower to stuff in my front. The rehearsal went fine. They said they wanted me to sing a duet with Mr. Smith and that was simple. The words were on cue cards and I just had to sing harmony. It did take my mind off "Far Away Places" and I had to sit in a dressing room by myself for half an hour to get it running again.

At eight the show went on the air. We stood in a tight little group in the wings while the band played the opening, Bob Smith did his monologue, and the first two acts went on. That did it! Somewhere in that five minutes, with all the music and applause, I lost the song. My mind went absolutely blank and froze solid. I groped frantically for a word or a piece of the melody, some clue, anything! "Far away . . . Far away . . . Far away what?"

To my horror I locked onto another song called "Long Ago and Far Away" and the needle stuck! I was on next and very sure I was going to be sick. In desperation I told myself that it was really going to be all right, because Mr. Smith would announce what I was going to sing and the band would play an intro and it would all come back. I stood there listening with all my little heart and soul.

The band played a fanfare, the stage manager pointed, and I held my breath as Mr. Smith said, "And now, ladies and gentlemen, Miss Mary Stuart." Then my little heart and soul sank. No title, no hint, no nothing.

The audience applauded, the band played some inane vamp that sounded like nothing I had ever heard, and I walked at least a mile to the mike, smiling and bowing, blinded by the lights, still running the wrong damn song!

"Long ago and far away . . . Long ago and . . ."

The conductor dropped his baton and the next two words fell automatically out of my mouth.

"Far away . . . PLACES, with strange sounding names!"

Miracle of miracles! I was at the right place in the wrong song! The next three minutes are a little blurred, but the rest of the words clicked into my mind like lemons lining up on a slot machine and I lucked out.

The Harbachs had watched the show. They said I looked real nice and sounded fine, but, then, they were friends. I gave Dougy back her dress and put the flower in my toothpaste glass at the hotel. A star had not been born, and if I'd had any idea how to go about it, it was time for some serious thinking.

"The Bob Smith Show" paid me $100 and I owed the hotel $40. The traveler's checks added up to $250, but the California Phone Company was threatening to sue for exactly that amount and I had a lot of time on my hands.

Being an actress can be a nebulous thing if you are not actually acting. You have decided to tell stories and create characters and fantasies as a way of life, and you have to create a character for yourself and believe a fantasy just to live. I was becoming a master at it. It said "Occupation—Actress" on my driver's license and the application for unemployment insurance. What did that mean? It meant I was good at play pretend, and so was every kid on the block. I was finally old enough to vote and even sign a contract—if there was one to sign—but I had barely skinned my way out of high school. For three years in Hollywood a lot of people had said I had Star Quality, but I had looked to the heavens and I'd been to MGM. Stars shine with reflected light or glow from within. I had no idea where the switch was.

The shows and the dinners and the parties were isolated little pools of light on a very dark stage. Like Jimmy Durante making a very long exit, I kept running to the next one. I wasn't earning a living and I didn't belong anyplace, certainly not at the Bernsteins'. They didn't know me and I didn't know them. I couldn't afford a cup of coffee at Sardi's and Yul liked me because I could sing harmony with him. I was seeing Richard, but he was hardly supporting himself and was definitely uncommitted. My room at the hotel looked like I was either moving in or moving out. That is the way I felt.

I had walked away from Hollywood because people I had never laid eyes on were controlling my life. Now I had a whole pile of pieces to a puzzle but I'd lost the top of the box, so I didn't know what the picture was supposed to be. I was very good at making up pictures and I was always trying to make the pieces fit. In two months I had erased Hollywood, Paris, and Central Park West. Now I was rearranging them again. The silhouette was definitely Park Avenue and the colors tended toward gray flannel, but too many pieces were still blank.

I had no idea in real-life terms what I wanted, so it did not seem unreasonable to want it all. I wanted love, perfect, pure, beautiful love forever filled with romance and surprise. Of course I wanted a career, but after Hollywood I didn't want the kind of stardom that takes up all the room in your life. Just a little stardom would be fine. I would do a play one year and have a baby the next. I would always be in demand, naturally, so the only problem would be choosing which play I wanted to do. You must admit it wasn't a bad plan, and I don't remember doubting for one minute it would happen. I remember fear but never doubt.

Since I hated my hotel room, I sat on the third floor at NBC a lot. That is where actors used to sit when they were between shows, and I had plenty of time between mine. One afternoon a young actor named Ross Martin stopped to talk to me. He was trying to get some people together, he said, for a new acting class. It was a new method developed by a man named David Alexander just for television actors.

Now I had never actually studied acting anywhere, anytime. There were drama coaches in Hollywood and dialogue directors, but "Method" was still a vague, mysterious word.

That first class met in a little rehearsal room on Broadway and about fifteen people showed up, fifteen serious, thoughtful actors. I recognized Leon Janney and Cliff Robertson from the third floor at NBC, and I had heard Jack Lemmon and his wife Cynthia Stone were preparing a new television show. Hal Cooper and his wife Pat had their own children's show on Dumont TV, and of course Ross Martin was my new friend. For the most part everybody there was already established and successful. It was a class for professionals—and me.

David Alexander was slight and dark and electric. He talked briefly in what might as well have been a foreign tongue about "Actions," and "Intentions," and "Images." Then he announced that we would begin, right then and there, with animal images! We were all to think of an animal, decide what that animal is feeling, and be that animal, right out in front of everybody, and nobody seemed to think that was odd. There was a bear, I remember, huge and awkward in the tiny space and humiliated by the imaginary chain around his neck. There was a very formal penguin and several elegant jungle cats. I was a frightened fawn, which in retrospect seems fitting.

I had no idea where David's ideas were leading us, but I knew immediately it was what I needed, whatever it was. David was so sure. There was knowledge in him that gave him power over himself, and by the end of that evening there was no doubt in my mind that I would pay the fifty dollars and let the phone company sue.

When I first knew Richard he was working for a research organization testing the new TV commercials. He would con fifty people into a dreary little theatre on Sixth Avenue and get them to sit there and react. If it wasn't raining that was difficult.

He lived in a second-floor walk-up on Fifty-second Street which he rented out in the daytime to his friend John. John was a writer, and he and his wife Jane had just adopted two baby boys, so home was no place to work. John wasn't at all pleased when I started hanging around. He made it clear to Richard that he was not concerned with his morals, but during the day the place was his.

Richard had a lot of friends. He had grown up in Scarsdale and kept up with, I think, everybody he had ever known. He had friends from high school, college, the Army, even the boys' camp he had gone to in Maine, and they were still close. They had shared college and a war and much of their lives. I had not been to college and I was younger, so I had missed their war, but being with Richard made me part of the group.

Being part of a group was a totally new experience for me. We went to his friends' apartments for dinner or met them for drinks and went out. Some of his friends had moved to the suburbs or to other states, but he had a car and we drove as far as Philadelphia to see his friend Bill Dickenson, who was editor of the *Bulletin,* or New Hampshire to stay with the McLanes. The McLanes were a beautiful family with six kids. When Charlie took them all skiing, one between his knees, one under each arm, and one on his shoulders, he looked like a Christmas tree. All Richard's friends were beginning careers and families, and I liked helping fix dinner and clear the table. I liked playing with the babies and the dogs. I loved driving to places far away and being with Richard.

Most of all, I liked Richard's mother and father. Albert was very thin and very tall and almost too perfectly cast as the gentle

Englishman. Helen was tiny and so full of indignant outrage she tended to explode fairly regularly.

Helen wrote letters to her congressman and sent telegrams to the President. Albert sat at the big old Steinway and played show tunes from sheet music. Sometimes his friend Stanley Holloway would be there and they'd do all the old music hall routines.

Helen was born in a time when well-to-do women were trained to do absolutely nothing. When she married Albert her mother told him:

"You know she can't boil water."

"Good!" he said, "I don't like boiled water."

I loved dinners in the elegantly shabby duplex and the cook who had been with them since Richard was a baby.

One night Richard mentioned, quite casually, that an old friend of his from Chicago, named Roy Winsor, was going to be in town and we would have dinner with him on Tuesday. On Tuesday I went to the restaurant and so did Mr. Winsor, but Richard never showed up. We waited over cocktails for an hour, then gave up and ordered dinner.

The hour of cocktails had eased the tension considerably, and Mr. Winsor talked a lot about Chicago. The great radio serials had nearly all come from there and he had worked with everybody. He had directed my favorite of all time, "Vic and Sade." He had written or directed "Ma Perkins," "Houseboat Hannah," and "Sky King." He supervised "Lone Journey" and "The Goldbergs." He had created and written "Hawkins Falls," which was the first nighttime show in serial form, and had written for "Garroway at Large," which was produced by another old friend of Richard's, Charlie Andrews.

Now he was in New York, he said, to develop new shows for daytime television. I will admit that I was not unaware of the possibilities that Mr. Winsor seemed to represent. He had just said that he was developing new shows, not a show, but shows for daytime television, and that meant he would probably be hiring actresses. In the three years I spent in Hollywood, I had met a lot of "big executives" and that little catchword "developing" sounded definitely indefinite. Still, what's an unemployed actress to do? What, after all, did I have to lose? Also, an hour of cock-tails can help a person rise to an occasion. As it happened, I had read an article in that Sunday's *Times* about women, what they wanted and what they needed. It was not my habit to read the Sunday *Times*, so that was a stroke of pure dumb luck. But it must have been more than that. I was, after all, one of the women the article was talking about. Even though I wasn't mar-ried and had no children, I was one of the women who grew up in the thirties and forties assuming that life really centered around a home, which is probably why I read the piece in the first place, and why it stayed in my mind.

Mr. Winsor said that Procter & Gamble was interested in moving some of its radio serials to television, but CBS didn't think it would work. Though women had listened to the radio while they did their housework, nobody was sure they would sit down to watch a television set in the middle of the day.

"They will if it's important to them," I said.

"What do you mean?" he quite naturally asked, and I knew very well it was just a nice round statement that meant absolutely nothing, but I had my article to fall back on.

A little information can be a wonderful thing. It does not cause you to question what you are saying. I had been living for three years in one room and cooking on a hot plate, but before Mr. Winsor's very eyes, in a crowded restaurant, I proceeded to build a very pleasant fantasy house and move into it.

I had a lot to say, as I recall, about creativity and the satis-faction of a home and family. After all, I did believe that no mat-ter what else she may want to accomplish, a woman needs a home and a family to feel complete. That was already a big part of my plan.

When he dropped me off at my hotel, he said he would like to talk to me about playing the lead in a show called "Search for Happiness" that he was working on. He didn't call, and I didn't think he would, but I remembered something I had read when I was just a little girl. It was a story in one of the radio fan maga-zines about leading ladies on the soap operas. It said they made $500 a week and only worked two hours a day. Five hundred dol-lars a week seemed like enough money to do anything, and if you as we were all leaving he came up to me and said, "Roy Winsor has hired me to produce a show called 'Search for Happiness.' He said he wanted you to play the lead, and I think he's right. Let's have lunch tomorrow and talk about money."

That was it! That was all there was to it. I had auditioned without even knowing it! We did have lunch the next day and when he asked me how much I wanted, I knew exactly, $500 a week, of course!

I signed a contract for seven years that next week. I did realize it was the fourth one I had signed in three years, and somewhere in my mind I tried not to take it seriously, but that was too much to ask.

Everything had magically fallen into place. I had a job and I was in love, but it was better than that, because the job and the man were both perfect. I had everything I needed for a perfect life. The show wasn't even on the air and Richard had never mentioned marriage, but those were details, and it was Christmas!

We did a kinescope audition of the show early in January, and except that the director had a nervous breakdown in the middle of it, everything went fine. Procter & Gamble was delighted, and decided that we would go on the air May 1, 1951. The only thing that had changed was the title. We would be called "Search for Tomorrow."

Richard's company folded in January, but that never worried him. We went out and celebrated, and he suggested we go to Europe and blow the $2,000 he had saved. I wasn't even tempted. I adored Richard, but I wanted to marry him and spend the money getting settled. The thought of just having a wonderful time was terrifying.

Sometime in February I went to see the doctor. I had pain in my left side and was bleeding intermittently. He suggested a D & C, so I went into the hospital for a couple of days. That didn't seem to help, and matters continued to get worse. I was in and out of the hospital for the next six weeks. Then two big decisions were made. "Search" would not go on the air until September and I needed a major operation.

While I was in the hospital the doctor told me they had re-

only worked two hours a day you could surely have a home
family, the best of both worlds!

The reality of my days that October remained the
bought *Variety* and *Backstage* and made rounds. I went
Richard and once a week I went to class, which got n
more involved. We had begun to work with different im
bright lights shining in our eyes, or floors that are une
slanted, cold showers and tight hats. We were expe
with "obstacles" and we used the images to color them.
stacle was a persistent headache, a tight hat would ma
specific.

Finally, we began to do little pieces of scenes
using the "Actions" and "Intentions," and to my abso
ment a scene could be about heliotrope bathroom
still be a love scene! It was like discovering the Ro
That was the key! Acting was no longer just saying th
whatever emotion you could muster, the simple kin
tive play pretend I had depended on. Acting was t
human behavior, human feeling, all there to choose
choice was yours. I was learning to understand the te
tion of the script, and finding that an action coul
mood from anger to love to fear, and an image coul
tire character or a word.

I will never forget Bernie Grant doing a sc
Lear using the image of an ox head hanging in
window.

Perhaps it was the excitement and discipline
every week, perhaps it was simply being in the c
people, working with them, being part of the gi
ally, being an actor was taking on more and mc
was at least learning how to learn, how to conn
my mind to my fantasy. I was learning how to
concentrate, on more than one thing at a time,
rivers flowing. It would be years before I put i
learned to choose wisely, years before I felt th
David, but at least I was beginning to understar

I had never really noticed Charles Irving i
there as a director to observe and rarely part

moved a fibroid tumor from the uterus and cysts from the left tube. He said it was endometriosis and would probably come back, but the other tube was fine. He was in the doctor business and I was not, so except for a nagging suspicion that he had sewed me together wrong, I didn't think much about it.

It also became clear while I was in the hospital that I couldn't go back to my little hotel room, so Richard's parents, who were leaving for England, offered me their apartment. Their housekeeper would be there to take care of me. John and Richard packed my things and moved me out. I didn't hear the end of what a slob I was for many months, but I was getting well, and the phone company had lost me again.

One evening early in July, Richard announced abruptly, "Let's get married on the first of August. That way I'll never forget the date, because the bills will come in."

I had absolutely no money after the hospital, so I scurried around putting together a dreary little trousseau. I bought a navy blue suit for twenty-three dollars and a pink felt hat for two dollars and fifty cents. Our wedding day was hot and muggy and my hair sort of twitched up on one side and under on the other. Richard was his tall, slim, elegant self, also in navy blue. John and Jane were to be best man and matron of honor and they met us at the church, dressed in gray. Jane was in silk and was the only one at least comfortable in the heat. John, however, was determined to lend as much dignity as possible to the proceedings. He wore heavy gray-and-black-striped flannel and kept the vest buttoned till he turned purple.

We were married in the Unitarian church at the corner of Eighty-eighth and Lexington, and I had always pictured a wedding in exactly that kind of church. It had high arched windows with clear panes letting in the sunlight, simple pale wood pews, and pure white walls. But in my picture the church was filled with soft spring colors and friends all misty-eyed and smiling. Somehow we looked so out of place in our somber clothes and solemn expressions. Our footsteps resounded throughout the empty church and a little trickle of perspiration ran down my cheek from under that idiotic hat.

"Dearly beloved, we are gathered together . . ." Gathered

together? There were four of us, Jane and John and Mary and Dick! The marriage certificate read like a first grade primer and we looked like we had come to view the body.

We stepped out of the church into the blazing sun and walked down Lexington, stopping to buy a pound of lox for the wedding reception.

Richard and I sailed into marriage on the *Queen of Bermuda*. I remember very little of that trip because I spent most of it throwing up and discovering that champagne, nervousness, and ocean travel combine badly.

I do remember running into two old friends of mine on the boat. I introduced Richard to Betty and Oliver just before I made a dash for the ladies' room, and by the time I got back a lifelong friendship had begun.

Having been on only one honeymoon, perhaps I have no right to say this, but I do believe they were devised solely to test relationships.

I spent my honeymoon with Betty. She and Oliver were well-to-do and had taken a beautiful little cottage at Pink Beaches. We were not well-to-do and had a room in a house. Every morning we would pedal the two miles to their place, have lunch together, then Betty and I would lie on the beach and talk while the men played golf. We got adventuresome once and tried the bike, but Betty wrapped herself around a lamppost in the driveway so we went back to the beach.

Every night we would meet again and go out to dinner, always together. Only once did we attempt to dine alone. I think it was Richard's birthday. I was never sure. His was the tenth of August and mine was the fourth of July; I added the two together to make sure I would never forget his birthday. I didn't forget it, but I was always four days late. Anyway, for our big romantic evening, as Betty called it, we both got dressed up, had a drink on the patio of the house where we were staying, and started walking the half mile to the restaurant. We were so romantic we didn't even ride our bikes, but halfway there the sky opened and within two minutes we were both drowned. We sloshed back to our room, had a couple more drinks, and decided to nap till the rain stopped. We woke up at three, and of course everything was

closed. We never got dinner, I had an awful hangover, and we resolved never to try that again.

I suppose my fantasies about weddings and honeymoons
came right out of the *Ladies' Home Journals* and *Saturday Evening Posts* of my childhood, and I was probably silly. Richard and
I were not strangers to each other; it was a second marriage for us
both. Still, I longed for moonlight and romance. I needed, I
guess, to feel that the two of us were enough for each other, that
I did not have to compete for his attention. I had no idea how
deeply disappointed and frustrated I really was; didn't even make
a connection when I developed little flat warts all over my chin
two weeks later, and the doctor said they were psychosomatic.

I was married, and married to the man of my dreams. Almost
one month later, on September 3, 1951, "Search for Tomorrow"
went on the air.

It is difficult to describe the tension that accompanies any
kind of theatrical opening, at least for me. The passage between
the mouth and the stomach seems to close to any manner of
nourishment, other that coffee, which in turn creates a tension of
its own which will eventually numb the extremities. The pitch of
a voice that is normally mellow and warm will rise to a decibel
level that would shatter glass, and a body which has been carefully trained to obey the commands of the mind begins to wobble
and heave.

There is, mercifully, an automaton—a kind of klone—inside,
that takes over. It has been rehearsed, it knows the lines and the
moves, and it has been programmed with all the ingoing and outgoing emotional patterns. It is always prepared to go on whether
I can or not.

On Monday morning, September 3, 1951, there were about
twenty such klones moving around an old opera house, called
Liederkranz Hall, on Fifty-eighth Street. We had rehearsed in an
office on Madison Avenue at eight in the morning and walked
over to the studio. The actors put on their makeup and fiddled
with their hair, and the brass began to assemble.

Bill Craig had flown in from Procter & Gamble's main office

in Cincinnati. He looked calm and handsome and debonair as Cary Grant, but he had bought the show and committed P&G. His neck was out a mile. Roy Winsor kept prowling back and forth in the control room, and before the show was over the agency supervisor had chewed his handkerchief in half.

Charles Irving settled his ample body into the director's chair and looked out through the glass control room window to the studio floor. He had been hired originally to produce the show, but after the fiasco on our audition kinescope he became producer and director. None of us knew that he had never, before that day, directed a television show in his life. If there was ever a moment when he hesitated we didn't see it.

The first task was to rehearse and set cameras on the two live commercials. A model had been hired, and she stood ready with her mop and pail, her linoleum, and a box of Spic & Span. We were not only introducing a new show that day, we were introducing two new P&G products, Joy and Spic & Span. The Joy commercials were on film and only had to be cued into the show, but Spic & Span would be live for many months. We had exactly two hours of camera time. One was to be used for the two minutes of commercial and the other hour for the show. There were other little technicalities, like the opening billboard, the film chains, the announcer, and the organ levels, all of which had to be timed to exactly fourteen minutes and twenty-two seconds, and we still had a show to rehearse.

At ten-thirty we went into the studio and began. There were three scenes and a little short teaser, and as we went through the lines and the moves for the crew, the stagehands began to build the set around us. They weren't sets the way you think of sets today, just pieces of sets. Doors and window frames were hung on piano wire from the grid to indicate walls. Then the furniture was grouped in the imaginary space. A black velour cyclorama was hung around the walls of the studio, serving, we hoped, to hide the clutter, absorb light, and give the illusion of enclosed areas. What this actually did was give every room we used, the offices, the living rooms, even the kitchens, black walls.

When the sets were "hung" and the furniture pushed into place, the lighting director tilted the trays of fluorescent lights directly down on us, and what looked like a surrealistic nightmare was complete. It was gloomy but expedient, and expediency was the important thing. We only had that hour and we had exactly $8,025.75 a week to do the whole show. That $8,025.75 had to cover camera time, sets, lights, salaries, even the coffee and bagels we ate in the morning. A lot of people bet Charles couldn't do it.

If the studio looked like a nice place for a nightmare, it was right in keeping with the way we felt. There are many sensations connected with live television that are reminiscent of mine. When you are about to go on, your heart is always pounding, and once you start you never dare look back. You know something's chasing you.

When we were not in our little sets rehearsing that morning we huddled in corners to run through the lines. I had a song to sing to the beautiful little auburn-haired child who was to play my daughter, Patti, and we went out in the hall to go over that. Even in the hall we could hear Charles's deep, rich voice on the talk-back. When Charles got nervous you could hear him a country mile.

When you are that nervous and excited you don't notice the clock till suddenly it's time. The hands have moved relentlessly in those little one-second jumps. You think your heart is going to stop, and maybe it does, but you have stepped outside yourself and into the show.

"But, Mommy, where is Daddy? Where is Daddy? Where is Daddy?"

Patti repeated the phrase in the singsongy voice of a five-year-old as Joanne tucked the covers around her and kissed her good night. Then the young mother moved to the window, being careful not to touch the frame. She looked soulfully out at the black velvet drapes, and the child began to repeat the words. This time a filter effect had been added and the child was not seen, so the plaintive question seemed to ring in Joanne's ears. The Hammond organ swelled, the scene faded.

Two of the three cameras lumbered to the other side of the studio to watch a young model dip a mop into a pail of Spic & Span! The announcer in the booth extolled as she effortlessly removed the grease so painstakingly smeared on a little square of linoleum. The other camera swiveled and waited in the dark as a portly man of about sixty wiped the sweat from his bald head, crossed himself, lit a cigar. Then he practiced glaring at the younger man cowering on the other side of the desk.

"And now we return to our story."

The floor manager pointed, the older man took a breath.

"I've coddled you long enough!" He sliced the air with an accusing finger that shook with frustration, rage, and panic.

The younger man bowed his head penitently, and the tirade continued for three and a half pages. The older man paced behind his desk, puffing, gesturing, and bellowing. His full, rich voice rising, falling, and ringing oddly familiar little bells.

"Hey, you know who that guy is?" a stagehand lounging against the back wall of the studio whispered in a voice clearly audible to both actors.

"That's Jack Pearl's partner . . . used to see them when I pulled the curtain at the Paramount. You know . . . 'Vas you der, Cha'lie?' . . . yeah . . . that's Cliff Hall."

The young man rose wearily, turned up the collar of his raincoat, and went out through the door. If you looked closely, you could see it swing gently on the invisible wires. He immediately broke into a cautious run to the end of the studio, picking his way through cables in the darkness, with camera three in hot pursuit. His foot caught the corner of a tripod holding a little branch of leaves in front of the pan of fluorescent lights designed to cast parklike shadows. The tripod crashed to the floor. He shrugged and moved on.

Camera two stayed with the older man, who sighed heavily, stubbed out his cigar, and wiped his head again. He couldn't see when the red light went out since the camera was on his blind side. He'd lost an eye in a gang raid in Chicago during prohibition, so he didn't relax until he heard the young man's voice come over the speaker. As the husky whisper explained his thoughts, the young man pulled his collar closer against the still wind.

"He had always wanted to be a photographer, but his father insisted he was wasting his time and should be in the family construction business. His wife Joanne and his little girl were at home waiting for him, but he was torn."

He stood in silent dilemma, the streetlamp casting harsh, shadowless light till the camera pulled away.

"Joy, Joy, Joy for your dishes."

The exultant words sounded throughout the studio from every speaker and a little gray bottle shaped like a woman's body appeared on the monitors through the magic of film. The camera crew had one minute to haul the umbilical cables and push the sound booms, like great mechanical giraffes, into position.

The minute was up, the floor manager pointed, the organ moaned, and the little red lights blinked on.

"But where is Daddy? Where is Daddy? Where is Daddy?"

Joanne shook her head sadly and searched the velour for an answer.

"Spic & Span," the model stood proudly on her sparkling square of linoleum, "and . . ."

"Joy . . . ," the little gray bottle appeared, "have brought you 'Search for Tomorrow.'" The organ played what sounded like was going to be "Beyond the Blue Horizon" but wasn't, and a list of names printed in white on black paper and wrapped around a fifty-gallon drum crawled past camera one.

Mary Stuart as Joanne Barron
Cliff Hall as Victor Barron
Bess Johnson as Irene Barron
John Sylvester as Keith Barron
Lynn Loring as Patti Barron
Sara Anderson as Louise Barron

Written by Agnes Nixson
Produced and Directed by Charles Irving

It was twelve forty-five and the show was over. That first episode included a couple of very clear, sharply focused pictures of the boom mike, but aside from that there were no major mishaps, and we'd gotten off the air on time. Freddie Simon, our production assistant, passed out the scripts for the next day's show and we met in the dressing room to read through it and get a rough timing. It was hard to concentrate. The butterflies had folded their wings for the afternoon, but nobody could settle down. We'd held hands so tightly all morning, we couldn't let go. I think we probably walked down Lexington together for a hamburger and beer. I actually don't remember. That's what we did so many, many times it seems right.

Every morning at eight we would start all over again. We met in our strange little office on Madison. We arranged the clumsy old dining room chairs that Charles had bought in the Salvation Army for a dollar apiece into little playing areas. We drank coffee and ate the bagels and cream cheese that Freddie bought on her way to work, and we made up another show.

Charles sat behind his desk with a floor plan spread out and a script, plotting camera angles with a little triangle. Then he would check his shots with a small viewfinder. We didn't have experience or knowledge, so we used everything else we had. We talked a lot about actions and intentions and obstacles, but I think mostly what we did was be ourselves. We were literally making up a new medium and the logical place to start was with ourselves, even if we didn't realize it at the time.

The first task every day has always been to adjust the script. It had to time out to the second, so sometimes we had to cut, sometimes we had to add. Nearly always in those days we made lots of changes. We began to put the dialogue into our own words early on. The principal problem the writers had was the switch over from radio to television. Words that had for thirty years sounded perfectly natural coming from the disembodied voice in the little box were suddenly ridiculous. In radio, time and space were irrelevant. The audience filled all the blanks with their own imagination. The heroines had beautiful voices, so naturally they were beautiful. The rooms they occupied and the furniture were all arranged by the listener. When the sound effects man knocked on an unseen door it did not seem odd for someone to murmur, "I wonder who's at the door," to no one in particular, as the organ swelled and the announcer teased, "Who has come to call on Olivia?" You could wait a week to find out.

We couldn't do that. When you are standing there, plain as day, and the audience can see that the door is ten feet from you and there is also obviously nobody around to murmur to, you just gotta answer that door. I remember Charles exploding when he picked up a script that had a scene that was supposed to be played "at the mailbox."

"What," he roared, "is behind the mailbox?"

We could only have played that scene in the middle of the night. We didn't have blue sky. We had black sky.

Our visual staging was unique. Charlie got the idea from a book on stagecraft by Lee Simonson. We were lucky; he was the first designer assigned to us. When Lee asked Charlie what he had in mind, Charlie said, "If you don't know, who does? I stole it out of your book."

The technique was later used by a lot of shows, like "Cameo Theatre" and "Matinee Theatre" as late as 1957, but we were the first. We were experimenting and there were hazards. Imagine how difficult it was to photograph sets you could actually see through. We had three playing areas, at least one commercial setup, three cameras, two booms, and a lot of people who wouldn't stand still. A stagehand was forever walking by outside a window that was supposed to be eighteen stories above the street, or just hanging around smoking a cigarette inside the closet of my bedroom when I opened the door. The only thing to do was stay so close on the faces you couldn't see anything else and try to get everybody to sit down.

That is probably why we earned the reputation early on as coffee fiends. Larry Haines and I very often start the morning rehearsal to this day by one of us saying, "Come in, sit down, have a cup of coffee, isn't anything wrong?"

It was hazardous, but it worked. When we had been on for three or four weeks Charlie asked a friend of his what he thought of the sets.

"Do they give the right feeling?" he asked. "Do the lamps and pictures seem in the right period?"

"I thought they were perfect," the friend replied.

We didn't have lamps or pictures!

What made it all work was the people who were playing those parts: not just their talent, but the people themselves.

Bess Johnson, who played Irene, was one of the great stars from radio. From 1930 to 1937 she was the leading lady on "Hilltop House," the voice of Lady Esther, and finally her own personal "The Story of Bess Johnson." She was tall and handsome, even in those tacky dresses some wholesale house gave us, and her awful phony hairpiece. She could walk across that linoleum oriental, sit on a filthy, torn couch, and make you believe she was a Duchess. She said one day that she had always dreaded the time when she would play secondary roles, so we saw to it she never did. She was always the star.

Cliff Hall was also a legend by the time he came to us. He was a star in vaudeville, burlesque, and on Broadway even before he joined Jack Pearl and that great comedy team was born. After twenty years of radio he came out of semiretirement in 1948 to do a new TV series called "The Front Page" for Franklin Heller and left "Crime Photographer," where he played the bartender, Ethelbert, when Charlie asked him to sign with us.

We believed in our characters, we believed in the show, and we believed in each other. We could see the many facets of Irene, and so could the audience. She was a lonely, desperate woman who could not let go of her youth and her son. She was a fascinating, sympathetic antagonist, because she always thought Irene was right!

After we blocked the show in our "rehearsal hall" we walked three blocks to the studio in Liederkranz Hall. Liederkranz had housed, in its time, besides the opera, the German-American Bund and a CBS recording studio. The decision to renovate and divide the building into four studios was made by William S. Paley, president of CBS. Bill Paley was the first man to bet several million dollars on daytime television. From the outside it still looked like it might be an opera house. The façade was weathered red brick with tall, arched windows on the second level and wide, marble steps leading up to the doors. The doors were the first clue that times had changed. They would have been more at home in a warehouse. Past those doors more marble steps and carved banisters led up to what had once been a lobby, and on each side great oak staircases swept up to the balcony level.

On the first level there were two studios, two makeshift offices, two cubicles we used as dressing rooms, and two bathrooms. Upstairs there were two more studios, two more cubicles, two bathrooms, and a long, narrow space used as a prop room. There were oddly beautiful moldings and mahogany shutters at the tall windows, but the plaster was yellow and peeling, and gray linoleum had replaced the thick red carpeting. Though everything was covered with dust and an acrid, musty odor hung in the air, it was a real theatre, a place where dreams were born.

Behind a desk at the head of the first flight of stairs, presiding over it all, sat Harry Cusick. Harry was a retired policeman with the face of an angel, who not only guarded the door, he guarded us, he accepted deliveries, took messages, answered the pay phone when it rang, and was our friend.

Daytime programming was a very new idea, but Liederkranz was already a beehive. Besides "Search for Tomorrow" and "Love of Life," which followed us on the air three weeks later, there were another dozen shows crowding each other in and out of the four little studios. Mike Wallace and his wife Buff Cobb did a talk show; "Bride and Groom" married a terrified couple in front of a live audience every morning; "The First Hundred Years" rehearsed, and went on the air at 1 P.M. daily; Margaret Arlen chatted for a half an hour and Mr. I. Magination played with the kiddies.

In the evenings the commercials for "The Ed Sullivan Show" and "Studio One" originated there, and on weekends "Lamp Unto My Feet," "Chromoscope," and "Bob Dixon's Chuck Wagon" took over.

All the scenery and equipment for all the shows was stored in the basement, on and around a full-sized bowling alley, left behind by the Bund. That's where contestants for "Beat the Clock" met every afternoon to practice playing the game. Everybody was cramped and hurried and nervous. Harry Kusic was the only totally serene face around, and when Ernie Kovacs and his tiny band of maniacs arrived in April, even Harry began to feel we had gone a little too far.

All the women on "Search for Tomorrow" got dressed and made up in one common room about eleven feet long and eight feet wide. The furnishings consisted of a long table against one wall with a mirror over it, and three folding chairs. Two small metal lockers contained our combined and obviously extensive wardrobe.

Joy Lange was our makeup artist from the first day. It was her first show, and she was as innocent as the rest of us. How far we would all go together!

Joy made everybody up every morning, but we didn't have a hairdresser, so we put in curlers or bobby pins for each other. Bess Johnson wore her hair smoothed back under a chignon. Bess couldn't see very well, so when stray blond hairs began to trail out behind her, it was my task to fix it up. After the first few weeks somebody decided that I looked too young with my own short hair, so I got a bun too, which looked like two day-old doughnuts.

It was when we went into the studio at ten-thirty that the tension began to mount again. It is hard enough to remember lines that have been very lightly etched on your memory the night before and rearranged that morning. It is not easy to move into the pretend reality of marriage and family. It takes a lot of concentration to keep a fight scene going with the pace and energy that will make it believable. It is next to impossible to do all that while a set is being built around you, a lighting man is working, three cameramen and two boommen are moving constantly and talking to the director over their headsets, and all the time Charles is on the loudspeaker adjusting the shots. That is, however, exactly the way it was. In one hour every day we built and lit the set and got all the rehearsal we were going to get.

We had problems and so did the crew. We had old RCA cameras with original iconoscope picture tubes and four turret lenses that had to be flipped and focused manually, and broke down constantly, since nobody had really learned to service them.

The equipment was new and strange and primitive and the technicians barely had time to read the instructions. The cameramen came from movies or the Signal Corps and the sound men from radio, but actors stand still in radio and cameras move on tracks in the movies. It was a very new ball game.

The only thing that made it possible was the people. Everybody tried so hard, everybody cared, and we were together from the first day, the cast and crew. I began in the first weeks to "good luck" everybody. We were out there together, depending on each other. The formula for survival, I decided, was one third talent, one third drive, and one third dumb luck.

We had wonderful people, and we had Charles, who was a genius. He had graduated from high school in Minneapolis when he was twelve and was thrown out of college when they found out he was only thirteen. Charles's problem all his life had been finding enough to do to utilize his talent and energy.

In the first few weeks of the show he listened to the technicians talking in the control room and realized he didn't know enough about what they were saying. That afternoon he went out and bought a kit for an oscilloscope. He had never in his life had a soldering iron in his hand. He had no idea that he had picked out the single most complicated piece of electronic equipment, but he went home and put it together. He used a lot of solder, and it worked. What was important to him was that he understood why it worked and what he could do with it. He could begin to experiment. If there was a problem, and every day there was a new one, by twelve-thirty Charlie had found a solution.

"Search" was an innocent little show about one family in those dear old days, and the plot was almost painfully simple. A press release from CBS will give you an idea.

"CBS TV's 'Search for Tomorrow' is the compelling story of the Barron family—father, mother, daughter-in-law and grandchild. It is the story of an American family dominated by the 'old-fashioned' elders, successful and secure. It is the story of a young widow and her child, and their pathetic struggle to voice the ideas of the young. It is the story of the folks next door, and the misunderstandings and heartbreaks that mar their lives.

"Son, Keith Barron, a year out of the Navy, and his wife, Joanne, come into conflict with the elder Barrons when they balk at following in the old man's footsteps. Keith's sister, Louise, is a sympathetic ally, as is young Dr. Ned Hilton. Keith's sudden death embitters his parents, who then turn their unhappiness upon their son's widow."

That is pretty much the way it was. If you accepted the notion that mothers-in-law, especially rich ones, are by definition evil, we were off and running. Irene constantly belittled and embarrassed poor Joanne, worshipped her son, and spoiled her grand-daughter rotten. Victor roared a lot, broke pencils in rage and frustration, and puffed his cigars, but his own sweetness gave him away every time.

What we were playing, actually, was the theme of *What Every Woman Knows*. The women were strong and the men were not. Even though Victor was powerful and successful, Irene controlled him, and Keith spent his year on the show ricocheting from his mother's corner of the table back to his wife's pocket. As for "voicing the ideas of the young," Joanne was twenty-two going on fifty from the day we went on the air.

There is one very large hitch in a seven-year contract. At the end of any thirteen-week period the sponsor has the right to cancel. You think you're okay, but you're never really sure, so it was a celebration at the end of the first thirteen weeks. Our options were picked up! We were a success! We were not only a success, we had money left over from the budget! Out of our $8,025.75 allowed for each week, we had $13,000 left over!

Charlie was pleased and proud when he breezed into the agency with the news, and totally dumbfounded by the panic that followed.

"For God's sake, don't tell anybody!" was the first reaction. "Go out and spend it," they told him, "and don't ever do that again!"

That afternoon he spent $13,000 on flats that he had painted dark green, and from then on we had sets. They still photographed black, but at least you couldn't see through them.

That was not the only lesson Charles had learned in the first thirteen weeks. He had learned how to get a lot for very little money and how to get the best out of everybody. Our sets were built while we rehearsed in them because it cost less; a stage crew of three could do it all. By the end of the first year we had a little recording booth in our rehearsal hall, and we did our own voice-overs on acetate discs. It was against union rules for the audio man to play an acetate during the show—that required an extra man. Our tech director just didn't notice.

Charles even worked out an agreement with the writer, on the front steps of Liederkranz. Irving Vendig lived in Sarasota,

Florida, which did not get CBS on its one station, so he never saw the show. He made a deal with Charles: "You don't bitch about the scripts and I won't bitch about the shows, okay?" He added only one stipulation: "If you cut two minutes out of the show in a chunk, let me know so I can use it again."

Melba Rae and Larry Haines joined us about six months after we went on the air as Stu and Marge Bergman. On the first show with Melba we were peeling apples, sitting at the ubiquitous kitchen table, when the floor manager gave us a signal to stretch two minutes! Somebody had skipped a couple of pages. Two minutes may not sound like a long time to you, but when you have nothing to say and five million people listening, it is eternity. We cut the peel into fascinating little curlicues, looked stupid, and everybody thought it was the writer's fault.

When Larry signed, he asked Charlie casually how long he thought the show would run. Charlie answered him just as casually:

"For the rest of your life."

What Larry Haines and Melba Rae brought to the show was fresh, delightful, and original. They brought comedy. Larry already had an enormously successful radio career, including roles on "The Columbia Workshop," "Inner Sanctum," "Gangbusters," "Suspense," and the title role in "Mike Hammer." After making a career as the voice of a tough guy he began to develop the character of Stu Bergman. The real Larry Haines emerged as the tender, quizzical, gullible man who knew everything was terribly important and was never quite sure how to do anything. All the delicious bits of business he had worked out in high school with his friend Art Carney slid into the character ever so subtly and Larry's own endless inventiveness added more each day. From the beginning he was genuine and wonderful.

Melba was pretty and feminine and bossy in her own ditsy way. She always seemed to keep her eye on the pitching hand instead of the ball, so she was surprised and just a little hurt every time she caught it.

After Keith's death at the end of the first year, Irene zeroed in on her granddaughter, Patti. She would get custody of that child come hell or high water. When legal channels failed, she started rumors that made it impossible for poor Joanne to get a job. Finally, in desperation, she engaged the services of a con man named Higbee, played by Ian Martin, who turned out two story lines later to be head of the local syndicate, capable of any dastardly deed, even blackmailing Irene.

Jo worked as a secretary in the hospital, briefly, and when she was fired, because of the "rumors," her boss, Arthur Tate, took her side. He believed so strongly in the defenseless young widow that he quit his job as business manager in protest. Arthur Tate was played by Terry O'Sullivan, who was tall, sandy-haired and straight out of the Nelson Eddy school of acting. He was married at the moment to, I think, his fourth wife, had several grown daughters, but still fell in love some time between April and June every year. Arthur was Jo's devoted friend, although everyone could tell, from the way he looked at her, there was more to it than that.

Jo wanted to buy an old house and turn it into a restaurant, but Higbee made it impossible for her to borrow money, so Arthur became her partner and together they bought the Motor Haven. When it looked like Jo had finally won, Irene began to go a little crazy, and as a last resort she kidnapped Patti!

The chase lasted several weeks and demanded more from everybody than any shows we had done up to then. Lynn Loring was only seven and had to play scenes with the grandmother she loved, but who was suddenly strange and unstable. The rest of us had to give the illusion of constant, frantic motion, with almost no place to go, getting in and out of cars that, of course, didn't move, and the last week was next to impossible. Irene had abandoned her car and disappeared into the woods, and we had to find her. We had five shows in the woods and all we had for a set was a little pile of dirt about twenty feet long and six feet wide with some artificial trees stuck into it, some clumps of brush on the floor, and branches wired to music stands scattered around the studio.

Eight actors had to keep running and talking and breathing hard for a whole week. Charles ordered a Chapman dolly and Stan Gould rode it. He would sit high in a searching long shot, on a very tight lens that did not expose bare floor, and sweep down for a close-up. Stan was great, but it was Charles who should have had a medal. He not only choreographed us so that he could cut from feet running on our little strip of dirt, to a face peering from behind a branch, to a carefully placed clue caught on a bush, he remembered where everybody was!

Jo and Patti were tearfully reunited and went home to the Motor Haven, and clearly the misguided Irene needed psychiatric help; but Jo would forgive her, and Victor would stand by her no matter what.

I said everybody believed in their characters. Nobody believed more fervently than I. I think I began to color in the blank spaces in my own life from the first day with her reality, and so much of that reality was left to me and my fantasy, I filled the space rapidly. The outlines given by the writers were strong and righteous, and Joanne's path always led through tangled underbrush. The light on the other side of the forest was clearly visible through the trees, of course, since they were only branches stuck precariously onto tripods, so it was a daily trial to continually lose the way.

In order to keep her wise and right, which to me was desperately important, I colored her vulnerable and caring. She stopped to listen so intently to every wounded bird or trodden wild flower, before you knew it night had fallen and she was lost again.

The plot had thickened, but by the end of 1952 tension had even eased a little. The morning rehearsal began when the stories and jokes were over and the afternoon read-through for a timing had deteriorated noticeably. Usually, Lynn read everybody's lines aloud while we took off our makeup. She was building a vocabulary and it was good practice for her. Her little eyebrows arched in concentration as she solemnly sounded out each passionate word. Some of her original pronunciations will be forever part of our folklore. They gave a fresh dimension to each continuing episode.

We were a close family from the beginning, the cast and the crew. There was affection and respect that held us together. If someone dropped a hat we had a party, and if there were cross words they were accepted and dismissed as natural outbursts of tension and emotion. It was truly a remarkable group.

That young man behind the soda fountain was Tom Poston. Rose Peterson, who was brought in by the nefarious Higbee to ruin Joanne's business, was played by Lee Grant, and Wilbur, the mute brother she protected so vehemently, was another friend of Charlie's from radio, Don Knotts. Connie Ford and Nita Talbot also played Rose over the years, but it was Lee when she and Marge Bergman had to pour the poisoned soup down the drain!

Our sets were no longer hung from piano wires, though they were still flimsy affairs, and the sink was not, of course, connected to any plumbing. The prop man simply hung a hose from the drain down to a bucket. We never rehearsed with real props, so it never occurred to anyone what would happen when that soup finally hit that sink. The scene was the climax of the story. Rose had to tell Jo's best friend and partner, Marge, why she had poisoned the soup, and why she couldn't let it be served to Joanne's customers, thereby ruining her Motor Haven business, thereby letting the syndicate take over her property to use as a dope repository. I told you it was a big scene.

Together they carried the five-gallon pot over to the sink and dumped it . . . well, if you can imagine what it would sound like if a horse relieved himself into a tin pail for four straight minutes, you know exactly what that was like. It never stopped. But they went right on with the scene as if nothing was wrong. They never missed a word!

Don had his trials too. After a year of having no dialogue to learn, it was discovered that his handicap was psychosomatic. He had been severely traumatized in a fire when he was a child, so the thing to do was reenact the fire, right? In an upstairs bedroom of the Motor Haven, which was really just a rooming house, we lit fires in the wastebaskets while sodium pentothal was administered. A doctor, who should have had his license revoked, was present, but no particular sanitary precautions were mentioned. We often stretched dramatic believability to its wildest limits.

What we did not anticipate that day, since—again—there was no technical rehearsal, was the smoke drifting into the air conditioner and being carried all over the studio, screening the courtroom, the hospital, and a lawyer's office. Everybody in the building was a little choked up.

There was another first in that scene. The Polaroid camera was the new toy on the market, and Charlie was the first kid on our block to have one. Now, in order to reenact the fire, we had to see that Wilbur had fallen asleep, then play out the scene that went on in his mind. This was long, long before the days of tape and instant replay, so Charlie took a picture of him with the new camera, in rehearsal, just as he turned his head to one side, indicating that he had fallen into deep sleep. Then, on the air, instead of cutting to a close-up of his sleeping face, he cut to a close-up of the picture which he had set up on a music stand.

As soon as the camera had cut away, the floor manager cued him, he leaped out of bed, ran across the studio and played the scene with Rose and their mean old stepfather. When the scene was over, Charlie cut back to the room, being careful not to see the bed, and we all worried a lot till he slid back into position. Then a hushed voice said, "I think he's coming to," and sure enough he did, and he could talk, and felt fine ever after.

The characters were only as interesting as the people who played them. When they were really fascinating they tended to last several story lines. Rose and Wilbur were around for four years, but Lee only played the part for six months. She was the first person to leave the show because of a publication called *Red Channels*. Freddie told me that when Lee got into a taxi in front of the agency she said, "I'll never work again." She didn't for ten years.

The specter of *Red Channels* hung over the whole television industry. Another wonderful actor, Ralph Bell, was fired from our show, and Charlie finally told me why his name never appeared on the credits. He said a man named Johnson, who owned supermarkets in Syracuse, had found his name listed and had gone after him. At least Charlie's face wasn't on camera, so his credit was taken off in an effort to hide him. Somehow, Johnson found out he was still working and started threatening again, so Bill Craig, from P&G, went further. Charlie was taken off salary and paid through the other companies that serviced the show.

Johnson still wasn't satisfied, and some months later Charles made arrangements through a "contact" to go to Washington and give his testimony in the form of an affidavit. It was a "favor," and the price was $5,000.

As a final gesture, Charles made a trip to Syracuse, New York, to see the man named Johnson, who bought a lot of products and had taken upon himself the task of guarding American television from the Red menace.

After a dinner of humble pie, Mr. Johnson walked Charlie back to his hotel. He'd had a lot to drink and was feeling expansive and confidential. It seems he had a daughter who was an actress but she'd never been able to get a job in New York. "Those reds would never hire her."

In 1953, CBS had eight of the top ten shows in daytime, and the viewing public was up 34 per cent in one year. In Liederkranz, "The Guiding Light," "Valiant Lady," "Rod Brown of the Rocket Rangers," and "The Continental" had joined the mayhem. There were always about half a dozen kids on the combined shows and the halls were open territory. If the game was cops and robbers, the water cooler and the banisters were good places to shoot from, and Harry Kusic was a kindly marshal.

"The Continental" went on late at night from our studio. A huge bed and a bottle of champagne were all he used for a set and props, but the bed was too big to take in and out every day, so we just worked around it.

Ernie Kovacs somehow always remained calm no matter what, and we gradually realized he wasn't calm, he was bored. He would arrive five minutes before air time with his hat and coat and cigar, and that's the way he went on. He never took the hat off or put the cigar down. For one whole show he hid behind the curtain and let the director try to find him with the cameras. After that, on days he was very late, the show went on without him. They would point the camera out of a window and pan the street while they waited.

"Bride and Groom" had just about scraped the bottom of the barrel when one of the wedding guests went beserk and wandered into our studio. He sat at the organ, making a dreadful racket, and it took us an hour to realize he wasn't there to tune it. Blessed Harry Kusic finally got him out of the building and sent for help.

On "Search" there were always new, fascinating, talented people. The kind policeman who found Patti in the woods when Irene kidnapped her was Ross Martin. The manager of the motel was Hal Cooper. He became our director when the part ran out and alternated with Charles, who was busy developing another show called "Heaven for Betsy," with Jack Lemmon and his wife, Cynthia. Don Knotts was still playing a tender, lost waif, but between scenes and in the mornings over coffee he did his routines.

"Nervous! Who, me?" His voice would crack as his eyes popped with the amazement and dismay of a newly hatched chicken.

When he finally did leave, he was out of work for quite a while. One day he asked me to meet him for lunch. He was broke, he had a wife and a new baby, and he'd been offered a job as a disc jockey on a little radio station in Texas. I remember looking at Don, knowing in my heart that he didn't really have a future. He was sweet and funny and winsome, but how many parts would there be for a man with that skinny little body and the high, whiny voice. I hated to tell him so, but I really thought he would be better off in Texas. Not long after, he did "No Time for Sergeants," with Andy Griffith, to rave reviews. Then he did his first stint as the man on the street on Steve Allen's old "Tonight Show," and the rest is history.

I may not have been right, but Joanne was. She was kind and thoughtful. She was loving and patient, and she was always right. From the moment I walked into rehearsal in the morning her sweetness and goodness became a part of me. She was everything I thought a woman ought to be, and for three hours a day that's what I was. I could rewrite and rehearse my life before I had to live it, and when my name appeared as the star of the show, it was the Good Housekeeping Seal of Approval. I was not only acceptable, I was accepted.

More and more Joanne sustained me. I made dresses for my fairy princess daughter. If Joanne stirred up a batch of corn muffins on the air for the restaurant, I stayed after the show and baked them. I kept trying to prove I was a woman and I was good at it, proving it in all ways I knew, and the most important way was in my own marriage.

From the beginning, Joanne and I have lived strangely parallel lives. Like railroad tracks, tied together, we give the illusion of being one person somewhere far in the distance, even though we've never gotten there.

After our wedding, Richard and I moved into our first apartment and I spent the next six months finding out how difficult it is to make a decision about something as large and expensive as a couch. Buying furniture, I realized suddenly, meant commitment. I had to decide not only how I wanted to live, but what I wanted it to look like.

The apartment was in a brownstone and had lovely high ceilings and a big window that looked out on a dark, dreary court. I had to decide on the paint colors before we moved in, so all by myself I chose what looked like a cool, smoky taupe in the little sample. What went on the walls was a hot, muggy brown that made you feel like you were drowning in chocolate cake batter.

The next week I hired a decorator. She was young and wise and elegant, and I followed her through miles of showrooms trying to imagine myself in every style from Ethan Frome to Mies van der Rohe.

What I finally wound up with was a room that looked just like Richard. It was lean and modern and elegant, all in black, brown, and white—a perfect background for gray flannel. If every ashtray was clean and no one had moved it an inch, and if magazines of just the right color were strewn, ever so precisely, it looked like the cover of a magazine. Otherwise, it looked like hell. I spent a lot of time emptying ashtrays and strewing magazines.

Richard had gone to work for Time, Incorporated, working for Arthur Tourtellot, producing the "March of Time," to play on television. He traveled a lot that first year, and spent long days and evenings at the office. Time, Inc., it seemed to me, went out of their way to provide a complete life for their employees, a life that rarely included spouses. It was a wonderful club which included at some time every famous photographer, every brilliant writer, every celebrity, and hundreds of beautiful, clever young researchers who had all graduated from Smith College and wrote in even, square, clearly legible hands. They also knew all those great, brilliant, famous people and made easy, witty conversation at cocktail parties. It was those parties I hated most. If he went alone, I was jealous and miserable. If he took me, I was shy, nervous, and miserable, and I remember one party too vividly to this day.

The hostess was a close friend of Richard's and already an assistant editor. She graciously brought me a drink, chatted for a moment, and became naturally busy. The room was crowded and noisy, and everyone was standing around in little groups. I stood too, smiling and looking hopeful, then I tried not smiling and pretending to be deep in thought, then I had another drink. I didn't know anybody, and it never entered my head to just join a group. Finally, I noticed a smallish, dark man also standing by himself. I edged across the room and introduced myself. He said his name was Stein-something.

"Well," I said, because I never know what else to say, "what do you do?"

"I'm an artist," he said, without smiling.

"What kind of pictures do you do?" I said.

"Cartoons."

I could tell by his monosyllabic answer, he was not easy to talk to, but I hung on.

"My husband works for *Time* magazine. He might be able to help you." It was a desperate attempt to ingratiate myself, and it failed.

"Thank you," he said, "but *The New Yorker* uses most of my things."

As his gaze went past me, my mind grappled for his name . . . Stein . . . Steinberg! Of course, all those *New Yorker* covers! It was too late. He had eased away. I felt foolish, and I knew it would be hours before we could go home.

Besides being graceful and charming, Richard had a wonderful memory for people and events. He could walk into a room filled with strangers, pick up the vibrations instantly, and move effortlessly into conversations about absolutely anything. He could quote from their books, he knew where they were working and what had been written about them in the papers. He also knew, it seemed to me, almost everybody in the world. He would be just a little peeved if he walked out of a movie and he didn't see someone in the lobby he knew, even if we were in Cleveland.

I, on the other hand, was so self-conscious when I met someone new I either didn't hear the name at all, or was so frantic trying to think of something to say I promptly forgot it. I had no small talk about anything except acting and had probably read twelve books in my life. Among my favorites were Van Loon's *History of the World*, and Teddy White's *Thunder Out of China*. So my literary conversation was pretty much limited to "Stop the China Lobby," or "Wasn't it a shame about Marie Antoinette?"

Besides the cocktail parties, we spent a lot of weekends with John and Jane. They had bought a beautiful old house in Bucks County about the time we made the kinescope for "Search." Richard had introduced John to Roy Winsor, too, and he had created "Love of Life." He was still head writer, so we had something in common. We also had nice, friendly fights, because John did not approve of my rather cavalier approach to the words printed on the page of my scripts.

We had traded in Richard's old Chevy for a secondhand, maroon Cadillac convertible, so the trip down was smooth and fun. That's the year I forgot how to drive, completely. I tried only once, late at night, but the car was too big and powerful and kept getting away from me. I never tried again, but it didn't matter. Richard liked to drive.

I love old houses, and that one was perfect, with fireplaces in every room, even the kitchen, and Jane had filled the rooms with beautiful things. Jane knew everything there was to know about furniture and gardens and houses. Jane, it seemed to me, knew everything there was to know about everything, then kept on learning.

Bucks County in the fifties was the watering place for the great names in the theatre and the literary world. Jane would point out the houses as we zoomed through the countryside, and very shortly they began to appear at John and Jane's. Besides writing "Love of Life," John had written a play called *The Grey-Eyed People*. It didn't run long, but it was good, and he was clearly eligible for membership in Kaufman and Hart country.

The Dartmouth Alumni Association had begun to distinguish itself, too. It seemed to me everybody had a big job in Washington or published or edited or wrote. Richard's roommate from college, Tom Braden, had written a book on the OSS that made the *Times*'s best seller list and married Joan, who was then assistant to Oveta Culp Hobby. His best friend, Ted Gates, was married to Richard's high school sweetheart, Dotti, and would shortly be taking home the national budget as weekend reading.

The weekends were, to me, often like a scene from a movie. The mornings began with beautiful little "do it yourself" breakfasts in the guesthouse, followed by Bloody Marys in the kitchen around the fireplace. We would stamp off the snow in the winter, before stepping into the library for cocktails and dinner.

There were lots of stories about college and the house parties, and I gradually made up a picture in my mind of what that must have been like. The pictures were wonderfully romantic. I remembered the Dartmouth winter carnival from an Ann Sheridan movie, and I could fill in the rest. They talked about college, and they talked about books and people and politics. Everything seemed to connect and the chain was endless. Nobody meant to leave me out, but the fact was I hadn't been there and I didn't know what they were talking about and I could never catch up. What seemed like the most important part of Richard's life didn't include me. Still, I was accepted. I was half of Dick and Mary. I was pretty, and everybody called me Mary Mouse.

I enjoyed the witty remarks and joined in the laughter. I admired the easy reach of knowledge and the way they all seemed to fit together, but I couldn't help it if occasionally the smile of pretended understanding would begin to cake and the defenses rise.

"And what do you do?" asked the pretty young actress, just out of Yale Drama and working at her first job in a summer at the Bucks County Playhouse.

"I'm on 'Search for Tomorrow.'"

"Oh, that's a soap, isn't it? Don't you miss real acting?"

It was a silly, callow remark at a cocktail party in Moss Hart's living room, and I didn't have a devastating answer. Later, when I didn't have to worry about the defenses or, God forbid, a tear brimming over, I would tell myself that their damn plays could run four years and not reach as many people as I did every day, but it wouldn't really help. I couldn't say it to anybody else, because they would think it was funny and I was being silly, which was true and I knew it and that didn't help either.

By Sunday afternoon, when everyone gathered in the library by the fire with the *Times* crossword puzzle and the reviews, I nearly always began to long for Liederkranz, and, all too often, driving home, the defenses burned through and erupted into an argument with Richard that had no resolution.

I was Mary Mouse on the weekends, but Monday morning I was Mary Stuart, and by Monday Mary had managed to glaze the memory, at least in the telling. In rehearsal, over coffee and bagels, or in the makeup room when I described that warm, intimate group before the fire with the puzzles, I was very much a part of it. It was nice to drop names like Moss Hart, and by Monday I had usually thought of something clever to say. What the hell, it was a shame about Marie Antoinette!

Long before we were married, Richard quoted from a poem he was fond of, by Byron: "Man's love is of man's life a thing apart; 'tis woman's whole existence."

I never really believed that he was one of those men and I was precisely that woman. I adored Richard. I loved shopping for groceries on my way home from the studio and fixing perfect little dinners for the two of us. He thought candles on the table and a smoky fire in the fireplace of an overheated apartment were silly, but I loved them. I made special long skirts out of gray flannel just for around the house, and by the time he came home Suzy sex kitten was purring. I thought Richard was the handsomest, smartest, most wonderful man who ever lived.

Actually, there weren't that many evenings to spend alone. He still traveled, we still saw his old friends and there were business dinners in restaurants. Arthur Tourtellot was one of the business associates in the beginning, but very soon he and his wife, Betty, were our closest friends. Richard worked for Arthur until they both left Time, Inc., and the Tourtellots were always very important to us. I loved to sit in Betty's rose garden in the summer or sip tea by the fire in Arthur's library on a winter afternoon. Arthur was an extraordinary man, who cherished language and literature and history. He wrote beautiful books and lectured at Harvard and Oxford. As a public relations director for a large, private company and later for CBS he affected policy and influenced the opinion of many great men.

Arthur thought the world of Richard. He also cared for me. He told me over and over that I had a special quality, something unique. I didn't really believe him or understand what he meant and I often dismissed it all as simply Arthur's fancy talk. Still, the fact that he had said it was important.

I asked Arthur one day what he wanted in his life and he said, "To contribute something and to live my days . . . with grace."

The times Richard and I spent with the Tourtellots were some of the best we had together.

Somewhere around the middle of June 1952, I had reason to believe that I was pregnant. More than anything in the world, I wanted to have a baby, have a family. We celebrated with champagne and I was already decorating a nursery when I began to hemorrhage. It didn't occur to me that I was in any kind of danger. I was only terrified that I would lose the baby.

Still, it did not enter my mind not to go to work. Actors just go to work. I still have fights with doctors about that. The compromise, then, was to have me picked up by an ambulance in the morning. The drivers would carry me in a wheelchair down the steps of our apartment house and put me in the ambulance. At the studio, they carried me up the front steps, then turned me over to the stagehands, who by union rule do all the carrying on CBS property. After the show they would pick me up and take me home. I was lifted to a regular chair for the show, which mercifully was a courtroom, so I never had to stand.

For three weeks it worked all right, but I was obviously not getting any better. I got so weak I began to faint and, what was an even surer sign that something was radically wrong, I started forgetting my lines. Richard was away in Chicago with the Eisenhower convention, so Charlie called my doctor and my lawyer.

My lawyer took me to the hospital and two days later they operated on me for an ectopic pregnancy.

I didn't know what that meant, and I had always felt that an
operation is the doctor's problem, so I didn't have sense enough
to ask. Coming to was my problem, but I was an old hand at
that. The trick was to never open my eyes as long as there was a
bottle hanging over the bed. I'd take a quick peek and go right
out again. When the bottles were gone I would ask for my Coca-
Cola. A few sips helped with the cobwebs and settled my stomach, and as soon as I felt like tasting a cigarette I knew it was
okay. I always took a Coke with me to the hospital, to make sure.

That time the bottles hung there for over a week, but I was
sitting up, dangling my feet over the side of the bed and feeling
fairly cheerful, when a chatty nurse started gushing about how
lucky I was to be alive and somehow let it slip that my right tube
was gone.

"That's what an ectopic is," she rattled on. "The egg lodges
in the tube, and when it begins to grow the tube ruptures."

I didn't believe her! She didn't know what she was talking
about! The doctor would have told me himself! But the tears
started to stream down my face. I had gotten used to the idea of
losing the baby, I was young, and there was plenty of time, but if
I had lost the tube, too . . . I knew what that meant. That spring
before Richard and I were married, when they had removed a
tumor from my uterus and the cysts from the other tube to try
and open it, they had told me it would probably close again. Now
the good one was gone! That silly nurse had to be wrong.

When the doctor came around that evening, he said he was
sorry and surprised that I hadn't realized before. He talked a lot
about how low my hemoglobin had been, how many transfusions
I'd had and how many CC's of blood they had to remove. Then
he talked about special therapy to open the left tube, and special
medication if it was still cystic. I knew it was all doctor talk to let
me know I would probably never have a child. He couldn't know
what that meant to me—the cold, sick feeling that woke me between three and four every night after that. I would never be a
mother, never be a real woman, never be a real wife.

I went to see five other doctors, and they all said the same thing: "Quit work, stay in bed for a year, and maybe." Quit work! It was the one thing I couldn't dream of doing!

Five weeks later I went back to the show. It was like going home. I loved the bagels and cream cheese in the mornings, I loved the jokes and the stories and I loved the work. I loved to act, and I was just beginning to get a little sure of myself. Of course, on the air the butterflies would begin to swarm, but the shows were good, and we were a success! We were the new family in the neighborhood in thousands of towns all over the country. We began to get letters that could have been from old school friends.

"I never answer my phone between twelve-thirty and twelve forty-five."

"The telephone operator in our town watches too, so she just unplugs all the lines."

"You are all so sweet, and Marge looks just like a cousin of mine from Toledo. Would you ask her if she's from Toledo?"

As the audience grew, and it did, from five million in 1951 to fifty million in 1960, the fan magazines began to spring up, answering all those questions. Those stories were not about stars, but about the new neighbors. We dispensed advice about marriage and decorating and recipes. Some of them were so sweet it's a wonder the pages didn't stick together, but I really believed every word. I believed it was totally fulfilling to make your own curtains, and I made my own to prove it.

Every day we got closer on the show. We needed each other for affection and survival. There were no teleprompters and there was almost no time. No time to finish rehearsing, no time to worry about our hair or clothes or makeup. At twelve-thirty we went on the air and did the best we knew how. If somebody forgot a line, somebody else said something, whether it made sense or not. Melba used to grab my hand and squeeze if that was all she had to say. Bess Johnson would give Cliff a sharp little kick on the ankle. Then one day I went so far up in my lines, I just never came down. I got a good grip on my bangs and said, "Arthur, I have something to tell you . . . I just can't think how to say it."

The floor manager whispered frantically, Terry O'Sullivan, who played Arthur, kept feeding me cue lines, but nothing helped. We were playing the scene on the front porch and I just dashed back and forth, groping for the banister and the corner posts and repeating, "Arthur, it's terribly important, I just can't find the right words," until we went into a commercial and mercifully to black.

After that I began to write key words from every line around the set. I wrote on everything, walls, floors, tabletops, napkins, plates—any place where my eye would naturally fall. Eddy Deverna, one of our stagehands, said once, "When Mary has a tough day, don't anybody bend over."

Writing on sets and the "good lucks" were my two rituals. I had to "good luck" everybody on the set, and it was just as important they wish it back. One day, Hal Cooper noticed four Boy Scouts in the hall, and at about two minutes to air he brought them into the studio. You cannot imagine the surprise on the faces of those four little boys when the star of the show wished them "good luck," then demanded their good wishes in return.

The "good lucks" for the cast and crew were special and individual. It wasn't just a ritual, we were out there together and we needed each other, and it wasn't just sentimentality. When you're proud of someone, fond of them, and your affection is returned, it feels good. Of course, it's possible to play a scene with someone you can't stand and make it work, but when you love them anyway, you can use the real to sweeten the make-believe and you get magic.

We had magic. We had talented people and Charles had a genius not only for inventing techniques. He could bring performances out of people they didn't know they had in them. It was a very special combination of affection, talent, and trust. Together they generated energy and a mellow atmosphere that allowed the cream to rise.

How many times have you heard it said about a great actor, that he could read the phone book and make you cry. Actually, you can make something good out of a scene that says almost nothing. I've always called those scenes a very thin slice of life, but when you infuse them with the feeling of the people for each other, and their relationship, which is the specific reality of that moment, something does happen. Out of those moments we begin to build a history.

We had been accepted and become part of other people's lives. The women of the fifties, the last generation, perhaps, of "stay-at-homes," were talking to each other. You see, we were stay-at-homes too, and every noon we shared a cup of coffee, a tuna fish sandwich, and our souls.

To give us due credit, there were hundreds of beautiful scenes sandwiched between the thin slices. You cannot put that many talented people together and not get something awfully good a lot of the time.

If actors have special gifts, it seems to me one of the most important is the ability to use their emotions, and to share them. If we make a contribution it is somehow related, not just to telling stories, but to sharing feeling. Surely everybody wants to feel, but not everybody has the chance, or the outlet, all the time.

Perhaps "Search" and other daytime shows that followed came at a time when we were needed. Something must have been simmering in those quiescent fifties, or it would not have blown the lid off ten years later. As girdles gave way to the polyester pantsuit, maybe our spirits needed more of an outlet. I know mine did. The show was not just an image of myself. It was a chance to work with thoughtful, disciplined, tender people who touch and lean and hold hands, and laugh!

I said we didn't have time to rehearse, and we didn't, but somehow we always had time for fun. Everybody played jokes on everybody else. If we had a scene to play in an airport, no matter how meaningful or touching, for dress rehearsal Tommy Buchanan, our sound effects man, would dig out a record of World War II planes and strafe the field, which was funny to everyone except the poor guys who had to do the scene. If we were supposed to hear a car pulling into the driveway, he would casually send it through the garage doors.

Eddy Deverna set the props and always managed to do something. He would glue the cup to the saucer, put a sandbag in the suitcase, or grease the sink so I couldn't write my cue words.

Nothing was too much trouble if it was funny. One day we were preempted. About five minutes to air somebody decided to make a speech so we would not be going on. Hal Cooper got a brilliant idea.

"Let's not tell Mary!"

Everybody stayed. I went around and "good lucked" and we started the show, but as the organist, Bill Meeder, swung into the theme, for the first time in his life he hit a clinker. Then other little things began to go wrong. Larry walked toward me and knocked a vase off the table. Without seeming to notice that, he started his first line, got halfway through it, and stopped. I gave him the next cue and he started again, but this time he jumped a whole page in the middle of the line.

Doggedly I tried to pick up the pieces, but no matter what I said, he would jump to the wrong place in the scene. I was racing around the set, trying to figure out where I had written the key words for the answer to that, when from out of the blue there was a knock at the door. Now, there wasn't supposed to be a knock at the door. Nobody was supposed to come into that scene.

"Open it," he demanded, and I was sure he had lost his mind, but I didn't know what else to do, so I cautiously turned the knob and Hal pushed the door open.

"Hi," he said, "just dropped by to tell you we're not doing a show today. See you in the morning!"

Of course, things went wrong, lots of things went wrong, and usually they were funny. Maybe not at the time, but eventually. If a camera broke down in the middle of the show, and one did at least once a week, the cameraman would just pull it out of the line of fire and the other two took over. Sometimes we could go on with the moves just as we had planned, sometimes we couldn't. There just wasn't a camera to cover it, so you slowed everything down till they had time to get there.

That's when those old turret lenses were handy. We could glance at the camera and know what the picture was. If the lens on top was a long one and stuck way out from the camera, they were on a tight shot, and you had to stay fairly still or move slowly, but the flatter they got the wider the lens and the angle. Now there was another trick I learned early on. When they were on the flat one, the fifty-millimeter, you couldn't let that one come in too close to your face, because it distorted. I would just stick my foot out and stop the pedestal. We lost cameras, we lost mike booms, we had sets fall down, and from time to time the generator went out and everything on the network just went dead.

The cameramen couldn't see us through the viewfinders, they lost contact with the control room and the control room couldn't see anything. When that happened, the trick was to stay the same distance from the camera you were on when the little red light went out, try to remember what you were talking about and keep going. You see, you never knew when you would be back on the air.

One day, Melba and I were playing a scene when the lights went out, every light in the studio except the little inkies on top of the camera. Now, when that kind of thing happens your mind flashes "air raid," "earthquake," or "end of the world," but what you do is go on with the show. We had rehearsed the scene walking around the room, but I grabbed her hand and pulled her down on the couch beside me.

All three cameras pulled in as close as they could with those inkies, no brighter than flashlights on a miner's helmet, shining just enough light to see we were still there. Two stagehands ran to get hand-held lamps and squatted down between the cameras, and we kept talking. Actually, we had gotten almost to the end and were just beginning to relax when my eye happened to catch the eye of one of the men holding the lamp. They weren't more than six feet away, and I was distracted for a moment to have a new face in my line of concentration, but it was more disconcerting for him. I guess he was embarrassed and certainly taken off guard. A self-conscious little smile flickered across his face and, with his free hand, he waved.

There were days when the crew saved us; there were days when another actor did, and little Lynn was the best. One day we were playing a scene in the kitchen, which had a porch opening off the back door. She noticed that a flat had fallen over where the porch should be, but I didn't, so when I started out the door, as we were supposed to, she grabbed my hand.

"Let's not go outside, Mommy . . . it's . . . er . . . too cold."

I assumed she had forgotten her lines, even though she never did, so I picked up the bowl of apples we were supposed to go outside and peel and started for the door again. This time she scooted around me, planted all four and a half feet firmly between me and the door, took the bowl of apples out of my hand, and sat down at the table. Only then did I glance at the door. There was probably a secret little smile of gratitude that day, as I looked at her and tried frantically to remember what the scene was about, but there was always so much more than that when I looked at Lynn. It was love, it was wonder and delight.

Then there were the days when nothing helped and nobody could save us and we just felt like fools. That's the kind of day it was when I had a scene to play that began as a picnic. In the middle I was supposed to remember something from the past and go into a dream sequence. The old Polaroid dream trick. The dream sequence was to take place in bed, so I underdressed. That means I put on my nightgown and put a sweater and skirt over that to hide it. At air time I climbed up on the papier-mâché rock and we began.

But that day we had a substitute floor manager who was a trifle deaf. When Charlie called "camera two," he thought he said "cue," so he cued me. I pulled off my skirt and sweater, revealing the nightgown, and was about to climb off my rock and dash when I noticed that the little red light was still glowing. There I was, for all to see, standing on that idiotic rock in my nightgown. There was nothing to do but walk across the set, get into bed, and say the rest of the words.

I mentioned a substitute floor manager. For seven years we had a young man named Joe Papp. The first year Joe began his summers of free Shakespeare, Charlie "borrowed" the lights and sets, commandeered a truck, and between us we helped set up the production in a park on the Lower East Side.

A year later Joe had moved to Central Park and he needed

more and more time to produce and direct the plays and raise money for what everyone thought was an impossible idea. Who, indeed, could imagine a young man wanting to put on plays in Central Park for a nonpaying audience, then travel them around to all the boroughs in a truck? That was Joe Papp's dream, and Charles agreed it was important, so he arranged for Joe to get afternoons off. Charles told them he would pay for the extra three hours, because anyone knows a floor manager needs time to prepare.

Joe is now by far the most important man in American theatre. His Public Theatre has been responsible for more hits, more new playwrights, more innovation than would seem possible. Then, he was a quiet, handsome, wildly dynamic young man who quoted Shakespeare all the time just for us.

When he left the show he said, "You're a fine actress, maybe a great one. I'll save *Much Ado* for you, but only for ten years."

Who knew what the next ten years would be like, what they would cost, still, I like to believe he meant it.

What we shared was a sense of commitment, and I still believe live television, with all the mishaps and clinkers, brought out the best in everybody. You only had one chance to do your best. Those cameras were heavy and clumsy, but as Stan Gould told me, "A man had a chance to really find out what his equipment would do and exactly what he was capable of himself." A long, smooth dolly across the set on a medium lens into a gentle arc around a face requires enormous skill and sensitivity. It was a kind of dance, as intimate and graceful as dancing used to be. Stan Gould was Camera 2 for the first five years. He used to practice his moves between rehearsals, and he's still the best.

What was it like? It was putting on a show, and every day was an opening. Elia Kazan came to watch us one day while he was working with Charles. He stood dumbfounded in the control room. He could not believe that we had blocked, timed, rehearsed, set cameras, and all the time they were building the set around us.

"Not only that," said Charles, "it's twelve forty-five. We've already been distributed!"

We'll never have a chance to work that way again, or feel

that way. But as Charles says, "They don't throw Christians to the lions anymore, either."

By the end of that first year, two deep and lasting friendships had begun for me. Joy Lange, our makeup artist, and I discovered that we had much in common. We had both grown up during the Depression in hotels and rooming houses. She was from New York. Her mother had worked for Ziegfeld and, until he died, her father had been his concertmaster. I was from Oklahoma, but it was the same thing. Our families lived with attitudes that their finances absolutely defied. Joy didn't find out till she was grown that her mother's restaurant in the Village had been close to bankruptcy for years. We both knew what it was like to live in one room, and took it for granted that when company is coming you throw everything under the bed. We had both tinted those years with affection. We were also married to men who had more than one similarity, and we both worshipped Charles.

Probably what brought us together was the conclusion we had come to, quite independent of each other, that a man's career, a man's point of view are rocks upon which a family is built. That may or may not have been odd, since we had both grown up in families kept together by a mother. No matter what we had lived through or seen, that is what we believed. We made a ritual of lunches at Schrafft's with the other ladies and practiced our attitudes over sandwiches and butterscotch sundaes.

Together we decided that it was much better in the long run to draw as little attention to our own careers as possible, on the theory that if we wanted to work then it wasn't really work, it was having fun. This was especially important for both of us, since we made more money than our husbands, and we both went through fairly long periods when we made all the money. It was, of course, all right to have a job as long as it didn't interfere with the home. We had vowed not only to love and honor, but to have dinner on the table whenever our husbands chose to eat, and we jolly well broke our necks to do it.

Dinners were especially difficult for Joy. She not only did the makeup for us, she had to do the early evening news, and she lived in the Village. She would run home, shop, put dinner on to cook, dash for a bus uptown, make up Doug Edwards, and race back to the Village. She finally moved to Sixty-first Street. It was the only solution.

Joy had the same beautiful face and sweet, mother-child expression her sister, Hope Lange, made famous two years later. We giggled a lot, but we took being women very seriously. We weren't really sure it was funny when we went to try on hats one day, and after an hour the saleslady said patiently, "Girls, do your mothers know where you are?"

Sometime during the first year we started calling each other Maud, and the name has stuck.

The relationship with Freddie Simon was quite different. Freddie was our production assistant, which meant she did just about everything. She brought the bagels and cream cheese in the morning, she timed the show, and when we decided during the early rehearsal what props we were going to need she ran out and bought them. She was bright, inventive, and decisive, and in 1951 that combination was abrasive.

Freddie spent the first few months out of college traveling through the mountains of Tennessee collecting folk songs for the Library of Congress. Then she got a job with the Biow Company. Her total list of qualifications consisted of one hundred assorted folk songs and three weeks of speed writing. She spent most of her time in the ladies' room hiding from the typing pool till she found Roy Winsor and Charles.

I remember standing on lots of street corners arguing vehemently with Freddie, but I have no idea what about. I remember stagehands knocking my wheelchair over when I was sick, determined to kill her. Mostly, I remember quiet afternoons in her sunny little West Side apartment. She could play a guitar a little, and she loved the way I sang harmony. She and Joy were my only contact with a world that was not Ivy League.

Gradually, we began to work the little songs Freddie taught me into the show, and on days that we ran short, or just got bored, I would sing one to Lynn.

Then she introduced me to her friend Ken Welch. They had met in college and he was just beginning to coach and write special material. Together we added lyrics to the little folk ditties and made them into real songs, and he taught me how to sing them. It took a year, and for that year those three times a week were the high point of my life. I adored Kenny, but I had no idea that in my dumb luck way I had waded into another puddle of gold. My lesson was just after Shirley Jones's and just before Carol Burnett's.

My relationship with Procter & Gamble, except that I have never learned how to spell it, has always been close and direct. In 1953 it was even easier because everything was smaller and simpler at P&G and at our agency, the Biow Company. There were family dinners at the Winsors' or the Bradleys'. Ev Bradley was the account executive who had sold the show to P&G. He was really responsible for bringing the whole group together and the group stayed close.

If the brass were in town from Cincinnati and gave a party, I was not just invited, I was an honored guest. When I saw Mr. Halverstadt, who was head of Advertising at Procter & Gamble, I called him Halvy—just as casual and friendly as could be. When I had something to say I never hesitated to call Bill Craig in Cincinnati. Bill was our own personal godfather, and my close personal friend, so when Kenny Welch and I had fourteen of fifteen songs together, I called Bill and asked him how he felt about my doing a record album of the songs I had been singing on "Search."

He thought about it for a minute or two and answered, "I'd like to do that. That's a good idea."

A few weeks later I had a contract with Columbia Records! The album was to be produced by Mitch Miller, with Percy Faith arranging and conducting. That was January of 1954. Kenny and I worked even harder. It was the first record album for either of us, and it mattered very much. I started studying with a real singing teacher two days a week, besides the three days with Kenny, and I started ordering the groceries over the phone. Afternoons were for me and music, and fantasies began to fill my head—new fantasies and the old ones that had led me out of Tulsa. At night before I fell asleep, or riding in the car on weekends, I would fall silent and dream.

The fantasies go back as far as I can remember. I was always pretending I was someone else. In first grade my teacher, Miss Mary, owned the little house we rented. I was aware that we were behind in the rent, though she was kind and never said a word to me. The reality of not having as much money as the other kids was my box of crayons. It was a nickle box and it didn't have a pink crayon. I tried, but there is no way to make the cotton candy color with white over red, or red over white, and the other girls had zippers in their store-bought dresses. Mother made all of mine.

It was that year, I know, that I started leaving Tulsa in my mind. I remember clearly walking home and counting on my fingers how many years it would take to get out of school. Twelve years! Twelve years of sitting in a room watching the clock and dreaming out the window. I remember the sick feeling in my stomach at the thought of those airless, numbing years stretching ahead.

One of the first plans of escape was to be adopted by somebody rich who would die and leave me all their money. So I began to visit a sick, old lady who lived in a big apartment house about ten blocks away. I spent countless afternoons sitting by her bed listening to her stories, and her nurse would always bring me a treat. I remember the piece of pecan pie with whipped cream and a perfect little crescent of maraschino cherry. It was sunny and cool and peaceful in her apartment.

That was the first year I was aware that Daddy drank too much. I usually managed to hang around on the sidewalk in front of Miss Mary's little house when it was time for him to come home, and I could tell when he turned the corner a block away if he had had too many beers on the way. The thing to do then was hurry in the house and be very cheerful and helpful while Mother fixed dinner, then maybe she wouldn't notice and be cross.

On summer mornings I would wait for the iceman. His truck would stop in the shade in front of the house, and I would ride in the back, up to the end of the street, licking the sliver of ice he always chipped off for me. But in my mind it was a covered wagon crossing the prairie.

Afternoons I dug for buried treasure under the garage, and when the hot, dry sun of Oklahoma summer melted the tar in the sidewalk, I lay on the floor of the living room and listened to "Ma Perkins" and "Pepper Young's Family," totally absorbed in their fantasy. Cool evenings I walked four blocks down Elwood and sat on the porch of a vacant house. It was high off the street and the porch wrapped around the side. Through the windows I could see the living room and dining room and the stairs. It had real stairs leading up to the bedrooms on the second floor. I knew there must be three, and one of them would be mine.

A room to myself. I imagined myself sitting on the landing of the stairs talking on the phone to all my friends. Even then I just couldn't accept the fact that I was really just a rather ordinary little girl who lived in the tiny house on Elwood. That was never enough.

I remember walking home from the store about five o'clock one afternoon. I was balancing on the little wooden step that kept the grass from growing onto the cement and I stopped.

"I must remember this moment," I thought. "It will be gone and I won't have it."

I stared at the sky and tried to memorize the little puffs of clouds. I wiggled my toes in the tough, Bermuda grass and looked at every house, trying to imagine what was on the other side of the dark windows closed against the heat. I still have the moment, I still look at the windows and wonder, and I never go back to Tulsa that I don't drive by the house with the porch on Elwood.

At least if I was a dreamer I came by it honestly from Daddy. Until I was four or five, Daddy sold Packard automobiles and we always had one of some vintage to drive. They were used, and they didn't belong to us, but they were grand. After that he sold stocks and bonds and "made deals." It was the middle of the Depression and there weren't any jobs. There wasn't any money, so Daddy did a little of everything; and he could do anything as long as he didn't have to do it with his hands. I don't think he could hook up a garden hose, but he could do anything with his mind.

He could glance at a long column of figures and add them in his head. He remembered the serial number of every car he ever sold. I was told he graduated from VPI with an almost perfect score, and he didn't own a book.

He said, "Hell, the man explained it in class, if you can't understand it what are you doing in school."

What Daddy did best was talk, and what he loved to talk about most was Virginia. He and Mother were both born in Virginia, and they felt sorry for anybody who wasn't. Daddy wanted to make sure my brother and I knew who our folks were, because who our folks were, and where you came from, was more important than anything else. He told the stories over and over, and it didn't matter that I got confused with aunts and uncles and cousins—there were a lot of keep track of.

Daddy was the youngest of seven children and he had sixty-two cousins in one county. I was vaguely aware, even as a little girl, that there was a lot of blindness on both sides of the family, and one year Daddy's oldest brother, Harry, came to live with us, and I realized what it meant. He was the first blind man I'd ever been around, but Harry could do almost anything. He'd come all the way out to Oklahoma in boxcars with a young mountain boy and his banjo. Harry was the only blind man I ever heard of who could hop a moving freight. Daddy talked a lot about his family because he was proud of them, and he had a lot to be proud of.

Daddy's grandfather was James Steptoe Langhorne, the seventh son of Henry Starbrook Langhorne. Henry had made a fortune in Cuban sugar and bought up land grants till he owned what must have been half of Patrick County. Grandpa was born in 1821, so it would have been about 1840 when he rode with his two oldest brothers back across the mountains to the headwaters of the Dan River. It was time to divide the land between his sons, and the eldest son, John, had first choice.

From a high plateau overlooking the river as far as he could see was the land he wanted, and there were thirteen thousand acres in that tract alone. Grandpa was already going blind, and he never saw that land again, but he always remembered it as the most beautiful sight he had ever seen. He didn't know it then, but he was meant to have it.

John's bride hated the place. She was used to living in town and going to parties. Back in the mountains there was not a soul for miles, and she was so miserable she stuck pins in her baby when she changed his diaper to make him cry.

"You see," she'd say, "even the baby can't stand this place."

That baby was Chiswell Langhorne. "Chilly" Langhorne built the C&O Railroad, and his five daughters would have made Virginia famous all by themselves if nobody else had. Irene married Charles Dana Gibson and became the first Gibson Girl. Nancy married Waldorf Astor and became one of the most famous women of our century. In our house she was always Cousin Nancy; to the rest of the world she was Lady Astor.

When Grandpa got the land he took his bride, six wagons, and a hundred slaves on the week-long journey. He built a home, put the land in chestnuts, and named the place Meadows of Dan, from the Bible. They had five daughters and one son. The youngest daughter, Evelyn, was born in 1866, and she was Daddy's mother.

Grandpa built the first grist mill in that part of the country. He built the first church, and preached in it, and he built the first school, where he taught, "to feed the mind, feed the body, and feed the soul," he said.

During the Civil War, when Virginia and West Virginia split, Grandpa lost most of the money he had invested in state bonds. Then the Yankees came through and took all the stock off the place, leaving only an old, lame mare. Somebody said that if you rode the horse into a millpond you could cure it, so his son got on the horse and rode it into the water. It was deeper than he figured and the horse got excited. She kicked the boy in the head and Grandpa's only son died instantly. That evening, Grandpa walked into the Yankee camp and told the Captain, "I'm a blind man and I need my horse." They gave it back.

When his daughter Evelyn married she and her groom came to live with him. In her early twenties, she started going blind.

Her cousin Chilly Langhorne took her to Richmond to be treated by a specialist. Evelyn became close friends with his daughter, Nancy, but in those days there was no cure for glaucoma.

When she died in 1900, Daddy was only two and his brother, John, was seven. The older girls were grown and gone, Julia to put herself through law school and Kate training to be a nurse. Daddy's father had gone to North Carolina to try to find work, and there was nobody on the place except the little boys and his oldest brother, Harry, and his grandfather, who were both blind. Daddy said they all learned to read when they were four because they had to. Grandpa made them read an hour a day from the Bible, but except for the hour of Bible reading the boys were growing up wild.

In 1906, Miss Eleanor Wheat heard about them. She needed someone to help on her place and she took them both for the summer. That was the year Cousin Nancy married Waldorf Astor and she was back in Mirador for a round of parties after her honeymoon in Europe. Miss Eleanor sent her a note about her two little cousins, and word came back immediately.

"You raise them and I'll educate them."

So she did. She sent a check every month and Daddy grew up with Miss Eleanor, whom he adored. She was brave and kind and wise. She was a deaconess in the Episcopal Church, she knew Latin and Greek, and she had designed the house she lived in all by herself. She had it built into the side of the mountain, with a cistern up above. It was the only house back in those mountains with running water.

In the summers, Daddy and Jack worked on her farm. They were both still part wild and Daddy had a temper. I can't imagine it, but they say he would get mad and run everybody off the place with a shotgun when he was nine years old. When he was twelve Miss Eleanor sent them both to military school. They still tended to get into a lot of fights, so she sent them to different schools. At the end of a semester, if things had gotten out of hand, she could simply switch them.

For a few weeks each summer, since she was a deaconess, she had the twelve little girls from St. Paul's in Richmond come and stay. Mother was one of those little girls.

Lady Astor was the first woman ever elected to the House of Commons. One day, when I was in school, the teacher was talking about her, and I piped up, "She's my grandmother." It seemed a natural conclusion from the known facts at my command. She had educated my father, which was a lot like adopting him, and if she had adopted him she was my grandmother. Everybody laughed, so I never mentioned her again, but in my heart I knew she was my family. It was a little confusing having a grandmother who was a millionaire and internationally famous and know your folks were behind in the rent, but an inventive child can rationalize that. After all, my father was much too proud to ask for anything!

What I remember is the way Daddy talked about them all, mostly his grandfather. Time and time again, he told us how Grandpa would get up whenever he woke and roam through the house, not realizing it was still dark, bellowing, "A little more sleep and a little more slumber, so shall poverty come upon you! Up, boys!"

When the house caught fire, he got excited and pushed the grand piano out the high parlor window. It crashed to the ground as he picked up a jug of whiskey, then went outside and gently laid it under a shady tree. After that, he ate his dessert before he ate his dinner. He didn't want to miss the good part, in case the house caught fire again.

Daddy had so many dreams, and most of them were for me or my brother.

"I don't care what she does," he must have said a thousand times, stroking my straight blond head, "as long as she's pretty and can play the piano."

Every time he got four or five dollars together we would "pay down" on a piano. Over the years there must have been twenty different pianos and all those five-dollar down payments might have bought one. He never quite managed that, but he did teach me how to sing. He taught me the harmony parts to all the old barbershop and mountain songs he knew. By the time I was seven or eight I could hold my own in a quartet, singing the tenor part a third above the melody.

He was only angry with me once that I remember. I had

gone to visit a little girl who lived down by the river and we went to play along the bank. It was a silly river really. In the summer the sun baked away the water and it was nothing but oily sludge with a little brown trickle between the bridges. But that spring there was still some water, and it cut off one little piece of the shore to form a tiny island. As I stood on the shore, I began to imagine that treasure was surely buried on that island, buried by the Indians and worth a fortune. There was an old pipe, half submerged in the slime, and shallow water leading out to it. Without thinking, I started across it.

I don't remember slipping and falling into the water. I don't remember dragging myself through the muck back to solid ground. I remember that it got dark, and I was too dirty to go in the little girl's house and get cleaned up, and I had to borrow money for a taxi. It was too far to walk. I remember feeling hopelessly late, and wrong and inadequate.

There were other rented houses. On South Main, for over a year, I had a room to myself, a new garage to dig under and a Dick Tracy detective kit. The boy next door and I stalked the grocer for the whole summer until we found out he was really a bootlegger, and we hid for a week.

That's the year Uncle Harry spent with us. Harry was blind, and Harry played the banjo and Harry chewed tobacco. The back yard sloped way down behind the house, so the back porch was almost a whole story high. Harry couldn't see that Mother and I had just hung out the wash one afternoon when he was sitting up there, with a nice, fresh plug, chewing and spitting. We just did that wash all over.

The next house was out on North Main, and Mother told me about something that happened there that I have absolutely no recollection of, not a glimmer. I was eight or nine, and if I knew Daddy was in trouble, I don't remember. Mother says he got mixed up in a phony stock deal. He'd sold shares, then found out they didn't exist, and Lord knows we didn't have enough money to eat, let alone make good on a bad stock. She said that one evening, just after dark, a big, black car drove up in front of our house. Two men got out of the car and walked up the steps to the porch. They didn't knock, just called out.

"Guy, we want you to come with us."

She said Daddy didn't move. He just sat there and looked at her.

"You'd better come on now, Guy. They want to see you down town."

Finally, Daddy got up and put on his coat. "I guess I better go," he said, but just as he was starting out, Mother says I appeared with my hat and coat on too. I took his hand and we walked out to the car with the two men on each side of us. Mother says she heard me say, "I'm his daughter and I go everywhere with Daddy."

They took us to a hotel where some other men were waiting, and I told them all that I was going to be an actress when I grew up, but I would be glad to sing for them right then and there if they wanted me to. They brought us home in the big, black car about three hours later, and we never saw them again. Mother was pale as she talked about it and had the frightened look I remember well from those days. She told me all she knew about that night, and what Daddy had told her, but I still don't remember. Whatever happened, I have blocked it completely.

After that, there were the hotels and the rooming houses and the housekeeping rooms. One Christmas, the church sent us a basket of fruit they distributed to the poor. I had to go to the desk and get the damn thing, but I saved face by announcing loudly and grandly that I had ordered some fruit for the help.

In that particular hotel, Mother and Daddy had not mentioned at first that they had two children, so my brother and I came in and out by way of the first-story window for the first week. They also neglected to mention the cat and the dog, who were both expecting. Inside of that first month, Fritsey had twelve puppies and Kukatchin neatly tore the bottom from the mattress of one of the two double beds in the room where we all lived and delivered to the world five kittens. From then on we had no room service, just towels and sheets outside the door, please.

I loved the evenings in the lobby. I talked to all the traveling salesmen, who were lonely and would talk to anybody, and I heard about the towns they came from. I ate in the Walgreen's drugstore and did very well, indeed. They would save the syrup cans for me and that was free dessert, and at the end of the day whatever was left over, for fifteen cents, I ate. I much preferred to eat alone. It gave me the freedom to be anyone I wished. With my folks I was just a little girl eating in a diner with a shabby family. Alone, I was anybody I chose, from a wealthy, eccentric runaway, to Orphan Annie in search of Daddy Warbucks.

Daddy was the world's greatest salesman, and during those years he sold enough of something to keep us alive. For two years it was soda pop and stale cigars. The pop went for a dollar a case and the cigars for a dollar a box. That dollar was what we ate on, including seven cents for my brother and me to take to school for lunch. He made the deliveries in a purple Austin, and somehow we all managed to fit into it, including the cat and the dog. But the dollars got scarcer and the cigars got staler.

By the time we got to the Reed Hotel, we had run out of just about everything. Mother was practicing typing so she could get a job, the room only had one bed for all of us, and the bathroom was down the hall. Even the lobby had lost its magic. Just before Christmas the man in the room next to ours jumped out of the window, and I watched my mother's face as she saw him die. The band of carnival performers stranded there had a fire in their room, and one of the girls I knew was suffering. It was hard to pretend they were international aerial stars on a lark.

One bitter, cold afternoon I met Daddy out front as I was coming home from school. He had hocked his overcoat the week before, but he didn't let me see him shiver. He was smiling and joking about the box of cigars under his arm, and was off to West Tulsa to sell them. West Tulsa was all the way across the bridge and the wind cut like dry ice. But he just smiled and waved and said he felt like going for a walk. As I watched him walk away, the holes in his socks blinked like silver dollars.

That Christmas, Santa Claus brought my brother a pair of roller skates. I got a fifty-nine-cent Ship & Shore blouse and my aunt sent me an aqua mohair sweater. It was the most beautiful sweater I had ever seen, but when we left the Reed Hotel, they kept our luggage. By the time I saw that sweater again, I had outgrown it.

Then in 1941, on December 7, everything changed for everybody. Tulsa became a boom town. There were two army camps a bus ride away and huge defense plants. Daddy went to work as a surveyor. I didn't know he had ever been a surveyor, but like I said, he could do anything with his mind. Mother had a job at the Oklahoma Tax Commission, so there was enough money to buy a real house. It cost three thousand dollars, and we gave them twenty-five dollars in savings stamps as a down payment.

I spread what furniture we had over the seven rooms, and had supper on cooking when Mother got home from work. She was frightened of the responsibility and wouldn't come in the front door that whole summer, but we were in a house! I bought paper drapes at the dime store, and after six months I found a secondhand set of dining room furniture for fifty dollars. It was painted white, and the top, for some reason, did not fasten to the base, just sort of rested on it. But I thought it was beautiful, and we were careful not to lean. The house didn't have a landing to sit on while I talked to my friends, but I had a room to myself!

Somehow, we were always a little shabby and a little untidy. Mother was great at cleaning closets, but she'd get tired and never get anything put back. If we had company I wouldn't let Daddy get out of his chair. "You sit right there and keep your hands over the holes in the slipcovers!"

The second summer we were there Daddy found a Christmas card under the couch.

"Goddamn!" he said, "hasn't anybody swept since Christmas?" "Okay," I answered him back: "You mow a path to the trash burner, and I'll be glad to sweep!"

That was also the year I tried out for my first play at the Little Theatre. I got the part, and I didn't think about much else after that except plays and boys. My school work began to suffer, because I was either rehearsing a play, or learning one, or just lying on the bed in that wonderful little bedroom, dreaming.

I spent the next two years hanging around the Little Theatre. I learned to smoke and say damn and felt quite grown-up. I must have been fifteen when I toured in a play called *Old Acquaintance* for the USO. We were in an army camp somewhere in Missouri. We did the show and I went to bed, but about three in the morning something woke me up. It was music. Somebody was playing music like I had never heard. I got up and went down that dark street in the camp to a recreation hall, where three soldiers were playing a sax and a bass and a piano.

It must have been the first time I had ever heard jazz, and I sat there listening until morning. Three musicians, all from New York . . . and I was right there with them. But it wasn't just the music I was hearing, it was people listening to each other and answering in a conversation that was pure and free and perfect.

That was the first time I stepped inside a fantasy, and it felt better than I had imagined. For the first time, the fantasies had a form. They weren't just a way to feel, they were now a place to be. From that moment on I had to be in New York City. The people I wanted to be with would be there, and they would know what I meant.

Meanwhile, back at the Motor Haven. Marge and Jo put aprons over their little cotton dresses every day and cooked lunches to serve to the customers. Rose and Wilbur were friends, and Rose helped out in the dining room from time to time. Stu dropped in to have a cup of coffee at least twice a week, when he wasn't busy selling cars at West Side Auto. Arthur Tate was Jo's partner and took care of the business, but most of the time he was a man in love. Ever so slowly, Jo had gotten over Keith's death and was beginning to realize she could love another man.

Life centered around the Motor Haven, which seemed perfectly natural. After all, what is a young widow with a child to do? Clearly, all she is capable of is cooking and sewing and making beds, so that is what she should do; and I agreed! It fitted right in with my own desperate belief in womanhood.

It was a little more difficult to rationalize Arthur's role in the business. He had been general manager of Henderson Hospital when we first met, so taking care of the books in our little establishment hardly required all his time or talent, but never mind.

That was what we did. Women were women, by God, and men had a lot of time to talk.

In 1954, Charlie had a new toy to play with, an electronic matting device. Against a black background he could use a picture of an exterior with live actors in front of it. We also had snow. TV snow never melts, but it's white. We were doing a Christmas show the first time we tried them together. Charlie got a slide of a picture of the outside of the Motor Haven. It was to appear electronically on a black screen behind us so when Patti and I played a scene at the mailbox the house was in the background. He finally had something to put behind the mailbox! The only problem was that the picture, which made an image only on black, also appeared any place else that happened to be black, like the inside of my mouth. Every time I opened it too wide, there was the Motor Haven, down my throat.

Charlie got around it by cutting away from me every time I got to a word with a broad A, or a short I. It may have looked odd, but we were making progress.

By then we were all receiving more fan mail, and one day Marge got a letter that threw us for a loop.

"What ever happened to Jimmy?" a woman asked.

We all stared at each other.

"Who's Jimmy?"

Then someone remembered. Way back, in the beginning, the Bergmans had had a little son named Jimmy. He had never appeared, since little children are hard to manage. He had always been "upstairs," either taking a nap, or put to bed early. Somewhere along the line, he had simply been forgotten. He'd been upstairs for four years! As it turned out, he stayed there for another three.

We had lost a character, we had gained a couple. Bess Johnson had a pet poodle, and when it had pups she gave one to Cliff. Cliff trained that dog as no poodle had ever been trained, with secret commands that he would work into his dialogue. The dog would even hit marks taped to the floor. So Victor and Irene had a dog.

Then I got a cat. I didn't go out and decide I wanted a cat, I just got one. We had a kitten in the prop room, and one day she slipped into the studio just as we were going on the air. When I went to pick up a sack of groceries the bag was moving! My heart began to sink, because what immediately crossed my mind in that filthy old studio was a picture of a rat, and we'd seen several. Still, I had to pick it up! I peaked, ever so cautiously, into the bag and there, to my immense relief, was a kitten. That is how I got a cat, and why we all played a lot of scenes with sardines in our pockets.

If things seemed tranquil with dogs and cats and friends, it was not meant to last. Jo's arch enemy, Higbee, was not a man to give up easily, and he had to have the Motor Haven!

Now, when Jo bought the Motor Haven it was just a nice, old-fashioned, two-story house where she could serve lunches and take in a few roomers. I had always visualized it being close to downtown Henderson, in a section that had gone downhill, as the suburbs moved out. Suddenly it was on the edge of town, right across the highway from a factory, and Higbee was determined!

He began to search Arthur's past for a vulnerable heel and turned up with Sue. Now, pay attention, there will be a quiz at the end of the chapter. Sue was an identical twin to Hazel, who was Arthur's ex-wife, who had burned to death in a fire. She appeared, pretending to be Hazel, thereby ruining any plans Jo and Arthur had for marriage.

Of course, Arthur had never mentioned to Jo that he had ever been married before, and Hazel had never mentioned to him that she had an identical twin sister! That is one of the problems actors constantly contend with. The story will change suddenly, the stage directions calling for a limp, and you discover you've had a wooden leg for ten years!

Credibility is a strange and wonderful quality. Ours did not depend, obviously, on the probability of the story, but on the moment to moment, day to day handling of each situation. When something happened, the news would travel deliberately in a five-day cycle around the little group. Each character reacted in his own way, thus achieving not only a recapitulation of the plot, but an elongation of the story. Both devices were used too often and too carelessly, leaving actors and directors to improvise to their wits' end, filling the holes. Again, it was the relationships that held. No amount of stretching could pull those lifelines apart. If anything, the knots got tighter and stronger.

But I was recapitulating. Nathan Walsh, played by George Petrie, who had defended Jo in the custody fight, now came to her defense again. He discovered that, indeed, Hazel had had a twin sister, and there was no proof that Sue was not truly Hazel. Ah hah! Time to use the old reenactment trick again. Nathan hired an "actress" to play the part of poor, dead Hazel, and the fire was staged. Hamlet had nothing on us! When Sue saw the "ghost" of her dear, departed sister, she screamed out the truth and ran off into the woods.

However, Higbee had one last trick up his evil sleeve. Joanne had run off to look for Hazel, knowing in her heart that even Hazel could be saved with enough love and kindness; but before she could get to her, Higbee did her in. By the time Jo stumbled over the limp form, an ice pick had been plunged into Hazel's back. The same ice pick that had been missing from Jo's kitchen and one that bore a perfect set of her fingerprints! Jo even had a motive, since everyone believed that Sue was Hazel and, therefore, stood between her and her beloved. The trial was brief and the verdict was guilty!

We had been on the air four years, and the affection that had grown between Lynn Loring and me was very real. Somewhere along the line we had all ceased to be just actors playing parts and become real people in real situations. As we often did, when the scene was very painful, we didn't really play it until air. We just went through the lines.

When Jo said goodbye to Patti before going to jail, the tears were as real as the sorrow. I would not be singing and dancing with my fairy princess for months, and I would miss her.

Telling the story of a show is really telling the story of the people who have done it. Everyone I have talked to had remembered something different. Like the blind men describing an elephant they all saw and heard and felt from a distinctly different point of view.

The drama in the lives of the actors was so often stronger than the story we were telling, but we had the benefit of both.

The act of dealing with personal problems colors anybody's mood and frame of mind. When you know someone close to you is troubled, you unconsciously pull a little more weight. Even by avoiding the subject you strengthen the bond. That unspoken understanding adds a dimension all its own. It could look and sound like strength or tenderness, even anger, but mixed into the batter of the whole show it was the salt that was real and human.

Melba Rae was ill so many days or in pain. She would always go on the air, of course, because she was brave and professional; and Larry Haines as her husband, and I, went with her, watching every move like hawks.

She would say matter-of-factly just as we were about to be cued, "Mary, if I faint, just ignore it," and I would say just as matter-of-factly, "Sure love, okay, don't worry."

Now, ignoring the fact that someone has just fainted and is lying on the floor, out cold, is one thing, but playing a scene that was written for two people all by yourself is another. It is possible to suddenly decide to make a phone call—that is, if there happens to be a phone on the set, and if you can keep your wits about you enough to think of doing it. It is also possible to suddenly start praying. The Almighty is always with us and always listening. Or you can just stand there and keep talking to your friend who has suddenly become not only speechless, but invisible. Thoughts of those alternatives tended to add a stern calm to a performance, no matter what the words or the situation. There was a constant undertone of "Don't you dare faint!" She never did.

When my father was dying, they took care of me. Daddy had been operated on for cancer, and for months I had gone home as often as I could. The doctors had said six months, but late in June my brother called to say Daddy was back in the hospital.

"Should I come home?"

"I don't think you'll make it," he said.

I called Charlie and told him I needed to go home, my father was dying. He said to give him half an hour and start packing. When he called back he said, "If you'll do the show tomorrow, we can work around you the rest of the week."

That day I had a scene with Larry. He was oddly firm, almost harsh with me. If he had been himself, or given me one of those dear, sweet "Larry" looks, I would never have made it.

Daddy was in and out of a coma when I got there, but he knew we were with him, and we were the pride and joy of his life. To hear Daddy tell it, people would cross the street when they saw him coming, because they knew he'd be bragging about one of us. He got a little confused and thought his nurse was his sister, Julia, and I was glad he believed she was there.

Julia didn't come to the funeral, but Harry did, all the way from Spray, North Carolina. He'd never been in an airplane and nobody told him that his seat reclined, or that the food was free. When I opened the little cardboard suitcase to put his things away, there was one shirt and one tie, both with the price tags still on them.

The church was dark, and smaller than I remembered it as a child, and the service seemed silly, just words out of a book that had nothing to do with him, so I didn't listen. I thought about a Sunday morning long before when Daddy was teaching Sunday school, and his class was in the front pew. He came in straight from the night before, sighted on the cross, and marched down the aisle.

One of the boys from his class leaned over and sniffed. "Sir, have you been drinking?"

Looking straight ahead Daddy said, "Young man, I was at early Communion. I didn't see you there."

Late in the summer Richard and I were driving in New Hampshire and we passed a wide, sunny field. Suddenly I saw Daddy there, as a little boy in Virginia, running free and happy, and I cried.

Columbia Records had scheduled the album for a Christmas release, so Kenny and I assumed they would record in July sometime. We kept working and singing and waiting. But August came and went, then September. Finally, the first week in October, unable to reach Mitch Miller on the phone, I called Percy

Faith. It was Monday morning, about ten, and he was pleasant on the phone, just said, "Come on over and bring me a demo."

I grabbed the little discs we had made and jumped in a cab and went straight to the record company. They were all so casual. The receptionist waved toward an open door.

"Mr. Faith is right in there."

He smiled and said, "Sit down," and took my little discs and put them on the turntable. He was so easy and so charming and had the sweetest face I'd ever seen.

"That's nice." He nodded and put on another one. "They're good," he said, sounding surprised. "Why is everybody so against making this record?"

"I don't know." I must have sounded stupid, because that's the way I felt.

"Well, let's do it." He looked at his schedule and sounded so offhand he might have been ordering lunch: "Let's do a session Wednesday and another one Friday."

It was settled. Just like that. All done! I flew home and called Kenny, so excited I couldn't sit down. Then later that afternoon the phone rang and Percy said, "How healthy are you?"

"I'm healthy," I said, feeling suddenly ill. "Why?"

"Because if I'm going to conduct, we have to do the whole album Wednesday, I have to go to the coast on Friday."

Well, if that was the only problem, that was simple. The thought of anyone else was impossible. He was the only man in the world, apparently, who liked our songs.

"I'm healthy enough," I assured him, but I had no idea what I was in for. I'd never seen a recording studio.

He told me to be in the Columbia studio on Twenty-ninth Street on Wednesday. We would do a "session" from two till five and one from seven to ten. Wednesday morning I managed to get down one egg and half an ounce of Scotch. I put two more ounces into a little medicine bottle and went to my voice teacher to warm up. At one, I met Percy and he played the changes he had put into the arrangements. I lied and said I understood what he was talking about.

Then we walked into the studio and I stopped dead. There

were two rows of string players, a whole row of reed players, and a harpist. Twenty-seven musicians waiting for us! Percy took one look at me and understood that I was either going to cry or throw up. He introduced me very quickly, then put big screens up so I couldn't see anybody but him. He tapped the baton and they started to play. When he nodded I started to sing.

My knees shook so violently that I had to lean on the stool. I didn't dare take my eyes off the lyric sheets, even though I knew the songs forward and backward, but I sang. Nobody ever told me they could splice tape, so if I messed up I started over from the beginning of each song. But sometime that afternoon I must have stopped shaking, and at ten that night we had finished. We had recorded a whole album in one day!

I went to work at "Search" the next morning and went through the motions of doing a show, and Friday I went to Columbia with presents for Mitch and one for Percy, two silver flasks. They gave me a dub of the album, then Richard picked me up and we drove down to see Jane and John in Bucks County. Saturday morning very late I woke up, feeling all right, except that tears kept streaming down my face. That went on all day Saturday, and most of Sunday. I ate and talked and smiled—just never stopped crying. I was having a nervous breakdown, but it was worth it. I had made an album!

About two weeks after the album was finished I found myself with a week of vacation time. Richard was busy, so he suggested I go to Warm Springs and stay at the Homestead. No, I had already tried that. We had gone together, and I had spent three months riding around an indoor ring on Twenty-second Street with a bunch of five-year-olds, getting ready. We'd gone to Warm Springs, and I had clicked through that cool yellow dining room in my new jodphurs and my brand-new boots, blissfully unaware that new clothes are a dead giveaway. I had climbed into that tiny English saddle and slipped the reins over my thumbs and around the pinky, just the way the five-year-olds did.

The first morning we went riding with a group, and as we walked the horses out of the paddock toward the trail everything went just fine. Then someone suggested politely that we all try a brisk little canter. They nodded quiet assent, and I started through the combination of heels and knees and little fingers that is supposed to get the damned horse in gear, but nothing happened. Everybody else was off down the trail, and there I sat, still fumbling, until I finally just gave him a good kick.

That did it! We were off! We not only caught up to them, we bolted right through at full gallop! I did finally manage to get him stopped and, by some miracle, I didn't fall off, but I had done everything else wrong. Of course, I had not held up my hand to signal that I was stopping because you can't hold up one hand if you're hanging on with two. No one said a thing, they were much too polite. They just rode past, looking straight ahead, and I walked the rear for the rest of the morning.

No thank you, Warm Springs was not for me. So I went off to the Catskills to a dude ranch.

It was a ridiculous place, built like the set in a bad western movie. There was a street and a long row of wooden buildings with the "saloon" and the "dry goods." The horses were old and calloused and cooperative, and the wranglers were sweet and lazy. They were glad I didn't insist on somebody going with me, and relieved that I didn't talk much and didn't fall off the horse.

I had a wonderful time. I rode all over the mountain all day without speaking to a soul. At night we'd all have supper together, and sometimes somebody would get out a guitar and we'd sing. Then I'd go back to my little cabin and read Agatha Christie. I was alone and at peace, content for the first time in a long while. The album was done, and Mitch Miller was talking about another one. The air was cool and fresh. My mind could turn off and drift through a good mystery, and when I turned out the light a fantasy sang me to sleep with woodwinds and strings and a harp. Richard came to pick me up on Saturday, and that was the perfect end of a beautiful week.

Less than a month later, I felt my body begin to change. I was so sure I called the doctor and made an appointment. He made me wait another three weeks for the test, but I was right. I was pregnant. I knew it immediately. I was going to have a baby, and I knew it was going to be all right.

The album didn't get released in time for Christmas. It came out on January 12, which seemed to me an odd time for a chil-

dren's record. It sold just fine, even got up to number 10 on the
"charts," only to fade quietly into history as the last ten-inch LP
ever made. They couldn't re-press it, they didn't make ten-inch
records anymore.

I guess I was disappointed, but how important is a record
when you have a baby to look forward to.

All winter long Jo languished in prison, her dreary gray uniform getting tighter and tighter, but Arthur was her true love and
Nathan Walsh was her true friend. They left no stone unturned,
and finally managed to unmask Sue's real killer. Again, it was the
nefarious Higbee who had poisoned the soup, who had black-
mailed Irene, and who, in a last desperate attempt to gain control
of the Motor Haven, had shot Arthur!

Jo was released from jail only to find that Arthur had a bullet in his heart. He feared that he would never be a real husband
to her, which was silly because in those days husbands and wives
weren't allowed in bed together anyway.

There were, however, several real problems:

Would Arthur live?

Could Joanne convince him that true love will conquer all?

Could Charlie fit Joanne, who was seven months pregnant,
into a two-shot without revealing that fact?

Would Arthur marry her immediately and get her off the
show for a while?

Yes.

Joanne married Arthur in June of 1955 in the hospital chapel,
and I was enormous. Having spent the winter in jail, clothes had
not been a problem, but the wedding presented some difficulties.
In those days, there was no such thing as a costume designer or a
hairdresser. I bought Jo's cotton housedresses myself, and most of
her aprons were gifts fans had made and sent to me. By 1955 my
hair had grown way below my waist, and I wore it wound securely
into a tight little circle of womanhood. I also wore hats! I perched
little flat discs on top of my head and attached them with hatpins
or combs.

In the maternity shop not far from where I live now, they

display a wedding dress in the window every June, but in 1955 things were different. It was a hot, hot summer, and I just didn't feel like walking very much on my thick, swollen ankles and my sore, swollen feet, so I went into a shop close to the studio that carried low- to medium-priced dresses. The saleslady stopped me as I walked in the door.

"Madam, we don't carry maternity clothes. I suggest Bloomingdale's."

"I'm not looking for maternity clothes. I need a dress for a special occasion. I thought perhaps something with a loose, matching coat."

"Well, madam, if you can tell me what the occasion is, I'll try to help."

"It's a wedding."

"I see. Well, they sell very dressy maternity clothes, if you'd care to try Saks Fifth Avenue. You're to be in the wedding party?"

"I'm the bride."

"I see." She looked me up and down and sideways, shook her head sadly and said, "Well, dearie, all the size sixteens are on that rack against the wall."

I found a princess line dress with a mercifully full coat that happened to be scarlet, but we were in black and white so who cared!

Even a sixteen wouldn't fasten in the back, so we held it together with shoelaces. I bought a bunch of daisies and some veil, and Maud stuck it all in my hair and I must have been the silliest-looking bride since my own wedding to Richard.

Marge was Matron of Honor, Stu was Best Man, and Nathan Walsh gave the bride away. They gathered carefully behind me. So Charlie could get a long shot and not see me full figure, Lynn stood in front. She was short enough for me to see over her and tall enough to hide all but my face with the daisies peeking over the cake.

Jo and Arthur were married at last, and went off on an extended honeymoon. Perhaps there is something about me and honeymoons. Arthur was the casualty that time. He decided he didn't want to hang around not working during my maternity leave, so he got another show and I didn't see him for three years!

July 29 I woke Richard in the night to say it was time to go to the hospital, and he reacted just the way all first time fathers do, poised and calm.

Without hesitation he called the garage, and I distinctly heard him say, "I forgot to put my car away. You can pick it up now." So we took a taxi to the hospital.

They brought Cynthia into my room sometime the next day, and for the whole hour I just looked at her. It never occurred to me to touch her. I just sat there and gazed at that mysterious little face, the exquisitely intricate ears, and the fingernails! There was a fingernail, a tiny transparent shell on every finger of her little fist.

As I watched that baby sleeping that first day, I remember having only two thoughts. She seemed to be smiling, and I thought, "Cynthia has a secret!"

Then a few moments later it occurred to me: "She's a stranger! I've never seen that helpless little person before in my life. My God, I hope we like each other!"

If at any time I had allowed myself to fantasize my role as a wise mother, and I probably had, from that moment on I stepped into the still, cold waters of reality. Parenthood is the one responsibility more people seemed to assume than any other. Is anyone prepared for it?

Jo and Arthur returned from their honeymoon the first week in September. He looked different, because Karl Weber was playing the part, but Arthur had changed in other ways. He was now suddenly restless to improve and enlarge the Motor Haven. He wanted to add a dozen cottages and a swimming pool. Where he was going to put it all was a little vague, since we had begun with an ordinary house on an ordinary city lot. However, since there would never, ever be a way to photograph it, nobody seemed to care.

He was unable to arrange financing at a bank, probably because the bank had sense enough to measure our back yard, but he was determined. It was important that he do something, make a decision himself.

It was the first time on our show that a man, at least a sympathetic man, had taken a strong stand. He was destined to fail, but at least he was trying. When the bank turned him down he made a disastrous mistake. He borrowed $125,000 from a loan shark. Little did he know that the syndicate behind that loan shark was the very same syndicate that had backed Higbee! When he could not repay the money at the end of thirty days, they had a legal right to take over the Motor Haven. What's a leading man to do?

Arthur turned to his rich Aunt Cornelia, played by Doris Dalton, who arrived with her money, her companion, Pearl March, and her bitchy little niece, Allison. All sorts of new folks were moving to town. Jo's mother died and her father, Frank Gardner, came to help out with all the new cottages. Then Jo's sister, Eunice, played by Marion Brash turned up. She was recently widowed, but obviously not in deep mourning. As if things weren't complicated enough, one morning in January Lynn's mother happened to mention that she thought I was pregnant again. In that little dressing room nobody missed much. I was so busy with a seven-month-old baby and the show, I hadn't paid attention. She was right!

Nobody wanted to go through nine more months of photographing me from the neck up, so Charlie called Roy, Roy called Bill Craig in Cincinnati and the three of them decided to try something that nobody else had. They wrote the baby into the script. Lucille Ball wrote hers in about the same time, but that was film. We were live and that made a big difference.

It should be noted that nobody actually asked me if it was all right, but they were very nice when they told me. I made only two stipulations. I was to have the last month *off*, and nothing would ever go wrong with the pregnancy or the baby in the script. I knew I couldn't handle that.

We had a lot of new people, and of course we still had our standbys. Stu and Marge and Patti and Nathan Walsh. I don't know who decided that Nathan needed a sister, but somebody did, and Charlie cast Kay Medford in the part.

George Petrie, who played Nathan for three years, was trim
and handsome and meticulous. Kay blew in the first day for rehearsal in something black and gauzy she found in a thrift shop
and had slept in since. She brought her moth-eaten airedale with
her, and when someone asked if he would bite she said, "No, but
he'll gum you to death."

My favorite story about George was the day he played a
scene on a front porch, and a twelve-foot ladder happened to fall
over. Now when a twelve-foot ladder hits a concrete floor, you
hear it. It makes a loud noise. But George saved the day. Without hesitation he said, "Those squirrels sure make a racket."

George spoke with the perfect American general accent,
standard to radio and television. Kay spoke pure south Bronx. She
could appraise a room full of people with one expressionless
glance—and drop a line the way her gaze hit the floor, sweeping
the corner for an instant, then, zap! Charles had cast these two as
brother and sister, because he had a sense of humor and a latent
mean streak.

We were moving into more complicated stories. Aunt Cornelia bore a resemblance to Irene, but she was much more sophisticated. She maneuvered other characters with a subtlety that
Irene was incapable of, and internal tensions built up in each
household. Allison, Cornelia's spoiled niece, and her jealous companion watched as Cornelia deliberately cornered Arthur. At the
same time they were always threatening to expose her.

At the Motor Haven, Jo's father, played so beautifully by
Eric Dressler, brought the gentle wisdom of another generation.
There were tender scenes between the two of them as they
carried fresh linen to all those new cottages out behind the trash
burner. He helped Jo understand Arthur's need to expand the
business and expand their life. Jo understood and continued to expand.

By 1955 the TV dinner had been on the market for a year,
McCall's had invented the word "togetherness," and "Captain
Kangaroo" had livened things up in Liederkranz considerably. So
there were all sorts of new folks in the halls, like a baby lion, a little panda, or a basket of snakes. You were liable to meet almost
anybody, and I remember, vividly, a very cross camel.

The phone booth in the hall was still our only link with the outside world, and no matter how busy he was, Harry Kusic never seemed to mind answering it and taking messages. As a result, he tended to know a lot about nearly everybody's private life, but Harry was as discreet as he was kind and generous.

Melba had fallen in love, but the romance was stormy, and many days after she had talked on that phone she would be in tears. So Harry would not always deliver messages for Melba right away. If it was close to air, he would decide to wait until the show was over.

When Cynthia was three months old, Larry Haines and his wife, Trudy, adopted a baby girl. Maud's first daughter was already nine months old, and by October she was pregnant with her second. She was always six months ahead of me, which made it very handy exchanging maternity clothes. When we had lunches at Schrafft's we talked less and less about husbands and more and more about babies, but the lunches were rare. It was no longer just running home to get dinner started, it was running home to the baby. Neither of us would leave them with a housekeeper a minute longer than we had to, and little pangs of guilt were a constant companion. Just the strain of working and running and throwing up was beginning to take a toll. Still, we agreed it was worth it. We had the babies and nothing was more important.

It was the year of the babies on the whole show. Freddie had gotten married and was pregnant, and one day I noticed that Melba's skirt wasn't fastened. We didn't know it, but she had married the man on the phone several months before. It was typical of Melba not to talk about her private life. She had always kept everything to herself, but this time she couldn't. With three of us pregnant in that tiny room, and getting dressed behind a twelve-inch locker door, nobody had any secrets.

I'm sure everybody meant to give me the last month off the show, but it just didn't work out that way. September came and went. We were well into October, and the baby was due around the twentieth. Finally, on Friday the thirteenth, I had had enough. I picked up the scripts for the next week, saw my name on three of them, and had a tantrum! In no uncertain terms, I told Charles I was not coming in! I was going home to have a baby.

The shows were all on the telephone, so he persuaded me to stay after that show and do an audio tape of the first one so they could play it on Monday and keep the camera on the other actor's face. That was as far as I would go.

The following Tuesday I began to experience all the signs of a busy afternoon and evening ahead. I was cool as a cucumber when I called Richard and told him he had probably better head on home. No big rush, I assured him, but today was definitely the day. Then I told my housekeeper that if she had any last-minute shopping for the house she had better do it, as I would be gone for a few days.

The phone rang only once that afternoon. It was Charles.

"Can you come in and do those other two voice-overs?"

"No."

"Why not?"

"Because I'm in labor."

"It'll only take about five minutes. How far apart are the—"

I hung up and went back to watching the clock. By three-thirty I was beginning to get anxious. The housekeeper was not back yet, and Richard was not home. Clearly it was time to leave, but Cynthia was sleeping in the next room. How was I going to get her out of her crib and into a cab when I wasn't at all sure I could move myself? So much for being brave and casual. I don't recommend it. I was actually on my way to her room, holding on to the walls, when Richard and the housekeeper got there. We left the house at four-fifteen, Jeff was born at six-ten.

When they brought me back to the room, Richard was reading *Variety*. He glanced at his watch and said, "It's only eight o'clock. Now what'll we do?"

What he did was get so excited he went to Sardi's and bought drinks for everybody in New York, and the only person he forgot to call was his mother.

The next afternoon Charles and an audio engineer arrived in my room and we taped the other two shows. The film crew was down at the nursery and Jeff made his television debut.

When Jeff was brought into my room I was not as timid as I

had been with Cynthia. I was used to holding babies, I suppose. Besides, he weighed eight pounds and was already a sturdy individual. He had come into the world screaming and furious with everyone and everything, and when I got my first good look at him there was a determination in the set of that toothless baby jaw that was unmistakable. I carried him over to the window, and one thought kept going through my mind: "I have a protector."

My first impression of both children has been a lasting one.

Two months after Jeff was born, Melba went into labor three months and one week prematurely. After a week of labor she gave birth to twins: a little girl and a little boy. She must have called us as soon as she was back in her room. It was morning and we were rehearsing.

She said, "Jo, I did it." She didn't call me Mary.

The little girl died sometime in the next twenty-four hours, and the doctors decided that the little boy had to be moved to New York Hospital if he was to make it. She said she watched them put him in what looked like a suitcase and leave. The baby was in an incubator for weeks, and the doctors advised her not to buy baby clothes or make any plans. All she could do was stand outside the glass and look at him. She came back to work and somehow we put on a show five times a week. I don't remember what it was about. It didn't matter.

When Eric weighed a little over four pounds, Melba finally took him home. She and her husband stopped by our apartment on their way, to pick up Jeff's outgrown baby clothes and a bassinet. They still hadn't bought anything.

"My God, you're fat!" Charles swatted me on the behind as I passed him in rehearsal one morning.

He was right! I was size 14! The morning talk was all babies. I always got up and fed mine before leaving for work, and usually had a little sour milk on my shoulder or backside from the last burp when I got there. Everyone had pictures and stories. Charlie listened patiently. No one knew then that his only child had died of crib death a few months before we started the show.

Charlie was born Irving Zipperman. In the old days in Min-

neapolis they had called him Zipp. He married Minnie Fruden-
feld, but I only knew her as Holly Irving, and Holly glowed in
the dark. Her red hair tossed around the exquisite little face of an
eternal child. I never knew her before the baby died, and I'm told
she changed. When I knew her she was fond of breakfasts at 21,
and if the impulse struck her she would call musicians to play for
dinner.

Charlie indulged her in every childish whim. Every piece of
furniture in the duplex on Sixtieth Street was covered with a
flowered chintz she had fallen in love with on sight. There were
toys and pets and people everywhere, and always a party. It was a
gay, extravagant life. Charlie, before he came with us, was the
busiest man on Madison Avenue and about to run himself to
death.

He was doing sixty radio shows a week, acting, announcing,
directing, and finally producing the Sammy Kaye show for television, with my old friend Willy Harbach directing. There was a
nice television first on that show. They were doing "The Saints
Go Marching In," and Willy wanted the band to march through
the audience.

Charlie said, "You can't do that, there is no way to get mi-
crophones out there."

"We don't have to, we'll just play a record." Bill had a commercial recording of the song that Sammy had already released,
and they very quietly anticipated prerecording by several years.

Willy and another young kid named Dwight Hemion had already distinguished themselves directing and producing the old
"Tonight Show" with Steve Allen. There was no budget for late
night shows in those days, but Willy knew everybody and everybody loved Willy. He could get Count Basie to drop in with his
band, just for the fun of it.

A few months before Cynthia was born we moved from our
modest little apartment, where we paid $128 a month rent, to a
lovely six-room apartment on Park Avenue. We took over the
lease from Mike Wallace when he and Buff Cobb got divorced,
and she took our old one. I had been to parties when they lived
there, and I remembered the white wicker and shuttered windows, the huge couches upholstered in white, and famous faces lit

by candles in tall, gilt torchères. My cheap, beige cotton carpeting never gave the same effect of the lush white wool it replaced, but the sun streamed in the windows in the afternoon, and I loved the big, square rooms. I bought a secondhand baby grand piano, and one day I spent two thousand dollars on French dining room chairs, a little silk love seat, and two beautiful yellow silk French bergères. The living room and dining room opened to make one big room, and it was a perfect place for all the beautiful parties we would have.

I finally lived in a real apartment on Park Avenue, and the day we moved in Richard took me to dinner at the Plaza and hired a hansom cab to drive us to our door. A few months later, his job at NBC ran out. Richard had been associate producer of "The Today Show" for a year, but he decided it was time to open his own public relations firm. He and Oliver Rea, one of the two old friends from our honeymoon, took an office together and Richard and I made a deal. His income was enough to pay his taxes and office expenses, and until the business got going I would take care of the rest.

Richard was in public relations and Oliver was just beginning to raise money to build the Guthrie Theatre in Minneapolis, so actually their two lines of work didn't make a whole lot of sense, but they liked each other's jokes and they had a great time together.

Richard signed Arthur Godfrey as a client, then the National Education Association. He was keeping up his side of the bargain. I was making enough to pay the rent and bills, but we had loaned the twelve thousand dollars we had saved to a friend of Richard's to make a movie in Europe, and no one had heard from him since. I still endorsed my checks as they arrived and left them on the bureau, but money started to become an issue.

In the dead of night, cold panic began to interrupt my weary dreams. Richard's charming habit of picking up dinner checks became a cause of irritation and a source of fear—fear of being dependent, of being poor. I had spent my whole childhood in cheap hotels or behind with the rent in dreary little houses. Now I was the star of the top-rated show in daytime, with an apartment on Park Avenue; but I was afraid to fly in an airplane, didn't have a bank account, and still pretended I didn't work for a living. I signed my checks and asked Richard for lunch money.

I was so tired most of the time I was sick at my stomach. The day began when Jeff woke at five and ended sometime between his ten o'clock feeding and Cynthia's last trip for a little playtime alone. In between I learned my lines, ran to the show, ran home, ran to the park with the children, ran back to bathe them, give them their supper and get them ready for bed so I could have dinner with Richard at eight.

Except for occasional Sunday afternoons at the Tourtellots, our traveling had ground to a halt. The Tourtellots were Cynthia's godparents and took the responsibility very seriously. John and Jane were Jeff's godparents and decided they would think it over until he was rational and civilized. I suppose to most people two babies are about as welcome on a weekend as cholera, and I was not about to go anywhere without them. My mother had never left us for a moment, except to go to work, and it never occurred to me there was any alternative. Of course, I did have to go to work, and that meant I had live-in help, but I couldn't get used to that, either. All the nice ladies who came to work knew so much more about how to take care of my house and my babies than I did. In my heart I hated them, and they tended to quit regularly.

When the nice ladies quit, they gave me very little notice, so I was a good customer at the employment agency. One day I came home to find the lady packing and both children raising Cain. Through the racket I called the agency. Richard was away on business and I had a show in the morning, so somebody had to be there.

"Yes," the voice from the agency assured me, "we have someone who seems just right in the office this very minute." Then she added a haunting little phrase, "Now, we haven't had time to check out her references . . ."

There was no choice. Either I hired her or took the kids to work with me in the morning.

About an hour later, Pearl arrived. She was a big woman, with a young, very beautiful face, and seemed absolutely sure of everything. She played with the kids for a few minutes and listened patiently while I talked about the job and the time off and things I thought I was supposed to talk about. Then she went into the kitchen and took over. When I went into the kitchen a little while later she was pushing the washing machine over to the sink.

"You ought to put casters on this thing, make it easier to move," she commented softly.

"It does have casters," I said. "You have to push down that lever."

Then she fixed supper while I bathed the children, and everything seemed just fine. Before she left the kitchen she took the stove apart and cleaned it. She said she didn't want to fix the children's breakfast on anything she didn't know was clean.

I gave Jeff his last bottle and put him to bed, and everything was quiet, so I went back to my room, but as soon as I turned out the light my mind went back to the lady in the employment office.

"We haven't had time to check her references . . ." she had said. I could see Pearl pushing the washing machine across the kitchen and a knot began to form in my stomach. "She's strong as an ox and I don't know that woman! She could be an ax murderess!"

I lay there in the dark, imagining untold horrors, until I couldn't stand it any longer. I got out of bed and crept into the dining room where Jeff was sleeping, lifted him out of his crib and put him in my bed. Then I slipped into Cynthia's room and got her. I felt a little better, but if she was really a killer I had to be sure. I tilted a chair and jammed it under the doorknob.

Of course, in the morning I had to face it all over again. I had to walk out of that apartment and leave my babies with a potential killer. I took forever getting dressed, dawdled over perfectly scrambled eggs, kissed the children goodbye until they thought I was really going to stay. Then finally, my heart pounding, I rang for the elevator. My only hope, I knew, was Martha. Martha would be there to do the laundry at ten o'clock. If they could just survive until ten o'clock!

I couldn't concentrate on the show. I snapped if anyone said good morning until the magic hour. At exactly ten I called home, and Martha answered cheerily, "Hello."

"Martha, it's me . . . is . . . is everything all right?"

"Everything's fine."

"Is Pearl there?"

"Yeah, she's here. She's getting the children ready to go to the park. She's nice . . . she's real nice."

The tears started to run down my cheeks. "Thanks, Martha."

"You want to talk to her?"

"No . . . just wanted to check . . . she's new."

"Yeah . . . well, she sure is nice . . ."

She was nice. She was wonderful, and she stayed for years. Everybody thought I was crazy, except Joy. Joy knew exactly how I felt. Joy felt so guilty if we had lunch, her heart would pound as she walked down the hall to the door. Surely God would punish her for leaving her little girls.

I was guilty too, but not just guilty. I was angry and frustrated because I couldn't get along with the nice ladies—tired and angry and frustrated as I went through all the motions of the perfect life I described in magazines and the makeup room—so tired and frustrated I started taking a tranquilizer on Saturday afternoon. That became my time off. I was furious with Richard when he left on a business trip to London and spent an extra week on the Riviera with Betty and Oliver. He was looking for the man we had lent our money to. Still, it was the Riviera.

I had a beautiful apartment, two beautiful children, a perfect husband, and a wonderful career. I felt like I had a bear by the tail. I didn't dare let go.

My lovely plan of using the dining room and the living room as one big space for all our lovely parties had not worked out at all. Cynthia and Jeff came into the world on totally different schedules that never changed. They insisted upon individual time alone, which I did not think was unreasonable, just impossible. The only way to get any sleep at all was for Jeff to move into the dining room, which meant that my lovely baby grand was closed off along with the hi-fi equipment and the dining room table. They both had a slight digestive problem for the first two or three years and could have no starch or sugar, so by the time they were

1. 2. My father and mother, 1918.

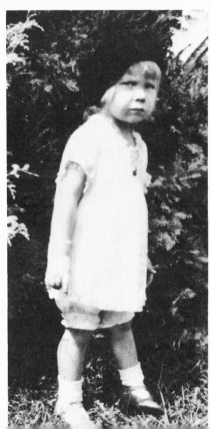

3. Me and my hat.

4. Bruce Hall, my first real love.

5. At Tulsa Central High School.

6.   Starlet with new teeth.

7.   Clark Gable and bathing suit no. 67.

8. My marriage in an iron lung, with dry-eyed close-up.

9. Hooray for Hollywood!

10. The ovalized face and home-made blouse from high school years.

11. Lester and me just before we moved in.

12. The new face at Warner Brothers.

13. The "dark beauty" in the Spanish shawl, from *Thunderhoof* with Bill Bishop.

14. "Cigars, cigarettes, novelties?"

15. With Errol Flynn in *Adventures of Don Juan*.

16. Three of us, going on four.

17. Richard and Mary as dudes.

crawling they were dragging a lamb chop bone in one greasy little fist across the beige cotton carpet, the silk love seat, and the French chairs.

We did give one party, and I invited everyone I knew so that would be the end of that. Of course, I had no idea how to cook for thirty people and was much too careful with a dollar to even consider having it catered. The solution was to have my two friends who ran the luncheonette on Lexington do it. On my way home from the studio I picked up a vat of pale chicken fricassee and gummy rice.

It was a very long evening. The noise woke both kids, and I was so busy running up and down the hall trying to get them back to sleep I let the rice stick in the bottom of the pan. It burned, but the people were nice. They all said they had a good time, and that I shouldn't be such a slave to my children.

I don't think I really cared, except that I was supposed to care, so I felt guilty and wrong not to. Parties weren't important and people weren't important, not then. We had two miracle babies, and no matter how upset or tired I got all I had to do was hold one of them or go into the room and watch them sleeping and everything was all right. When Richard was away I'd eat my supper when I fed them, then we'd watch "Kukla, Fran and Ollie," or snuggle in the big bed and read the little picture books over and over again.

Somebody offered me a part in a Broadway show that year, and I remember thinking, "No, there will be other plays, but only two babies. I don't want to miss a minute of them." I've never regretted that, and the nights I fell asleep with one of them in that rocking chair are among the sweetest I remember. Somewhere along the line my original fantasy of a baby one year and a play the next got mislaid. I was finding out that kids take a lot longer than a year.

Everybody said I spoiled them rotten from the day they were born. I don't regret that, either. Jeff had a temper and demanded what he wanted when he wanted it. Cynthia seemed to retreat, but she would always reappear, ever so softly, when the noise died down. Long before they could talk they were saying something. I didn't know what it was, much of the time, but I knew it was important.

There was no time for plays or parties and almost no time even for friends, but mine were as busy as I was. Freddie left the show when her son was born, and Maud was on her hands and knees with two little girls, two shows, and no help except a babysitter when she was gone. Not seeing each other except at work didn't affect the friendship. As a matter of fact, it would be years before we realized how strong the friendship really was. Perhaps I am particularly slow, but it's usually ten or fifteen years before the thought occurs to me that, yes, we are friends.

One of those long trips began just before we moved out of the apartment on Park Avenue. It was a Sunday afternoon and the sun was streaming in the windows when Barbara Carroll came by for a drink. Richard had gotten to know her when he worked on "The Today Show." We'd been to clubs to listen to her trio, and he talked a lot about how talented and beautiful she was. I had mixed feelings, a mixture of admiration and pure hatred.

Barbara played jazz piano like no one else I'd ever heard. Somewhere between her mind and her fingers, those unbelievable passing tones said all there was to say about a song. She was married to her bass player, Joe Schulman, and when they worked together they listened and smiled and answered each other in a conversation so complex and so simple, it said all there was to say about everything else that's really important, like trust and love and talent.

I thought they were the two luckiest people in the whole world. Then Joe died, suddenly, tragically. They had gone to Fire Island for a little vacation. It was out of season and they wanted to be by themselves. Joe had a heart attack. There was no doctor for miles, and he died in her arms.

That afternoon Barbara was sitting on the little beige love seat, talking about Joe, and she was talking to me. I don't know why that moment stands out, but it does for both of us, and it's been twenty years. I think, perhaps for me, the way she looked at me let me glimpse, for a moment, her world, her magic circle.

Barbara's music sets images flickering through everybody's

mind, and I think unconsciously I went back to the three soldiers playing in the army camp when I was a kid. It was the same kind of music, the same kind of listening, and they were the beginning. They were the first New Yorkers I had ever met, and somehow I thought that when I got to New York everybody would be just like them, but then I also thought that New York looked like one great big Rockefeller Center. That was the postcard that had made the lasting impression. When I finally arrived, it was a surprise, but never a disappointment.

When I got out of high school I talked my way into a job on the local newspaper. I had convinced them I would be a good roving reporter, collecting fascinating tidbits on the streets of Tulsa. They handed me a Speed Graphic and a pad of paper, and out I went. I had inherited my father's aptitude for anything mechanical, so I spent the whole first day fiddling with the camera. The only people on the street who stopped were trying to show me how it worked, so I had to sort of fake the stories.

The film came back from the lab blank, and the editor turned back my copy with a little note, "Don't put your whole life story in the first paragraph," and moved me to the obituary column. That lasted almost a week, but since I couldn't spell or type they decided my writing style didn't yet deserve an assistant to proof the copy, and my newspaper career ended abruptly.

I had, however, met the man who ran the American Airlines office, because he came up to visit with the sports writer. I went straight from the paper over to his office and conned him into giving me a job. I had to lie about my age and my schooling, but by the time I left that office I had even convinced myself that what I really wanted more than anything in the world was to be reservationist for American Airlines. They were to send me to New York for a three-week training course. One week later I left home with thirty-five dollars from the newspaper and a free ticket to New York.

I also had a suitcase containing one black evening dress

a lady had given me, one red velvet suit that had been cut down from a size 16, and thirty or forty ascots. An ascot was a little square of colored material that someone clever could do wonders with, changing her costume from casual to dressy in an instant.

One night, while Mother and I were cutting and hemming the scraps of material, Daddy looked over his paper and asked innocently, "Exactly what part of the anatomy does an ascot cover?"

I also had a pair of light-green tweed pants my brother had outgrown and a thick black Navy issue sweater.

I never used my free ticket. There were no vacant seats available, and after three days of hanging around the airport a private pilot asked if any servicemen wanted to go east. No one answered and I said, "Take a civilian?"

He looked at me and smiled. "You bet," he said without hesitation.

I had never been in any kind of plane before, and wouldn't have known about automatic pilots if I had. In North Carolina I decided to get out and take the bus the rest of the way.

It's hard to see much of the city coming in through the tunnel in the middle of the night to the bus terminal. I got into a taxi with my suitcase and gave the driver the address of a friend I had met on a USO tour. We started up Broadway toward 116th Street and I saw my first taxi meter ticking away. I had only four dollars left, and fifteen dollars in a traveler's check, so when it got to $3.85 I asked him to stop.

"Why, kid, what's the matter?" He turned around and looked at me.

"That's all the money I have," I said. "I'd better walk."

He looked at my suitcase, he looked at me, he shook his head, then he turned off the meter and took me to 116th Street. He even waited until they let me into the door of the shabby apartment hotel. He was awfully nice, but then I knew people were going to be nice in New York, so I wasn't really surprised.

I was, however, surprised, amazed, and a little frightened when my friend opened the door. The light was behind her, shining through her thin little wrapper, and it was immediately apparent that she was very, very pregnant. It was a shock, because I knew for a fact that she was not married, and in my young eyes, forty was very, very old to be doing that sort of thing. As she spread pillows and a blanket on the floor of her one-room apartment, she explained that she had decided this was her last chance to experience childbirth. She had picked out a suitable father, gone through all the necessary preliminaries, and now, with the event just a week away, had no qualms about her decision.

Thirty years ago, people did not do that sort of thing. I had no idea how to react or what to think, so I didn't. It was late and I was tired. I just went to sleep.

The next morning my friend had to go to the doctor, but before she left she gave me a map of the city and pointed me toward a bus stop. I rode down Central Park West on top of a double-decker bus and before we turned at Fifty-ninth Street I was in love. It was early October, and the leaves were just beginning to turn in the park. People were dressed in the rich shades of fall and seemed to glow against the solid wall of brown, beige, and gray apartments.

The bus went all the way down to Washington Square, and that's where I was going. Besides my pregnant friend, I knew only one other person in New York, and I called her Grandmother. I knew she had only educated Mother, but when I was growing up that's what we always called her, and that is the way she had signed the cards and letters that came from all over the world. Her name was Susan Volmer when Mother was young. Now her name was Susan Woodruff.

If Daddy's upbringing had been strange, Mother's was stranger. While Cousin Nancy was making news in Parliament, Grandmother was making news in another way and from the other political pole. Riding down Fifth Avenue that morning I tried to focus on all the pictures I had formed from the stories Mother had told and the stories in the magazines. She would be tall, with big bones and a strong, husky voice, I decided.

"Bring back one of those Virginia blue bloods and I'll raise her," Grandmother had said to a friend who was going to Richmond, and Mother was the blue blood.

Mother went to St. Paul's when she was eleven, and at twelve the beautiful little girl with big brown eyes and long, wavy auburn hair was on her way to New York. She was so shy the soft, southern accent was rarely heard.

In 1912, Grandmother was one of the leaders of the Women's Suffrage Movement. Her farm in Huntington was a meeting place for all the radical leaders of the time. Dr. John Dewey, the father of modern education, lived on the farm next to Grandmother's and the assortment of children they had acquired were Mother's playmates. Sabino was about Mother's age. The Deweys adopted him when they were in Italy, and since he was allowed to drive at twelve he and Mother could roam fairly far afield. Mother met him the day he turned the car over in front of Grandmother's house and came to the door to ask casually if he could borrow hers.

It's hard to imagine what it was like for Mother, who was born in the mountains of Highland County and had never even seen a Yankee. She was dressed up as Miss Liberty and marched down Fifth Avenue in a suffragist parade. She was sent door to door collecting money for the movement, and since nobody had time to notice if she was there or not, she and Sabino would sneak into the city and go to shows.

In the summer Mother studied with all the Dewey children under a tutor. One afternoon a breathless maid announced, "Sabino's building a fire under the bed!"

"Move the bed!" was Mrs. Dewey's instantaneous solution.

Mother, who couldn't read or write when she was eleven, took special courses in Latin at Columbia University when she was fifteen and graduated from high school when she was seventeen, fluent in a second language. But it had been a lonely childhood. If Grandmother went to Palm Beach in the winter, she spent Christmas at the Cosmopolitan Club. She was still too shy to go into the dining room, so she spent her allowance and bought hot dogs.

By the time I could read, Grandmother was a Socialist. She sent us postcards when she traveled in Russia and lectured in universities. She sent us a subscription to a magazine called *Soviet Russia Today*, which my yellow-dog Democrat parents used to burn in the dead of night. In those days you didn't want that kind of literature, even in your trash.

Once she sent us a fur-lined opera cape, which my practical brother surveyed and immediately put to use. "It'll make a good cover," he said, and somebody slept under it for years.

Now Grandmother was one of the three ladies who owned *The Daily Worker*. I had her phone number and her address on Eighth Street. I rang the bell marked Woodruff in the old-fashioned apartment house and a door opened at the back of the dark hallway. I walked back and peered into the gloom and there stood Grandmother, not the Valkyrie I had expected at all, but more the Good Witch of the East. She was tiny, and her round little body was wrapped in a black shawl. Her hair was soft and white, and she gazed back at me with steel-blue eyes that had seen everything.

"You look like your father," she said in a quiet New England accent. "I told your mother when she married him she'd never be happy but she'd never be bored."

She didn't hug me or even offer her hand. She just said, "Come in, child."

Later that afternoon we sat in the cluttered little back room where a dozen French clocks made the only sound. She folded away the envelopes she had been addressing to libraries, offering them a subscription to the *Worker*, and said in her absolutely matter-of-fact way, "Now my dear, we must plan your life. First, you will get a very good education. That is essential. Then you will choose a cause. Take your time and choose the cause carefully, then you will devote your life to it."

She smiled and folded envelopes and assumed that was settled.

While my friend was in the hospital having her baby, I stayed in her apartment and tried to go to the American Airlines school. But years had not lessened the frustration of a schoolroom and, whether by design or accident, I rarely got there. The New York subway system brought back all the old terror of the river I had tried to cross as a child, and each day the feeling grew. I was late, I was wrong, I was inadequate.

The last day was a nightmare. They took us all in a bus to LaGuardia Airport, sat us down at desks in long rows, and we were actually supposed to make reservations. I was given four huge, heavy books with schedules of planes and cities arranged alphabetically. At the far end of the room there was a big blackboard with flights chalked in and the number of seats available. At least I think that is what was written on that board. I never got all that quite straight. I was much too busy trying to figure out what the books were for.

I have always been what you might call an original speller, and only had a vague kind of general idea of geography—sort of a nice general picture in my mind. If you can believe that I got all the way through World War II with France sort of behind Germany, you will understand the problem.

I only succeeded in making four complete reservations that whole morning. By the time I had fingered my way through the alphabet and looked up the flights in the books, they had hung up and called another airline. The last straw was the supervisor coming over to tell me I had booked an overload and overhearing my conversation.

"Sir, where are you now? . . . Uh, huh—could you just tell me one more time where you want to go? . . . Uh, sir, would you happen to know offhand if that's to the right or left of Dallas?"

They were perfectly within their rights to fire me on the spot. I really wasn't cut out to be a reservationist. They were nice, though, and paid me a whole week's salary, which came to sixty-five dollars. I gave forty dollars of that to my friend, who had had a beautiful baby boy, and put the two of them on a bus back to Tulsa. Then I made a deal with the hotel where the other reservationists lived to stay on in the dormitory for the rest of the week, but that was awful and lonely. Most of the girls had graduated and gone, and the rest of them were still busy with their books and maps.

I had flunked out. I didn't want to be a reservationist, but knowing you have failed is not a nice feeling. To make the day complete, Mother called to see when I would be home. Home? The thought had not crossed my mind for three weeks, not since the first morning in New York. She took me completely by surprise.

"Well . . . ," I lied, "I'm going to stay on in New York reservations for a few weeks. They think I'm pretty good, and it'll be a good experience." I didn't fool Mother at all, and she was worried sick.

I went into a bar near the hotel and ordered a drink. I didn't drink, but I needed someone to talk to. Someone turned out to be two nice young men who not only talked to me, they bought me dinner, and a week later, when I was without a place to live, let me sleep on their couch. I was too dumb to realize that picking up strangers can not only get a person in trouble, it can get you killed. I was trying so hard to appear sophisticated and grown-up, and I fooled no one.

Not once did anyone say an unkind word or even seem like he might take advantage of the kid. Only at odd moments, late at night, did a cold finger of terror go through me. If I was missing, no one would know.

The next night I went back to the bar. It was friendly and a cheap way to eat. A nice man bought my drink and took me to a real restaurant for dinner. That dinner was the first turning point. When we got to the restaurant, that nice man checked his hat and I noticed he gave the girl a quarter. After we had been shown a table, and I was feeling very grown-up indeed in my made-over velvet suit and my ascot, I excused myself and went back to the hat lady.

"Excuse me, ma'm. How do you get this kind of a job?"

She looked at me tolerantly and answered, "You gotta be a member of the union, honey."

"How do I join the union?"

Her practiced eye examined the suit and she said, "How bad do you need the job?"

"I need it."

She paused a moment, then she asked, "Do you have a black dress?"

"I have a long one."

"That'll do." She looked around to make sure we were not overheard. "Tomorrow at five o'clock go to Queens Terrace, on Queens Boulevard. Ask for Benny, and tell him Flo sent you. He's gonna need somebody."

Three weeks later I not only knew how to check hats, I could sell cigarettes, flowers, and I had even learned how to use a Speed

Graphic, so I could take pictures of drunken customers. I was also very adept at hiding under a table when Benny came into the kitchen, or when the cooks started throwing knives and boiling water around.

The next job was much grander. I was the camera girl in the Roosevelt Hotel, and my little purse full of quarters was enough to afford a room. I saw the sign, ROOM FOR RENT, on Lexington. It was seven feet wide and eleven feet long and I was afraid to turn out the lights standing on the floor for fear of creepy, crawly creatures, but for some reason I wasn't frightened when a perfectly strange man casually opened my door one night and walked in.

He turned on the light, looked at me, surprised, and not a little stupefied. "Guess I got the wrong room. You new?"

That was all he said, and left.

The next day a terribly pretty girl, who lived on the second floor, asked me if I had anybody steady, and I said no, having no idea what she meant. Then she said they always needed an extra pretty girl and invited me out to dinner. It was a big group of strange people, and the man I was sitting with got awfully drunk, so the subject of why I was probably there never came up.

At the end of the week the pretty girl asked me to share her apartment. It had a private bath and she seemed nice, so I moved in with Lynn. I worked at the Roosevelt until three every morning so I never had a chance to meet any of her friends, but I knew she had a lot because I was nearly always locked out when I got home. I sat on the steps the first night and fell asleep. Then the second night a nice man she called Polly, who had the only real apartment in the building, invited me in for coffee and talked to me until I fell asleep on his couch. After that, I began to hope the door would be locked.

New York winter came as a surprise. I had seen snow once or twice back in Oklahoma, but nothing like the cold in New York. I was still wearing a little spring-weight coat, and at night when I went to work I wore little ballet shoes with my "evening gown." I must have been very lucky not to get sicker than I did. I don't remember passing out, but I remember the sleazy doctor's office they took me to.

"Call Polly," I pleaded. "Tell him to come and get me."

He came and took me home and took care of me until I was well.

I had never seen an apartment like his. Polly's real name was Lester. He was a painter and a set designer, so it was also his studio. He had painted everything gray, even the furniture, and stretched a wire across one whole wall, with white sheets hung from the ceiling to the floor. The ceiling was domed, and he'd painted that pale blue with floating clouds. On a brick wall that the bedroom looked out on, he had painted a country landscape. He was wise and patient. He was tender and Jewish. When I brought in a scraggly little tree at Christmas he cut out marvelous designs from a deck of playing cards, and I had a home. I was in New York, I lived someplace, with somebody, and I had a job. When I looked from the streets or a taxi at the walls of yellow squares I still wondered who was in each little box, but I had a window too, a real window, even if the view was only paint.

Lester and I spent a lot of time alone, and usually at odd hours. He was teaching at Sarah Lawrence, besides designing and painting, and I was working nights. Still, we managed to go for long walks throughout the city and to museums.

He had lots of fascinating friends who lived in all the funny spaces you can find only in New York. Most of them were painters and many of them were famous, but I didn't know that then. We only went to one apartment that made me uncomfortable. He had been in love with a very beautiful woman named Virginia before he knew me. She had just married a young producer named Bob Whitehead. He and his partner, Oliver Rea, were putting together a new company to do Broadway shows, and Lester was one of two resident designers. We went to their apartment for dinner once or twice, and often for meetings. If they were having a meeting, I waited in the anteroom all evening.

Everything in the apartment was perfectly beautiful, and I studied every inch. The walls were painted pale, pale yellow and the couches were covered in brown silk satin. Virginia was tiny and blond. She always suggested that she walk with Lester if we were going out. I was taller than Lester and very aware that she was just right.

Late in March, Joe Pasternak came into the Roosevelt one night and quite casually asked me if I would like a Hollywood contract. I said, "Sure," and moved on to the next table. The headwaiter whispered to me a few minutes later that the gentleman sitting at ringside was a very important producer at MGM. I made it my business to hover nearby until he noticed me again.

Two days later I did my first screen test. They told me to bring a tight sweater, slacks, a skirt, and a blouse. I took my red velvet suit, my brother's green tweed pants, and my sweater was still Navy issue. They also asked for high-heeled shoes, so I bought some with ankle straps at a store on Lexington that stayed open late and I practiced wobbling around the apartment.

My first encounter with professional makeup men and hairdressers should have been an omen. My hair was long and thick, and I usually wore it on top of my head. They curled it and brushed it till it looked a lot like a horse blanket slung around my shoulders. They slimmed my nose, arched my brows, rounded by chin, and sunk my cheeks until I looked like somebody else altogether, and we began.

The director gave me a mark to stand on. I was to look directly into the camera, say something charming or witty, hopefully both, turn slowly and walk straight away from camera, turn, smile, and do a quick pivot. Then I was to change clothes and repeat the process. What I didn't understand was that they were going to do a camera cut in the middle of the pivot, and when I came around I would be dressed differently—from simple elegance to glamour, from young and vulnerable to the siren—displaying my many potential facets.

Since I only had three changes of clothes, the test was mercifully short. All went well with the red velvet until the quick pivot, which was too difficult to negotiate in the new ankle straps, and I stumbled completely out of the frame. Then came the green tweed, Navy issue number. When I turned to walk back to my second mark, there, marching down my back, was a line of clothespins. The wardrobe lady had clipped the sweater and the pants together to give me some shape. I pivoted gravely, staggered out of the picture again, and everybody fell on the floor.

"You can't sing, you can't dance, and you probably can't act," Mr. Pasternak prophesied, "but you've got something."

They signed me to a seven-year contract the next afternoon in a suite at the Waldorf Towers.

"Don't get married or engaged or anything," Mr. Pasternak said, "and I want you to meet Bullits Durgom, he's your new agent."

Lester and I were married, secretly, two weeks later at City Hall and left together for Hollywood.

The first six years "Search" was on the air was a time for growing and discovery. The technical medium itself had become part of every scene. The three cameras edging around the perimeter of the set were not mechanical, they were live eyes and ears. As the moves in a scene became locked to the dialogue, the cameras became part of the dance.

Somewhere along the line I had realized it is pointless to raise an eyebrow in a long shot, and instinctively I knew to telegraph with a glance what I was going to do next. The communication had become refined to a point that was often so perfect it helped fill the scene. When the little red light blinked on at the precise second I turned into the close-up, it was almost as if the cameraman and the director had reached out a hand to help me.

We had real lights after the first couple of years, and Frank Olson became part of the family and part of the drama. We didn't have to have marks on the floor, we could feel the lights. I remember very clearly walking across the kitchen one day, with tears streaming down my face, and feeling the light grow cold. I had walked a little too far. I automatically stopped and backed up.

The music, too, became personal and integral, with a theme for each character. Bill Meeder knew before we did what we were thinking and feeling. If there was not enough time to prepare, and I had a scene that called for tears, he would play Patti's theme for me and it always worked, bringing back memories and releasing tenderness. Like the red light holding out a hand, a melody began when the thought occurred, often in counterpoint and always right.

As an actress I was growing, too, and discovering every day. Despite the nervousness, I began to love that magic moment when the fourth wall comes down and you're on the air, really playing the scene. That fourth wall for us was time that enclosed us, and somehow completed the reality we were creating. The silly stove that was never plugged into anything would suddenly become hot enough to burn my finger as I solemnly stirred a pot of cold water. A blast of chill wind through the trees painted on the backing would make me shiver when I opened the front door. If we had had time to rehearse, the way Broadway shows and nighttime television were prepared and thought about, those reactions would have been programmed and set. For us, they had to occur spontaneously.

More important, by far, than cold winds or hot stoves, were the images of remembered awareness and emotion that kept welling into consciousness and filling the space around the words and between the actors. I was learning to listen. I was learning to be totally receptive to a moment. All by itself, a moment would ignite and catch fire to the next moments from my own experience and moments from Joanne's life, from her growing history. The past and the present were beginning to mingle and the deep currents of the third river were beginning to flow.

I was learning my craft and I was learning discipline. No matter how tired I was at the end of the day, I pushed my head through another script. I always learned my lines so well that I could think through a scene like a monologue. We were live, and that was scary, so until I had the script in my mind I didn't feel secure enough to rest. When I did turn out the light, I would force myself to check each scene one more time before I let my mind turn off or change the channel to something pleasant and private.

Joanne was the pivotal character in those days, and I was on nearly every day. There were many nights when the effort made me sick to my stomach. I would lie there, staring at the page with my mind a total blank, the clock ticking away the sleep I needed and the frustration making it more and more impossible. It had to be done, and I always did it, and if I woke in the night I would check it again, running a difficult scene or a long speech in my head to make sure I had it.

After the children were born I was more often exhausted, so I had to spend even more time memorizing. Being tired makes it more difficult to retain, but being tired also puts you a little closer to the edge, and I was terrified that my mind would simply turn itself off.

It was at the beginning of the seventh year that everything started to change. There were more daytime serials on the air and the competition had gotten stronger. "The Guiding Light," "The Secret Storm," "A Brighter Day," "Valiant Lady," and "As the World Turns" were all vying for the ratings and audiences, and everything had begun to change for us.

Our advertising agency, the old Biow Company, went out of business in 1956, and we were moved to Leo Burnett. They were based in Chicago, and unaccustomed to producing live dramatic shows, so the beginnings were difficult. They surveyed our autonomous little operation and decided immediately that things had to change. I suppose that was natural. They couldn't take over the show and leave everything just as it was; they had to contribute.

The problem—or one of many—was that they didn't know quite what to do. The first move was to send in a producer who liked to sit in the rehearsals in the morning. Possibly our early morning coffee klatch looked a little haphazard, and probably very unprofessional. Possibly the fact that Charles owned the company that supplied our sets and our furniture seemed irregular. That was the old system that had been arrived at by Bill Craig, but Bill had left Procter & Gamble and was an agent with William Morris.

Our most serious problem, and one that was hard to hide from the new agency, was that Charles was very often not in New York at all. His wife, Holly, had been hired as the second lead on "Blondie," which was filmed in California, and Charles was commuting. The trip was not four and a half hours in those days, it was twelve, and by 1957, Charles was only around on Tuesdays and Wednesdays.

Our writer had left to develop the new half-hour show, "The Edge of Night," and the new set of plots and characters was not making it. Irving had let the story simply run out. Melanie, whoever she was, had gotten lost in the woods. The search was funny in rehearsals, because Larry Haines planted falsies all along the trail and would hold one up triumphantly every time he had to say, "I think she went this way!"

But when Nathan disappeared and Arthur Tate and Stu had to poke around with long sticks in a tub of water that was supposed to be a pond, we knew we were in trouble. For an entire week we moaned and mourned poor, dear, dead, soggy Nathan until the closing shot on Friday. If only we could have used the dress rehearsal of that show, we'd have been all right.

There was a knock at Jo's front door and when she opened it there stood Nathan! He looked just fine for a man who had been at the bottom of a pond for a whole week, but as he walked in the door, straight toward the camera, a steady stream of water kept spurting out of his mouth.

Jokes were not enough to keep spirits up, and certainly not enough to keep a show alive. The faces were different, too. Freddie didn't come back after her son was born. Sue Slade took her place. She was clever and bright but she wasn't my friend. We staggered along for months, piecing together shows and waiting for something to happen. If Charles's plane was late, we would start rehearsal without him, or Hal would rush in and take over.

One day nobody showed up until dress rehearsal, so I blocked the actors and Joe Papp talked the camera crew through the moves from the floor. We got the faces on the air, but that's not doing a show.

One afternoon during that period, Irna Phillips, whom I knew to be the single most powerful writer at Procter & Gamble, and also the best, came up to me in the hall.

"You and I together could do the greatest daytime half-hour show of all time," she said. As she proceeded to tell me about this great and wonderful show, I started backing away, partly from the force of her enthusiasm and partly from terror. She had already announced that she did not want to have anything to do with fifteen-minute shows. Her show, "The Guiding Light," followed ours. It only took a moment to add our fifteen minutes to her fifteen minutes and see exactly where she was heading.

For months we drifted, Charlie flying back and forth to California desperately trying to keep the home fires alight, and keeping us afloat with the sheer strength of his bravado and the genius he will always have. Even then he and Hal were putting together new shows, but we no longer had the safety and assurance of the one station markets and the ratings slid.

The last straw was a bitter fight between the new Procter & Gamble representative and Charles. Their ideas about television, people, and power had clashed from the first moment they met, and finally exploded into an anger that was personal and irrevocable.

We met as usual that last Friday, in our rehearsal hall upstairs over Longchamp's restaurant. The door to the inner office was closed, but we could see Sue and Charlie's silhouettes through the opaque glass. Sue came out for coffee with tears streaming down her face, and nobody said anything.

Finally, Charlie came out, smiling, only because he is an unbelievably brave man. "Well, this is it, kids. The son-of-a-bitch finally got me."

We had known it was coming, but the sudden reality left us stunned.

"Okay, let's do it," he said, and sat in his chair behind a table. He fanned the pages of the script with his thumb, making a rude remark about its contents.

We went through the motions of the first act mechanically. There were the usual jokes about the dialogue, but that morning they did not ease the tension; they only seemed harsh and grating. That flimsy little script was all we had. Everyone in that room loved Charles more than they knew how to say, but he had gone too far away from us. We knew we couldn't get him back.

Finally, he marked the last shot on the last page. "Well,

we'll give them one to remember; they'll see, the show will be off
the air in six months."

It was too much. "God damn you!" I screamed at him.
"You've taught us all we know, and it's enough! We'll go on forever!"

Why do you always cry when you talk on the phone?"

Cynthia was sitting in her high chair at the kitchen table playing with her supper and watching me with big, solemn eyes.

"Oh, it's just business. Business people get cranky and mean because they don't have any babies to come home to and play with."

I cut a little chicken off the bone for her but kept the best part on, hoping that would keep her interested long enough to eat it, and went back to feeding Jeff. That was more of a project. He was securely wedged into a low feeding table, but I'd gotten into the ridiculous habit of letting him play while he ate. Every night I would try to find some new distraction, and I was running low on inventiveness. He had been turning a bunch of keys on the ring and was close to figuring out how to get them off altogether when he decided it was more fun to push them close to the edge of the table and let them fall, because, of course, Mother would pick them up. Every time I bent over and retrieved the keys he rewarded me by taking a bite.

The phone rang again and both children looked at me. They were just babies. Cynthia was two and a half and Jeff was just over a year, but they were so aware. There were no arguments on the phone, just long, tense conversations. That time it was a voice out of the blue.

"You'll never guess who this is, it's Terry."

The voice was right. I had no idea who that was.

"Terry O'Sullivan!"

"Oh . . . hi. How've you been? I heard you were in California."

"I'm back! I'm really back. They just hired me to do the show again."

"To play Arthur?" I hoped the dismay didn't show in my voice.

"Of course to play Arthur. Would you believe it, those bastards made me audition! Audition to play Arthur Tate! I *am* Arthur Tate!"

"Well, Terry . . . I'm delighted." I felt sick and helpless and sorry, but that wasn't his fault, so I also felt guilty for wishing he had blown it.

"I just called to let you know how grateful I am. I know you had a lot to do with getting me back and I appreciate it."

Oh my God, I thought. If he only knew.

"Well . . . see you in rehearsal . . . and welcome home!" I hung up and debated whether it was too late to call Frank one more time, try just once more. It was six o'clock. The agency would be closed for cocktails.

"Was that a friend?" The kids had not moved since the phone rang. Cynthia was watching me, one little hand poised in midair where it had stopped when the phone rang.

"Yes, a nice old friend." It was no fair what I was doing to them. No wonder they didn't want their dinner. The damn show was not their problem.

"Let's have dessert and go watch 'Kukla, Fran and Ollie.'"

Jeff took half a banana and Cynthia had a little bowl of raspberries. I wiped their hands and faces to make room for the new mess, but Cynthia methodically mashed a raspberry between her first two fingers and her thumb before she tasted it, so there were three new, tiny pink smears on the white wall where she turned the corner into the living room. I started to clear the dishes as Pearl came out of her room.

"I'll do that, you go on now. You've been up since five this morning."

"Thanks, Pearl. Richard will be late, so put the potatoes in to bake at seven-fifteen."

Cynthia looked like a Christmas fairy in her little white nightgown and her long red bathrobe. Her walk was so light and graceful, even then, floating to tiptoe, a tiny capsule of a woman, and always her fingertips touching the air. Her hair was cut short in a tawny cap, and her long black lashes gave the baby face oddly exotic moments of expression, so pensive, always listening.

Jeff made his way across the room, too, still a little unsteady, but with undeniable determination. It was a new skill he had discovered only a couple of months before, and discovered is the only way to describe it. He had gone through the motions of pulling himself up in the playpen, of course, but standing alone had been a specific moment of achievement that I had to believe he planned.

"I did it!" he crowed one night. I was startled because it was a whole sentence with no trace of baby talk, and that was a first, but as I turned smiling and pleased with this accomplishment my heart stopped in panic! What he had done was stand, also for the first time, and the place he had chosen was the top of Cynthia's high chair. He did manage to stay balanced on his first mountain for the two seconds it took me to get across the room and grab him. There was not another moment of peace for years.

All three of us sat on the floor in front of the set and I looked forward to the shows as much as they did. In the afternoons, especially in cold weather when we didn't stay in the park so long, we'd watch the Mickey Mouse Club and sing, "M-I-C— See you real soon . . . K-E-Y—Why? Because we like you . . . M-O-U-S-E."

Then it was bath time and I always put them both in the tub in our bathroom. The one off the other bedroom was too full of drying laundry to use for anything else. It was a sloppy process and they liked to play in the water, of course, so the floor and I very often got soaked. There were tears and screams if it was time for a shampoo, but the smell of clean children has to be the sweetest one I know. The mix of baby powder, the touch of cot-

ton flannel and tender, tender skin is a miracle-soother at the end
of the day. No matter how your back hurts leaning over the tub
and lifting them out, over and over, there are wonderful places to
kiss while you dry them off—on the neck, just under the ear, or
the crease of a silky little arm that has a dimple for an elbow. For
that you can do anything.

Watching the show, they sat cross-legged and leaned forward
totally absorbed, concentrating. Cynthia's eyes wide and round,
her rosebud lips open in anticipation, Jeff edging even closer, his
round little jaw set, almost glaring, and his brow a straight line as
he strained to catch every new word. The strange convention of
the woman talking to the puppets, the box within a box—where
did that fit into their reality? I didn't think about it then. Ollie
was simply a dragon who happened to have feelings like anybody
else. Perhaps that is what they saw. By the end of the program,
they would begin to tire and lean against me, and I could rub my
nose in the baby brush of Jeff's crew cut. Then it was time to
read. One book, one story before bed.

The Little Train That Could was Jeff's favorite. Cynthia
would want *Lonely Doll*, so we very often would read both, or
Sam and the Firefly, because it was my favorite. Then it was really time for bed, the last lift of the day, as I carried them one at
a time and settled them into their cribs. A kiss good night, and
one for my "bottle." I always got an extra kiss for my bottle, and
over and over I would have to tell them, "Some day you will grow
up and I won't have babies to kiss, but I'll have my bottle, and
every time I want a kiss all I have to do is open my bottle and
take one out."

Neither one of them ever asked me where I kept the bottle,
or what color it was or how big, but every night the moist little
faces would press my cheek one more time.

If I was anxious or frightened, sometimes I squeezed them
too tight or held them an extra long moment. Just the fact that
they were there, warm and loving, made everything else possible.
That was how it was on a perfect night. When it was good it was
very very good, when it was bad it was awful.

Sometimes the phone would not stop ringing, or one call
would last too long. I would talk on the kitchen phone, trying not

to lose my temper, trying not to cry, but trying too hard, while tension filled the air like the smell of scorching potatoes.

The worst nights were the ones when Richard and I had to go out. Then there was the added pressure of time—everything by the clock, and the kids picked up the vibes the minute I got home from the studio. They had to get up from their naps on time, instead of when they woke, and get to the park. I had to learn my script while they played, instead of chatting with the other mothers on the bench, or swinging them. We had to leave by four o'clock, even if it was warm and sunny and they were still absorbed with a pail in the sandpile. If they were tired and full and bathed and asleep by the time I had to leave they would never know I was gone. But if they were up and restless and anxious, there would be a scene.

They never seemed to mind when I went to work. I had always gone to work, so it was part of the routine, but I was usually home at night and especially Jeff would not let me leave. He would cry till his little face was red and swollen the minute he saw me start to get dressed. Richard would be ready to go while I was still trying desperately to get them to fall asleep, and the desperation alone was enough to wire them for the night.

Cynthia never seemed to mind. Maybe the year she was an only child gave her a different kind of security, or maybe, as my mother always said, "*Women come into the world trying to please, men come into the world expecting it to please them.*"

No matter what it was, it was real, and I never learned to handle it.

"Richard, you go on. I'll get them to bed and come later."

"No," he said, and he had every right. "They are fine. He'll stop crying the minute we're gone. I'm not going alone and it's time to leave."

Sometimes Jeff stopped crying, sometimes he didn't, and Pearl would still be rocking him when we got home. The sound of Jeff sobbing as the elevator doors closed stayed with me no matter where we went. He was spoiled, whatever that means. How can someone be spoiled when they've only been around for a little over a year? He knew what he wanted and he felt needs, and he said so in no uncertain terms. That did not seem unreasonable, even if I didn't understand what it was he wanted or needed, or why he was afraid. My being there made it all right, and that was enough for me.

My mother had never left us, except once that I could remember. My brother got burned that night and she never went again; but times were simpler, and she didn't have any place to go. I knew that. What difference did that make? We had a family, we had each other and two children. Why wasn't that enough? Why did we have to sit through an evening with a lot of people who didn't really matter? What was so important that you could leave a baby crying? I could not stand the look on Richard's face. I couldn't stand to hear Jeff crying. I was not living our life together the way Richard wanted me to. I wasn't handling the house and the children, even the help, the way the other women did. Motherhood had also done nothing for my wit and charm at a party. I may have given up on the China lobby, but I knew a lot about diarrhea.

If we were going to a party it was probably at the Reas'. We were invited to two parties at the Harbachs', but I got the date wrong on one of them and we showed up a night early. Willy and Dougy were divorced, and Willy had married a very beautiful girl from a rich social family. Their two little girls were the same age as our children, but they had a nanny and Fay's apartment was always perfect.

The dining room opened into the living room, just the way ours did, and they had built the hi-fi into bookcases too, but somehow it worked better for them. Maybe the fact that a kid wasn't asleep in there had something to do with it. If Fay's apartment was perfect, she was more so. Ice was always on the bar, food was always ready, and she moved with the athletic grace of a woman who is very sure. Her clothes knew just what to do. Her children came in to say good night and were not heard from again.

We were, however, probably going to the Reas'. They had moved in from Stamford to a duplex on East Seventy-second, and it seemed every time we saw them there was something new. One night the party was to celebrate a new Steinway baby grand and it was beautiful. It was a light walnut, very simple and modern. Almost all pianos, almost all instruments are beautiful. The form itself is perfect, and that simple, elegant instrument would have been beautiful no matter where it found itself, but it was wonderful in that room.

All the delicate French furniture and the exquisite faded Aubusson had come from Oliver's grandmother. Betty's decorator had chosen soft, pale textures for the love seats and the long, modern sofa, and an almost casual blue and green checked silk for the Louis XVI chairs. The bar was set up on the French Provincial sideboard in the dining room, and a buffet supper was served from the dining table Betty had made out of a base from a French butcher block and a long slab of marble.

All the regulars were there. They were Betty's old friends from the Junior League, but by the time they moved to Seventy-second Street a whole new group was beginning to gather. Sir Tyrone Guthrie had arrived from Ireland, and it looked like Oliver's dream of building a theatre might really happen. Oliver had produced *Medea* and *A Member of the Wedding* on Broadway, with great success. He had credibility, he had knowledge, he had a wonderful idea, and Betty was a perfect partner.

She had been president of the Junior League and Queen of the Mardi Gras. She could charm anyone, but she also made lasting friends. If she was ever frustrated in her role of helpmate and eternal hostess you only caught a glimpse late at night after a few vodkas. She might begin to dance, her slim body taut as a wire in skintight velvet pants, and her face flashing by. Betty was not beautiful, but she seemed beautiful, always in motion, always smiling. That night the pants were vivid bitter green, and she wore a pale green silk shirt and a wonderful little vest embroidered and appliquéd in gold. That would have been from Tiger Morse's shop. The chic women bought their clothes from Tiger, and Tiger was there, the black satin priestess.

The new faces were all from the theatre: Jessica Tandy and Hume Cronyn, George Grizzard, Eileen Herlie, and Chris Plummer. Chris's wife, Tammy Grimes, made her entrance in a white fur coat with a voluminous hood which she never took off. She made a beeline for the new piano, sat down, and played her repertoire of nine chords in different variations for quite a while. Even if she couldn't play, she looked fascinating with the white fur framing her face, and I'd have given my soul to have had that kind of guts.

It's funny—I can remember the names, the color of the upholstery, and I remember clearly the gazpacho served in cups with croutons floating on top, I remember Tony Guthrie, tall and commanding, towering over everyone, but I can't remember me. I probably wore a black dress because I always did. I probably spent most of the evening sitting at one end of the big sofa. I know that's where I was sitting all the time Tammy was banging on the piano. I remember the sound of the group, the rich voices demanding attention, and occasionally the high-pitched arc of laughter.

I remember leaving and feeling through the pile of mink on the bed for a cloth coat. That night I remember very clearly that Tammy was desperate for something to wear to an opening the next night, and Tiger was going to open her shop so everybody was going to help. It was midnight and I was tired—and I sure as hell didn't want to watch Tammy put on another show. I wanted to go home.

I can't even remember Richard that evening, except the way he looked. We never talked to each other at a party. I would catch sight of him in a group, every now and then, animated, laughing. He always held his Scotch in his right hand and touched the glass with the fingertips of his left. It was a graceful gesture, Richard was a graceful man. But I don't think I ever really saw him. I saw what I wanted to see, and I watched for the flicker of approval. It was there, but so many other thoughts and emotions crowded each expression and the picture moved relentlessly. I was not wise enough to catch it as it went by, and we never managed to slow the motion.

Richard was charming and witty and graceful, but Richard was also a very bright and thoughtful man. While he was absorbing the trivia of the world he had also absorbed the literature and the history. No one knows what someone else's mind is like, but it seemed to me his was as neat as his closet and his chest of drawers, or his suitcases. He could pack for two weeks in one little case and be perfectly dressed for absolutely anything. I would leave with everything I owned in three cases, a cardboard box, and two shopping bags and never be right for anything. He had filed his knowledge and his experience and could put a finger on it any given moment, fit it into any context or conversation.

Richard was always at his best around people, and I've never known anyone with so many really interesting friends. He also had a great instinct for originals like Walt Kelly and Jim Moran. Chet Huntley and Walter Cronkite were his close friends, and it seemed to me all the writers and photographers on *Life*, like David Douglas Duncan and Gordon Parks, were much closer than drinking buddies. Somehow, he managed to keep in touch with them all. He wrote letters, had lunches, and always had the time to do somebody a favor. He could always put somebody in touch with somebody they needed to meet, help them find a job, or get a kid into school.

Richard loved great jokes. He loved his friends, he loved me, and he loved his children. He saw absolutely no reason why everything didn't work out simply and graciously every day. He was not fond of getting up with a kid who cried in the night, and I don't think he ever did. He also saw no reason why I got up, since Pearl slept in, but if I wanted to that was up to me. He wasn't really concerned unless I was cross from lack of sleep.

I only remember him giving Cynthia one bottle. He lifted it out of the pan of warm water, stared down at his daughter, thought for a moment, then banged the bottle on the side of the pan to get her attention, "Here baby, eat," he said in a kind but matter-of-fact tone of voice.

Feeding babies should work out like everything else. If they would just cooperate everything would be nice. Of course she didn't cooperate. The sharp clang startled her and she started to scream bloody murder, so he decided that was not really his province. Women seemed to like that sort of thing and they were good at it, so that was what they should do and he would do what he liked to do.

He liked to stay in his office until six, walk home if the weather was nice, stopping for a drink with a friend along the way, see his children for half an hour, and sit down to dinner about eight. He was absolutely right, it was gracious, it just wasn't simple. It meant that Pearl didn't get out of the kitchen until ten and had to be fixing breakfast by seven. I usually finished what was left on the kids' plates at six, so it was a fourth meal for me that was ruining my figure. When he was away, Pearl and I both were in bed by eight.

On good days I looked forward to his coming home. I listened for the elevator and got out the ice. He always had something interesting to talk about, and between the show and the babies and the ladies in the park my life was pretty narrow. But on bad days I didn't look forward at all. He was just someone else to relate to, and because he was my husband, and because he was Richard, he was the hardest of all.

I could measure my energy all day and parcel it out. On days when the show was very difficult, or if I had been up late with a child, I would sit very still when I wasn't working in a scene. On the bench in the park with the ladies I would pretend to listen, only getting up when disaster seemed imminent in the sandpile. I had to do the show, and I had to do it as well as I could. I had to take care of the children, and babies don't understand that Mother is tired. You can't tell people you work with, or people who work for you, to go to hell. When you are so tired and irritable you are ready to scream and you have just gotten two small children dressed for the park in two sweaters, a snowsuit, and boots, threading their arms and legs which suddenly have the resiliency of overdone pasta through all three layers, and they both decide they have to go to the bathroom, you cannot say or do anything that comes immediately to mind. You cannot yell at them, shake them, or throw yourself on the floor to have a good tantrum. They can, because they are honest and forthright, and supposedly don't know any better, but you can't because you are an adult and responsible, and those are the rules. I also assumed it was a rule that I was supposed to be glad to see my husband when Daddy came home, and all too often he was not only the last person on the list, he was the last straw—but that was against the rules.

Maud and I had rehearsed our attitudes so carefully over so many tuna fish sandwiches. We wanted to work, we wanted the children, and we loved our husbands. So it was up to us to keep juggling. We just hadn't realized how much it was going to cost or how much each one needed every day, whether we had it to give or not. We had wanted work. Now we couldn't quit, the money was a necessity. The money was a necessity and a major issue. One day I found a little pile of bankbooks in Richard's drawer. Every one—and there were seven of them—said, "Richard in trust for Jeff or Cynthia." My name didn't appear on any of them, and it was money I had earned. That day I walked around the block two or three times, trying to think. I couldn't think rationally. All that kept going through my mind was that if I died, the children would never even know I had existed. They were too young to remember me, and I had nothing to leave them. That night I told Richard I wanted the accounts changed, all of them. He thought I was out of my mind, because if we were married everything we had belonged to both of us, and it didn't make any difference whose name was on it.

"If it doesn't make any difference, I want it to be mine." I said it coldly and calmly, and the next day we went to seven banks to change them.

The other thing Maud and I had rehearsed so carefully was not talking about work too much. For years that had not been really difficult. The show was fun to do. We worked hard, but it was rewarding and we felt satisfied at the end of a day. Now, things were different, totally different.

After Charles left, the show came close to falling apart. We didn't even have a place to rehearse. A couple of mornings we used old radio studios and one morning in desperation everyone met in my living room. We finally settled into an unused restaurant on the lower level of the Lombardi Hotel.

The new team arrived on "Search" all the same week. Frank Dodge was our new producer, Dan Levin was the new director, and the new writers were Frank and Doris Hursley. Frank Dodge had been with the Burnett Company since the early fifties as coordinator for the commercials on Arthur Godfrey's shows. He was a gentle man, with soft, gray hair and a strikingly handsome face. I was told he'd had a skin problem working for Mr. Godfrey and wore white cotton gloves most of the time. Frank and Doris

Hursley were from California and had written successfully in day-time for several years. Doris was a big woman, taller than her husband, with a strong face tanned and lined from the California sun. She always wore casual skirts and expensive sweaters, and the first day she admired my coat, which was tweed and lined with rabbit. After two pregnancies it never hung straight, but Doris said she wanted one just like it. She was enthusiastic and talkative about all the changes she had in mind for the show.

"Jo has always been too good. We want her to make mistakes, be human!"

I agreed with her. "As long as they are in character," I said, and she paused for just a second before she swept on to the next point. She did say she wanted to spend a lot of time getting to know me, because I had always been so important to the show. I didn't know it at the time, but when she signed her contract she insisted that I no longer be billed as the star of the show. My name was to appear in the crawl with the other cast members, and the Hursleys' names would be first. I had no recourse. It had never been in my contract that I had star billing. It wasn't necessary, it had always simply been understood.

I met Dan Levin the first time in the hall at Liederkranz. I had heard about him when he worked for Ted Corday on "The Guiding Light." He was moved from there when problems developed with the actors, and Irna Phillips suggested him for our show. The Hursleys were also friends of Irna's, and the three of them were hired on her recommendation by Doug Kramer, the Procter & Gamble representative who had had the problem with Charles. He was an interesting man, but he seemed out of place in Cincinnati. He was so sophisticated, so handsome and so distant. He was single and he was Jewish. It was a combination one didn't expect in a company that had always seemed like a close midwestern family.

I knew Irna had put together the new group, and I remembered my conversation with her in the hall. I could not believe that she would really have wanted to help us when she had already announced she would no longer do a fifteen-minute program. Her show, "The Guiding Light," and "Search" were among the last remaining fifteen-minute programs and they were back to back. The ploy seemed obvious to me, but nobody else noticed. Perhaps when I met Dan I had preconceived misgivings.

It was also not the best possible moment. It just happened that we were moving that day from Park Avenue to the East Sixties. I had been up packing most of the night for a week. When I left at eight that morning both kids were wandering around the apartment, which was drafty with all the doors open for the moving men, and both running a temperature. When I called home at noon, just before the show, Pearl told me Richard had taken them out for a hamburger, and they had just sent for the second moving van. The kids should not have been out in bitter cold weather, and the extra van was going to cost another six hundred dollars. I was exhausted and anxious. Tears of frustration were running down my cheeks as I emerged from the phone booth in the hall.

Dan was standing there watching me. He was wearing a beautiful English suit, his thin brown hair combed straight and flat. His mouth was small and when he smiled his lips got wider but his mustache did not move and his eyes squinted just a little. He wagged his head from side to side ever so slightly when he said, "You really shouldn't take this show so seriously."

The story the Hursleys had come up with did exactly what Doris had promised. It also took the character about as far afield as anyone could imagine. When last seen, Arthur was sent off to Puerto Rico as punishment for having an affair with Jo's sister, Eunice. They had brought Arthur back with a drinking problem. Joanne and Arthur were reunited, but Joanne insisted that they have separate bedrooms. Every night he would make a move toward her, but she would bustle upstairs and he would head for the kitchen cabinet where the liquor was kept, as any self-respecting alcoholic is bound to do.

They also decided that Jo needed more of an outlet for her own psyche, her own personality, so she went to work as a private secretary for a very handsome foreign correspondent who suddenly happened to live down the road. It did not seem to matter that she had a two-year-old baby at home, and nobody to look after him, or that supposedly she really loved her husband and wanted to be reconciled. The handsome correspondent apparently could not find anybody who typed as well as Jo, and he really needed her. That was their explanation. Jo is the kind of woman who goes where she is needed! So, every day she went to work, leaving Arthur, who was naturally jealous, and her little boy. The baby was never seen, so I simply visualized Jeff, who was almost two and getting into everything. It was hard to believe he napped all day.

The first days of rehearsal with the new group were, to say the least, difficult. Dialogue from new writers sits uncomfortably on the tongue and is hard to memorize. It's like wearing a new dress that hikes up when you sit down, or dancing with a new partner. Poised on your toes, you have to keep your balance and be ready to turn, but you don't know which way he's going to go. The palms are always a little sweaty, too, just because you are anxious to please, and I've never known an actor who wasn't. We had been dancing with each other for so many years and felt so comfortable together. When someone changed a line to make it easier or more conversational, or simply to time better with the business, everybody automatically adjusted. If it meant the next line had to be changed, or even cut, it was not a big deal. A hand to hold was always somewhere in reach, if the moment felt the need, and our bodies had always fit together in affection or sorrow.

If I make it sound like an improvisation, make no mistake. It was never casual. We were as structured and highly disciplined as we knew how to be. We were a company, and we spoke to each other with our eyes and our bodies and our silences as clearly as we spoke the words. We had also, over the years, developed behavior patterns that were as much a part of the show as our names. Charlie and Hal had never marked a script until the morning. They knew what they wanted to happen, of course, but they preferred to let things develop, and if somebody had a good idea they went ahead with it. They got bored with the same shots and we got bored with the same moves, so it was always a kind of group choreography.

The first morning Dan walked into rehearsal changed all that. He had marked every shot in his script and every move. He called the actors for the first scene and gave them the blocking as they ran the lines, without once taking his eyes off the page to glance at what they were doing, and every time he wanted to indicate a camera cut, he snapped his fingers. If someone had made a change in the dialogue he corrected them, and if someone felt a move was awkward or came at the wrong place, he became impatient.

"Don't stop. I'm timing this," he would say, and we would soon learn that time was his consuming passion.

When the show is put together it is timed and back timed. Notes are made in three or four places on every page to indicate exactly how many minutes and seconds you have to go. There are padding devices for safety, of course. There is always the option to use the credits or not, and there are at least two closings with a long or short musical background. The announcer has the copy in front of him and, on a signal from the control room, can add or subtract as much as thirty seconds. If there is a serious problem on the floor, if someone had skipped a page or two of dialogue, or someone fighting for lines had slowed down, the floor manager would give us a signal. He would get somewhere in your line of peripheral vision and hold up one finger, making little circles if he wanted you to speed up, or hold the fingers of both hands together in a motion like pulling taffy if he wanted you to slow down. Needless to say, it was a distraction and only used when absolutely necessary.

Charles and Hal usually let us know during a commercial that we had to speed up the next scene or slow it down, so we had time to adjust. Dan did not believe in working that way. From the first day he wanted the timing to go just as it had in rehearsal, so we got constant signals on the floor. It was a little like being conducted by a bandleader.

The signals made us nervous, the new dialogue was uncomfortable, and almost no changes were allowed. But the biggest problem was fitting a performance into Dan's preordained framework. If the moment you felt was important to your character was not on camera that was tough. As it happens in life, usually something someone else says is what makes you change. So very often it is more important to watch the person who is listening to catch the reaction. But Dan had chosen the moments he wished to see and that was that. He never saw the reactions anyway. He sat there every morning glued to his script, glancing at his stop-watch occasionally and snapping his fingers. His only comment would be a request to take a beat between speeches so his camera cut would be clean and neat.

For the first couple of weeks we went along that way. We made jokes among ourselves. "Hit, click, talk," was the comment on the rhythm suddenly imposed on us, but it was the story that began to close in and become impossible.

Jo was not only turning her back on Arthur, she was becoming a shrew. She made no attempt to understand his problems or even talk about them, and in those days if you didn't talk about a problem you had a problem. Arthur felt guilty and sad about his behavior. He needed understanding and forgiveness. Jo responded by reminding him of his mistakes and his drinking. It seemed to me that if Jo had agreed to reconcile, she should at least attempt to leave a door open now and then, especially the one to the bedroom. That was the first one she slammed.

At first, I used her humiliation and hurt to justify the anger, but it began to wear thin. Arthur was trying desperately to rekindle their old love, and Jo did nothing but punish him. Finally, one Friday, she stomped up the stairs toward the room she would not share and the script called for her to stop and turn back for one last, particularly hateful line. I crossed toward the pretend stairway of the rehearsal space and made a decision.

I turned, quite deliberately, to Dan and said, "I won't say it."

He squinted back at me without smiling, and a battle began that we never completely resolved. From that day on, I began to write speeches for myself to justify Jo's behavior and motivate her actions.

To be as fair as I can be, Dan is a brilliant, sensitive, extremely thoughtful man. He has knowledge, taste, and a great feeling for the theatre. There are actors on the show who still think he was the best director we ever had. I can only tell what I saw, what I felt, and what happened to me. It was not one-sided. I was threatened, and I was fighting back every way I knew. Whether my name came first or not, it was my show, and I believed that what they were all doing had to be damaging. If I could prevent it, I was going to. I could not have been easy to deal with, but I wonder if anyone is when they are going through hell.

Since time and neatness were so important to Dan, it was hard to understand why, after only a few weeks, he began to arrive late for rehearsals, but he told us his wife was in and out of the hospital, so we did the best we could. By the end of the first two months he was arriving exactly one hour and fifteen minutes late every morning for a rehearsal that was scheduled for an hour and a half. That meant we barely had time to get through the show once before we went to the studio. That also meant there was no time to work with the scenes, only time for Dan to give us the blocking and gallop through it while he snapped his fingers.

We did compensate as best we could by running the lines before he got there. I would arrive with new dialogue, which I managed to work into my own lines, retaining the cues, because there would be no time and Dan did not believe in erasures. Any changes I made had to fit into the format already preordained. It was just a little like trying to change all the words in a crossword puzzle and make it come out with the same answers.

The main problem for me every day was to try and stay cool. If I lost my temper, I would not be able to get back into the mood to play the scene. When I forced a line change I had to be right, and God help me if I faltered. In order to keep Jo vulnerable, I had to keep her protected during rehearsals and at the same time I had to keep Mary alive. An argument drained energy, and I couldn't afford to lose a drop.

The story with the foreign correspondent ended in a gasp of melodrama. Whoever he was supposedly doing a story about got very cross about the whole thing and held us captive at gunpoint for a whole week before we were rescued. Arthur was rightfully angry. After all, he had told me so, hadn't he? It was decided that what Jo really needed was psychiatric therapy, but first they had to make sure her odd behavior wasn't caused by some physical problem.

So, a very pretty young actress was hired to play the part of the doctor. Unfortunately, no one had told her what doing a daytime show was like. She burst into tears the first day when she found she had to use a stethoscope and say lines at the same time. But she had a sweet quality, and a lot of people need time to adjust to the pace of a daytime schedule. I had played several scenes with her, and if they weren't great, they were adequate. Then we got to a big one with a number of long speeches that I knew were going to make her nervous. To make matters worse, I was coming down with a sore throat. In the morning it was just beginning to tickle. After running the lines thirty times it was definitely worse, and by the time we got on air I was beginning to cough. That, I knew, would be a problem because it would distract her, and I got nervous too.

Naturally, I had my little page of cues placed where I could see them, just in case, and we started the scene. Sure enough, halfway through, the tickle started and no matter how hard I swallowed, it would not go away. I managed to stifle it till I got to my own line, but I was practically gagging, so I stopped to cough before I went on. It happened two more times. I kept watching her face and the little list of cues and holding my breath till I got to a good long speech of my own, twitching with little stifled coughs, but, by golly, without mishap we got all the way through! She had been fine, I had a dandy cold and never thought about the scene again. It was just another show, and we had done seventeen or eighteen hundred by then.

When they called me to come into the agency I had no idea what it was about, but there was an unfamiliar edge in Frank Dodge's voice.

"Some people from the agency and Procter & Gamble are here, and we'd all like to talk to you," he said.

"What about?"

"I'd rather not discuss it over the phone, but I think you know."

"You sound very serious." I tried to laugh but that didn't work and after a moment I said, "Should I bring a lawyer?"

"I think that would be a good idea."

Steve was my lawyer and my friend, so when I called he walked out of whatever he was doing and met me at the agency.

We just stared at each other in the waiting room. I couldn't tell him why we were there, because I didn't know.

When we went into the office I nearly fell over. There were five men there, from Procter & Gamble or the agency. Bob Short was the new head of P&G productions and I'd never met him before. I knew Doug Kramer, and I had met Milt Slater from the Burnett Company, but only at a cocktail party. Frank Dodge and our story editor, Leonard Reege, I saw every day, but they were so stern and formal my heart began to pound. Nobody said anything for fully two minutes, just a lot of cigarette packs rustling and lighters clicking, till Steve said, "Well, I have to get back to work. Why are we here?" and dispensed with amenities.

"We've had a very serious complaint about you, Mary."

I think it was Milt Slater, though I'm not sure. I only knew someone said it and my heart sank. All those script changes! That was why we were there. I had forced them, there was no doubt about that, and I couldn't deny it. But it had been going on for months. Why was everybody so upset all of a sudden?

Steve didn't know any of that so he simply asked, "What?"

"Dan tells us you've been making it very difficult for a young actress on the show, because you know she is there to replace you."

I was dumbfounded. What were they talking about, and who on earth was there to replace me?

"You even went so far as to cough on the air, trying to make her look bad."

The light dawned. The lady doctor! I'm afraid I laughed. For an instant I was relieved. How on earth could I be afraid of a kid who couldn't walk and chew gum at the same time! It was, however, a short instant. They were very serious. I suppose I can't blame them. If it had been true it would have been a lousy thing to do. If they had known me they would have known better, or should have, but they didn't know me.

For half an hour I had to sit there and defend myself. I had to explain that I had done the best show I knew how to do under God knows what circumstances for seven years, and that, believe it or not, I had no idea that girl was there to replace me. I had to do it without letting the tears show, until Steve couldn't stand it any longer.

"Just tell us right now, do you want to fire her? Is that why we're here?"

There was a very long pause after that, then Doug said, "No. We don't want to go that far," and Frank said, "We just want to go on record that we won't have that kind of behavior on the set," and Milt said, "We expect professional attitudes from everyone."

Bob said nothing. He just listened.

Afterward we went to a bar. Steve bought me a drink and I started to cry. Steve listened as long as he could, but he had to go back to work and I had to stop crying. I had kids to go home to, another script to learn and another show in the morning. It turned out the girl really had been hired to replace me. A year or so later I ran across a whole pile of publicity pictures and stories about her. Luckily, I didn't know that then. I had enough to contend with.

Every night I would stare at the script until I figured out something to make it work. The one big thing I had going for me was Jo's long relationship to most of the characters—her history. I also had the skills I picked up from Charlie, and finally, let's face it, I had no choice! I simply couldn't remember the words if the scene didn't make sense.

Even Dan began to respect what I was doing. He never admitted it, but he accepted changes more and more readily, and when the scene went well he even seemed pleased. Still, there was no doubt who had made the change. Dan hadn't even been there for rehearsal, so surely he wasn't responsible. If there were mistakes or repercussions, they were not his fault.

It was not just the pressure of knowing I had to be right and I had to be perfect that began to take a toll. The battle began every evening as I fixed the script, and every morning we went to our corners. As a fighter keeps his belly tight for a body blow and his guard up at all times, I began to learn to keep control of my lines of defense. The results were as inevitable as they were disastrous.

Remembering lines that you have learned the night before requires an incredible amount of concentration. I memorize sort of photographically; I see the page in my mind, and I use the thoughts to propel the dialogue. When my mind is working, even if a word is illusive, the thought is there and I can substitute. It also helps when somebody else forgets a line. I can see the page, I have the sense of what the other person is supposed to say, and I can usually blend it with my own and get on with the scene. But when the pressure is very intense there is always the danger that the mind won't work, won't hum along from thought to thought. Those days are like climbing a steep sandstone hill. You reach for a word at a time and they keep slipping out of your grasp, crumbling in your mind. They didn't happen often, but I always knew they could. Add to that the distraction of a few time cues and it was a day in Hell.

Dan not only changed the feel of the show, he redesigned all the sets. Each living room had a fireplace upstage center and a couch directly downstage facing the camera. This meant that everybody sat with their backs to the fireplace. He liked all rises and crosses to go straight up and straight down, so if I entered from outside he would always ask me to put my purse on the mantel. Arthur also kept his pipe and tobacco on the mantel, and anything else we needed was conveniently there—except, of course, a fire. Dan preferred even, clean, direct moves, and he would always ask that we take a beat between speeches to give room for the camera cut he had already written in. Over the years, without really trying, I had become so aware of cameras that I knew, almost subconsciously, where they had to be in dry rehearsal in the morning, just as I knew where a shadow falls. If I wanted to make a move he had not indicated, and he said, "I can't shoot that, I don't have a camera," I could tell him, "Camera One hasn't had a shot for two pages and he's right in line."

I was right, and I hated being right as much as Dan hated me for it. I began to hear the edge in my voice. I could feel the rush of pride and determination, and I knew well the sour aftertaste. I won the rounds often enough but the price kept going up, and Dan still had the final weapon that he alone controlled.

He never told us what the timing of the show was until we were on the air. If my joke was that he conducted the show, it wasn't funny. It was a daily battle that I prepared for so many times it began to seem natural. I never knew when I would get a time signal, but I knew at some point I would. Sometimes he would give four or five cues, sometimes he would wait till it was almost too late. In the control room, tension would grow as the seconds passed, and everyone knew we were running long, but Dan would put off making the decision.

One day we got to the last scene in the show with five pages of script and two minutes of time. It was a scene between Arthur and Jo in the bedroom. I was supposed to wake up, talk to him, get up, put on my robe, cross to the window where a voice-over would play, then cross down to the dresser. Arthur was then to get out of bed, cross down, and we were to finish the scene there. I had almost all the last two pages of dialogue.

During the last commercial the floor manager said, "Cut three minutes."

"Cut three minutes how?" I said. "Where do we cut?"

He listened over his headset for a few seconds. "He says just speed it up!"

"We can't do it. Do we cut the top of the scene or the end?"

"He's thinking about it."

Actually, Dan had left the board and was standing in the back of the control room.

I thought frantically for thirty seconds and made the decision, "We're beginning at the dresser, we both have bathrobes on. Camera Two has the first shot." Wildly I tried to focus on a way to get into the speech without any prologue while I put my bathrobe on. The red light went on. I turned from the window and crossed to the dresser to find that it was gone. The only decision he had made in that minute and a half was to remove the piece of furniture that had all my cues on it, as well as the marks for our positions. I did it! I got through another one. I earned respect from the crew and the technicians and, as if I had spent an hour in the gym, I added another microscopic layer of muscle. I was faster technically than he was, if only because I had to be, and every day he made me prove it.

When I tried to talk to Frank he would say, "Now, Mary, that's just the way Dan is. The shows are good and the ratings are fine. He must be doing a good job. You and Dan just don't get along, but that's not the show's problem."

He would have one drink too many and wait for the lunch to end.

I had grown fond of Frank and his sweet, mannered ways, but the silences made me furious. He created a vacuum and I invariably got sucked into it. He also admired Dan. Just the fact that Dan was so intractable and stubborn was a kind of strength that he was drawn to, and there was nothing I could do. I couldn't complain to P&G without being disloyal to Frank. There was nothing I could do about anything, except learn the script at night and go to my corner in the morning. The muscles were beginning to harden.

By the spring of 1958, the stories had definitely swung away from Jo's character. Aunt Cornelia had a stroke and Jo's sister, Eunice, being handily a nurse, was hired to take care of her. Eunice had fallen in love with Rex Twining, who worked for Aunt Cornelia. The other characters in the dark old mansion were the secretary-companion named Harriet, played by Vicki Vola, a tiny, vivacious woman and wonderful actress, and Aunt Cornelia's bitchy niece Allison, who stood to inherit all her money. Aunt Cornelia still controlled her nephew, Arthur, and everyone else, with an iron hand. So as the poor lady lay helpless for weeks, she was surrounded by several folks who had fairly good reason to hope she did not recover. Sure enough, somebody did her in. That was a good ploy. The audience did not know who had cast the ominous shadow that hovered over the bed and caused the dreadful look in the eyes of the poor, speechless woman when the dirty deed was done.

This time, it was decided by the Henderson police that Rex and Eunice together had plotted the murder, so they were both arrested and we had lots of scenes in the waiting room while the lawyers tried to talk and the lovers were momentarily reunited. You may begin to note that in those days it was a standing rule that every two years we had a trial, and if you keep score you will see that, in every instance, it was an innocent victim. So much for justice in Henderson in the 1950s. In this case, Jo suddenly appeared and discovered, somehow, that it was really Harriet who had caused Cornelia's demise; but as soon as Harriet knew that Jo knew, she whipped out her handy revolver and we had another week at gunpoint.

That week was much more embarrassing than the first one. Vicki Vola was five feet tall and I was five feet six. I still am, for that matter, and Vicki probably hasn't grown either. Anyway, there we were, alone, in a close two-shot much of the time. I was younger, taller, and stronger, but apparently a lot dumber than my adversary since I never even tried to grab the gun and had a dozen chances. The climax of the story took place in a car. I was unconscious with the motor running and Harriet sneaked out, leaving me to die of carbon monoxide fumes. You will forgive me if my memory is hazy about how I got out of that one. For Heaven's sake, how could I remember? I was unconscious.

Rex and Eunice were reunited, married, and sent immediately to Puerto Rico, which is where everybody went when they weren't in the story.

As soon as Aunt Cornelia's bitchy little niece inherited all that money she began to change. She was suddenly no longer a tall, redheaded kid of fourteen. She was in her late twenties, blond, and four feet ten inches high. In order to make the change believable, she was, of course, recast, and Ann Pearson took over the role. I liked her, although I was a little afraid of her. She could be warm one minute and turn to ice the next, but that was not only true of Ann.

The whole cast began to change with the new regime. We had been a close family with Charlie and Hal, united against the writer. Now it was every man for himself. Everyone knew, certainly, that I was in trouble. My name had been taken from the starring position on the credits. There were the constant battles with Dan, and my character was used only peripherally. More than one actress got the idea that I was on my way out and they might be the new leading lady. I suppose to some I was a troublemaker and they simply didn't want to be caught hanging around with me.

Something very subtle and frightening happens when a character is dying on a show. It is as though the disease is real and contagious. The same thing was happening to me. Conversations that were close and animated tended to exclude me, and once or twice there were overt signs of hostility. Even Lynn and Terry became short and cross. Lynn and I had always been so close, and Terry had grown and matured as an actor and become a real friend.

One morning, just before we went into the studio, Bill Meeder, the organist, passed me in the hall.

"Watch your back," was all he said, and I made a joke, "I can't. I'd have to wring my own neck." But I was upset and I couldn't imagine what to look out for.

Then all of a sudden, in the middle of camera rehearsal, Terry blew up. "Stop upstaging me!"

I stopped dead in my tracks and stared at him.

"Stop what?"

"Everyone's been telling me how you always upstage me!"

At that precise moment I was about two feet downstage of him, and the accusation was so far from any truth I could fathom I wanted to laugh. But tears welled up instead, and I knew I was losing control. I have never been able to fight with anybody without getting so upset I either cry or get sick.

"Please, Terry, let's just do the scene. Stand any place you want to."

He wasn't expecting that, and he picked up the script he slammed down on the table.

"Well, this is all right for now . . . but actors watch the show. They tell me what you do, so be careful!"

I was shaking as we went on with the scene. He knew, and I knew, that we had never in our lives had a problem. I was sick and he was sorry. The incident itself wasn't important, but it was a symptom. The disease had spread. Nobody slammed a script on a table again, but I simply wasn't included in the jokes before rehearsal in the morning, or the girl talk during makeup. If the show had not been so important, or if I had not needed it so much, that may not have mattered, but I did. The show had been like a family for so long. We all worked hard, and were scared and nervous, but we did it together. We supported each other, and the satisfaction made up for the butterflies.

By 1959 I was making the decisions for every move I made by myself. I think that was the worst part—having no one around to depend on or trust. During all the years with Charlie it had been all right to experiment and expose. I knew I could rely on him to push a performance a little further or pull it back. He was the director and he was responsible. Now, there was no one to rely on and, besides being frightened, I was lonely.

Also, I had to learn to work in a totally new way, exposing only enough to let the other actors know how I was going to play the scene so they could build their own performances and saving the real emotion until we were on the air and it was too late to change. It was difficult. Letting yourself be vulnerable enough to cry on cue is a delicate process. It is, for me, a little like peeling off skin, a layer at a time, all day, till you have nothing left between you and the painful moment. I had to learn to protect the self I left so naked.

I was not the only one who had problems. Technicians refused to work on the show, and actors got too upset to do their best work. Frank Overton quit one day. He said, "I use two thirds of my energy every day to keep from killing Dan and go on the air with the third I have left." Frank was nominated for an Oscar the next year, so maybe it was all for the best.

Dan walked into the makeup room one day and said to Maud, "Now you know as well as I do, actors are all just children. Why won't you admit it?" and she said, "Get out of this room and don't ever come back."

Tension and anger became a way of life, but somehow, in a bizarre way we all settled in. At least we knew what to expect.

Probably the strangest thing of all was the adjustment I began to make in my mind toward Dan. He made doing the show as difficult as possible, and every day I took the dare. I would show him! After all, when the performance was good, the show was better and he got the credit.

Christmas came, and we had the first Christmas party at my house. When Charles was with us he always gave one, but the new agency didn't want to bother, so I took over. Of course, when Charlie gave the parties the money came out of the show budget. When I gave them it came out of mine. But it seemed important, and it made me feel that way. Everybody came, from the show and the agency, even Procter & Gamble. The apartment was big enough to handle a lot of people and I was proud of that. It even looked pretty with just candles burning and nobody could see how dirty the dining room rug was.

Doug Kramer was especially nice that Christmas, and as he was leaving he said, "Let's have dinner soon. We haven't had a chance to talk in a long time."

It was a couple of months before Doug called, but I was pleased and looking forward to it. Just like the old days, I was being taken out by the sponsor. Actually, that night we had dinner in. Richard must have been on a business trip, because I remember being alone after the kids went to sleep.

After dinner I poured him a brandy, and we sat down to talk. Out of the blue he said, "There's a story coming up you probably are not going to like, but we feel it's important. I just want to kind of prepare you for it, so you won't be too upset."

I made a joke about being held at gunpoint again, but I was nowhere near ready for what was coming.

"Duncan Eric is going to die."

Duncan Eric was the show name for the baby Jo had when I had Jeff. He had never been seen, so every time I leaned over the crib, picked up the toys, or talked into the playpen I had always visualized my own son. It would be like playing his death, and they had promised me that as long as Jeff was the child in the story he would not even have a bad cold. He was going to die!

I started to shake so violently I made myself a drink and tried to argue in a calm, rational voice. "That is a breach of contract."

"Well, actually, it was never written into the contract."

"They gave me their word."

"Well . . . it's difficult when you change writers. The Hursleys feel it will pull a very strong rating."

"Killing a child couldn't pull ratings. No one will want to watch."

"I just wanted to tell you as a friend that it will be coming up."

When he left I went to the typewriter to write a letter to the company. Surely they would respect my feelings. Then a thought crept into the back of my mind. I never read my scripts ahead, just picked them up the night before I went to work. There were several in the bedroom, and I went back to get them. It was a Thursday when Doug came over. I didn't have a show the next day, so I picked up Monday and read through it. On the last page, Jo was in the kitchen fixing supper. She turned to call out the open back door for Duncan Eric to come in for his dinner. He didn't answer, so she crossed to the door to call him again and the stage directions read, "Her face freezes in horror. Sound effect, car brakes, tires screech. Jo screams."

There it was. Too late to change. All I could do was refuse to play the scene, and that meant I had to quit the show.

It was a long night. It was late when I went to bed. The sky was turning gray when I went to sleep, but I had made up my mind. The Hursleys said it would pull a rating. No, I would give them a week of shows that nobody could watch, and that is exactly what I did.

They did not kill the child instantly. He needed brain surgery, which lasted the whole week. Every morning I went through rehearsals and said the lines in an absolute monotone. It was hard on the other actors, but there was no one who did not understand. Dan only asked me once if I was going to cry and I just looked at him.

I cried, of course, but I remembered my mother the morning Daddy died. She was smiling when she came out of his room, and she said, "He looks better this morning, don't you think, sister?" She had never accepted the fact that his death was inevitable, and Jo never accepted the reality of her son's thin thread of life. Maud could not go in the control room at all that week and the men on the crew, who all had children, could not get through a show without tears. But somehow we all made it.

On the day of the funeral Dan had ordered white flowers for every inch of my living room set, even a garland up the stair rail.

"Get every flower out of there or I won't walk in," I said, and it was the most emotion I had shown in rehearsal all that time.

It ended and was forgotten, and perhaps you think I was a fool to feel so strongly. It was, after all, only a story. Perhaps that is the substance of daytime, it is never quite just a story. In order to prepare and make it real, you have to use so much of yourself, your own emotions, your own experience. You can't hold back, and there is no time to find other sources. I think it must be the substance of all acting, but I only speak from my own experience. Playing the death of your own child is too real. If I had not been so angry I never could have done it.

After Duncan Eric died the story shifted to the young people. My daughter Patti and the Bergmans' daughter Janet were blossoming and ready for teenage trouble. Janet, being a few years older, had even run off and gotten married to Jo's cousin Bud. She'd had a baby just before he deserted her, and that's enough trouble for any young woman who is barely eighteen. Then she fell in love again, this time with a nice, stable young doctor named Dan Walton.

Bud had been in an automobile accident and was presumed dead so Janet and Dan decided to get married. Everybody was pretty upset naturally, when Bud suddenly reappeared, but that time the cast was more upset than the audience. The young man who played the part never knew his lines and always forgot where he was supposed to stand. You needed a butterfly net to play a scene with him. Stu went to talk to him and persuaded him to give Janet a divorce, but they got into a fight and Bud knocked him out cold. The next morning Bud's dead body was found in the courtyard below and, wouldn't you know, the poor befuddled Henderson police arrested Stu. The magic two years were up and it was time for another trial of yet another innocent person.

The trials tended to be a lot alike, so there is no point dragging you through each of them. The principal members of the cast sit right behind the table where the accused and his or her lawyers sit and worry a lot. Each of us has overheard one line of incriminating dialogue, and under oath we have to admit to it. Nobody has much to do, except the lawyers, so it's boring, but it's restful, and it was a relief for me. All I had done for months was take a basket of fruit to everybody's mother. I had made a remarkably quick recovery from Duncan Eric's death and he was not mentioned again for several years.

Things looked dark for Stu as the evidence piled around him. I had a bad case of conjunctivitis, and Dan insisted on lots of close-ups, so everybody must have thought Jo was sobbing into her pillow all night every night. Not so! Not Jo! She was not just sitting on that hard little bench with her swollen eyelids doing nothing! At the last moment, while the jury was out deliberating, she went back to the scene of the crime! Like Nancy Drew at her very best, Jo studied that courtyard and, sure enough, she found the missing clue! The drainpipe! The drainpipe was pulled loose from the building just the way it would be if someone had tried to climb down it. Sure enough, they found Bud's fingerprints along the top of it, so obviously he had not been pushed out of the window. The dumb cluck had fallen. Stu was released, and again we had "Another Bride, another Groom, another Sunny Honeymoon," and Janet went to live in Chicago.

Now it was Patti's turn. My beautiful little auburn-haired princess had grown into a beautiful young girl. She was beginning to date and experiment with makeup. The clothes tended to swing radically from little girl to extreme sophisticate, with the same unpredictable rhythm of her mood.

Children who have grown up in theatre have been exposed, and are accustomed, to all kinds of emotion, real and dramatized, from the people around them. Most actors are naturally affectionate people, and most of us cannot resist the feel of soft, shiny hair on a sweet, young head. They are used to being hugged and petted. They have also grown up with discipline, but I suppose no amount of experience, however varied, can prepare young people for the new feelings of apprehension and joy that accompany young adulthood. Everybody just has to get through that the best they can. Possibly because she was an actress and very, very bright, Lynn managed to tip the scales at both ends, and as I said before, what was happening in each life off the show became inevitably a part of the daily episode in some way.

Patti started running around Henderson with one of the town n'er-do-wells, and wound up in an automobile accident, paralyzed from the waist down. For weeks, Jo hovered at her bedside, bereaved, but brave and strong. Now as it happened, the accident took place during a period in Lynn's personal life when she was going out with a boy a few years older, and she was suddenly very sophisticated and blasé—so sophisticated and blasé one day I could have strangled her on air. Jo tiptoed into the hospital room to gaze tearfully down at her daughter's drawn little face. There she lay, unconscious and still as death, wearing bright red lipstick, false eyelashes, rouge, and blue eyeshadow! She had a big lunch date and she was all ready to go!

Makeup or no makeup, the doctors gave up in despair. There seemed to be no cure for Patti's paralysis. It was some strange trauma to the nervous system. Patti would have to want to walk herself if she was ever to get well. Arthur and Jo took her home in a wheelchair and turned a downstairs room into a bedroom for their invalid daughter. Jo and Arthur had obviously given up too, since no therapy or psychiatric help was sought. Except that I went out and bought some books on the subject so I could carry them around as props, nothing was done at all, for months. Then, quite suddenly, we discovered two things: Behind the picture over the mantel was a wall safe—it must have been there all along, we had just never looked—and the prodigal n'er-do-well was back in town, desperate for money!

The minute we found that wall safe, we started to stash large amounts of cash in it without bothering to close the blinds or turn out the lights. Any aspiring n'er-do-well could easily have peeked through the window and seen us doing that. It didn't take any brains at all to hide in the bushes and hear Arthur open the front door, suitcase in hand, and call back to us that he would be home from Chicago in a week. With the setup so neat and complete you may be able to predict at this point what happened next. That was the format in the old days. The audience knew what was going to happen long before the characters did, so the only suspense was waiting to see how they would react. There we were, for the third time in four years, AT GUNPOINT FOR A WHOLE WEEK!

On the final day the entire show was the three of us: Patti, Jo, and the boy. The tension had to build as the boy grew more and more desperate. Then, just as he raised the gun to shoot Jo, Patti would miraculously rise from her wheelchair and manage to get behind him. The momentary distraction would allow Jo time to get control of the gun and we would be saved. It was a good, melodramatic situation, but when I read the script I knew we had to make major changes. The dialogue simply did not make sense with the action, and of course until I knew what the blocking was going to be we couldn't adjust it.

I walked into the gloom of our restaurant that morning and noticed someone sitting at the table besides the two actors, the floor manager, and the assistant director, who belonged there. It was Stan Potter, from Procter & Gamble. He was staying in the hotel and had just dropped in to say hello. We all just sat around that morning and chatted. We couldn't run the dialogue, because we didn't know what it would be. At nine-fifteen, as usual, Dan arrived, and before he saw Stan he said, "You're all going to have to help me, this dialogue doesn't work."

Stan stayed for the whole rehearsal. He heard us writing our own lines and literally making up a show. He called me to say he would turn in a report, but he doubted it would help. The agency had to make those decisions. So nothing changed, really, except that Patti learned to walk again.

A couple of months later Lynn decided she wanted to leave the show, maybe go to California, as soon as she graduated from high school. I sat with her mother and father at her graduation and cried, because I always cry when they play "Pomp and Circumstance"—and because I knew she was going. She stayed in New York for a year and went to college at Hunter, but every time she dropped by to have supper with the kids she talked about going to the coast. When I looked at her I couldn't imagine anyone that young going to Hollywood, but wasn't that silly. She was doing just what I had done, and I was almost the same age when I arrived at Metro-Goldwyn-Mayer.

I had, of course, prepared myself for my first day on the lot of Metro-Goldwyn-Mayer through years of assorted fantasies and two months of concentrated visualizing. I had seen myself quite clearly, walking into a huge, beige and brown plush office, settling myself into a chair, crossing my legs and lighting a cigarette with just a hint of an enigmatic little smile on my face, while all eyes turned to stare at me.

"She's it!"

"She's perfect!"

"She's just what we want."

"She's a natural."

"She's a star!"

In my mind, the whirlwind of activity that usually followed that scene got a little hazy because I wasn't sure how they did it, but the result was always dazzling. I would appear on the set with my hair down and softly brushed, wearing a long, white chiffon something, and walk to my place. It would be a simple, unassuming walk, but filled with grace and power. Rita Hayworth had done it almost as well in *Gilda*.

The day I actually arrived was a lot more like enrolling in a new school. Bullits Durgom drove his huge, red convertible through the gate and stopped in front of a low, white frame building.

"This is Lillian Burns's office. She looks after all the kids and she'll set up your appointments." Bullits climbed out of the car and I trotted behind. Inside the door was a large comfortable waiting room, a sweet English secretary, and lots of big, chintz-covered chairs filled with very beautiful young people. As I looked around that room I became acutely aware of my clothes, my shoes, my hair, my stockings, my purse, my fingernails, and the extreme length of my legs, which just seemed to be in the way.

The other girls lounged in simple peasant skirts and low-cut blouses. Their tan skin glowed through sheer cotton. Their silky, stockingless legs were stretched lazily in front of them, one tiny, slim ankle over the other, each ending in a strap or two of pale leather, the same pale of the fluff of hair that grazed the damn tan shoulders.

My basic, light brown hair was pulled back into a barrette, my stockings sagged at the knee, my feet wobbled in the black ankle-strap shoes from my screen test, and I was wearing a navy and white tailored dress and jacket, just right for traveling and a steal at $14.95.

The nice English secretary said Miss Burns would be tied up for an hour with Margaret O'Brien, and Bullits said I should wait. He would meet me in Mr. Pasternak's office after I had made appointments with the other teachers. It was a long hour of listening to the tanned voices and wondering what they were giggling about.

Miss Burns's inner office was like a big living room, complete with a baby grand piano. She was a small, bosomy woman who gestured with a cigarette and walked with very deliberate steps in very high heels and did both constantly. She told me that if I had any questions or problems I should always come to her. Then she told me there was a group class every Friday for all the contract players and I would be expected.

She called the vocal coach. "Joe wants to know if there's anything we can do with her singing voice," she said into the phone as if I were not there. ". . . Well, try your best."

She told me how to get to Harriet's bungalow and I started walking. It was farther than I had expected, past two big sound stages the size of airplane hangers, into a kind of miniature suburb of bungalows. Harriet's was small and she didn't have a secretary, but she was warm and easy, a big woman with short, blond hair, and a deep, husky voice. She sat down at the piano and began to play.

"What do you know?"

I didn't really know any current songs, but I remembered the one I had sung in the contest when I was nine, so I said, "Mood Indigo."

She looked surprised. "What key?"

I didn't have any idea, so we tried several. After about fifteen minutes she said, "I think we'll start over, but I like your voice."

The third stop was the dance studio, and my heart began to sink. Dance! . . . Never! As it turned out, I never did. I spent the whole time standing next to Janet Leigh during the warm-up exercises. Then, while they did all those pretty little turns and leaps, I did extra drill just walking toward the mirror trying to make my feet go in one direction at a time—both feet, one at a time, straight forward, no little extra flip-flop, just straight toward the mirror.

Finally, it was the French teacher. It was another hopeless cause, but she was absolutely enchanting, a tiny, feminine, gray-haired woman. I used to wonder about all of the teachers. Were they disappointed actresses? Had they wanted to be stars some-time? I kept trying to ask, but none of them ever gave me an answer.

About three-thirty I started back along the winding paths, past all the bungalows, stopping to read the little signs in front of each one. The composers all had bungalows, as well as the writers and some of the directors. I had to ask directions all the time, because you couldn't see where the paths ended, only a big long street lined with those enormous sound stages. As I ambled, star-ing at the buildings and the signs, I saw a most astounding sight. A very beautiful young woman with reddish blond hair was walk-ing toward me with two afghan hounds on leashes. She was wear-ing a bright print dress that stopped at her knees in front and touched the ground behind her. She had a parasol of the same material and a long fox stole flung across her bare shoulders. As I stood there gaping, and marveling that anyone could manage all that at the same time, I got a good look at her fine, handsome face. It was pale gold and wise.

The last stop was the dressing room they had assigned to me, and that took longer to find. There was a whole building of new dressing rooms right behind the makeup department, but they were for the stars. I had been assigned one of the old ones, dating back to silent pictures. I thought it was wonderful. There was a long, two-story frame building way over behind the last stage, right against the wall that surrounded the lot with a porch all along the front and outside stairs to the upper level. It reminded me of the house from my childhood on Elwood. It even needed paint.

Inside the door was a plain little room with a worn rug and an old-fashioned daybed. It had a couple of wicker chairs and a little dressing table with lights around the mirror. That did it! I had an actress's dressing table! I had a place to go, if I could just remember where it was.

It was probably about four when I finally got to the Thalberg building. I was walking down the hall looking for Mr. Pasternak's office, when he popped out of a door.

"Sir," I said, moving toward him, "I'm Mary Stuart, I just got here."

"Well," he beamed at me, and his gravel voice was truly warm, "glad you're here. Haven't got time to see you today, but drop by tomorrow and we'll see about everything. We'll get you a car and a place to live . . . I hear you're staying with friends, but you don't have to do that. We'll take care of you."

Just then a heavy-set man with thick black hair opened the door on the other side of the wide, marble hall and stepped out.

"Henry," Mr. Pasternak said, "I want you to meet Mary Stuart, and I want you to put her in a picture."

"Oh?" said Henry, turning to look at me and extending his hand. "I'll be glad to," and without pausing or smiling he said, "and what will she do for me?"

"She'll do nothing," said a quiet, firm voice with just the trace of an accent. I was startled, and as I turned to see who had spoken, a hand took mine and steered me directly toward the other end of the hall and out the door. It was the woman in the print dress. She didn't have the dogs and I wondered where they were, but she still held the parasol.

"Who are you?"

"My name is Linda Christian."

"I'm Mary Stuart. I just got here."

"I know," she said, and left as abruptly as she had arrived.

There I was, on the steps of the building, wondering what had just happened and, since I had no idea where Bullits was, how I would get home. Lester and I were staying with his friend Tina, in Laurel Canyon, and somebody would drive down the hill to pick me up, but first I had to get to Schwab's Drugstore. I hung around for a few minutes and noticed that everybody seemed to go the same direction, so I went that way, too, and it led to a parking lot. I didn't know what else to do, so I just sort of stood around, and everytime I saw somebody get in a car I asked them if they were going anywhere near Schwab's Drugstore. Finally, somebody said he was and drove me into town. He was a nice man. His name was Islan Auster.

One of the first shocks upon arriving at MGM was the discovery that a contract for a year is not really a contract for fifty-two weeks. It is a guarantee of salary for only forty. The studio has the option of putting you on layoff for twelve weeks if you are not actually working in a picture. I was put on layoff immediately. That circumstance made two other problems infinitely more complicated. We had to have a place to live, and living in Hollywood without a car is next to impossible. So Lester signed up for work in a scenic studio painting sets. It took a couple of weeks for his union card to be straightened out, and things were tight, but after that we had a little money coming in. A couple of folks at the studio offered to lend me money, but I didn't think that was such a hot idea. If nobody was using Tina's car, Lester drove me to the studio and I stood in the parking lot till I got a ride home. Actually, I met some nice people that way. Mr. Auster, it turned out, was Mr. Pasternak's associate producer, and he drove me in several times. One day I found out he lived in Cold Water Canyon, and that was nowhere near Schwab's.

After six weeks, I got my first check and we found a little apartment in a private house on Laurel Hills Road. It was only a couple of blocks up the hill, so it was possible to take buses and walk the rest of the way.

When we had saved three hundred dollars, we bought our first car, a 1935 Ford. It stopped dead two blocks from the used car lot and we had to spend another twenty dollars on a battery, but we had wheels! The upholstery was all torn on the doors, so we just ripped that out and exposed the works. The springs were gone under the front seats, so we stacked bricks under them. The only major problems were the brakes and the steering gear. We had to pump up the air brakes till the pedal felt tight if we were going down any kind of hill, and sometimes the wheel would stick so you couldn't make a right turn. Lester's solution when that happened was to turn left in a complete circle. It was a tricky maneuver in the middle of Sunset.

Our apartment was just one quite large room, a bath, and two closets. We put everything we owned in one closet and a hot plate in the other. There was no kitchen, but there was a wonderful tennis court, so we both learned to play tennis. That is not true. We bought two tennis rackets and a can of balls and batted them around a lot.

The first scene in a picture I did was with Van Johnson. They had finished the picture, but they were adding a few shots. I was to be a secretary who comes in to whisper something in Mr. Johnson's ear. Nobody told me what I was supposed to whisper and I didn't find out till I saw the movie. I was telling him his wife just had a baby. It might have changed my performance a little if I had known that, but I didn't know who to ask. I walked over to him, whispered and left.

They said, "That was fine," but then everybody was very busy and after about an hour they said I was to do it again. I assumed I had not done it right, so I tried to improve. I walked a little faster, I hesitated before I whispered, and the director yelled, "Cut!" I tried several more times to improve, and every time they stopped until I ran out of embellishments and went back to the way I did it in the first place, and they said that was okay. Nobody had thought to tell me that we were doing a close-up of the shot we had done before, so it had to match.

The first real part was in *Good News*, with June Allyson, and I even had a name. I was to play Flossie. When I got to Wardrobe, there was a whole rack of clothes with a sign on top that read FLOSSIE, but there were about six other girls picking through them. I wasn't sure what that meant. Perhaps there were to be several Flossies. I didn't care, I had a copy of a real script. I was excited, thrilled, and delighted. Then I put on the first dress they handed me. The thrill was gone.

The movie was set in the 1920s, and all the dresses were way above the knee. A fact that I've managed to hide all my life is that I am knock-kneed. I have always managed to approach a swimming pool like a crab, moving sideways. In a short dress that is not only short but full and flouncy, I knew I had to look ridiculous.

The next stop was the hairdresser and the situation deteriorated totally. The horse blanket coif from my screen test was nothing compared to the mass of ringlets they achieved for Flossie and me. I looked like Shirley Temple with her finger in a light socket. My worst suspicions were confirmed when I walked on the set. Chuck Walters, the director, took one look at me and laughed so hard the tears ran down his face.

I didn't have any real scenes in the picture, but I had a few lines and I was in the background for almost a month. I spent most of that time just trying to stay out of sight in the little canvas dressing room the lesser folk were supplied with. The stars had trailers with bedrooms, a dressing room, and even a little kitchen—actually more of a kitchen than I had at home.

I discovered that mostly what you do on a movie set is wait around for hours at a time. Those days would have been endless if I had not found a friend. It was on *Good News* that I first met Willy Harbach. Willy was gorgeous, funny, and about as ill at ease as I was in his first acting job. It was, incidentally, his last.

Willy and I hid together, for different reasons, but he and his wife, Dougy, became good friends to both Lester and me. They knew Helen O'Connell, who lived up our hill about halfway and had a swimming pool. George Platt Lynes, who was a famous *Vogue* photographer, lived at the top with a wonderful terrace for sunning. Between the three houses, we had a whole country club. We just had to keep the brakes on the Ford pumped up for the trip down, and watch out for the right-hand turns.

We had been in California almost three months and begun to settle in. We had a pleasant place to live, a few friends to play with, and our marvelous tennis court. We both got tan enough to look like we belonged, and I learned to make stew on a hot plate. Then in July, Virginia called from New York to say they were going into production and Lester would have to come back for conferences. When Lester was there, I felt fairly sure, but when he was gone it was as though he left all the doors open. Just the fact that he was with Virginia made it worse, but there was nothing I could do about that.

When I wasn't in a picture, which was most of the time, I went to all my little classes. I sang with Harriet, who was teaching me very sophisticated songs by Rodgers and Hart like "My Old Flame" and "Glad to Be Unhappy." I walked toward that damn mirror in ballet and noticed how straight everybody else's legs were and how round their figures were in other places. On Friday we all went to class with Lillian Burns. We would pair off and prepare a scene to do in front of class. Willy never made it to

the Friday classes, but Linda was there, and Barry Nelson. I loved
to watch Linda work with Barry. She was like a continental Jean
Arthur. Barry was fascinating and more experienced than everybody else, and after a couple of months he even did a scene with
me. He was very exacting and directed every breath and every
move, but I was grateful and began in a quiet way to worship
him.

I guess I sort of worshiped them all. I watched every move
they made, especially Gower Champion. I loved the way he
stepped out of his Continental on one long, graceful leg, wheeling and slamming the door at the same time. Mostly, I worshiped
Cyd Charisse. She was, I decided, the most beautiful, and obviously the smartest, person in the class. She never opened her
mouth and she never did a scene, but it was just the way she sat
there—her body at ease and arranged so perfectly, her lovely face
always so calm and serene. She didn't have to talk or act, because
obviously she knew all there was to know.

Lillian Burns's waiting room was never a comfortable place
to be, even after I'd been on the lot for months. I knew I never
looked right, and God knows I tried. I copied what everybody else
was wearing the best I could, especially Cyd Charisse. I went out
and bought a beige silk dress that draped up on one side and even
had a matching turban, but I never could figure out how to press
it, so it always looked like I'd slept in it. Of course, just as I was
beginning to catch on to the peasant look, the hemlines went
down and I had to start all over.

The one day I remember most vividly in that waiting room
was in the fall. Elizabeth Taylor was sitting in one of the chintz
chairs, wearing a soft, white cotton dress. With her white, white
skin, the famous violet eyes, and that jet-black hair, she was the
most beautiful creature I had ever laid eyes on. That day she was
slumped in the chair, dangling her legs over the arm and pouting;
but even pouting she was lovely. It seemed she had been invited
to a party and met the captain of the football team at Beverly
Hills High and she was in love, but there was nothing she could
do about it. She had no way to see him again. I felt so sad for her
that day, and I had always envied her in the makeup department.
Her mother was there to brush her hair and see to her makeup,

and she seemed protected and safe. Of course, she was married by the time she was eighteen, so maybe it didn't make that much difference after all. I may not have had a mother, but I had Linda.

I never really knew who Linda was, but she was beautiful. She wore incredible clothes and jewelry, and every time she picked up a telephone she spoke a different language. I thought she was wonderful, and she did look out for me. Two or three times I was invited to parties, but around twelve or one she would send me home. I was never quite sure why, but I remember standing at the door one night and glancing back. Nearly everyone was gone, and under every piece of furniture there was a pair of shoes.

When I had been on the lot about four months, I got a call to go to the wardrobe department for a fitting, and just before she hung up the secretary added, "Mr. Gable will meet you there."

Mr. Gable? She must mean Clark Gable! Oh, good grief! It had to be important if Clark Gable cared enough to look at a costume! With fantasies flying, the Ford and I sped out Saint Vincente.

Sure enough, he was there, sitting in a big chair in one of the fitting rooms reserved for stars. He stood up and thanked me for hurrying and explained that it wasn't a big part, but he thought it was important to the picture and that's why he wanted to choose the costume himself. I was to play a model in his new picture with Greer Garson, and the scene would be with him.

Gazing up at a legend, who also happened to be very nice and very handsome, I was too awed and excited to ask questions. I just followed the wardrobe mistress into the little changing room. I couldn't wait to see the costume! I was wrong. I could have waited. The entire little room was lined with bathing suits! Dozens and dozens of bathing suits! For the next three and a half hours I sidled back and forth from the big room to the little one wearing a total, I think, of eighty-three different bathing suits, while Mr. Gable watched and nodded and smiled.

In the picture, I had to lie on my back, holding up a bottle of suntan lotion, waving my legs in the air, then mutter a line to the photographer as I left, while Clark played a scene with Miss Garson. I didn't think it was that important at all.

Besides taking lessons and playing bit parts in pictures, the one other thing a starlet does to earn her $150 a week is to assist on other people's screen tests. One day I was called to do a scene with Yul Brynner. I only had to listen to his voice to know he was very special.

When we walked out of the office I said, "Mr. Brynner, I'm not very experienced, so if you want to coach me and show me what you want me to do, that would be fine with me. I'll work anytime you say."

"That's a good idea," he said. "I'll take you to dinner this evening and we'll work on the scene. But you'll have to pick me up, I don't have a car."

That was a truly fantastic evening. We worked on the scene for two hours, and he filled it so completely I felt as if I was doing something too. I probably wasn't, except that I was mesmerized by him, but the combination was enough, and he loved my car!

After dinner we went for a ride in downtown L.A., and he showed me great old houses built by Frank Lloyd Wright in the twenties. Then we sat on top of a mountain and sang French folk songs. I didn't know the words or the tunes, but all I had to do was sing harmony. Every time he came to Hollywood after that he would call, and I'd meet him at the airport. He looked so strange with his elegant clothes, his capes, his gold-handled walking sticks, climbing into that silly old Ford, but that's the way it always was.

When Lester came back from New York, we decided that paying rent was a waste of money and we started looking around for a house to buy. He had the G.I. Bill, which would help with the financing, so we got the paper and off we went. We looked for two or three weeks before we decided that no matter how much financing we had, we just didn't have enough money to buy anything we really wanted. Then we just happened to see an ad that sounded intriguing: "Half acre, partially built house. $7,000." Now that was in our price range.

"Partially built" turned out to be a trifle misleading. Actu-

ally, there was a foundation, and the half acre was a ribbon of
clay four hundred feet long and fifty feet wide, just treetop level
above the valley in Laurel Canyon. We decided that if we built it
ourselves we could earn the money as we went along, and the
man was willing to take a mortgage himself for most of the
$7,000, so we signed the papers. Every time we got paid we'd go
buy some lumber, a load of bricks, or a keg of nails. We didn't
have any power tools, but Lester could saw as fast as I could hammer a two-by-four cross brace.

We decided we wanted to cantilever the roof, and it took
several weeks to figure out how to do that. Only the fireplace had
us stumped, so we went to the library and checked out a book by
Benjamin Franklin. It had everything we needed to know after
two hundred years, except where to buy the stone. That was my
project, because I was the one who insisted on pink granite. The
man in the stone yard just shook his head.

"You pick out any rock you want, lady, but if it's at the bottom, you gotta move it."

Every rock I wanted turned out to be at the bottom, of
course, but it was worth it.

We had to build the outside chimney first, and being on the
downhill side of the house it was almost two stories high and
took us two months. I would mix the cement in our rented mixer,
pour it into the wheelbarrow, and let the weight pull me down
the hill, while Lester stood, day after day, on the ladder laying
bricks. We didn't realize how tan we were till we got a note from
the man in the big house at the top of the hill: "We don't want
coloreds in this neighborhood."

If I had felt my appearance left something to be desired
when I arrived in Hollywood, four months of spending weekends
and days off working on the house had done nothing to improve
matters. The addition of the cement in my hair and the grime
under my nails charmed no one, but perhaps building the house
was doing something for me. At least, much of what went on at
the studio began to seem pointless and stupid.

I had appeared in several movies. I had gotten married in an
iron lung in a "Doctor Kildare" picture, which was naturally a sad
situation. When they did the whole scene I felt sad and senti-

mental until the tears rolled naturally. But when they came back two days later and just pointed the camera at me and said, "Cry," they might as well have said turn green. I lay there, looking at everybody backward in my little mirror, trying to feel sad, and squeezing my eyes, but nothing happened. I tried staring into a light. That only made me blink. I didn't have the skill to re-create the moment for myself, and nobody even suggested a way to do it. So it was a dry-eyed close-up.

I had played a part in a box of a huge theatre, but my only clue to the character was her name and the way they dressed me up. I was wearing a green satin strapless dress, and my hair was smoothed into a lot of big coils on top of my head, and I had a white fox stole. I was not important enough, of course, to have a stand-in, so I sat in the box all morning while they lit that whole theatre and arranged all the extras who were seated in the orchestra section below us.

I sat there and stared at the two pages of dialogue they had given me, wondering who I was going to play the scene with and how in the world I was supposed to say those lines. Then gradually I became aware of the extras sitting in the box right next to mine. There was a handsome woman just on the other side of the little brass rail. She had the velvet voice and precise pronunciation of a trained actress, and after a while I got up the nerve to lean over and say, "Excuse me, ma'm. If you had to say these lines in a scene, how would you do it?"

That lovely lady looked at my little script for a few minutes, and for the next hour she coached me in that scene. By the time they got to us, I was a fairly believable New York sophisticate, or at least the Hollywood version of the late forties, which is closer to a Barbie Doll than a Brenda Frazier, but I did do the scene in one take and the executives were impressed.

The only other thing a starlet does when she is not in a picture is put on a bathing suit and a pair of high heels and have her picture taken doing something improbable. I had spent a whole day on an air strip somewhere, standing sideways, of course, pretending to lead a toothless old lion into the hold of a Flying Tigers' airplane . . . some press agent thought the Metro Lion and the Flying Tigers were a natural combination. I felt ridiculous, and somewhere in the back of my mind was the constant nagging suspicion that that's how I looked.

In the makeup booth every morning there were three drawings on the wall. One of an oval face, one round, and one square. The lady who made me up had been the makeup artist for Jean Harlow and kept telling me stories about her as she pointed out to me that I was not anywhere near a perfect oval, so she would have to shade and highlight me until I was. It may be one of the reasons so many people looked exactly alike.

After the makeup it was the hair department. It took two ladies to get me out in time, because I had so much hair. They would stand there with their curling irons, clicking away, while I sat trapped in front of the mirror, staring at the ovalized face with the starkly arched brows and the pencil thin nose. Somehow, the face staring back at me never looked anything like the way I felt. I couldn't raise an eyebrow—they had already done that. I felt too self-conscious to smile, because the studio dentist had covered my two front teeth with porcelain caps and I felt like my upper lip stuck out a mile. All I could do was try to feel like I looked, so I would copy everybody else who looked like that.

The best place to watch the other young actors and actresses was at the lunch table in the commissary. The girls would arrive in costume and makeup and make entrances. They would jump up from the table constantly and move around the room chatting with directors, returning breathless with secret excitement and news. Young men like Dick Derr, Cameron Mitchell, and Gower Champion would sit calm and poised, saying little, but also holding a secret it seemed to me. What was it they all knew that I didn't?

One day, Mickey Rooney came in particularly high and obstreperous. He was in the middle of an Andy Hardy picture, and he had been rehearsing a scene in which Andy was supposed to tidy up his room and worry about getting the girl. They had decided just before they broke for lunch that the scene wasn't working, so they had added a soliloquy from *Hamlet* that he was supposed to be learning for school while he straightened up the room and worried about the girl. He had a copy of the soliloquy, and occasionally would glance at it, but all through lunch he was "on" and hardly stopped telling stories for a minute. I was curious, and after lunch I went over to the set where he was shooting.

"Let's do it," he called as he stepped from the bright sunlight into the huge, dim sound stage.

"We're ready," the director called back from the corner of the studio where the bedroom was set up, surrounded by a jungle of lights and equipment.

"Let's rehearse it."

"Let's do it," Mickey repeated. "I have a date this afternoon." And that's exactly what he did.

It was a long scene, probably three minutes, and he remembered every move, hit every mark, and said every word of the soliloquy. But he wasn't just saying words and hitting marks. He was Mickey Rooney, being Andy Hardy being Hamlet. He was doing three things at one time and making them all seem like one. All that carrying on at lunch had somehow just been charging up the batteries. He had really been concentrating on the scene, learning the words, and putting it all together in his mind. Mickey was real genius.

Whenever I got a chance, I went out to wander around the back lot, and that's where I went that afternoon. The old back lot at Metro was wonderland. You could walk down the street where the Hardy films were shot, with the house and the church, turn a corner and be in Pompeii, move on and see the mast from an old schooner above the roof of a London townhouse, then look over your shoulder to Shangri-La. It was a place to let fantasy run wild, or feel momentarily at peace and complete. I tried to see myself in those settings, but I could catch only a glimpse. I was still standing on the corner watching, not actually there. I could smell the salt air blowing from the basin where the schooner floated, but I had not learned to hold the breath, so I would wander on to Pompeii filled with a vague uneasiness.

By the time I got home, if Lester was in California, everything was all right. I loved to tell him everything that happened and play all the parts. For a while, he designed the sets for a production of No Exit and about that time I started typing some pages about how it felt to be a starlet. Lester always started designing a set by doodling. For days he would just think about the show and his brush would make designs, almost as if it had a mind of its own. The doodle for that show was a spiral that went endlessly in on itself in shades of yellow and orange, getting hotter and hotter as it coiled.

Every now and then he'd say, "Want to look at something?" and after a while I'd say, "Want to listen to something?"

I called my scribblings "Want to Look, Want to Listen."

But when he was gone, things were not all right. I hated to go home to that empty, dark apartment and cook a hamburger on a hot plate in a closet. The bushes brushing against the window looked like faces, and the wind sounded like footsteps. I was terrified, and it was impossible to sleep with my heart pounding so loud. When I did fall asleep I couldn't wake up, even with two alarm clocks in tin wastebaskets across the room, and one morning I even slept through a call.

Of course, no one at the studio knew I was married. I never had the nerve to mention that, but I knew it, so I couldn't go out on real dates and I was lonely.

One night I did go out to dinner with my friend Mr. Auster from the parking lot. That was fun. We went to Ciro's on Sunset and stopped for a drink at the Players, and it was really a night out in Hollywood. The next day, Mrs. Burns called me into her office.

"You should speak to me before you go out with one of the executives," she said. "I happen to know someone else is interested in you."

I wasn't really sure what she meant, but I had enough of an idea to get angry. I called Islan and he was furious, so that night we went back to Ciro's and a few weeks later we were great friends. He had a wonderful house in Cold Water Canyon with a gorgeous view and a wonderful cook. He drove a Cadillac convertible and told the most wonderful stories about the theatre I had ever heard. Sometimes the stories would last a long time, and I would fall asleep on the big, deep couch in his living room and he covered me up with a cashmere blanket. I had never seen a blanket made out of cashmere.

It's hard to explain why I decided, quite suddenly, that I didn't want to be at Metro anymore, because I really don't know.

It's a little like my last year of high school. I remember standing outside one classroom door, knowing that I was too far behind and would never catch up. I didn't go into that room ever again, and I didn't go to my math class, but I don't know where I went. I still dream about the deserted halls and the empty smell of school. I also dream about an agent's office in Hollywood, with a desk up on a little platform and blue neon lights around it. I dream about old men unzipping their pants and coming toward me with soft penises hanging down from white shirts that had little hand-embroidered monograms on the tail. I dream about wanting to go home and not knowing how to get there.

About two months after we went to Ciro's, Islan was let go from Mr. Pasternak's staff. I don't know if I was part of the reason, but he was my friend and he would not be there. I remember having that old feeling I'd had down by the river when I was a child, the feeling I had every time I went down into the subway. I was lost, and late, and inadequate.

When I went to Mr. Pasternak and told him I wanted to leave he was furious. He said I was foolish, that I had a future at Metro and several people agreed with him that I was talented and had star quality. He was very nice to me, really. He always was. He believed in me, and in his own way he supported me. He had no way of knowing how I felt—but then, I didn't know that either. Of course, I still had a contract, but my parents had never signed it and I was under age, so it wasn't valid. I asked them to write a letter, saying they thought I was too young to be away from home, and walked out the gate of Metro to the parking lot. I got in the Ford and drove home.

Being unemployed gave us a lot of time to work on the house, and just the fact that we had no money coming in made it important that we stop paying rent. We started to work from early morning till evening most days. The walls were up and roofed over. We didn't have enough money for the electric work yet, so we decided to go without. At least we had plumbing. We finished laying the floor about eleven at night, and put the stain on by Coleman lantern. It had dried by the next day, and we moved all our belongings into that funny little house. We had a double bed, a redwood picnic table with two benches, two canvas

lawn chairs, an unpainted coffee table, and one end table we had
actually bought with one real lamp. The lamp didn't work, because we had no electricity, but the fireplace kept us warm and
we cooked in it for the first few weeks. Lester had given me a
German shepherd puppy I called Eleanora Duse, and all three of
us slept in the double bed.

Lester's easel was always up, and my typewriter was nearly always on the coffee table. I could sit cross-legged on the side of the
bed and write, and the space and light were good for Lester's
painting. I put sheets across the big corner window, and he hung
costume sketches on the braces where the walls would go when
we got around to it. The one big painting he had done of me was
hung on the only wall we had finished. It was a full-length portrait of me standing in the door to the big closet of our old apartment, wearing black slacks and a shirt and sweater that belonged
to him, with all the paraphernalia of our life tangled into the
background. There were tennis rackets, suitcases, stockings, and
nightgowns draped and stacked everywhere, even a girdle on top
of a shirt on top of a laundry bag, all hung from a hook. The expression was benign, perhaps a little challenging. "If you don't
like it, that is your problem," it seems to say. He always knew me
better than I did.

We were both living on our combined unemployment, which
amounted to fifty dollars a week, so it took some planning. The
first priority was our foster child, and that was fifteen dollars a
month. We bought one quart of gin a month, gas for the car,
food, and with anything left over tried to move ahead on the
house.

There were two other houses going up on the muddy hillside.
Mr. Welby, on our left, seemed to stay in the tar-paper stage forever, but the Mitchells, on the right, were really moving along.
They had spent the winter in a trailer with their two small children on the site and moved in about the same time we did. They
had no interior walls, but they did have a stove with an oven. So
if I bought something big, like a ham, I carried it up the hill and
cooked it in their house. Otherwise, it was stew or soup, or anything else you can cook in a pot. We didn't have a door on the

bathroom, and we had to learn to bank the fire every night to keep from freezing, but it never seemed to be a problem.

We got to know other couples who were building their own houses and traded skills and dinners. Mostly we were alone. We didn't have money to spend on movies, so we read and went to galleries.

We talked about the books, but when we went to a gallery, Lester would say, "Don't tell me what you think. Try not to think at all. Just look."

It took a long, long time to realize what he meant, and he was right. I learned to see, really see. It was the single most important gift I have ever received.

When Lester got a commission to paint a portrait of two little boys, that eased the financial situation, though not enough to buy clothes. So I decided to learn to sew. It seemed the natural addition to the days I spent mixing cement to build the steps and cutting up a dishpan full of vegetables for the soup. Mother had made my clothes when I was little, but she never could teach me, because I was left-handed. The fact that I was also awkward and impatient, I assume, had little to do with it. I needed clothes, we had no money, so I would learn to make them.

The first pattern I picked out was a lined, fitted suit, and I bought some natural linen to make it out of, with tiny pearl buttons. I did not, of course, have any idea that I had chosen to begin where most people graduate. I did not know about facing or interlining, or anything else for that matter. I also did not know that linen stretches and frays. I will admit that tears spilled frequently, but two weeks later I was almost finished. I had lived on cookies and coffee and the only detail left was to make the buttonholes. I read my little sheet of instructions, picked up the scissors and whacked holes around the little tailor tacks. I cut three tiny squares of linen and tried my best to stitch them to the front of my suit. I made an unholy mess, but I couldn't afford to give up, so I kept making them over. Each time, of course, they got a little bigger, but before that sewing machine rental was due, I had a suit—a suit with three huge, flat buttons down the front. A week later I wore it on my first interview at Warner Brothers.

Perhaps I'd changed. Perhaps it was the different lot, or just different people, but the change was miraculous. From the first day, everybody treated me like a person and an actress. I was never a starlet. Their drama coach, Sophie Rosenstein, directed the first screen test and somehow made me feel I could do anything.

When I went to see the test, the screening room was full of executives and they were all talking about pictures I would be right for. They said I was a young Greer Garson, and just as I was leaving somebody asked who designed the stunning suit I wore in the test, the one with three big buttons down the front of the jacket!

Even the makeup department was different. A makeup man and hairdresser were assigned to me, and they spent a whole week experimenting with styles and makeup colors. No more curling irons and oval faces. They just pulled my hair back and clipped it with a barrette, and when the makeup man was finished I looked just like myself, only better.

They took photographs of me, blew them up to 11×14, and put them all over the studio dining room so everybody could see me. Every day, it seemed, there was a new director to talk to. I met Raoul Walsh, and he said I would be good in a western. He wanted me to play a tough girl. Bill Orr didn't think I could, so Raoul wrote a scene to show him. I threw a gin bottle at the leading man, rolled a cigarette, and said damn, and they dressed me up in gay-nineties underwear. Actually, it was pretty good, and I really could roll a cigarette because I had done it for Daddy when I was a kid; but I rolled it with my left hand, and for the first time I realized how odd that looks. That was for a picture called *Colt .45*, with Errol Flynn, and they were talking about shooting in September. I couldn't believe it! Then they talked about a picture called *Adventures of Don Juan*, also with Errol. Somebody said I was too young to play the queen, so I did more tests with wigs and beautiful gowns, and every now and then I felt like a movie star for a moment or two.

That was July. The first of August, Lester got a call from Virginia to come back to New York and work on a production of *Crime and Punishment*. He would be gone for months, and for months I would be alone. Well, not quite alone. Besides my German shepherd, who had grown into a good-sized lapdog, I had acquired two cats and two parakeets, who preferred to fly around the little house than to stay in their cage, and three possums! When I turned into the dark little dirt road off Laurel Canyon at night, the headlights would catch at least three pairs of eyes shining in the dark. They could cut across the field and get to the house before I did, but if I had hated going home alone to a real house with people living right upstairs, the dark hillside was a hundred times worse. I'm not sure what I was afraid of, but the ritual was to look behind even the clothes in the closet and the dilemma was whether or not to close the front door before I checked for hobgoblins. The evenings were long.

I decided one day that it would be nice to have a rug on the floor, so I went down to Ventura and bought a crochet hook and a thousand yards of rags. I could see myself in front of the fire, with a nice classical record on the little player, my dog and my cats at my feet, quietly crocheting through the fall and winter evenings. It was a nice picture. As it happened, I cranked up the record player with Joe Mooney records, put the coffeepot on high, and had an eight-by-ten rug finished in two weeks. I was crawling around the damn thing at two o'clock every morning, so hyper I couldn't have slept if you'd hit me over the head with a mallet.

At the studio one morning in September, I was called in to meet a new producer. When I got to the office a tall, nice-looking young man got up from behind his desk. He introduced himself and said to call him Mac, then he introduced me to a young woman named Ruth Brooks. They asked me to sit down, and for the next half hour they talked about the tests they had seen, and how good they thought I was, what a lovely quality I had. Then they told me I was going to play the lead in a picture that Ruth had written and Mac was going to produce. It was her first major credit, and it was the first time he was producing. They made it seem so easy and natural I don't think I was even surprised.

They had decided I was exactly what they wanted the minute they saw my screen test. They weren't in the least bothered by the fact that I was an unknown; they thought that an advantage. They knew that I had two other pictures coming up in the next year and they wanted theirs to be the first. They kept saying

I was exactly right. That seemed to mean that, just as I was, I was enough. It was a very new idea to get used to. I didn't have to try being sexy, I didn't have to make a smart-alec remark, I didn't have to do anything—I was enough. Amazing.

Mac invited me out for a drink to celebrate, and by the time we left the Players Club my head was swimming. Everything had fallen miraculously into place. I was in Hollywood working as a real actress. I had three pictures to do and nobody seemed to have any doubt that I could do them, and this enchanting, witty, wonderful man was going to begin it all.

Two days later I went to meet the director. He was tall, dark, and quite good-looking. He sat behind his desk and did not smile when he told me, quite frankly, he did not think I was right for the picture at all. I was too young and too inexperienced, and he thought Veronica Lake would be a much better choice. When I told Mac what he had said, he and Ruth just laughed.

"It's his first big picture, and he wants the protection of a star. Don't worry, Bill Orr, Jack Warner, and Collier Young, everybody agrees you're just right."

They wanted to make a test and I was worried, but Mac kept telling me it was just a formality. Actually, the rehearsals went very well. I went up to the director's office and he blocked the scene. We went over it several times. I went through it with Sophie Rosenstein, and the night before we were to shoot I felt comfortable and secure, and very, very happy.

In the morning, I went to my regular makeup man, but he said I had been assigned to someone else. After a whole week of makeup tests, that seemed odd, and strange makeup people made me nervous. But someone else was going to do the picture and there was no choice. During the week of tests they had made up special colors of makeup for me. I heard someone say that my skin absorbed light, so they used lighter shades on me. The new makeup man didn't have any of the colors they had made up, and the dark color made my face look hard and muddy. By the time I went to the hairdresser I was upset. Another strange face and another shock were waiting. She got out her scissors and began to cut my hair!

"It's what the director wants," she said, "he doesn't want you looking like a kid," and the two or three inches she took off made it impossible to pull back into a barrette, so it fell over my eye and I knew who I was supposed to look like.

By the time I walked on the set I had had more than enough trauma for one day, but Mac and Ruth were there. They said I looked lovely, and the test was not important. Again, they told me it was just a formality. In the shadows behind the lights and cameras I could see that Mr. Orr and the executives had all gathered to see me do my first production test.

The scene itself didn't worry me. We had rehearsed it, I knew it backward and forward and felt easy and natural. I was surprised when the director stopped the first take and said, "No, that is not what I told you to do there. On that line you move to the chair."

We had not rehearsed it that way, but I assumed he had changed his mind. Then he stopped the next take and criticized the way I read the line, and the take after that for some reason. By noon we had tried the scene twenty times and he still was not satisfied when we broke for lunch.

I ran to the cafeteria and got a sandwich and took it to the makeup department. My own makeup man and hairdresser did everything all over. By the time I got back to the set I was looking like myself. I had even had a few minutes to see Sophie and go over the scene, and I was feeling better about everything.

Mac wasn't there and Mr. Orr didn't come back after lunch, but we did get the scene in one take, so I was pleased when I called Mac to tell him. He asked me if I would mind waiting around till he was through, he wanted to have a drink with me.

We didn't go to the Players that night. We went to a little place in the valley.

After a while he said, "We've canceled the picture. Ruth and I don't want to do it without you, and you're just not experienced enough to do it with a director who is fighting you all the way. We all saw it this morning. He'll kill you . . . so we've put it on the shelf."

He looked so sad, and I knew how much the picture meant to both of them. I was crying for me, but I was crying for them, too.

"You don't have to worry. As soon as Errol gets back they want to go ahead with *Colt .45*, so you'll be working—and we'll find another one for you. Don't cry . . . we all believe in you."

Before I got in the Ford to drive home, we sat in his car for a while. When Mac kissed me, the disappointment seemed far away and less important. He was, after all, protecting me. He hadn't fired me, he had taken care of me. He had made me believe I could do the picture, and I believed he was right when he told me not to.

Then he smiled at me with his funny mouth that wasn't quite big enough for his face, and his funny eyes that were almost too big.

"Since we're not going to be working on a picture, it's all right to spend more time together, if you'd like to." Then he said, "There's only one problem—I'm married."

"So am I," I said, but Lester was much farther away than New York.

Lester had never actually asked me to marry him. He just said, "I'm not going to California with you unless we're married," and to me the idea came out of the blue.

"You shouldn't go out there alone," he said. "You'll never make it. You're not very good alone."

But married! It had never entered my head that we would get married. Marriage was children and a real house and forever, and I had no idea how that was supposed to feel—but whatever it was, I hadn't felt it. Marriage was a honeymoon on an ocean liner to Europe. It was a beautiful hotel room with champagne and a white negligee. Marriage was being wildly, madly, totally committed to love. I had certainly felt wonderful love for Lester. There had been days that seemed so perfect, so beautiful, and evenings that were warm and peaceful. He laughed at my jokes, he liked my silly stews, and I loved the way he looked at me. Sometimes in his mind he was sketching, but there was always love. I liked the way I felt when he was around, but the minute he left, and that reflection was missing, the feeling began to ebb and I was lost.

It certainly wasn't that I was particularly sexy. Oh, I pretended to be, and went through all the motions, because it seemed to matter so much to everybody else and—Heaven knows! —everybody talked about it all the time. To me, it was friendly and harmless, and that's as far as it went, unless I was in the front seat of a car. Emotionally I suppose I hadn't passed the petting stage, but that simply would not do when you are in the movies, married, and petrified of being alone.

Lester and I had exchanged friendship rings, little gold link chains instead of plain gold bands, and in many ways that's where I had stayed. When Mac looked at me I was a newly interesting woman. He was not a man who had casual affairs with actresses, and I knew I was very special to him. We didn't have a lot of time together, but the time we did have was perfect. Usually, it was only a drink after he left the studio. But when the big red Chrysler pulled in the parking area my heart would pound.

We only went away for a weekend once. It was romantic and it was beautiful. Mac loved to sail and he had a little Swedish fishing boat in the yacht club at Newport. When we first drove past the forest of masts in the harbor it was just sunset, and he explained to me very carefully that you could glance at the boats and tell immediately if anybody was making love. The mast would tip ever so slightly if both folks were on the same bunk.

Then he grinned at me, "So you'll just have to leave me alone," he said, stroking my hand.

"If I can," I said solemnly, "and if I can't, we'll put the mattress on the floor in the middle."

"You're oversexed."

"I'm underprivileged."

He laughed and kissed my hand.

Checking into the motel was the difficult moment. I sat in the car and slumped down so no one would see me till the man carried the bags in, but if the moment had cast a shadow it was gone the instant I walked into the cottage. It had a little kitchen with ice and a bottle of champagne. It had a real fireplace with a real fire going. The only thing possibly wrong was the pair of twin beds in the bedroom.

"We'll just have to put the mattresses on the floor in the middle," I said, and he laughed.

"You think we can make the whole room tip?" He kissed

me, and it took a little while for the strangeness of the new room and being alone together to wear off, but we managed.

In the morning I put on the shirt he had left on the chair and went out to try and stir up the fire. He watched me from the doorway.

"Oh no you don't," he said. "No matter how goddamn cute and sexy you look, we are going sailing." But I knew he'd debated for at least a minute.

I had never even seen a sailboat up close, let alone stepped onto one. Mac's was beautiful; all natural teakwood and polished brass. I wasn't much help as he took the covers off the sails, and the ropes that lashed them to the spars, but I loved watching him do it. I adored the tiny little cabin below with everything fitted into place. There was a tiny oil stove, a tiny icebox, tiny cabinets, and two bunks.

"Let's sail to Mexico."

"Okay," he agreed. "But today let's see how good a sailor you are."

I did not, of course, know what he meant by that. I thought he was telling me I should learn to help with the ropes and the tiller, and in a way he was saying that. He was also very wisely not mentioning any other possibilities, which might put the notion in my head that more than likely I was going to get sick.

The water was calm in the basin. Even in the heavier water outside the boat sailed steady with the wind behind us and the sails bellied above our heads. For an hour we sailed straight out, and when I looked back the shore was gone. We were absolutely alone. We could have been a million miles from anywhere. There was no sound except the waves, the wind, the gulls, and the creaks and groans of the little wooden ship straining through the water. I had always been so terrified of water I couldn't even swim, but that day I was afraid of nothing.

"Hold this," he said, putting my hand on the tiller, "and hold it steady."

He started unwinding a long line lashed to a cleat in the deck.

"Keep your head down!" he yelled, and suddenly the boom

swept across the cockpit. The boat leaned over and swung into the wind.

"Maybe we should go to Mexico." He smiled at me and wound the rope onto a cleat on the other side of the deck. The front sail began to flap a little, and he hauled that line in till it stopped. We were no longer sailing directly into the sun. It was definitely on the right, so we were going in the direction of Mexico. I knew he was kidding, but still it seemed like a wonderful idea to just leave, take off, be absolutely nowhere.

When he took over the tiller again he did kiss me, but with a line in one hand and a tiller in the other he was pretty busy. After a few minutes I was feeling much less romantic myself. The change of direction, besides moving the sun, had done something to the motion of the boat. We were rolling, and the horizon was rising and falling in regular, sickening dips. Wise, thoughtful Mac was alert to the possibility of the problem.

"You go below and lie down for a while," he said. "We'll go to Mexico another time."

It was dark when we drove back along the highway. The headlights flashed in our faces and the taillights glowed in a long, red line. At night, cars don't seem to have people in them, so we were still alone.

By the middle of October the leaves were off the trees in North Dakota, and Errol was still absent. He was having trouble with the studio, he was having trouble with Internal Revenue, and had apparently decided to stay on his boat, where nobody could find him. *Colt .45* was shelved, *Don Juan* was postponed indefinitely, and the career which three and a half months before had been about to take off was definitely dusty.

I was back to my old routine of making tests for other people. There was nothing coming up for me, and there were a lot of experienced, expensive actors on the lot who weren't working either and would certainly be used before me. The magic moment had passed, and, actually, I thought they were just trying to get rid of me when they sent me to Columbia to audition for a low-budget picture called *Thunderhoof*. There were only three characters: a young man, an older man and his young wife, who was described as a hot-blooded Mexican. The fact that I had dirty blond hair and gray eyes didn't seem to bother anybody, and I got the part! I was loaned out to Columbia and for the first time at least I had a real role to play.

The character's name was Maria, and after dying my hair as black as they could and experimenting with makeup, it was decided she was a half-breed. Wardrobe was simple, since she only wore three outfits in the whole picture. But it's never that simple in Hollywood. I tried on the blue jeans she would wear most of the time. When I went for the final fitting, to my utter amazement, they were padded! I was used to padded blouses, padded evening gowns and bathing suits. Any dress I had ever worn looked just the same with nobody in it—but blue jeans!? I guess I had never had occasion to notice that part of my anatomy, since it was on the wrong side of me when I looked in the mirror. By Hollywood standards my bottom was apparently skimpy, so I was padded. Actually, after a long day on a horse I learned to be grateful.

The only dress was a piece of cake. That was just a blouse and a long skirt. The long underwear that went under it was pretty special, what with the low-cut neck and all, but it was cold and, again, I learned to be grateful. The real hoot was the Spanish shawl she was supposed to find in the abandoned house. When I read the script, I assumed she put it over her head. When the costume department got through with it, it was complete with bust pads and would have been perfect for Dorothy Lamour. None of that mattered once we started the picture.

Almost all of the five-week schedule would be shot on location, so every morning I got up at four, ate breakfast with the truck drivers at a drive-in, and arrived for makeup at five. From there we went to the ranch to begin shooting as soon as the sun was high enough, usually about eight. Pancake body makeup in an open truck at seven-thirty on the desert in October is a shock, but the rest of the day always made up for it.

The cast was tiny and close from the first day. Preston Foster was the star and played the husband, and Bill Bishop played the "Kid," a young western drifter. Bill had just finished two years of Shakespeare, in New York, and had never ridden a horse in his life. An actor will try anything.

The crew consisted of the cameraman and lighting director, the grips and technicians, the sound men, makeup artists, and dressers you have on any picture. On a western you also have animal trainers, wranglers, and stuntmen. Jock O'Mahoney did most of our stunts, and he was my special friend through the whole picture. I always tried to sit near him riding out to the ranch, or home late at night.

"Why do you do it?" I asked him after the first time I saw him do a particularly dangerous fall.

He thought for a minute and said, "Because I probably should have spent my life riding around on a white horse saving damsels in distress. It's as close as I can come. I was born in the wrong time." By the time we finished shooting, I would understand what he meant, and by the time we got to my stunt work in the picture, Jocko had taught me so much I could do most of my own. Only the bareback mounts were too much. I never was strong enough to do the trick with my elbow.

The ranches we worked were huge tracts of land designed just for western pictures. There were streets, and whole towns with saloons and hotels and stores. There were isolated cabins and stage stops. Of course, there were other pictures shooting, and occasionally we had to wait till their posse rode through. Sometimes on a cheap picture they'd get a shot of it anyway and probably use it. It was the feeling that mattered. We were a little troupe out in the desert, most of the time, just us and the sun and the wind and the sand. Part of the time it was snow, but we hoped it photographed like sand.

We had a simple story to tell, about three people out to catch a wild stallion. Of course, the younger man became attracted to the older man's younger wife, and that made for complications. The old man was hurt trying to break the stallion. That meant they had to find shelter. Every day it all became more real. Preston did ride the wild horse, and he was really thrown. Everybody got hurt on the picture, but everybody kept right on working and it almost seemed we had moved into a different world, another time.

When the story called for a dust storm, the wind blew so hard we couldn't put out the lunch tables and one of the trucks blew over. We kept right on shooting. In Bill's death scene, we only had set up for one shot, but it was so good when he staggered down the hill I went after him and the cameraman just pulled the camera tripod out to the sand and followed us. It was cold, and we were so tired we were limping, but so were the people we were telling about.

It was the first time I had ever felt making a movie made any sense. We'd done it all in five weeks, I'd never worked so hard in my life, I loved the actors, I loved the mountains and the little pretend towns. I loved making up our own society and living it. I hated to see it end. I didn't want to go back.

After the picture was finished everything at Warners seemed different, or maybe it was just me. Seems like every time you take a step in any direction it changes the view. I found out what it feels like to work in a picture, really play a part, and I hated the idea of going back to just hang around.

It was getting close to Christmas and Lester wanted me to come to New York. I was afraid of that. I had gone so far from Lester I almost dreaded seeing him again. I didn't want to leave California. I kept thinking something would happen and I wanted to be there, but the idea of spending Christmas alone on the hill was more than I could handle.

Finally, it was Mac who made the decision. He said it would be better for him if I was away for a while, and it would be better for me if the studio realized I had somewhere to go. So, I left the animals with the Mitchells and flew to New York.

In January 1960, Richard and I bought a tiny house on three beautiful acres in Weston, Connecticut. By sheer coincidence it was twenty-five feet square, the exact dimensions of the little house on the hill in California. We saw it about eleven-thirty in the morning, and before we stopped to give the kids lunch we bought it. We took possession the first of June. I had been up every weekend during May to get the vegetable garden in. I had never in my life grown anything, but the lady who sold us the house insisted I could do it. She helped me stretch the strings, hoe the trenches, and hill the corn. I had no idea that three vegetable patches, each measuring thirty feet by thirty feet, was rather a large undertaking for a lady with two small children who was only going to be around on weekends. She said it would be easy if I mulched! So I mulched, and I mulched, and I mulched. I also scrubbed and sanded and painted.

The next problem was learning how to drive all over again. I had only touched the wheel of a car once since I met Richard, and the fear of driving had grown into a phobia. I never got farther than the train station, but at least the grocery store was on the way, and after a few months I found out how to get to the beach. Of course, I always had to find two parking places side by side, and I always had to go the same way past my landmarks so I wouldn't get lost. I didn't find out for two years that I was making a long dog-leg out of the trip to the station.

Truthfully, even after I found the short way I tended to avoid it. There was a long, narrow bridge, and whoever said, "We will cross that bridge when we come to it," should burn forever in Hell.

About the third weekend we had the house, Richard had to be away on a business trip. We got a friend who lived down the road to drive me to the house, while somebody else drove his car. The plan was to leave the car at the station on Sunday night, admittedly a long, involved, fairly ridiculous plan, but the alternatives were absolutely out of the question. I hated feeling helpless and stupid, but not nearly as much as I hated driving.

Actually, the weekend was going very well. The lady down the hill showed me how to plant the rosebush I bought and what not to pull out of the perennial garden. The kids were still intrigued with the novelty of playing outside and were happily tired when it was time for bed. I had driven to the store without incident, and I had decided that what the kitchen really needed was new linoleum on the cabinets. So while I was in the little shopping center, I bought two sheets of bright red vinyl.

As soon as the children were asleep Saturday night, I began taking off the old, worn-out linoleum. I had, of course, no tools. I used a piece of string to measure and rusty scissors to cut, after removing the old surface with a beer-can opener. Like my ninety-foot garden, I was blissfully unaware that what I was undertaking was impossible. I read the instructions on the glue, which were full of warnings. "This glue adheres instantly!" "Do not inhale fumes!" "Cannot be removed from clothing or skin!" What they did not say was how to get all four sides of the damn stuff into those little metal edges at the same time, while you were holding your breath and worrying that you would spend the rest of your life with a square yard of vinyl stuck to your thumb.

As it happened, I never quite got to that point. With my piece of string and my rusty shears I couldn't even get the stuff cut right. So, about ten I decided to take a break and make myself a cup of Sanka. As I ran the water into the kettle I noticed the faucet was spurting and grumbling, and I knew just how it felt.

When I sat down at the kitchen table with the instructions to look for one more clue, I was just tired from a day with the kids and the garden, and irritated with my project. So tired it probably took me two seconds to react when I felt something run across my bare foot and saw a gray tail disappear through the open doorway to the basement. Okay. That's it, I decided. That's absolutely all. I had seen what was at least a mouse! I had seen the tail of a living creature going into my basement. It was definitely time for bed!

To make matters just a little worse, while I was brushing my teeth the water spurted again a couple of times and quit altogether. I decided to swallow the toothpaste. I was not going down to that kitchen maybe ever, and certainly not in the dark.

Bed, however, was not restful. Now that there was no running water the pipes began to rumble and bang, and it suddenly occurred to me that the hot water tank did not know we had run out of water and was probably still hotting away. The only hot water tank I had ever seen was the one with a little gas jet from my childhood, when you heated the water as you needed it. Obviously, I had to turn off the heater, which meant that I had to go down into the basement where "you know what" was lurking. Still, it had to be done. I had to go down to that basement and I did, holding my nightgown around me and wearing a pair of high boots I found in the closet.

I turned on the lights and crept down the stairs with my heart pounding and my eyes searching every shadow. The hot water tank was over in the far corner, and I had to tiptoe all the way across that damp, cement floor to get to it. But then what? I stood there and stared at the thing for what seemed like an hour, with no idea what to do next. It didn't have a little gas jet, and I suddenly remembered why. The house didn't have gas! It didn't even have a little door to open, or a switch, a plug, or an off button. It didn't have anything, so I went back up the stairs and got back into bed.

By two o'clock, the situation had definitely worsened, and I knew I had to make a decision. The rumbling had grown so loud the house was beginning to shake. I had visions of the water tank exploding, sending the whole place into orbit. The only thing to do was carry the children out of the house and put them in the car before the holocaust.

At three, I was still debating the awful alternative when I remembered. The garden hose! It had been running since three that afternoon when I planted the rosebush. It had to be turned off, and of course the turn-off valve was outside.

If our forefathers had dreaded crossing unknown territory as much as I feared walking into my yard in Fairfield, Connecticut, the West would still not be settled! But for my sleeping babes, I went. Actually, when I got outside, it wasn't bad at all. The moonlight was soft and surprisingly bright. The air smelled sweet, and the instant I turned the little knob on the side of the house, the rumbling stopped. I didn't hang around to enjoy the night air, but I didn't run back to the house, either. When I took off my boots for the last time I was satisfied and sleepy.

Having the "little house"—which was always the way we referred to it—was a totally new experience which Richard and I viewed from diametrically opposed points of view from day one. He saw the house as a wonderful place to escape to after a busy week in the city. It had a wide, sunny space in back, sloping gently down to the woods, and it was surrounded by great, shady trees. It was a perfect place to enjoy the sun in the morning and a

martini at eventide. I saw it all as new space to conquer and man-
icure, and a constant challenge. He saw giant maples majestically
enclosing the land, and I counted dead limbs.

Suzy Sex Kitten had moved away, and Hannah Homemaker
was taking over. Every weekend I worked in the vegetable garden
dragging out great lumps of field grass that had not gotten the
word about mulch, and the garden grew. Oh my God, it grew! By
the end of July I was bringing in bags of tomatoes to anyone who
would take them, and throwing cucumbers and zucchini, which
had grown to obscene proportions, into the tall grass. In August it
was a daily war with the squirrels and the woodchucks for the
corn, but it was a constant miracle when the eggplants formed in
tiny perfection beneath the gray-green leaves, swelling and dropping their shiny purple bellies.

Toward the end of July the plumber came to fix the pump,
and when I asked how much I owed him he said, "Mary, to tell
you the truth, it's five dollars . . . but if you don't mind, your garden is in and I'd rather take it in vegetables."

Both children were in the kitchen and that moment was easily worth all the hours in the sun, the blisters on my hands, and
the backaches. They each took a basket and went with Ed out to
the garden, those two little people. They had a new respect for
what we had grown on our own land, with our own hands.

It was a new and strange environment for both kids and they
met it, each in his own way. Cynthia danced after fireflies and
enchanted the neighborhood. Jeff established the boundaries of
his territory and his inestimable rights with his fists and his lungs.

The ride out every Friday became the weekly horror, and
both of them can still do a very good repeat of every game and
every fight.

"Let's play addition. Let's play subtraction. Let's play license
tag."

"She's got her doll on my side."

"Daddy, he hit me!"

"She hit me first!"

The principal ploy was how to get into the front seat and
into Mother's lap. Jeff was a master at that. He also tended to get

car sick, so it wasn't all phony. He did actually get sick, but he wasn't sleepy. Cynthia would lean over the back seat, watching and waiting for his eyelids to flutter.

"He's not asleep! He's faking! I want to sit up front!"

At some point in every trip, Richard would pull over to the side of the road and threaten to leave us all sitting there. It was a wonderful way to start the weekend.

It was also difficult, I discovered, to keep two houses going. There were usually four bottles of mayonnaise in one house and seven bottles of ketchup in the other, and lots of odd shoes in both. My mind, like my clothes, now spread itself over three places: the studio, the apartment, and the house. The rest of me just tried to keep up. I would fly home on Friday with a list of groceries, clothes, and chores. I backed out of the door in Connecticut every Sunday with a mop in my hand, and only once did I lose track of where I was completely. It was a pitch-dark, moonless night in Connecticut when one of the children cried out. Of course I sprang automatically out of bed, but on my side the eaves sloped down to about four feet, and I cracked my head so loudly I woke Richard. He says he waited ever so long for the wail of pain, the cross word, or falling plaster, but all I said after a very, very long pause was: "Wrong house."

Once we moved to the new apartment, living in the city became a lot easier. At least everybody had their own room. That apartment was just one of the many gifts from Richard's mother, Helen. We had always been close, and when I told her I was getting desperate she simply said, "Leave it to me. I'll find you an apartment." Helen never in her life learned to boil an egg and has always believed that she is absolutely useless, but whatever she has ever had she gave to me, like her taste and education. Also, whatever she set her mind to, she accomplished. She found the apartment in two days, called me at the studio, and I signed the lease before I ever saw it. It was beautiful and it was just what we needed, but I had to face decorating again, and too much was happening everywhere else. I just put that off.

The dining table was lost in a real dining room, so I shoved it in a corner with the white shutter-door cabinets from the old apartment along the walls. I shortened the old white curtains and decided in a moment of childish whimsey that if I hung ribbons from the curtain rods I wouldn't need drapes, and it would be fresh and young and different. It was all of that, and it looked just awful. With two kids banging tricycles into everything, it didn't seem to matter.

The living room was large and formal, with beautiful proportions. I simply closed the doors and walked around it until we gave a big party six months later. Then I had to deal with it. I remember lugging the coffee table home in a taxi in the middle of a snowstorm.

Things went well for Richard that year. Time, Inc. had been a client of the office for over a year, and in 1960 he went on staff. They had acquired several television and radio stations, and "Time-Life Broadcast" was a full-time job. In two years he would be a vice-president. We still needed both salaries to keep up with schools, rent, and help, but we did begin to save a little. So with our combined financial wisdom and the advice of Richard's barber, we bought mutual funds.

By 1960, both children were in the Town School. We hadn't planned it, that's just the way it worked out. Cynthia went to school at three, because her brother was demanding, and getting, too much attention. She needed space of her own. The next fall, when Jeff was not yet even three, it was decided that he was lonely and needed companionship, so he went too. So much for Cynthia's space.

Richard and I both thought it was ridiculous to have Pearl full time and Martha coming in every day, besides spending $1,400 sending the children to nursery school, but like a lot of decisions, that one got away from us.

New York children live such isolated lives. They are taken to the playground at a certain time and brought home. They are picked up and taken to school, picked up and brought home, with no chance to test their own resources. So actually, it was a good day when I came home after a late rehearsal to find them both sitting downstairs in the lobby—although at first it scared the daylights out of me.

"What are you guys doing down here?"

"There's nobody home," Jeff said matter-of-factly. "Pearl went out and didn't come back."

"We can't go in the house if nobody is there," Cynthia added. They obviously had discussed the situation.

"You are absolutely right!" I agreed, and as we got in the elevator I thanked Al for looking after them.

"No trouble, they were fine," he said, with his quick, nervous little smile. Then a thought struck me.

"What would you two have done if I'd come home even later?"

"Oh, we had that all planned!" Both little faces lit up, and the way they told the story, they were obviously disappointed that I had.

They had made a deal with Al to stay after his shift and walk them across the street to Phoebe's Hamburger. They knew Spry would give them their supper if they told him Mother would pay later. Then Spry would walk them back across the street, and they had promised Al they would watch the ballgame instead of the cartoons if he would stay with them.

I was proud of them, and so happy and relieved I could have hugged them and kissed them and cried. I probably did, and I don't think I felt quite so guilty for a while. They were becoming very independent, thoughtful people. They understood that they couldn't cross streets alone until they were tall enough to be seen over the hood of a car, and they accepted that. It had nothing to do with how smart they were, just how tall.

Days and weeks and years when children are small tend to get lost in routine, but I will always have the feelings and pictures of the moments in my mind, obviously pictures that I have deliberately chosen.

They had between them one nice, big bedroom and one tiny one, and they traded several times, so the pictures go back and forth. They liked to put on shows, like all children, and put sheets over a pile of boxes and chairs to make a tent. I can see Cynthia in the little room, playing with her dolls by the hour, murmuring quietly to people smaller than she was. Jeff had trains and trucks in the big room, and rode his tricycle all over the house. Later, when his anger began to build, he started to draw the pictures of a war he imagined. He also started going to sleep in our bed. We would move him later, but the routine was rigid. The covers had to be smooth, the closet doors had to be closed, and the light in the bathroom left on.

On rainy days, or especially cold ones, as long as they could both fit, they went grocery shopping with me in their twin stroller. If it was raining, they held the big, black umbrella between them and looked out at the world from their dark blue chariot.

Cozy house was the end of every day. Cozy house was reading aloud with each of them leaning on a shoulder. Cozy house was my bed in the city, or the couch in the little house. By the time they were four or five, we had read E. B. White's *Charlotte's Web* and *Stuart Little* so many times, both of them had memorized long passages, and we had finished Frances Hodgson Burnett's *Secret Garden*. They were smart little brats. They knew I'd get interested and read till eleven if they stayed awake, so they did. I wasn't so dumb, either. I knew they'd sleep a little later in the morning, and I loved the books as much as they did.

Among the pictures I think I treasure most is Cynthia's face as she watched her first Broadway show. We went to a matinee of *My Fair Lady*. She wore a red velvet dress Mother had made for her, with a white lace collar. She seemed almost incandescent, and her little hands, always the hands, touched every moment. She was just six, but by then she could sing the lead to absolutely anything, while I sang harmony with her. All the way home from the theatre that day, we sang the songs from the show.

Of course we sang together lots of times. We sang when we did the dishes, just the way I had sung with Daddy when I was her age, and sometimes we'd make up new songs to fit whatever we were doing. She was wonderful at the rhythm and the story, though I always had to come up with the rhyme. The game was not to falter, never to drop the beat. Sometimes we sang folk songs that I could play on the guitar. I don't think she ever liked to sing if anybody else was listening, but she did it anyway. She knew how happy she could make me feel.

I see Cynthia at the piano. I see Jeff the only time I think I ever hit him. He had pushed me right over the edge, and I whirled to swat him on the backside. In turning I accidentally caught him on the face with the back of my hand. We were both so surprised we stopped dead in our tracks. He put his hand to his mouth, looked at his fingers for a trace of blood, and with stern calm said, "Mother, you've gone too far." Like all the battles, that one dissolved in tears and laughter.

I had never felt like a good wife, but being a mother felt the way I had always imagined it would. I remembered how tired my mother was, so when I got tired, that was right and natural and to be expected. I loved calling school to say, "This is Cynthia's mother . . ." "This is Jeff's mother . . ." I loved picking them up, when I had a day off, and I was proud walking down the street, each hand in one of theirs; just the way I know my mother had felt. At the fancy East Side private school, I usually thought I looked a little tacky, and in a way that was Mother too. I don't remember my mother as the kind of woman who would have had that kind of awareness of herself. I remember Mother as someone who was there for me, and I was there for mine.

When I walked away from the school with my two children, I always stopped for a moment to watch the beautiful brunette woman who always wore brown. She was the only mother who was always there. Her little girl, Fifi, was in Cynthia's class, and that year she had a little boy in a stroller. The next fall, she had another girl in the carriage. She was always there, in a perfect brown coat, her hair short and straight and simple, and I always thought, "If I could only feel the way she looks."

A few months after we moved, Pearl left. We didn't understand why, but she left abruptly. Martha said she knew why, and would say no more. Martha was still there every day, and several other ladies came and went. I can see them all, and I can see Martha.

Martha Grey was a constant friend from the first year of our marriage until she retired. With a gentle dignity I never saw disturbed, she somehow managed to take care of us and raise her own three children. When her son died, she took the child of a young friend to raise. I don't think I had any idea then how much her patience and kindness affected all of us. We tended to take that for granted, like her habit of putting things away where no one else could find them. I know how many times I wondered at her strength and her ability to accept, or at least live with, tragedy.

Every time we hired somebody new, Martha would say, "She's nice. She's real nice." And when we hired the fancy Swiss cook she said, "This white one, she's nice too."

"Martha, she's not nice! We're all scared to death of her."

"Well, she's strict with the children, but that won't hurt them."

"She's strict with me! No matter what I ask her to do she says no."

Martha laughed and imitated the Swiss dialect, "Oo-a nooa," and from that day on the Swiss cook was called Ooa Nooa.

If I suggested steak for dinner, she would say, "Ooa, nooa, ve have veal und noodles," and that's what we got. We had veal and noodles till the Alps looked level.

It was during the Cuban Missile Crisis in 1962 that she finally went too far. She got the children's stroller out of the basement, filled the shopping cart with canned beans and canned fruit, and prepared us all to walk to Connecticut. Our shoes and blankets were piled in the hall and we had our instructions. For three days we stayed at the ready! Needless to say, we did not walk to Connecticut, but we ate beans and canned fruit for two years.

In 1962, I went to the doctor for a checkup, and he told me there was a mass in my left breast that had to be removed. Anyone who has been through it knows that no matter how many times they tell you they are sure it is benign, you know perfectly well they don't know or they wouldn't be removing it. I went home and picked up the children and took them to the park, because that is what I always did. I talked to the other mothers and watched the kids. I pushed them in the swings and caught them at the bottom of the slide, and all the time I was more aware of my own body than I had ever been in my life.

Reaching up to guide the swing, waving as Jeff wheeled around on his bicycle, leaning over to tuck Cynthia's doll into her little carriage, I couldn't help imagining what each moment would be like without a breast. I was so terrified I couldn't even cry, and I couldn't think about anything else.

Another opinion, I decided. Maybe he's wrong! I found a dime in my pocket and went to the phone booth just outside the playground and called Richard's friend, Dr. Goodman.

"The gynecologist says I have a mass in my left breast that he has to take out."

"Well, he isn't going to," he said. "If you need an operation I'm going to do it. Be in my office at five."

In some bizarre way, I was relieved! It was only four, and I had a whole hour before there was any real decision. Ed sounded so sure of himself, and so definite, it was as though he had taken the problem on himself. At five-fifteen that had changed.

I called the producer to ask when I could have Monday and Tuesday off, and he called the hospital to arrange for a bed.

It was a long ten days, and ten very long nights, with too many hours to imagine what might happen. Mother came up from Oklahoma to stay with the children.

When the day finally came I went to the show and, as usual, took the children to the park. I had been to the hospital once when they were very small, and that had frightened Jeff too much. His eyes were big and round, and his little mouth was quivering when I got into the elevator. He had nightmares for weeks. So I thought if I didn't make a real exit with a suitcase, they would think less of the whole thing. They were both playing and happy when I kissed them and walked on home. They knew I would be gone for a few days; I just hadn't mentioned where I was going. There were tears in Mother's eyes, but of course I was still her baby.

The look and the sounds of an operating room are always the same: that big light shines down in your eyes; the hard, cold table; and the smell of disinfectant that always gags me. Then there's the casual blur of voices as the nurses and the anesthesiologists go about the routines of sliding the paper boots onto your feet and taping your arms to the board.

"You're going to feel a little stick, then I want you to count."

"I know. I never get past ten." I can tell I'm going out when

I hear the fans. Always the fans in my head, getting louder and louder . . . till nothing, except the dreams . . .

Later, the voices are far away and the room is dark. White shadows move across the darkness and brush against the bed; but the voices are somewhere else, fading in and out of the pain and the nausea.

"She's coming to."

"Does she have a special?"

"Dr. Goodman ordered one."

"She can go down."

"Careful, she's draining. Leave her on her side."

The bed moves, and the light changes to green. No. That's the hall. There's a bump and a scrape. Now it's white, and the elevator doors close. They open again, and there's a bump as the wheels go over the ledge, another bump turning the corner into the room, and another white shadow rustles.

"Do you need something for the pain?"

The pain is somewhere under all those bandages, and pale pink blood has soaked through onto the sheets.

"Am I . . ." you want to ask and you think you have. You know they won't tell you, and you want to go back to sleep.

"You're all right. It was benign. The doctor will be in to see you later."

You feel a sharp sting in your backside, and it's all right to melt away again.

In 1962 the Hursleys finally came up with another story for Jo, and it was almost as appealing as killing Duncan Eric. They had read through the old histories and discovered Jimmy Bergman, who, you'll remember, had been napping since 1953. Everyone agreed that was no way to treat a small boy, so he was reintroduced. However, by some strange twist of fate, he was no longer the Bergman's son, he was their nephew, and obviously they had been silly and forgetful to ever think otherwise. He really belonged to Stu's sister, and Barbara Baxley joined the cast to play some brilliant scenes, and teach us all some new words.

Now, Barbara did not play the kind of mother one had

learned to expect on a daytime serial. She had not even been around to pick up his laundry in nine years. But it was more than that, much more.

Actually, it was a beautiful relationship. Barbara played a mother who simply didn't enjoy motherly chores, and Jimmy was a very self-reliant child who looked after her. They were very close to each other in a refreshingly unsticky way.

Jo had spent some time with Jimmy when his mother was busy, but that was natural. Jo always liked kids and Mary always enjoyed working with them. Then, quite suddenly, the relationship began to take on strange new colors. Overnight, Jo became harshly critical of Jimmy's mother, even making remarks in front of the child. Then, Barbara began to talk about leaving Henderson, this time taking Jimmy with her, and Jo started going completely around the bend.

In the Wednesday show, she announced that she thought Barbara was a totally unfit mother and did not deserve the child. I began to get very nervous, so I read ahead and, sure enough, by Friday Jo was on her way to court to start a custody fight. That night, for the first time in my life, I wrote a memo, with copies to Frank, Dan, the writers, and P&G. I typed it and spelled it myself, and I am told there was a hushed silence in the office while they all puzzled their way through it, broken only by Stan Potter's quiet plea, "Does anyone have any idea what the word is that has three M's?"

What I talked about was our long investment in Jo, and our commitment to some kind of honesty and continuity. This was the kind of childish, frantic idea Irene would have had back in the fifties, and did. Irene had taken Jo to court to fight for Patti. If Jo was to continue to be a rational woman, she could not follow the same pattern.

Sometime over the weekend, the story was canceled and the scripts were thrown out. They even canceled calls for actors, who had to be paid. I was grateful and relieved, but what was more important, a new level of trust had been restored between me and the company. We'd come a long way since the day in the office after I'd coughed on the air.

There was only one script of the old story that still had to be played, but with the story canceled I could turn it around and make it work in character. Yes, Jo did love the little boy, and she had lost her own son. She couldn't help wanting him so much. That was human and real. Yes, Jo was wrong, but for reasons that made sense.

That was the last story they wrote that involved Jo at all. I was back to taking baskets of fruit and serving coffee, if I was there at all. Most of the time I wasn't.

When Lynn Loring left the show, the search for a new Patti was long and trying, and there must have been at least thirty young women who still list on the résumés they present in casting offices, "role of Patti Tate, 'Search for Tomorrow.'" Trish Van der Veer, who, I thought, was one of the sweetest, was gone in a week. As it turned out, probably for the best. Sometimes they came and went in one show, and I remember distinctly fading out on a Tuesday in a scene with a tall, blond Patti and fading back in Wednesday with a short brunette. Unfortunately, my first line upon entering the darkened room was, "Patti? Patti, is that you?" I thought it was funny but nobody else did.

In 1962, Abigail Kellogg was playing the part, and the story centered around her affair with Dr. Everett Moore, played by Martin Brooks. In order to complicate the situation, Dr. Moore decided to marry a patient of his, because he knew she was dying. After all, she did love him and he was a nice guy. However, she complicated him one better by deciding she wasn't so sick anymore, just had terrible headaches from time to time.

The wife, Isabel, was played by Lenka Peterson. Lenka is a wonderful actress. She is also married. She also has five children, who were young then, and a large house and, like a lot of us, self-confidence that would have room to grow in the belly button of a gnat. She said one day that when she had a big role to study she'd find herself thinking, "Now, if I just give the kitchen a really good cleaning it will be all right to go and work on the play." I understood exactly what she meant.

She is also a wonderful friend, and a pro. She was the only one who made it to work on time during a blizzard, and her last day on the show she was there, being a corpse on the floor, but she had to lie so we could only see her back, because the oven had blown up in her face the night before.

Patti and Dr. Moore went on trial for Isabel's murder—but I have gone a little too fast and didn't mention that somewhere in that year we changed Pattis again. Gretchen Walther was playing the part by the time Patti discovered she was pregnant. So, unless I'm counting wrong, Dr. Moore went to bed with one lady and got another one pregnant! Little mistimings like that continued to plague us as long as the show was live. There were just too many people to coordinate, too little time, too many words to learn, and too many little technicalities that could go wrong and turn a simple episode into a shambles when you least expected it. Like the nice, simple day when there were three phone calls. We were a little long at dress, so one of the calls was cut, the one between Arthur and the Bergmans in the second act. It was a good, clean cut and on the air everything was going smoothly. Arthur had nothing to do in that act, so he was lounging in the Tate kitchen, not even listening. The Bergmans got to the place in the script where the call had been cut, and were just about to sail past it when . . .

"Ring . . . ring . . ."

Everyone in the studio froze. Everyone, that is, except Tommy, our sound effects man. Nobody had told him there was a cut.

"Ring . . . ring." Nobody moved. They just stared at that silly black instrument that had suddenly lost its little mind.

"Ring . . . ring." Terry did manage to galvanize his body into action and bolted for the phone in the Tate kitchen, knocking over a chair on his way in a lot of wasted motion. There was no mike and no camera there.

"Ring . . . ring." Finally, Marge made a decision and managed at the same time to dump the situation squarely onto Stu.

"I think it's for you," she said, just as if that made sense. He shot her a look and started toward the phone much the way he would have approached a coiled rattler. He picked up the receiver and, in the husky whisper of a man who has recently received several threatening phone calls, said: "Hello?"

He waited. Everyone waited. There was only silence. Slowly the color came back to his face. He even smiled, a little smile of triumph that may have seemed odd if you didn't know what he'd just been through, and he said:

"Wrong number."

That was the trouble with phone calls. They were almost too easy and got very little rehearsal. If you were on a show that had a teleprompter you could read them, and you may have noticed that a lot of actors put their glasses on every time it rang. Phone calls were easy, and they could also be forgotten altogether.

One day I was on my way to the dressing room when I noticed the actor I had just played the scene with walking out the front door with his hat and coat on, and a little thought buzzed me.

"Hey, Andy. Have you done your phone call in the third act yet?"

I did hear the name of our Lord spoken without reverence, as a body flashed by me, tearing off clothes as it went by. I could only assume he had not done his phone call at the end of the third act. Since he had to make that call from his bed, he also had a change of costume. The Lord had apparently heard him, because he did get there, and he got into bed and said all the words, breathing a trifle hard, but audible. The only detail that may have seemed out of place was the hat. He forgot to take that off.

Timing went wrong, and technicalities, but always it was the lines that plagued us, and the wildest day I can remember was Allison's wedding to Fred Metcalf.

Weddings are nearly always happy affairs. Everybody gets all dressed up, nobody has much to say, so it's like a party. The champagne is only ginger ale, but the cake is real and there is an extra one to use for dress rehearsal, so everybody gets a piece. Sometimes we even have funny presents for the bride and groom, because the love affairs have usually dragged on for a couple of years, and it's a relief to get it over with.

The ceremonies are always Protestant, because most of the people are. Stu Bergman, one would assume, is Jewish, but his son and daughter are not. Oh well, what do casting directors know about heredity? Our ceremonies are Protestant, though for some reason most of our ministers, through the years, have been Jewish, and on the occasion of Allison's wedding to Fred Metcalf, that was the case.

The minister was Jewish, he was far-sighted, and he was, I think, a tad vain, because he decided not to wear his glasses on camera. He held the book, but he had memorized the service and was only pretending to read. The rehearsals went smoothly enough, and nobody paid much attention until we got on the air. The floor manager cued him and he took a deep breath, but the hesitation before the "Dearly Beloved . . ." was a little too long, and there was a distinct quaver in his voice.

It had happened so many times before. The final squeeze of tension that accompanies a live air show had loosened the glue.

Of course, we still assumed he was reading. It didn't occur to us that he couldn't see the page in front of him till he started ad-libbing the Book of Common Prayer.

"We are gathered together in the sight of God . . . to join this man and this woman in the state of matrimony and Holy Jesus." He knew that was wrong, and the involuntary giggle from one of the pews would have distracted him further, but I doubt he heard it, as his eyes frantically scanned the blurred page in his hand.

"If anyone knows a reason . . . why . . . then forever hold your peace!"

It made absolutely no sense, but he said it with great sincerity and conviction, and, having dispensed with the opening of the service, got straight to the meat of the scene.

"Do you, Fred?"

Fred was puzzled but agreeable. He couldn't say, "I do." That, he knew, came at the end. So he just said, "I, Fred."

"Take this woman . . . ?"

Fred nodded, then realized he had to say more. "Take this woman."

"To love?"

"To love."

"And honor?"

"And honor."

"In sickness, and in health . . . ?"

"In sickness and in health."

"Forsake all others?"

"Forsake all others."

"Only keep her . . . ?"

"Only keep her . . ."

"Till . . ." The furrows in the minister's brow deepened as he searched the void of his mind for a clue.

"Till . . ." He was so close, and he had the right idea. He just couldn't nail the words. "Till . . ." Then, in final desperation, he blurted: "Till you're both dead."

It took a very long moment, but Fred did manage to look him in the eye and say, with an absolutely straight face, "Till we're both dead."

The heads of the dearly beloved were bowed low, and handkerchiefs covered faces. Tears had formed and streamed from the eyes of the immediate family, trapped with the miserable couple on camera, and it wasn't over. No. They had to do it again, the whole thing, more or less the same way, and he did it, too, all the way to the last.

"Only keep him?"

"Only keep him."

"Till you're both dead?"

Allison repeated after him with a demure solemnity that did her proud, "Till we're both dead."

When the organ mercifully drowned the noise of the crowd, heads were still bowed, but not in silent prayer. That day it was helpless hysteria.

Out of the blue, in 1963, I got a telegram:

"WE ARE PLEASED TO INFORM YOU THAT YOU HAVE BEEN NOMINATED BY THE TELEVISION ACADEMY OF ARTS AND SCIENCE AS BEST ACTRESS IN A CONTINUING SERIES."

It was absolutely unbelievable! I had been nominated along with Mary Tyler Moore and Shirley Booth. Those wonderful actresses on big, nighttime shows, and me! It was an honor, and even though I don't think I ever really believed in my heart of hearts that I would win, I sure did have some dandy fantasies. I admit, I wrote a speech.

Besides being an honor, it was a large help to an ego that had slipped through a hole in my pocket and had been lost in the lining for a couple of years. I also knew being nominated was bound to bolster my standing on the show. It was the first time anybody from daytime had been nominated for anything. I had won six or seven TV Radio Mirror Awards, but that was only in a daytime category. This was quite different. Incidentally, it was not only the first time it happened, it was the last.

The freeze was still on, and I wasn't sure what the reaction would be inside the cast, so I didn't mention anything about it until it was announced in the papers, but I did call P&G. Stan Potter was excited, and of course my family was ecstatic, especially Cynthia. She began to plan what I would wear and went with me to pick it out. We spent fifty-nine dollars on a blue and white cotton evening dress and for twenty dollars we bought a little white cardigan to put over my shoulders. I paid ten dollars for white kid gloves, and fourteen for navy patent sandals. Betty Rea loaned me her ten-thousand-dollar diamond and sapphire bracelet and I was complete.

The only people who were genuinely upset, and with some reason, were the writers and the producer. The Academy asked for film of a scene to run during the dinner, but I hadn't had a scene for weeks and none coming up. So there was no film available. The solution was to write a scene and jam it into the show. The result was, necessarily, awkward, since it wasn't planned, and I played it with Martin Brooks. I had written the key words from my dialogue, as usual, on the floor in front of the porch swing we were sitting on. At the precise moment Marty went up in his lines, the cameraman pushed in for an unexpected close-up and parked his big fat pedestal right smack on top of my words! Some day I would like to write a book called, "How to Act in 8,000 Very Difficult Lessons!"

I didn't win an Emmy, but it was a wonderful evening. Hal Cooper sent me a dozen red roses and a beautiful note. Cynthia had stars in her eyes when I left in the blue dress, and I promised both children they could stay up and watch the show. I went over to Maud's house to get made up, and her little girls danced with me down the hall to the elevator. There was one moment during the evening that would have stopped my heart, but I was so nervous I never did hear it.

There were two simultaneous award dinners, one in New York and one in California, and they kept switching back and forth, so when Best Actress in a Series was announced they said, "In New York . . ."

Stan Potter thought I was the only actress here, and he jumped up out of his chair. I missed the whole thing, but when the audience started applauding I knew the spotlight wasn't on me, and I could see Shirley Booth moving toward the stage.

Oh, well. I did get nominated! And Cynthia has saved the blue dress all these years. Cinderella went home from the ball in her blue patent sandals, and they felt just fine.

A few months later the phone rang about 3 A.M. Richard picked it up without turning on the light.

"Hello?" he said groggily, trying not to wake up. There was a pause and he said, "Eddy, how the hell are you—and why the hell are you calling at this hour?"

Another short pause.

"Of course, she's here . . . just a minute." He turned on the light and handed me the receiver.

"It's Eddy Binz . . . says it's important."

"Eddy? . . . Hi," was all I could manage, and he said:

"Hey, why do your writers hate you so much?"

Well, that sat me up.

"I don't know, Eddy, but I know they do . . . Why?"

"Well, I just had dinner with them—a little group, just eight people—and one of them had a lot to drink. Her husband tried to shut her up, but she kept talking."

"What did she say?"

"Well, it seems P&G won't let her kill you off, but she figures by the end of the year the character will be so useless they'll be begging her to."

There was a long pause, and I said, "Thank you, Eddy. It's sad . . . but you've helped me a lot. I knew that's what they were doing. Nobody believed me."

The next day I called Stan Potter, who just happened to be in New York, and Frank Dodge, the agency supervisor, and said I had to have lunch with them. I told them about the phone call, and I remember the incredulous look on Stan's face. He was becoming the kind of friend Bill Craig had been, and I could tell he was sad and angry for me.

Then I heard someone mutter, "God damn Eddy Binz." I think it was Frank.

Actually, I doubt the phone call from Eddy had much to do with it, but by the end of the year there was talk of the Hursleys leaving. I remember having lunch with Frank.

He said, "I feel like I'm crawling out to the end of a limb." He took another sip of his drink.

"I'm crawling out there with you, Frank. They have never been right for us. They have never believed in the show. They say they don't believe in melodrama, and we've had more in five years than the rest of the time put together. Held at gunpoint three times! And you know how they feel about Jo."

When they left us, they went straight to "General Hospital" and did a beautiful job. Their ratings went up, the stories were good, and they were there for a long time. I never understood why they felt the way they did about me. They forced me to fight and God knows it's the last thing I wanted to do. But when I have to I will, and I did. Jo had become too important to me. When I protected her, I protected myself.

Changing writers is always an adjustment, but when Julian Funt and Dave Lesan took over it was the easiest one we ever had to make. They had written radio for years. They were old friends of Charlie's, and they were thoughtful, kind men.

One of the first stories Dave and Julian came up with was the dearest, funniest we ever had. Marge discovered she was pregnant! With a grown daughter and a grandchild, she and Stu started all over. First, they went through the initial shock, the disbelief, and the embarrassment. After that came months of anticipation, very tender rejuvenation and pride. Marge got used to the idea, but Stu never did. The last weeks before the baby was due, he began to make trial runs to the hospital to make sure exactly how long it was going to take under varying circumstances. He would try it before going to work at West Side Auto in the morning, then set the alarm and dash out in his pajamas and overcoat in the middle of the night. During one of his runs, Marge realized it was time, calmly called a taxi, went to the hospital, and by the time Stu got home and found the note, Tom Bergman was sleeping quietly in the hospital nursery.

Credit where credit is due. It was a wonderful story, but what Larry and Melba did with it was magic.

With Dave and Julian, the relationship between Jo and Patti was richer and warmer, too. Gretchen Walther brought a more mature quality to the role, and that alone gave us more possibilities to explore and use. Patti was pregnant with Dr. Moore's baby, and we had difficult emotional material to play. For me, just having somebody who was tall enough to look me straight in the eye was a huge help, but Gretchen and I always had a lot going for us. She and Lynn Loring are the only Pattis who became my close friends.

We had all the right ingredients for a wonderful working relationship and a beautiful show, except for our ridiculous rehearsal schedule, which had not changed in all that time. Most days, we managed. If an actor only had one scene to play out of the three, he could even get some makeup on. Of course, if you had two scenes, that was doubtful, and if you had all three, you went on the air with your heart in your mouth.

The problem on any five-day schedule is that actors tend to be written in heavily for days at a time if they are carrying the story, and by Friday they get a little weary. Your head is too full of words. That is what happened to Gretchen and me the week Patti lost the baby. We had both been on all week. The scenes had been long and draining, and by Friday we were tired. Friday was, in those days, always the big one, and that day the two of us had almost the whole show.

Patti was just coming out of the anesthetic and Jo was by her bedside. She didn't know she had lost the baby, and Jo had to tell her.

Dan was, as usual, about one hour and fifteen minutes late. He never varied that. We had, of course, been rehearsing for the hour and fifteen minutes, but it was a complicated script and the spaces for the camera cuts changed the rhythm so much the rehearsal was useless. We ran to the studio. Maud made us up and we started camera blocking.

We were pretty much on schedule, though it was difficult, disjointed dialogue and we were both nervous. Then, to make matters worse, Dan announced after dress rehearsal that we were long. He must have known that all day, and it was typical of him not to mention it till he was fully covered. So at fifteen minutes to air, we got cuts, which made the scenes even more disjointed.

We had ten minutes to rearrange the dialogue in our minds and try to rethink the emotional changes, the pauses, and the looks. It's damn hard to play that kind of scene at best, and with cold panic freezing all the switches in your mind, it's next to impossible. There is often a moment when you simply think, "I can't do it," but there is no stopping the hands of the clock, and nobody famous was making news that would preempt us. I hate to admit it, but there have been days when I found myself thinking a tornado would be a nice distraction and we wouldn't have to go on the air. They never happened on those days, so, ready or not, we went on.

In the middle of the first page I could see her getting into trouble, so I took her hand. That's a good thing to do when you are out there and nobody can help you but each other. Since she was coming out of the anesthetic it was natural for me to prompt her, "Honey, do you remember?" and give her part of her line. I had words scribbled on the side of her pillow to cue me into mine, so at least I knew where we were going. She got halfway through the next one, and I could see her eyes beginning to glaze. She was gone again, but the hands held firm. The little notes I had on the pillow didn't help me with her lines, and with the cuts they were difficult to follow, but from somewhere I managed to focus in on the pages in my mind.

My mother once lifted a fallen tree because Daddy was caught under it. She weighed a hundred pounds. You can do anything if you have to, and for the next fourteen minutes I said my lines and most of hers. She came back for moments, but just the act of playing groggy made it more difficult for her to concentrate, and the strain of doing five shows straight, with virtually no rehearsal, had taken its toll.

I had perspired straight through my shirt and my jacket. When I could move I went to the ladies' room and threw up. I washed my face, took Gretchen a cold paper towel, and then had a tantrum. I went right through the roof of the control room. I think if it had happened to me I could have stood it, but it had happened to my girl. Dan had gone too far. I told him and everybody else between Park and Lexington that I would never work that way again.

That afternoon, Frank called to say P&G wanted to have dinner with me on Monday.

"You know this is going to cost me my job," he said.

"Come to the dinner, Frank. I don't want anybody to lose their job. I just don't want to work this way. Please, come to the dinner."

"I'm the producer. I should never have let this happen."

"Please, dear. Come to the dinner. We'll work it out."

On Monday I asked Richard to go with me. I was nervous, and he always knew how to handle people. We went to the Tower Suite, on top of the Time-Life Building, at seven, and when we sat down there were seven men around that table, and me.

The Tower Suite prides itself on serving endless courses, so besides having a couple of drinks, we had sat there for over an hour without anybody saying anything about why we were all there. Actually, they were serving the coffee when I couldn't stand it any longer.

"We have a lot to talk about," I said. There was a pause, and Richard jumped in. Why he said it I'll never know, but he did:

"You guys think you have trouble! I have to listen to what a son-of-a-bitch Dan Levin is every night."

Nobody laughed, and I was in such a state of shock I only felt the bullet graze me.

Then Bob Short turned to me. I didn't know him well then, and his expression is often reserved. He said very quietly, but very firmly, "We cannot accept ultimatums from actresses."

I remember the feeling of absolute panic when everything stops, but I had no time for that. I had clawed my way through too many scenes. I would get through this one. Almost without hesitation I said, "It isn't an ultimatum. I didn't mean I won't work. I meant I can't, and it's true. I am taking tranquilizers every day now. You all know what happened to Gretchen on the air. It could happen to me. I'm just telling you, I'm not making it. We get the shows on the air every day, but at what cost?"

Then I described our routine, which obviously came as a total surprise.

"Frank, is that true?"

Frank was white as a sheet, and I said, "Frank has been after Dan constantly. He keeps promising he'll be on time, but then he has an excuse. It isn't Frank's fault."

The agency supervisor added his two cents:

"We've always felt that, since the shows look good, he must be doing his job, so maybe he doesn't need all that time."

If looks could kill, mine would have, and I repeated, "We do the shows, but at what cost? There are too many times when we do the show in spite of Dan." I had quite a lot more to say, once I warmed to the subject—I always do when I'm nervous—but finally I excused myself to go to the ladies' room, and Richard escorted me to the door.

"Honey," I said, "get back to the table first. I'll be gone exactly ten minutes, but you go back and listen so you can clue me as to how it's going."

I went back to the table exactly ten minutes later, and there was no sign of Richard. Someone had ordered me an after-dinner drink. I was afraid to touch it. The smoke hadn't cleared and I didn't know how the battle was going.

When Richard did arrive, he said in a delightfully jovial way, "I thought the deal was for me to get back and let you know how things were going."

There was nothing to do but laugh at the joke and feel more alone than I think I had ever felt in my life. I know I looked around that table and realized I didn't know where I stood with any one of those seven men, and the only person I knew I could depend on was myself.

Then Bob asked me a question: "Do you want Dan fired?"

The answer was easy: "My God, no. I don't want his career or anybody else's on my conscience. I just want to work and do the best job I can. But I can't do my best without a little help. I just want him to show up and do his job, and we'll do ours."

Two days later, Dan was sent on an extended leave of absence. I think he was gone five or six weeks. His personality never changed, but he was never late again, and everything had changed for me and the company I have spent my whole adult life with. Perhaps it was worth it. Perhaps it had to be.

While Dan was gone, Jack Wood and Len Valenta came to direct the show, tell jokes and listen, and ever so quietly become dear, close friends. It gave us a chance to breathe, and let the family regroup. Six years of tension had pulled at the seams but, thank God, there was no damage that couldn't be mended.

There was another new face in the control room about that time. A young man who looked remarkably like Richard, and had even gone to Dartmouth, began to arrive for dress rehearsal every day. His name was Ernesto Caldiera. He rarely said anything to me, but I often felt him looking at me, and when our eyes did meet I could see through the reserve to something I felt I could trust.

Everything was changing, and the biggest change of all was the move to the big new production center across town. Our tacky little wardrobe was packed into lockers and we got ready to leave the dear, familiar filth. Our stage crew was going with us. Harry Cusick was being transferred to our floor, but Maud would not be going. That was the hardest part. She had separated from her husband and felt that by herself she couldn't make it in New York with three little girls. Her sister and mother lived in Vermont, so she rented a little house in Woodstock, bought a secondhand car and an enormous parka with a fur-lined hood. The trick to loping through deep snow, we decided, was to keep very low to the ground. We would miss the daily contact, but as things turned out we had been so wrong about so many things, perhaps it was time. Yes, it was definitely time.

The production center was almost too good to be true. The studio was big and clean, the bathrooms were new and sparkling.

There was a real office for Frank and Ernesto, and we had real dressing rooms. They each had a long makeup table with mirrors and a sink, and lockers. As a very nice gesture, which meant more than he knew, Frank assigned me one all to myself.

The biggest, most important change, however, was the stunning cast that had gathered to play the new stories. Dino Narizzano played Dr. Len Whiting, who was in love with Patti. His mother, Andrea Whiting, was about to arrive from Paris, and would be played by Virginia Gilmore. The regulars were all there: Marge and Stu, Allison and Fred Metcalf, Patti and Arthur Tate. But it was the character of Sam Reynolds that would change the show. Robert Mandan played Sam, and he did more to change Jo, or maybe allow her to change, than anyone before or since.

Perhaps we were a little late catching up with the sixties, but we would get there, and we would be an honest reflection of the times as we had been in the fifties, because we were part of those times ourselves. Besides being actors and writers and directors, we were people who were part of families and communities and constantly affected by them—a chain reaction, like the nursery rhyme about the old woman who found a crooked sixpence: the rope hung the butcher and the butcher killed the ox, we all lived together in a little bitty box.

When a very short person is systematically battering down a door and simultaneously screaming his head off, if you happen to be the presiding adult and therefore in charge, you will probably decide that something has to be done.

One of the choices open to you, especially if the door is still holding, is to remove yourself from earshot, light a cigarette, pour yourself something cool and refreshing, and think the whole thing over. You must be aware, however, that you do not have time to dawdle, because even if the door is strong the sound will carry and the neighbors downstairs, probably even the superintendent, will be arriving soon. They should not catch you drinking before five.

You quickly ascertain that the price of a new door will be forty-five dollars, because the last one was forty and the price of things keeps going up. You agree, in your mind, not to haggle. What, after all, is five dollars?

Soothed by the drink and armed with calm resolution, you start down the hall toward the scene of dissension, hoping against futile hope that the short person has, in the meantime, found something to distract his attention and when you open the door all will be serenity and peace. But from thirty feet you know pretty well this is not to be the case. You will, after all, have to do something. That was always the hardest decision for me when I found myself in that situation, because all the way down that hall I found myself thinking, "Oh, thank God, he's doing it!"

Jeff got angry and he let you know. It was just hard to find out what he was angry about.

All little boys fight with their sisters, and probably all little sisters are masters at baiting them. Jeff and Cynthia were so close in age it probably aggravated the situation. I could sympathize with both of them, because I remember vividly wanting to ring my brother's neck.

Jeff's trucks had been put away in favor of soldiers, and he would spend hours constructing battle lines. He drew pictures of battleships with planes overhead dropping bombs, and he would press so hard on the crayon it often tore the paper. There was a major eruption almost daily, which usually coincided with Richard's arrival.

Cynthia had started to take piano lessons. She was too young, but she had asked Barbara Carroll and if Barbara could start at five, why couldn't she. Of course, if she was going to take piano lessons, she had to practice and that meant I had to listen. I loved to watch her sit at the big piano. The light made her little face glow and she gazed so intently at the music, but of course she wanted the doors closed. That was her time, and Jeff could stand that for about fifteen minutes. He would start a rukus somewhere else—which was a great excuse for ending the session.

Every time I gave in to either one of them, I got a lecture from Ooa Nooa. Her father would never have allowed children to behave like that. As she said herself, she despised her father. Still, she had her little say daily.

Then, one afternoon Cynthia said, "Mother, Ooa Nooa

doesn't like Jeffrey. When you're not here she makes him go to his room."

They had fights, but when the chips were down they stuck together. That was that. The three of us went into the living room. We closed the doors and had a council of war. We all listed our complaints and decided unanimously she had to go. Then we decided that what we really wanted was to get Pearl back. I tiptoed to the kitchen and called Pearl.

It took her two hours to get there, because Pearl always took special pains getting dressed, but then she looked it. She had always worn wigs, we knew, but we weren't prepared for the red one she had on that day. Still, it was Pearl.

She was hesitant about coming back, although she obviously wanted to. She said she hadn't been well and might need an operation. We all agreed that, especially if she wasn't well, she should be back with the family, and we would face the operation when we got to it. She started work the next morning. That afternoon we explained to Ooa Nooa, as we helped her pack, that it was really Pearl's job and, if she was free, it was only right that she come back. We haven't had veal or noodles since.

Jeff was going into second grade the next fall and had decided he wanted to change schools. He wanted to go to the one that was all boys. I spent a month sitting in lobbies of every private school in New York, listening to the kids talk and watching them, and decided I thought Trinity was the best place for him.

It was a big, old red brick building on West Ninety-first Street, and it looked the way an old-fashioned school ought to look: a little seedy, a little dirty, and crowded with men from three to six feet tall, all wearing wrinkled blue blazers and filthy black ties.

School began the end of September, and every morning Jeff got up early to put on long flannel pants and the blue blazer. The first morning I wanted to take him, but he insisted that he go alone on the bus with the other men. It was a forty-five-minute trip, and the first few days he got sick and almost threw up, so after that he refused to eat breakfast. With that little jaw set, he marched out to the corner every morning and waited for "Sir."

"Sir" was the high school senior who was in charge, and to my best knowledge he never had any other name.

Every night Jeff worked over his homework for at least two hours. When he was ready, I would hear his spelling words and check the multiplication. He was so tense and nervous he woke nearly every night with a nightmare. When I went to tuck him in, his little face was damp with perspiration and he was always grinding his teeth. There is nothing you can do when the youngest man in your life sets out on his own, except ache for him every time he starts out the door.

The choice was the first of many Jeff insisted he make himself. All I could do was hear the little spelling words, which were mercifully printed on the page, and be there to love him when he got home.

About the first week in November, Richard announced that there was a conference of CBS affiliates in San Francisco that he had to attend, and he wanted me to go with him. Immediately I said absolutely no. It was no time to be away from home. I had hardly ever been away from the children, and certainly that was not the time to start.

Richard was insistent to the point of making it sound like an ultimatum, and after a week of arguments I gave in. After all, we would only be gone for six days. We would leave on Monday the eighteenth and come back the following Sunday. Richard's parents agreed to come by every evening to see that everything was going all right, and, after all, Pearl was there and the children loved her.

Actually, after I talked myself into the whole thing, I was determined to have a good time. I didn't like the idea of going to an affiliates meeting when I hadn't been invited, but that was just ego and not important. It was important to be alone with Richard. We hadn't tried that in a long time. It turned out to be a lot more difficult than we thought. We were, for one thing, almost never alone until we closed the door to the hotel room somewhere between two and three in the morning. There were endless dinners and cocktail parties, hospitality suites to attend, and hundreds of names to remember or forget.

The days were pleasanter, but I never saw Richard. I met Terrance O'Flaherty, who did a column for the *Chronicle*, and he showed me his version of the city: the antique shops and warehouses full of great junk you could buy for a dollar. Every evening I called home. The first night they all sounded fine. They were doing their homework, and Pearl had cooked fried chicken. It was an adventure to be on their own. The second night, Richard's mother got on the phone and told me that Jeff had torn up Cynthia's paper, and I could hear her screaming in the background. It took twenty minutes and a fifteen-dollar phone bill to calm everybody. Thursday night when I talked to Jeff I recognized all the signs. He was being very brave, and he assured me that everything was perfectly all right, but the tears were in every breath. The next morning I was on the first plane out.

I walked into the kitchen on Friday, November 22, about two-thirty. Both kids were home. Things had gotten so completely out of hand they hadn't even gone to school. Richard's mother called to say she had never seen a child behave that way —I should do something about it immediately. She was certainly not going to set foot in my house again until I did.

Pearl's first words were, "I'm quitting. I can't stand any more of this." She was watching the "Ann Sothern Show" on the television set in the kitchen. Both kids were bellowing for attention, and I hadn't taken my coat off, when the announcer cut into the program:

"Unconfirmed report, the President has been shot."

"Oh, my God! All of you hush! Let me listen."

At four o'clock I took the children to church. They were so quiet and solemn as we walked up the street. I didn't know what else to do.

When I woke the next morning, for a moment I thought it was all just a nightmare. There had been so many, surely I had dreamed it all. It was the first time I remember a morning darker than the night before.

I suppose I didn't realize for a long time that the strain of getting through each day was catching up with me. I tried not to talk about the show when I got home, but it was impossible to leave the feelings behind. The anger, the fear, and the daily chill had produced a fine case of paranoia. Or, as the tag line of an old joke goes, "You'd be paranoid too if everybody hated you."

I made too many decisions all morning and too many decisions all afternoon, but at least I'd gotten a little better at running the house. I walked around with lists on the back of scripts and nearly always managed to get it all done. I could plan a meal, order the groceries from the studio, run to Bloomingdale's after the show with a list of sheets and socks, and get home in time to make Halloween costumes for the kids and order a load of manure to keep the pipes from freezing in the little house. I could get the kids to a birthday party, rain or shine, Hell or high water, learn a script, and get them ready for bed.

If I was having people in for dinner, I would stay up after the kids were asleep and cook so it would be ready when I got home the next day. But, too often Doris-do-it-all had to circle the block a couple of times before Martha-mother-love could walk in the door. I kept telling myself it would only last a little while. Things were bound to calm down on the show, the kids would get older and, once our incomes equalized, Richard and I would get along better.

It wasn't so much that we didn't get along. We were always a good pair, just never a very good team. We looked good together walking, but we weren't going in the same direction. His work and his nature constantly drew him into crowds of people, and mine seemed to draw me more into myself. At any rate, by the end of most days I was too tired to care. Part of me was in the room doing what I was supposed to do, but very often part of me was not there at all.

One evening, Richard and I were walking down the street, and he stopped to chat with friends of his on the corner.

As always he said, "You know so and so."

And as always, I smiled and said, "Of course." But that day, as we started away, I said, "How nice to meet you," and Richard stared at me.

When we were out of earshot, he said, "For God's sake, they were at our house for dinner last night!" I felt awful, but I didn't remember them. They had just been faces that I didn't see.

Children are incredibly sensitive to grown-up feelings. They always know when something is wrong. While mine were growing up they always kept a candy bar hidden to bring me in moments of ultimate stress. But sometimes even when they want to help they don't know what to do. Like the day I was trying to change a light bulb at the top of the landing in the little house and fell all the way down the stairs. I wasn't seriously hurt, but I had scraped the underside of my arm and side, and was sort of massaging the pain. Cynthia watched me for a moment and then ran to get a bottle of deodorant.

"That's what you always put there. It will make you feel better," she insisted. In a way, she was right. She did make me laugh, but it didn't take away the bruise.

I remember Jeff coming home from school one day, his little lip trembling as he pulled me into his room and closed the door.

"Why do I cry sometimes and the other boys don't," he said, and a big tear washed a fresh streak down his face. He asked the question so seriously he obviously needed to answer something about himself that he doubted, so it was no time to hug my little boy. I had to give him the kind of answer I looked for myself when I felt the same way.

"Maybe you feel sadder than the other boys, but it's all right. Maybe it's even better to be that way, because if you feel sadder than they do sometimes, you'll probably feel happier sometimes, too." It was true and I did believe it, but I knew how hard it was to really believe when you can only see the bottom.

When I am frightened and lonely, like anybody I guess, I need a little more reassurance. I look harder into a face for a glimmer of affection, or just plain contact, which only makes everything worse. The more you need the more you turn people off. Or maybe it just seems that way. When I had a show to do, I couldn't let it get me completely down, so I tried to put the disappointment somewhere else. I forced myself to think about other things that needed no reflection.

When I wasn't on the show, I tried not to think about it at all, and I began to learn to keep to myself, to withdraw. I could not turn off, but at least I could pull the curtains, and behind the curtains I began to write. They were children's stories. The first one was about a little girl whose birthday is on the Fourth of July and she thinks all the fuss is for her. Since my birthday is also on the Fourth of July, there just may have been some connection.

Then, quite by accident, I started to write, of all things, history books. I looked at the books the kids brought home from school. Granted, I had not read enough of anything to have a basis for comparison, but even I was offended by what sounded like the Bobbsey Twins on the *Mayflower*. I got so curious I took myself off to the library to see what really did happen, and it was like discovering a whole new world. Within a few months, I had read everything I could find and had worked my way backward to original source material.

Every time I had a day off, I ran to the New York Historical Society as soon as the kids left for school. All morning I sat at one of the long, smooth tables, in a highbacked oak chair, holding books in my hand printed in the seventeenth century, with notes in the margins, until I had memorized the names and stories and dates. Then the people began to come alive for me, and I spent hours trying to imagine how they felt, what they thought, what they wanted, and what they were afraid of.

Time and time again, I asked Richard to drive me up to New England so I could walk around the tiny houses and measure for myself the toy-size ship they had sailed in, and ponder the kind of bravery I could not comprehend. The people haunted me. They were, after all, only people who ate and slept and loved and needed. Their moment was forever suspended in a wave of destiny, but what was each of them looking for? What did they expect to find for themselves? It could not have been comfort, so was it peace, joy, freedom? But then, what did those words mean to them? What, indeed, do they mean to anyone?

In many ways, it was a wonderfully quiet time in the library, or sitting at my desk, looking down Madison Avenue. Eventually, both kids got involved. Cynthia loved the birthday story, and Jeff began to call the history "Our Book." He read it over and over, and went to the library with me several times "to help" with research.

When we went to Concord and Lexington, the family went together. Granted, Richard got the brunt of those trips. He had to drive the car, find a place to eat and a place to stay, and to him the whole thing was a miserable waste of a perfectly good weekend.

"Why do you have to walk around every damn house in New England. They're all exactly alike," he said, not so much with impatience as real curiosity.

I didn't have an answer that made sense, so I said, "I think I'm looking for something that wasn't finished."

The books were a wonderful place to retreat to, but what I didn't realize all that year was that besides being the decision machine on the show and at home, I had added more pressure when I started them. It was a pressure of my choice, but still pressure. All I had done was add one point of contact, without relieving any of the others.

The days were still too long, too tense, and too one-way. Without really noticing, I slipped past the point of exhaustion. All I looked forward to every day was oblivion. The formula was two martinis and two five-milligram tranquilizers. I took one pill at bedtime and left the other on my night table to take when the nightmares started, sometime between two and three.

Every night it was the same. I would wake with a start, trembling with fear, my nightgown soaking wet. Usually the tears would come as soon as I realized where I was, and I would lie there sobbing in the dark. Sometimes even the pill didn't help and I would cry for what seemed like hours. It went on for months.

The mornings were the same as they had always been. Richard brought me coffee when he was through with his breakfast, and either I went to the show or I went to the library. When the first history was finished, I had it typed and sent it to an agent. I was already far into the next one, absorbed in the clothes and even the recipes of another time and place.

Then, out of the blue, I got a letter from Viking Press saying they liked the birthday book and wanted to talk to me about the history.

"Richard, look! Look what came in the mail!" I called out the minute he got off the elevator. He read the note and I know he was pleased, but unfortunately his first reaction was a joke.

"Hey," he said, "you wrote a book and you never read one."

That morning when I woke I watched the moon till it crossed the window and disappeared, without taking my pill. Staring into the darkness, I could see a body in deep black water. It was a girl who had fallen, or jumped, from the *Mayflower*. I could see her dress floating around her and feel her agony and terror as she sucked the water into her lungs. Then I could see her floating and finally at peace. By five o'clock I had stopped crying and even managed to smile at my spasm of melodrama and self-pity, but I knew I was very close to being in serious trouble. I was treading water at the bottom of a well, and I needed help. In the morning I called my doctor.

"Do you have somebody you send patients to when the window is looking good?"

"I sure do," he said immediately. He didn't even know how many tranquilizers I was taking. I lied and got them from him and the gynecologist, the dermatologist, and even occasionally from my dentist. Two days later I went into therapy at forty dollars an hour, and it was worth it. I had somebody to talk to.

I took special pains getting dressed and arranging my hair for the first appointment. I sat on the deep, down sofa in the waiting room instead of the more formal side chairs. It was a pretty room at the back of the parlor floor in a brownstone. The colors were soft greens and cream, and I knew immediately there was a woman in his life. The doctor's office was at the front, and narrower. There was a desk, a spare Scandinavian settee and two chairs. I chose the one that did not face the doctor.

I began to talk in a light, I hoped uncomplicated, kind of vein. I would present myself the way I really was, warm, sincere, witty, reasonable, and certainly more attractive than the woman who had decorated the waiting room. The banter lasted, I would say, seven minutes, at which time the tears began to stream uncontrollably down my hopelessly contorted face. The doctor handed me a box of Kleenex, and the work began.

"Do you remember dreams?"

"I am in a barn, up in the hayloft with the children, and a storm is coming. The sky is dark and yellow, and the wind is so strong I can't close the doors. I struggle to pull them in and I fall."

"Do you sleep well?"

"I take tranquilizers. Every night . . . I drink martinis."

The doctor wrote something in his book.

"I want to turn it all off. I want to forget."

"What do you want to forget?"

"Mistakes. I made so many."

"What kind of mistakes?"

". . . I spent forty dollars on a yellow feather hat."

"That doesn't sound serious."

"It was a mistake . . . I looked like a fool, and I talked too much at the party. I talked all the time. I couldn't stop."

"What did you talk about?"

"I talked about Daddy and Mother."

"What did you say about them?"

"It doesn't matter. I was boring."

"Did you enjoy talking about them?"

"I don't know. Richard says I don't know how to enjoy."

"How do you feel about that?"

"I think he's right."

"Why?"

"I try, and I fail."

"How do you fail?"

"I forgot to pick up the dessert for the party . . . Richard's friends were all there, and I stayed up all night cooking the food, but I forgot to pick up the dessert. He got three little cakes from Cushman's and they were ridiculous."

"You were embarrassed."

"It wasn't important. He was right."

"It was important to you."

"No. It was silly. Everybody was dressed in evening clothes, but I don't believe they had a good time."

"Did you have a good time?"

"No. I felt foolish . . . That made me angry."

"At Richard?"

"At myself, and Richard, and Dan. He makes it so hard every day. He makes me hate him. He pushes me till I scream, then I can't stop screaming. I scream all the time."

"Do you scream at Dan?"

"No."

"Do you scream at the children?"

"No."

"Do you scream at Richard?"

"I just bitch all the time."

"Why?"

"I feel disappointed."

"What did you expect?"

"More."

"More what?"

"I don't know . . . I have so much, and Mother never asked for anything."

"How do you feel about your mother?"

"I always worried. Sometimes she didn't get home from work till two in the morning, and she ran all the way along the railroad tracks."

"Where was your father?"

"Daddy couldn't make money because there was a depression."

"Wasn't your father an alcoholic?"

"Mother said he needed other women because his mother died when he was two and no one woman could make up for the love he didn't have. Mother cried a lot . . . Sometimes I knew where he was but I didn't tell her."

"You felt responsible?"

"I see young men sleeping like a pile of rags blown into a doorway. I see old women rocking between their shopping bags. I want to bring them home. If no one is looking I give them money . . . I see their faces all the time."

"You can't be responsible for them all."

"I'm stronger and luckier. My children are healthy. I have a nice warm apartment and a good job."

"Do you feel strong?"

"I feel afraid. I'm afraid to make decisions. I'm afraid of the dark. I'm afraid to drive a car. I want Daddy to drive. I want . . ."

"What do you want?"

"I'm not sure . . . It's a feeling. I'll know it when I find it. And if I don't . . ."

"If you don't find it?"

"I'll be afraid of growing old, of growing old not knowing, dissatisfied. I'm afraid I'll hate my children because they're young and hate myself for feeling dissatisfied. I'm terrified of growing old and realizing it's all over and I missed it, never felt it, don't have it to remember. I'm terrified of growing old, feeling angry all the time."

When I got home every day, things continued to go from wild to borderline hysteria. Pearl had her operation, and about three weeks later I walked into the kitchen to find her out cold on the floor. There was something so strange about her position it occurred to me immediately that she had not just fainted, and I called the hospital to see if they could tell me anything that might help. Of course they wouldn't, and if it had been a heart attack she would have died.

As it turned out, Pearl was epileptic. That was why she left when the children were younger, and that was what Martha was talking about. But we all decided we could cope with that, and we got pretty good at anticipating the signs. Richard and I thought, at first, that it might upset the kids, but as usual we were wrong.

The first time Cynthia saw her in a seizure she was just on her way to school and Pearl had fallen in the front hall. Cynthia kissed me, then she kissed Richard.

"Bye, Mom. Bye, Dad," she said cheerfully. Then she glanced at Pearl's inert form on the floor and added, "Bye, Pearl, wherever you are," and stepped over the body to get in the elevator.

A few weeks later in Connecticut I came out of the supermarket and noticed a small knot of people on the parking lot. When I got a little closer I heard Jeff's voice:

"Just stay back. She's having a seizure. I know what to do."

It was a totally strange woman, but he was right. He knew just what to do. I stopped worrying.

My doctor did think Jeff should see a psychiatrist, but Jeff didn't agree. For three months he played Monopoly with the doctor at sixty dollars an hour and never opened his mouth. It was an expensive experiment, but he got to be a great Monopoly player.

Even if the weekends at the little house were exhausting, they were an enormous pleasure and satisfaction. Nancy Neat scrubbed the kitchen floor and polished the copper pots and Phoebe Farmer watched for the first sprouts in the garden. The jonquils were always the first delight and always a surprise. I tossed handfuls every fall and wherever they landed I dug the hole. I enjoyed it all but I took it very seriously. I worried about the birds and filled the feeder. If there was a stray cat or dog, we drove around the neighborhood on Sunday till we found it a home. When it seemed like the raccoons were having too much trouble opening our garbage, I left their food on little tin plates. Then there was the crow. The children and I found the crow while we were out walking down a back road one Sunday morning. He was over by the side of the road with his head all flopped over and both kids told me his neck was probably broken and there was nothing we could do, but I thought we should at least try.

We ran to get a box and took him home. Nora Nurse knew that we had to have some kind of splint for his neck, so Jeff unrolled all the toilet paper off the little tube and I slid it ever so carefully into place. He still didn't look exactly happy about the situation, but he could drink water and we were all quite cheery. We started thinking about names and planning to teach him to talk as soon as he was well.

The only problem with a crow on the kitchen table was our cat, Sodie. She didn't care if he could talk or not. She thought she would just eat him then and there, so we had to put him out of reach. The only place the cat never went was the top of our station wagon. It was parked in a nice shady place under a big tree, so that seemed perfect. We put the crow in his box on top of the car. We went out to give him water a couple of times but then it was time for lunch. It must have been two in the afternoon when we went out again and discovered the station wagon, crow and all, was gone.

By the time Richard drove in half an hour later, both kids

were upset and I was in tears. Before he turned off the motor the wail went up.

"Daddy, where's the crow?"

"The crow?" Richard is a patient man but we often pushed him too far. "What crow?"

"We put him on top of the car." Jeff's voice was rising out of control.

"You put a crow on top of the car?" Richard looked helplessly from one accusing face to another.

"Why?" he asked, trying hard to be reasonable. "Why did you do that?"

"Because its neck was broken."

"You put a crow on top of the car because its neck was broken?" Richard just stared at us, his disbelief almost cracking into a smile. "Oh, for Christ Jesus' sake!" He got out of the car and surveyed the empty rack.

"Well, it's not there now," he said, hoping that would be the end of it.

Of course it wasn't. I worried about the crow for weeks. He'd already had a pretty rotten day when we found him and I can still see that poor bird hurtling through the air with that idiotic toilet paper tube around his neck the first time Richard swung around a curve.

In the spring, we took the children to Florida for spring vacation. It was the third year we had been to the same small hotel, and the third year the other couple had been there. Each year we had spent more time with them. That year, I went to the window of the room we shared with the kids and looked out toward the pool. There he was, with the silly straw hat he always wore, the pipe that was never lit in a strong, graceful hand, and the smile. It was as though hot liquid had suddenly arrived in my stomach without waiting to be swallowed.

I wanted to run out to the pool, but I stayed to get the kids ready for their first swim and change my clothes. Of course, I wouldn't put on a bathing suit! Exposing winter-white skin for the first time in a resort where everyone is gorgeous and golden is an ordeal that one prepares for. I put on slacks and a shirt and tried to seem nonchalant, even surprised to see him.

But the minute the kids were in the pool and out of earshot he said, "I've been watching that door all day. I called to check on your reservations so I could be here at the same time."

Then he just looked at me, and I looked at him. I thought I had remembered how handsome he was, how red his face got when he sat in the sun, and how many little lines there were around the blue, blue eyes. I'd remember the gray hair, because it was incongruous with the young face, but I'd forgotten how the long sideburns softened the crew cut. I'd forgotten how it suited him, like the pipe and the hat. And I'd forgotten how strong his body looked.

What he had just said and the way he was looking at me seemed to say he felt the same way I did, but that wasn't possible. He couldn't know how many fantasies I had shared with him those other springs. Still, he was saying something and the hot liquid had come to a slow boil. It was the most exquisite discomfort I can imagine. For the next two weeks we managed to quietly drive each other nuts. We nearly always sat next to each other when we all went out to dinner, and our hands would touch under the dinner table like schoolchildren, guilty and secretive. He was married, I was married. Nothing was going to happen, but, oh my God, just to feel so strongly and want someone so much made me feel alive.

Before we left for home, he took me for a walk on the beach and he said, "I wish we could just keep going on."

"We can't."

"I'm in love with you. I want to marry you." He kissed me and we both cried. "I'll call you in New York, and, remember, wherever you go, I can get there and I will."

He did call two or three times a week, always on the hall phone in the studio. He could watch the show and tell if I was there, and he'd call just as we'd come off the air.

After a couple of months he said, "I have to see you. Can't we go somewhere?"

In a moment I said, "I could go to Boston and do some research for the books."

"I'll meet you there."

By the time Saturday morning arrived, when I was to leave, I was swimming in guilt. I got up at six and watered the plants, dusted the house, and cooked food for the weekend. I was sure the plane would crash to punish me for my sin, and then I felt guilty for taking all those innocent people down with me. Checking into the hotel was an agony, and when they gave me a room with a single bed I didn't have the nerve to ask them to change it. After all, why would a single woman alone need more than that?

He wasn't supposed to call until five o'clock, so I went for a walk around the common and through the old graveyard, taking notes and trying very hard to be Agatha Author, but it didn't work. Adele Adultery walked back through that musty, old-fashioned lobby, and there were tears of shame when I fumbled with the key outside the door. Five o'clock came, and I began to imagine reasons why he wouldn't call. He was probably busy. He had said he wanted to meet me, but that was easy to say over the phone. He probably hadn't really meant it. After all, he was a long way away. It was expensive to fly so far. He'd probably changed his mind, and who could blame him. I knew there had been other women in his life. He'd probably found another one, a beautiful young stewardess on the plane today! He'd told me they all made a fuss over him. The phone rang.

"Yes . . . ?"

"Hey, you got here all right."

"I got here fine. Where are you?"

"You're not going to believe this."

"I'll try."

"I'm in a dinky little town, and the only plane out of here till nine goes to Washington."

"I guess that would put you in pretty late."

"I'll come if you want me to, but I know you have work to do on the book."

"Yes . . . I took some notes this afternoon."

"I'll come if you want me to."

"I know it's a long trip."

"That's all right. I just wasn't sure you really wanted me to come."

"It's probably silly for just one day."

"I guess . . . If you say so." There was a long pause, and he said, "I don't know how I'd explain a trip to Boston on Saturday to my secretary anyway. She watches me like a hawk."

It occurred to me he might have thought of that before.

"Well, I guess you won't have to."

"I didn't really believe you'd go."

"I needed to work on the book."

"I'll call you next week."

"Okay."

"Bye."

"Bye," and I lay face down on the damn single bed for a long, long time, running the conversation back through my mind. It seemed he was saying he wanted to come. Why hadn't I said I wanted him to? Why couldn't he have gone to Washington and taken the shuttle? He just didn't think of it, the ninny. But I didn't have any idea where he was. It was too late. I ate dinner alone and caught the first shuttle home in the morning. I was one of two consenting adults, and neither one would say yes.

When I told the doctor about Boston, he said, "You didn't really want to meet him."

"I thought it would be perfect."

"Maybe that's why he was afraid to come."

"He wants to marry me. He wants to build me a house."

"He's already married and he's an alcoholic."

"He's in love with me . . . He wants to take care of me."

"In a little town a thousand miles from New York. You know you couldn't do that."

"I want to be loved."

"You want to believe he loves you. You're afraid to find out if it's true."

"My brother said I didn't know the truth from a barn door."

"Did you make up stories when you were a little girl?"

"I told Mother that I found a baby bird on the ground, and I climbed up the tree and put it back in its nest. Then Mother said, 'If you had found a baby bird on the ground, you would have climbed up the tree and put it back in its nest, wouldn't you?'"

"Why did you tell your mother that story?"

"I don't know."

"Were you disappointed when your mother didn't believe you?"

"I don't think so. I think I was satisfied. It was such a nice story."

"But it wasn't real. It didn't happen."

"It happened in my mind."

"The man in Boston happened in your mind. Were you disappointed?"

"Yes . . . no."

"What is real to you?"

"My children. The way it feels to hold them, to see them sleeping, safe and secure . . . And trees. Trees against a winter twilight . . . And houses . . . a farmhouse across the snow, with lights in the windows, snug and self-contained. My guitar . . . holding it in my arms, singing harmony, feeling the notes lean against each other. Acting . . . locked together with another person, filling time and space outside myself."

"You want to be outside yourself?"

"No! I want it all inside!"

In December, I went to the gynecologist and he said I had developed another mass in my right breast. It was another week of waiting, another week of imagining. Daddy had died of cancer. It could run in the family. It's not knowing, and not wanting to know, that keeps you off your guard.

The night before an operation there is not much you can do, and you certainly don't need sleep. The night before that one, long after visiting hours, there was a little tap at my door and in walked Len Valenta with two enormous shopping bags. He had brought a projector, a hand-cranked phonograph, and two old silent Tarzan reels. He showed movies on those awful green walls till it was almost time for surgery. It was a good night, and the next morning the operating room didn't smell quite so bad.

The operation was longer and more serious than the first one, and I was out for a couple of days, but, again, I was so lucky I sipped my Coke when the bottles were gone and thought, "Dear God, I am the luckiest woman in the world. Thank you."

In every way I knew I had learned to structure my life with

no time left over to feel or just be. In the city I worked, spent time with the kids, wrote on my little books, practiced my guitar and, finally, with twenty minutes of idle time every day, Rita Renaissance started to restore furniture. I bought an old Italian sideboard for two hundred and fifty dollars and refinished it myself. It was beautiful, but unfortunately I also made drapes out of green and white toile and put down green carpet, and the total effect was still just awful. It was a little like eating under water. The dining room was the one I seemed always to care about the most, and I could never get it right. Maybe it just looked like I felt.

In the country I cleaned and gardened, and cooked and cleaned again. On my way from the station I stopped at the Goodwill and poked my way through the dust for bargains. There were many times when the yard looked like the end of a tag sale or the beginning of a junk yard.

When we decided to add a wing onto the little house, I talked to architects and contractors. I talked to everybody in the neighborhood to find out about building materials, and I cut out pictures of old New England houses to copy roof lines. Every day all that summer I got up at five-thirty, drove to the station, and caught the seven-ten. I was on the two o'clock in the afternoon and was blocking out furniture arrangements on a concrete slab by four.

Richard made it clear, constantly and patiently, that he could not visualize houses and did not want to visualize houses. Just as constantly, and probably less patiently, I showed him the plans and asked his advice. Should we put in a bath upstairs? Should we have a front hall? The strings on the ground had looked enormous and the concrete slab didn't have enough room to turn around. Finally, the man down the hill told me that for resale I had to have a bath upstairs, but by then the house was framed in and the bath had to be jammed into a corner.

Richard had wanted the addition to be small and simple. The architect didn't like my roof line. The contractor said the house cost by the square foot, then the man down the hill told me that the extra five feet I wanted would only have come to five hundred dollars.

I had listened to everybody and taken their advice, and I hated what was being built with all that money. I called the contractor, and when he got there we stood in the driveway talking. The kids were inside watching TV, Richard was sitting out by the garden having a drink as we went over the list. The quarry tile floor was wrong; it would be too cold in the winter. Cutting off five feet for a covered porch made the living room too small and left the downstairs powder room pipes exposed. There would be room for an upstairs bath if a dormer was added, and at one very precise moment I remember looking at Richard and making a decision.

Until that instant I always said, "We want the porch enclosed. We want the wood floor and the old brick for the fireplace," but quite deliberately I said, "I want the dormer added to the plan. How much will that cost? *I've* changed *my* mind, *I* want the living room extended. *I* am worried about the exposed pipes. *I* don't want a great big expensive porch on the back of a tiny house."

Such a little thing, a different pronoun. The first person plural to the first person singular. It shouldn't even have been a ripple in fourteen years of high and low tides, but somehow it washed away a bit of sand and exposed bare rock.

"You've finally admitted it," the doctor said when we began our conversations that fall. "He forces you to make a decision and when you do, even though you are right, you feel you have failed, because you're not being a real woman."

"I don't know what a real woman is supposed to feel."

"So you pretend. You've pretended all your life. You probably learned how to act by making up a reality when you were a little girl and playing your part. You wanted to depend on Mommy and Daddy, and when you were disappointed you learned to pretend. You want to depend on the men you work for. You're disappointed and angry when they won't let you. Perhaps Richard is afraid you don't need him, and if he lets you feel like a woman you'll finally know, too."

"If that's the way he feels, it's my fault. Maybe I don't give him a chance."

"You don't feel loved."

"What is love?"

"I think it is understanding someone's needs and trying to fulfill them."

"Can anybody do that?"

"I didn't say succeed, I said try. The important word is understand. If you understand, you are beginning to accept. Does Richard accept you the way you are?"

"I don't think he's ever seen me . . . but that's my fault too. I shattered the mirror, and the faces change."

"Do you want to stay married?"

"I have to. I can't fail again."

It was a long flight from California at the end of 1948, and cabs were still the big, old DeSotos. Lester was sharing an apartment with his friend Ben. I had never met Ben, but I had heard hundreds of stories, and the whole first winter Lester and I were together we had expected him to arrive any minute. A letter came in January, saying he'd left California hitching East and would be there soon. We didn't hear again until May when we were leaving to go West ourselves. It was a postcard from New Orleans saying the weather was wonderful and he would be along any time.

The new apartment where Ben and Lester lived was on Thirty-sixth Street, in Murray Hill. The evening I arrived there was a light snow on the streets, and the light from the bay window was warm, yellow, and welcoming. Lester opened the door and smiled, but the hug was hesitant and shy. His breath was sour from nervousness, and I felt tall and awkward. Then I met Ben—dear, shaggy Ben—and he eased the moment.

He carried my suitcase into the front room of the long, narrow apartment and set it down in what was a combination workroom for them both and bedroom for Ben. There was a drawing table in one corner, an easel in another, and a rumpled cot, where Ben slept, along the wall. Through the arch was the combination living room and bedroom for Lester and me. In the back was a filthy little wall kitchen and a bathroom. The layout did not allow for much privacy, but as it turned out we were all sound sleepers and Ben tended to be gone a lot. He would go to a party on Thursday and not be heard from again for a week. Once he went for cocktails with the Duke and Duchess of Windsor, and when he got home a week later he had a beautiful Jamaican tan.

That evening there was no time to feel too awkward or test for feeling. We barely had time to get ready to go over to the Whiteheads'. Oliver would be there with his new bride, and they were sure I would like Betty. We were going to have cocktails at the Whiteheads', then we were all going out for dinner, and for the first time I almost looked forward to an evening with Bob and Virginia. After all, I had done something myself since I had seen them last. I had been in the movies, and I had met some famous folks. When I told it I could make it sound a lot better than it was. For the first time I would have something to say.

I may have had something to say that night, but the opportunity never presented itself. *Medea* had opened in London with great success. *The Member of the Wedding* was playing in New York and they were all excited about that. I did like Oliver's new wife, Betty. She sat next to me on a couch in the study, wearing a rose-colored suit, a little black tam, and beautiful black shoes. I didn't know they were French, but I knew they were beautiful. She didn't have much to say, but she smiled and seemed to know what they were all talking about. I didn't know that she was uncomfortable, but I did notice how many times she crossed and uncrossed the legs with the lovely shoes.

It was as if I had never been away, as if I had gone nowhere, done nothing. It was as if I wasn't there that night. They talked about *The Member of the Wedding* and told stories about Judith Anderson. I kept thinking somebody would ask me about Hollywood or the house or something. I don't know what I expected. Whatever it was it didn't happen, and the old anger stirred the old defenses.

Virginia never did or said anything rude to me. She hardly spoke to me at all. She greeted us at the door, and the smile was quick, the "hello" was bright. The cocktail hour lasted two and a half. Virginia sat perched on the edge of her chair, leaning into the circle of light, or moved on her exquisite little feet around the pale, yellow room, settling now and then on the arm of a chair, like a bird, to share a word and a smile. She spoke only to the men, and she knew that no one took his eyes off her. Her handsome husband and his young partner were the brilliant new team on Broadway. She had brought them together, and she stayed in the middle. She kept control. I admired her, and I hated her. Almost as much as she made me hate myself.

That night as we were leaving she handed me a box.

"It's a very pretty nightgown," she said, "but it's too big for me." Then she kissed Lester good night.

Ben didn't go home with us. I had hoped he would. I didn't want to be alone with Lester. All the way from California I had dreaded being alone with him. It had been too long. Too much had changed. There was too much distance to cross in one evening. Now the anger seemed to justify it all. I had started the evening flushed with a little success and in three hours I was back to being the gawky kid off the bus from Tulsa. It was not hard to direct the anger at Lester. If he hadn't left me alone in California I wouldn't have had an affair! I wouldn't feel weak and cheap and guilty! It *was* his fault! If he didn't love Virginia I wouldn't hate her, and him, and that damn nightgown! Why did she have to give it to me that night? Well, I would show her—I would show them both who was sexy!

I took it out of the box and, of course, it was yellow, pale yellow. I went into the bathroom to put it on and I looked at myself in the mirror. I'd had a brandy and that always made me dizzy, so the reflection was soft around the edge, but still the face was too starkly drawn. It was a child's face, done in heavy pencil. It was late. It had been a twelve-hour flight from California, and I never did know how to put on makeup anyway. I didn't want to wear the nightgown back into the room, but I hadn't unpacked and it was silly to get dressed again. So I just stood there, wishing I was anywhere else in the world, wishing to God I could just go to sleep, let the dizziness and the anger pass.

I hadn't felt guilt or remorse in California. When I was with Mac, Lester was simply not part of my life. It was as if he didn't

212 BOTH OF ME

exist. Now he existed, and all the love, jealousy, sweetness, and guilt were churning in my stomach with the brandy, making me sick. For a moment I prayed I would just get sick! That would take care of one evening, anyway.

Lester was sitting on the side of the bed when I finally walked into the room. "You look beautiful," he said, and I knew if I got closer to him he would touch me. I couldn't stand that and I couldn't look at him. I knew that expression. Way in the back of his mind he would be sketching me, but his hands and his face would be loving me. No, I couldn't stand to think about that. I couldn't think at all. I just opened my mouth and the words fell out:

"I've had an affair."

Again, I tried not to look at him. I knew his reaction would be a sudden, absolute silence. His mouth pressed into a line, his eyes blinking back the tears before they welled. I tried, but it didn't help. I knew too well what I would see. I knew what I had done, and the instant I said the words I wanted to catch the arrow, but it was too late. At least if I looked at him I felt the pain with him, and in that moment, as if the arrow had punctured an abscess, the anger drained away.

I suppose I had to tell him before I could sleep with him; had to have the absolution. It could not all have been anger, although it helped. He listened, and the silence went on forever. When he finally spoke he didn't look at me, and only his hands moved. He always did that, describing the perimeters of feeling the way he would enclose space, gesturing with strong, meticulous hands, fingers close and straight, palms in, squaring the distance to his body. He was not denying emotion, or hiding it. No, never. He seemed to be reasoning with it, trying to make it make sense.

"Is it over?"

"I don't know. He's married." There was a long silence, then I went on: "I've been alone a long time."

"I know . . . you work there, I work here."

"Do you have to work here . . . with her?"

"She has nothing to do with it."

"She has a lot to do with it."

"I love you." For the first time he looked at me, and I could see the tears.

"I love you." I put my arms around him, but he was empty and gone. "You left me out there! What did you think would happen?"

"I knew I was taking a chance."

"Then why did you leave me?"

"I had to leave for myself. I can't hang around and paint scenery because you have a contract. I have to paint! I have to design! My God, I don't know which I have to do . . . I walk down a street and every time I look at a door I have to decide who I am! Am I a painter? Am I a designer? Do I see light and shadow? Do I see form and space? . . . I can't do that and follow you around. I can't be a painter and wait for you to come home from the studio and do your little dance around the room. I love you, but it isn't my life—not my whole life."

"But Virginia is?"

"Virginia happens to be involved in the things I have to do."

"Do you love her?"

"Not the way I love you." He sounded so tired, and without saying any more he got undressed and went to bed. If I had wanted to get even I had succeeded, but that wasn't what I wanted at all, and I was drowning in regret. That old, sick feeling down by the river and the subway. I was late and lost and wrong, and terrified.

"Lester, I'm sorry." He did not move, he did not speak.

"Lester, please forgive me." I kissed his face and tasted the tears. "Lester, please. Please forgive me. Oh God, Lester, talk to me!"

Sometime that night we made love, and he was not cold, but he was distant. We went through the motions of starting over, but I think he knew I would never be able to finish. He was going to stay in New York, and he had said in the beginning, "You'll never make it by yourself." After Christmas I went back to California alone.

At the end of my first six months at Warner Brothers, a decision was made somewhere in a big, plush office, at eleven-thirty at night, by someone I did not know who nevertheless controlled my life. Columbia Pictures had decided they liked *Thunderhoof* and wanted to put me into a series of westerns, but only, of course, if I was under contract to them. Warners had paid no attention to me for several months and did not even seem to notice that the option period would expire at midnight. I was to start work the next week at Columbia. At a quarter to twelve my agent called to say Warners had picked up and that contract was legal. Mother and Daddy had signed it.

For weeks I scarcely went on the lot. I made a test or two for Bette Davis, playing her part while they cast the movie. I was told she didn't want me in her pictures, and I took that as a compliment. Once, I got to use her trailer with the pink mirror just beside the door. The last look she had just before she stepped in front of the camera was ever so slightly tinted. Why didn't I learn from that wonderful, wise woman that the self-image is all that matters! Who knows, who cares, if you tint it every now and then!

Then, a couple of months later, Jerry Wald called to tell me they were finally going to make *Adventures of Don Juan,* but I was not going to play the queen. I would be playing the first love interest. I was disappointed, but at least it was work, and at last I would meet Errol.

Actually, the first time, we were in makeup and he was sitting under a dryer with a blue hairnet on. It was a shock, but everything else about the man was pure delight. He was handsome and charming and elegant. The first day of shooting he sent flowers to my dressing room, and nearly every evening he would invite me across the street to the little pub for a drink. He talked about everything under the sun except sex and movies. Mostly he liked to talk about his boat or his father, or John Barrymore. He was patient and helpful, and we managed to negotiate some very passionate embraces—even though we were encumbered by the fifty yards of blue chiffon they made my nightgown out of, the two thousand pearls they sewed all over it, and one long red wig. There was only one moment of near disaster. I still had to wear the little porcelain veneers on my front teeth, and after one particularly soulful kiss they stuck to his lip.

It was a pleasant, relaxed time and nobody seemed to care that it took forever to get anything done. It simply meant there was more time to sit around and tell stories, or play jokes on each other. In the middle of one of our kisses a woman's voice came stridently from out of nowhere:

"Errol, is that the only thing you know how to do?"

It was Ann Sheridan on a bicycle, riding toward us over the drawbridge!

It was fun and, like the little western movie, we were somehow removed from reality. We were in a castle with a moat, there were horses and swordfights, and romance. I felt pretty, and I suppose I was sexy even, because a lot of men noticed me, and one of them was the tall, craggy man who had written the picture. I don't remember the precise moment we met, but I do recall seeing him on the set, mumbling jokes that seemed to put everybody on the floor.

The first time Harry Kurnitz took me out to dinner he thumped his long, black Continental in my muddy parking area and climbed cautiously down my steep cement steps.

"I think I just parked in your swimming pool," he commented mildly before he came in. He glanced around my makeshift house, with the assortment of porch furniture and animals.

"You're probably a very nice girl," he said. "Let me take you away from all this."

"Sit down. Let me make you a drink."

He looked at my low canvas slings, and from six feet four it was too far. "I don't think I could ever get up. Why don't we just go to dinner?"

At that moment the birds decided to take a little spin around the room, and he was so startled he sat down whether he meant to or not.

"I'm not quite ready, but I will be in a minute. Sing something."

"Why on earth would I do that?"

"Because I don't have a door on the bathroom."

"Oh, for God's sake! Where did you come from?"

"Oklahoma."

"Then everything Steinbeck said is true."

"Probably. Are you going to sing?"

"I'm better on the violin. If I wasn't double-jointed I could be making fifty dollars a week in a gypsy cafe in Philadelphia." Harry struggled to his feet. "I'm sure the restaurant will have indoor plumbing. Why don't you just wait?"

We went to Romanoff's, in Beverly Hills, a gorgeously elegant, very private little restaurant where nobody seemed to have reservations. They were just expected. We got out of the car in front and somebody came and drove it away. Prince Romanoff greeted us at the door and escorted us to a table with a very grand gesture.

"He's not really a prince, you know," Harry said as he left to order our drinks.

"I asked him once how he got his title, and he said, 'Oh, there are many ways. One can be born with a title, one can marry one, or buy one. For myself, I had cards printed!'" Harry smiled at his joke and his face softened into all sorts of funny lines and crinkles. He peered at me through the glasses that seemed almost attached to his slightly overlarge nose. With the long fingers of his right hand he pulled absentmindedly at a short, tightly curled forelock.

"You were good in the picture," he said. "You'll probably do all right out here, if that's what you want."

The comment slid by quickly. Since I left Metro, it had not occurred to me to question whether Hollywood was what I wanted, and at that moment I didn't question anything. I was in a famous restaurant with a famous, successful man, and I was learning to enjoy it.

The dinner was amazing. We had butterfly steaks they cooked at the table and Caesar salad, made just for us, with a lot of flourishes. He signed the check, and by the time we got outside his car was waiting.

"We'll drop by the Gershwins' for a nightcap," he said ever so casually as the big car crept into the wide, solemn streets of Beverly Hills.

There were already a number of cars in the driveway, so we left the Continental on the street and walked up to the door. The Chinese houseman opened the door, but Lee Gershwin was there to meet us as soon as we stepped inside. She was so warm and so gracious, and seemed truly glad to see me.

"Come in, dear. You must meet everybody." She took me by the hand and led me into the huge room full of big comfortable couches and flowers and people.

"Ira, dear, this is Harry's friend, Mary Stuart."

The short, stout man with round glasses who was sitting just a little apart from the group around the coffee table took the cigar out of his mouth and beamed up at me. "Aren't you pretty," he said.

In the next few minutes I had met Oscar Levant, who was playing the piano, and I think he smiled. It was hard to be sure. Then I met a handsome young man named Richard Brooks. I didn't know whether he was a writer or a director, but I assumed he was one or the other. I met Irving Lazar, and then I really lucked out.

"I want you to meet someone else who's new here. He just arrived from New York. This is David Davidson."

And for the first time in my life I could honestly say to a real author, "I loved your book."

It was true and I had really read it! It was also obviously the right thing to say, because he hugged me, and with genuine delight he said:

"That's why I wrote it. I wanted a pretty girl to come up to me at a party and say, 'I loved your book.'"

Somewhere in that first ten minutes I became aware that I had stepped into a very special place.

I think it was Ira who suddenly got up and started toward a door at the far end of the room.

"Come on, Harry, let's play."

Harry unwound his legs and got up from the couch to follow him. I followed too, into a whole room that had nothing in it but a pool table and for the next hour, I was privileged to watch some very fancy playing. Harry had grown up on the Lower East Side, where, as he used to say, "You walk once around the pickle barrel for the salt sea air," and you also pick up a lot of skills because you have to. Now, his suits were tailored in London, his shirts were monogrammed, and his pajamas were silk.

The next time Harry called me, which was only a couple of days later, he suggested I drive my car to his house, if I didn't mind. I didn't mind if the car didn't, and, as a matter of fact, it wouldn't quite make his driveway, so I parked it in the service area.

It was a beautiful house, built obviously for one person to live in, one very special person, or one couple. On the main floor the three large rooms opened into each other so the library, the living room, and the dining room could all be used as one. There was a guest room and bath, a big kitchen, a maid's room, then upstairs there was just one big bedroom, dressing room, and bath. The walls were studded with Harry's collection of French Impressionist paintings, and the furniture was expensive English and elegant. The kid from the Lower East Side had come a long way. He also seemed to like the way the kid from Oklahoma looked in his surroundings.

I don't think Harry was quite forty. He was just one of those people who was born middle-aged. When he was young he'd been a newspaperman in New York and during his last years there had been part of the Algonquin Round Table, so he knew all those wonderful, witty people. Fanny Brice and Dorothy Parker had been friends of his; so had Benchley and Perelman, Ring Lardner, James Thurber, and Harold Ross. His first big movie success was the *Thin Man* series with Myrna Loy and William Powell, but he also wrote mystery books and Broadway plays. He was a busy, very successful screen writer, and he was a great, delicious, tender, witty man.

When I knew him, his closest friends were Groucho Marx, Charlie Lederer, Frank Loesser, and, of course, Lee and Ira Gershwin. For the next few weeks I found myself in a number of famous living rooms.

I started to see Harry nearly every night, and every night there was something different to do. We went to Chasens and Romanoff's for dinner, either by ourselves or to meet friends of his, and nearly always to the Gershwins' later. They never seemed to go out, so everybody went to them. Every writer, every actor from New York, directors, and musicians seemed to find their way into that living room to mix with the regulars like Harry, Irving Lazar, and Oscar Levant.

Sometimes we just had dinner at his house, served by his old German cook, in the big dining room at the end of the house. The table was polished mahogany, the silver and crystal shone, and the Picasso over the sideboard winked at the kid from Oklahoma who was eating very high off the hog.

Harry always called me "Kitten" or "Pisherka," which is Yiddish for "little wet one." He liked my being young. I liked it too, and as the weeks went by I got younger. Once or twice a week after dinner we would go to somebody's house to screen a picture. Sometimes, there was a real screening room, but usually an Utrillo would slide aside, exposing a projector behind the wall, and a screen would drop from a hidden slot in a white ceiling. Occasionally there was a real party, and they were incredible. At any given moment I could look around the room and see half the famous faces I had ever heard of.

If the party was at Groucho's, they started early, because he liked to go to bed at ten. The party didn't end at ten, of course, and he often came back down after he had napped awhile. He was married to a lovely young girl named Kay. We didn't have much in common, but we were close in age, and sometimes if the party was at somebody else's house and Groucho left early, I would drive her home. Groucho had a pool table too, only his was in the dining room. He considered a table for pool much more important than a table for eating, so if dinner was served they just put a big board over it and a tablecloth. Except that the plates were right under your nose, nobody seemed to mind.

Of course, everybody had a swimming pool, but only at Charlie Lederer's was it customary to go for a swim late at night. As Harry said, describing one party, "The lawn was littered with evening gowns."

Charlie was Harry's best friend, and Charlie loved practical jokes. He would go to almost any lengths for a good one. One night he decided that it would be fun to change the time on the clock that hung out over Sunset Strip in front of Utter McKinley's funeral home, because he knew that everybody who drove to work along Sunset automatically checked their watches by it. He had to hire a truck with a crane on top to reach it, and he had to stay up all night until the street was deserted, but the panicky surge of speed the next morning when everybody noticed they were fifteen minutes late was all he wanted.

It was also Charlie who decided one night after we'd all gone out to dinner that he was in a mood for high adventure. We'd probably had too much wine, because we started by drawing mustaches on our faces with burnt wine cork. Nothing seemed outrageous enough after we completed our disguises, till Charlie had an idea. We would rob Irving Lazar! In very high spirits we cruised by the Gershwins' to make sure his Jaguar was in the driveway.

Next, we went to Charlie's to get tools and make our plans. Finally, the long black Continental slipped silently into the driveway of the apartment house where Irving lived. Charlie's girlfriend, Ann, was elected lookout and waited in the get-away car. I was the most agile, so when the screen was unhooked I crawled through and opened the door. We didn't want to hurt anything, just play a joke, so we decided to hide everything in the bedroom —everything! We took the beds apart and put them into closets and the shower, we dragged the chests into the guest room and jammed them into a closet, we put the pictures in the oven, and nearly had heart attacks doing it.

As a last touch we spelled out, "We Love You," on the rug with bathroom tissue and stole away into the night terribly pleased with ourselves; too pleased, and too flushed with success, because, like all criminals, we made one, fatal mistake. We went too far.

As we swung by the Gershwins' to make sure the Jaguar was still there, Charlie had one last inspiration.

"Let's steal the car!"

We knew the keys would be in the lock, they always were, so Charlie tiptoed into the driveway, released the brake, and let it roll downhill. We gave him a little push, so there would be no sound of the motor starting. He eased the car along the dark street, without turning on the lights, because he couldn't find the knob and had just sailed across Sunset to freedom and safety when a police car pulled out of the shadows and forced him to the curb. Not because it was a stolen car, not because Charlie was driving with no lights, but because Irving's license plates were a year old. And there is justice!

Being Charlie's good friends and his partners in crime, we did the only sensible thing and drove right on by. But by the time we got to Charlie's drive we realized that the situation was probably quite serious. Charlie would be making up a good story, but he had that idiotic mustache on his face and all those house-breaking tools on the front seat. Also, any minute, Irving was going to notice his car was gone and call the police, and Charlie was going to be in very hot water. Somehow, Irving had to be detained in that house until the car was back in the driveway!

Harry sped away to the Gershwins', and just in the nick of time! When he opened the door, Irving was standing there with two little watercolors Lee had just given him. He was on his way home to hang them in the bedroom! That was close! But Harry was clever. He hadn't written all those mystery books for nothing!

"You can't leave," he said, brushing by Irving. "I've just had a great idea for a picture and we have to line up the people!"

On the spot he started making up a movie that would include every one of Irving's clients, calling Paris, London, and New York checking availability. He sat there, sweating and inventing, for over an hour, till the phone call came from Ann.

"Charlie's out of gas and needs you to pick him up!" It was the code message meaning the coast is clear and the car is back in the driveway.

It was an extravagant, childish prank. They were extravagant people. One party ran late and there was too much to drink so they called an ambulance and we inhaled oxygen before we drove home.

If they were extravagant with money and games, they were more extravagant with talent and wit. At parties, after dinner, everybody went on. Groucho would sing "Show Me a Rose" or "Captain Spaulding," with Harry Ruby at the piano. Frank and Lynn Loesser would do the songs from *Where's Charley?* or "Baby, It's Cold Outside." Martin Gabel loved to do his very special version of Cassius's speech from *Julius Caesar* with a Yiddish accent. Benny Goodman played duets with Piatigorsky. Danny Kaye did all his double-talk routines, and Jack Benny was the best audience anybody has ever had. He would laugh so hard the tears rolled down his cheeks. The musicians played and the singers sang.

One night I remember Judy Garland singing at the Gershwins'. Something frightened her. Like a haunted child, in the middle of a song, she ran out of the room.

For the first month or two I knew Harry, I don't think I opened my mouth. I was audience, and decorative, and occasionally dumb enough to be straight man for Harry and Groucho. Then one night in the poolroom at the Gershwins', Frank Loesser started to sing an old barbershop song, and I automatically filled in the tenor part. Groucho sang the baritone and somebody sang bass. I don't remember who, but it sounded pretty good. We were a quartet. Frank started another one. Then he moved into more complicated songs, some I'd never heard, but it didn't matter. Without thinking, the harmony just comes out. From that night on, we sang every time we were together, and when Groucho introduced me, he'd say, "This is Mary Stuart and she's a third away from everybody."

Frank Loesser especially liked the funny harmonies I heard. He was going into production with *Guys and Dolls*, and every time I saw him he'd sing me a new tune and say, "Sing with me."

"Frank, what is it? Let me hear it first."

"No, just sing with me."

I'll admit, "My Time of Day" was too much for me to fake, but one night at Groucho's he and Frank and I sang "Fugue for Tin Horns" for the very first time as a round. There weren't any words yet, and we sat on different couches, bouncing up and down to keep the rhythm, until three in the morning.

It was the heady, inner circle of Hollywood, and I certainly had not earned my way in, but "Harry's girl" was admitted free, and, because Harry's girl could sing funny harmony, she was pretty much accepted. Also, Harry's girl wasn't much of a threat to the other women. She washed her own hair and it looked it, she didn't wear makeup because she didn't know how, and her clothes looked homemade because they were.

Actually, the clothes got to be a problem. I was going to too many fancy places and I just didn't have what it took. Harry suggested he give me a charge account at Saks. I wasn't ready to handle that, but it brought up a lot of subjects we had both avoided.

"Kitten," he said one night, "you've been separated for three months. What are you going to do? You've got to make a decision."

I knew he was right. Lester had called and was coming out to California. I was either going back to him or I wasn't. Being separated had been the best of both worlds. Lester was my family, almost like a mother and a father. I could go out on a date, even have an affair, without feeling guilty and still have a place to go back to that was secure and safe. I didn't know how to let go of that. I was afraid to. I didn't feel independent, and I wasn't sure of Harry. No matter how grown-up I tried to seem I had never dared go past the rope that marked the deep water. I was still in the shallow end.

For several weeks Harry persisted. He didn't talk about marriage, but he didn't want to go on seeing me unless I was divorced. Lester was only going to stay for a month. It would be the same thing all over again. I don't remember deciding to get a divorce, I just did it. I don't think I felt I was divorcing a husband, but I knew I was saying goodbye to my best friend.

The night before I was scheduled to go to Santa Monica for the hearing, I couldn't sleep. I stayed up all night. At seven-thirty I went to pick up the woman who was going to be my witness. She was building a house down the road, and when I drove in she was out in her garden in a pair of jeans and an old shirt. She waved and called out for me to wait in the car. Then I saw her lean over and pick something out of the dirt. It was a piece of string she used to tie her hair back and, satisfied with her appearance, she wiped the dirt off her hands on her pants and got in the car. That's how the morning began.

I had asked her to be my witness because she knew more about divorces than anyone I had ever known. She had been divorced four times and was married to her fifth husband. All the way to the court she told stories about the other husbands. One smoked marijuana, and would get high and ride his bicycle to Palm Springs before breakfast. One was a saxophone player who would sit in the bathtub and play so nobody else could get in, and he kept her from having any friends. One was an alcoholic who made her go to AA meetings in his place. I think the other one was gay, though I really don't remember. I didn't know anything about marijuana, except that the men in a band I sang with when I was a kid had smoked something funny in the bus coming home. They called it tea. I had no idea she was growing her own, although I did think it was odd that she insisted on buying a sack of doughnuts before we went into the court.

It was ugly, gray, and foggy in Santa Monica. It was the last place on earth I wanted to be. I must have been just a little crazy myself, because while she was buying the doughnuts I saw a little banjo in a pawnshop that was open twenty-four hours a day. It was only fifteen dollars and I bought it.

We sat in the back of the courtroom for over an hour, listening to the cases that came up before mine. If I was a little crazy when I walked in, I got a lot crazier. I heard somebody talking about walking in and finding his wife with a sailor who was washing her hair, and I didn't notice that the grease from the doughnuts had soaked through onto my skirt. I began to hear tunes that I would play on my little banjo, and all the stories my friend had told me about her husbands kept running through my mind.

I had rehearsed everything the lawyer told me to say about Lester. "He had sworn at me if I made noise when he was painting. He interfered with my career. He was cruel and abusive." That was silly and ridiculous. I was going to get a divorce because we didn't really live together. He was going to keep the house and I was going to keep the secondhand Studebaker he had driven out from New York. That didn't mean I didn't love him. I couldn't say ugly things about him in that ugly place with those dreadful people listening.

When they called my name I went up to the witness stand still holding my banjo, and my lawyer began to question me. The questions were all rehearsed and written down, and the judge had a copy in front of him, but I couldn't come out with the answers they had given me. They weren't true. Then suddenly I heard myself talking about my friend's husbands, only I made them all one. I described a man who played the saxophone in the bathtub and went to Palm Springs before breakfast till it all seemed to make sense. At least the stories were true, and it didn't matter whom I was talking about.

My lawyer just stared at me and apologized to the judge. I don't know what the judge thought. Maybe he decided the strain had been too much, because he called my witness. She was the only one who understood. She had all the other stories and she told them well. The divorce was granted.

When I got home I fed the animals and played the little banjo for an hour or two. Then I went to sleep. I slept all that afternoon, all night, and all the next day. Somewhere around dinner there was a tap at the door. Harry had come to get me.

When I left Warner Brothers, I started to work more than I ever had before. I went almost immediately into a picture called *Caribou Trail* at Columbia, playing the ingénue opposite Dale Robertson. My old buddy, Jock O'Mahoney, was doing stunts for Randolph Scott, and an interesting young actor named Blake Edwards was the bad guy who got killed. I was back playing cowboys and Indians and keeping the wagons in a circle. I learned how to hold a gun and how to look like I could ride a horse a whole lot better than I really did. Actually, that turned out to be an almost serious mistake. In the final chase there were sixteen stuntmen and me. We were all riding in a tight pack, with the camera truck driving alongside, when someone brushed my leg and kicked my stirrup loose. I did that whole ride with my toes curled under the horse's belly, hanging on for dear life, and it's a wonder I lived.

Then I did two really quick pictures with Ray Walburn and Walter Catlett, but I think I learned more in those two weeks than all the rest of the time I was in Hollywood. Ray was a short, round man with big, round eyes and hands that articulated every sentence. He'd grown up in Vaudeville and knew every bit of schtick in the business and every trick.

He said to me the first day, "Little girl, you're going to have trouble finding yourself in this picture, because a lot of the shots they take of you are not going to be used. But it will be good experience."

He was absolutely right. Every time his hand went up for a gesture, it was between me and my light. There was not one close-up unless I was with the other young love interest and Mr. Catlett, and Mr. Walburn was nowhere around. But by the time we started the second picture, I began to figure out why, and I was ready to give them a run for their money.

Shooting a one-week picture is very different from any other kind. For one thing, it is faster for actors to change clothes than it is to change a camera setup, so that is what you do. There were, in that picture, probably six scenes with the family around the dining table. There were two dinners, two breakfasts, and a couple of lunches. The director would set up for the master shot of the whole table, and we would do all the eating scenes in the long shot, one after another. We'd do a dinner scene, then run change clothes and do a lunch, change and do two breakfasts in a row. When they had all those in the can, they would change the camera setup for the two shots, and you started all over again, trying to remember what you wore and how you had fixed your hair.

When the two shots were done, they moved in for the close-ups, and that's when things got tense. You see, the trick is not just to remember the dialogue and what you wore, you have to remember the business. If you had butter in your hand when you said your good line in the master shot of the first dinner scene, you had better have the butter when they get around to your close-up, or they can't use it. Now, everybody else knows this, and they are not really in favor of your having a close-up, so they will be damned if they will let you get your hands on the butter. What you learn to do is grab! You grab, and then you hang on! Mr. Catlett wants his close-up too—maybe he'll make a deal when he needs the mashed potatoes! The director doesn't have time to referee. He barely has time to turn the pages.

After that, I did two half-hour pictures for a new company called Review Productions. My agent at MCA called me in and explained that the company was small and didn't have much money. They just wanted to experiment with movies for the tele-

18.   Mother and Dad.

19.   Jeff and Pearl.

20.   Jeff and friend on Martha's Vineyard.

21. The Christmas doll.

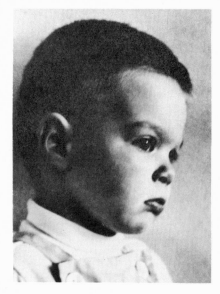

22. A determined young man.

23. Lynn Loring and the children.

24. Cynthia glowing.

25. My first guitar, a gift from my family.

26. Cynthia.

27. Jeff.

28. Richard and Jeff in Connecticut.

29. Jo and Marge in their ruffled aprons—not pleased.

30. Jo and Stu.

31. Jo and Arthur and Patti in a black kitchen.

32. Maud with Maud (Joy Lange).

33. At home in the kitchen.

34. On the show in the kitchen.

35. Jo and Patti.

vision market that was beginning. They couldn't afford to pay much, and they only had one day to shoot the whole picture. I was getting a small reputation for being a quick study who could nearly always do a take the first time, so they had chosen me for their first two ventures. I was flattered, so I accepted the fee of $150 and no residuals for each picture. I didn't find out for over a year that MCA owned the fledgling little company we were beginning.

The term "one day" was correct, as it turned out, if a trifle misleading. It began at 7 A.M. and ended at exactly 7 A.M. the next morning. We wouldn't have gone so long, but two elderly actors had a card game with a lot of complicated dialogue, and that took five hours all by itself. Then, the makeup for the automobile accident took forever, and at 4 A.M. somebody remembered that I had to go back into regular makeup for the last scene.

The second picture was shot mostly on the beach, and we'd have finished that one on time if the ocean had cooperated. There was one scene with a page-long speech. I was sitting, leaning against a rock, with the waves breaking just beyond. By the time we got to it, the tide was in and the third breaker kept crashing over the rock, nearly drowning me. Three times we had to wait until my hair dried to retake. The last shot was me running down the beach at sunset, but the light was going and we didn't have time to rehearse, so I just started running.

They got all the footage they wanted, the director called "cut," and they started packing the equipment. I couldn't hear, so I kept running. I was halfway to Santa Barbara before I dropped in my tracks. They thought it was funny. I guess it was.

At one of the parties Harry took me to I met Howard Hawks. He kept watching me all evening, and the next day he called Harry to ask about me. I don't know what else Harry told him, but he gave him my phone number.

"I have an idea," he said when he called, "and I'd like to work with you."

Mr. Hawks's house was different from any of the others I had been in. It was a huge movie version of a farm. The floors were wide pegged and polished boards. Half a dozen big, sunny rooms opened into each other and a cool breeze seemed to follow me everywhere I went, even into the bathroom, which was as big as my whole house and had a separate little room with louvered doors just for the toilet. When I drove into the driveway he was working in his woodshop making a table. He had sanded the wood till it was like satin, and at that moment he was beating it with a length of chain and shooting holes in it with a BB gun.

"That will make it look antique," he explained.

He showed me the barn out behind the house, with horses and dogs and puppies, the garden and the white-fenced paddock. Then we went into the big, cool house to talk. He told me all about his method of building a star, and I couldn't help thinking of the way he made antique tables.

"I gave Betty Bacall a line to use every time she went to a party, something that people would remember. I told her what to say and what to do."

I thought about the only time I had met Betty Bacall. Harry had taken me to a party. It was Christmas, and Bogey had given Betty a sable jacket. When she opened the box she hugged the jacket, then she put it on the floor, took off her shoes and scrunched her toes in the fur. I didn't think anybody had told her to do that.

"I'm going to give you some scripts to read aloud, because I don't know yet what I want to do with you, but we'll find a character."

For several weeks I drove the twenty miles to his house and read the scenes he gave me. Sometimes it would be from a movie, sometimes a play, and sometimes it was just passages from a book.

Then one day he said, "You never do anything the same way twice."

"I thought I wasn't supposed to."

"How can I find a character for you if you change all the time?"

"I'll be anybody you say."

"But I have to know who you are first."

It turned out to be a problem he couldn't resolve. I don't wonder. Mr. Hawks was very kind and very patient, but he was building with Silly Putty. One day he said he had to go to New York and he would call me when he got back. I didn't think he would. He didn't.

The next director who took an interest was Jed Harris. I met him at the studio when I was working on one of the fast pictures, and he took me out for a drink. He had a script with him and said he wanted to take me to dinner and talk about a part for me.

"You have an instinct that I feel I can trust," he said, and I was immediately on my guard. I knew he was a great director, but I had a feeling it was not my instincts that interested him. However, I had learned one thing from Mr. Hawks, so whoever I decided to be should be consistent! She was, and she was a lulu!

We went to dinner at a restaurant near the beach, and when the waiter brought the menus Mr. Harris started to order for me.

"The young lady will have chicken curry," he said.

"No," I said, "I think I'll have the shrimp," and when the waiter had gone I turned to him and said very seriously, "I think chicken is too delicate a flavor for curry sauce."

It was an opinion I arrived at on the spot, because I had never, ever, heard of chicken curry. Two hours later, just before leaving, through the door of the ladies' room I could hear him talking to the maître d'.

"The curry sauce is too strong for chicken," he said very seriously.

After dinner we went to his house to read the script, and his butler brought in a box of cigars and a bottle of brandy. Ira Gershwin had taught me how to smoke cigars because he thought they were better for me than cigarettes. Whoever I was being reached for a cigar, bit the tip, dipped it in the brandy and lit it. Mr. Harris was in love!

I was having a pretty good time myself. I managed that night to smoke almost all of the cigar, and I listened to one of the great directors of all time talking to me. Just to me! Most of the time he talked about "red lines." The red line was the pure path through the dialogue and action that carried the idea. He talked about entrances and exits. They were not just to get people on and off the stage, they were doors to open, letting the drama expand, and the red line had to follow or lead the way. Then he began to read the play, and for the first time I found I could hear the way Lester had taught me to see, until I almost tingled.

Once I shivered, and he said, "What's the matter?"

"I keep getting goose bumps," I said. Besides being true, it was obviously the right thing to say. From then on he made a note every time I got goose bumps.

I feel sure that the brandy helped that first night, but to this day red lines and goose bumps are invaluable barometers, and I will always be grateful to that brilliant, wonderful man.

I was learning to see, I was learning to listen, but it still wasn't enough. When I was called to test with William Holden for the comedy lead in a picture, I knew I was in trouble.

"You're a funny girl," the director kept saying.

"That's different from playing comedy."

"You'll be great. You're perfect for the part. I knew it when I first saw you at the Gershwins'."

It was the part of a very sophisticated lady agent, about thirty years old, and who I was being the night he saw me, God only knows, because I never got a handle on that lady again. In the scene, the lady agent was supposed to walk into Mr. Holden's apartment, which was in a state of wild disarray that she never seemed to notice. The dialogue was crisp and caustic, but she was really letting him know she wanted to have an affair. She was supposed to comment on the mess by stepping over it from time to time, lobbing the dialogue but never letting it bounce, and still come on to him.

"You want me to do three things at the same time! I don't know how to do that!"

"You'll catch on," he insisted, and to him it seemed so easy. He would walk through the scene to show me, and I tried with all my heart and soul to do what I could see him doing. Mr. Holden was an angel and spent an entire Saturday trying to be helpful. It was a lost cause. I simply didn't have the skill. I knew it, and I didn't know how or where to get it.

A week or so later, about three in the morning, Charlie Lederer called. I had been asleep but something in the sound of his voice was so strange and hurt. It cleared the cobwebs and wakened an old, restless fear.

"There's something you have to know about," he said, "but I
don't want to talk about it over the phone. I'll meet you in the
gas station on the corner of Ventura."

"Why don't you come by here?"

"I don't think I should."

I put a bathrobe over my pajamas and got in the car. I was
so upset by the time I got there I scraped the paint off the side of
my Studebaker on the damn gas pump. Charlie drove in a few
minutes later and parked his car. The station was closed, and he
walked across the dark drive and got in with me. He sat there for
two or three minutes without saying anything.

Finally he said, "It's trouble. Jay's had an affair with Mara,
and he got scared he'd got some kind of female infection from
her. The dumb cluck went to his wife's gynecologist to check, and
of course everybody in town saw him and half of them called his
wife. When she asked him what he was doing there he said he
was asking questions for me."

"Why?"

"He said I'd had an affair with you and I was worried."

"Why did he say that?"

"Because the four of us were alone the night it started.
Remember, Harry went home early and you were going to drive
her home?"

"I'm Harry's girl, and you're his best friend . . ."

"We're the only ones who aren't married."

"And I'm dispensable."

Charlie nodded, I think, and looked very sad.

I said, "I have to tell Harry before he hears it from somebody
else."

"Maybe he won't." That was silly and we both knew it.

When I told Harry, he was so angry he wanted to start a
fight, but after a while he realized there were two marriages at
stake, and they were friends of his. About a week later we were
having dinner alone, and Harry looked very far away.

"I've been thinking, Kitten . . . I'm not going to marry you,
and maybe it would be better for you if we didn't see each other
anymore."

"I thought you were happy with me."

"I don't really want to be happy. If I wanted to be happy I'd have gone to a shrink years ago. If I was happy I wouldn't write good jokes and I wouldn't make five thousand a week, and I couldn't buy all the things I like." He twisted the curly forelock with the long double-jointed fingers. "You're so young. You'll be better off. Of course if you need anything, I'll always be there."

Harry and I broke up and all the friendships ended as abruptly as they had begun. No more parties, no more Romanoff's and Chasens, no more screening rooms. No more dear, wonderful Harry—or Harry's girl. Just Mary, whoever she was.

I called Mac and we had dinner. All the old sweetness was still there, but that was all. He was trying very hard with his wife, and I didn't feel the same, either. Besides, I didn't want to hang on to the edge of somebody else's life again. It was just good to see him and have a friend. Jocko came around a time or two and took me riding. The second time when I came home, before I took off my boots, I built a fire. I was reading a book with my feet up on the hearth, my dog and my cats, and smoking a cigar that Ira had ordered for me, when my agent walked in.

"Jesus!" he yelled. "Don't let anybody see you looking like that! You'll never work again!" It did seem that Mr. Hawks's image was still eluding me.

Then an old friend called to say he wanted me to meet a friend of his who had just come back from Europe. Norwell was the first man I think I ever went out with who was close to my own age. He wasn't tall, and he wasn't handsome, but he was different from anyone I had ever known.

He lived with his father and mother and two sisters, and three of their children, in a big, old house in Beverly Hills. They all screamed at each other in Czech and German and French and Italian, or whatever language seemed appropriate or handy. One day I couldn't get to the laundromat and I borrowed a sheet from his mother. When I got home and started to make the bed I thought she had made a mistake and given me a tablecloth. I had never seen a linen sheet.

Before we could play tennis, Norwell suggested I take a few lessons and buy a pair of white shorts. Red, he said, was not appropriate. When we went riding I hung on to the English saddle as best I could, and he had the best horse in the stable. Afterward, we had brandy milk punch. Once we went away to La Jolla in his father's Cadillac. Then he told me he had to go to Paris for a couple of months.

"I would like you to be my wife," he said, in the serious, matter-of-fact way he presented anything romantic. "There are some diamonds in the vault in Paris, and Papa says to take one and have a ring made."

"For me?"

"Of course, madam." He smiled at himself. Even he knew when he was being a trifle pompous. "We'll go to St. Moritz for our honeymoon and we'll live in the Paris apartment for a while. We'll probably settle in London."

It was dazzling. It was ridiculous. It was a linen tablecloth on a cot, and it was the best idea anybody had had all week! At least it was the honeymoon in Europe and maybe a white negligee. Surely love was in there somewhere. So I said, "I'd love to marry you." Kiss.

That was the end of August 1950. A week later my agent called to say that Ida Lupino was directing her first picture and wanted to see me. The interview was brief, and they told me I had the part. I went to fittings for wardrobe, I learned the script. They gave me a starting date and I called my stand-in.

On the Saturday before we were to start shooting on Monday, my agent called to say he was sorry about the contract, they just hadn't sent it yet and not to worry about shooting on Monday. He called again on Monday to say they were a day or two late, and again on Tuesday and Wednesday.

Thursday morning my stand-in went to the studio to see what was going on. She called me about ten. "Mary, they're shooting the picture. They've been shooting since Monday."

"Are they shooting around the character?"

"No. Somebody else is playing it. She's new and they're not sure she can do it. But they know you can pick up at the end of the week and make up the time . . . Well, you are fast—everybody knows that."

I hung up the phone and sat there for a long time. It had been three and a half years. I was fast and everybody knew that. I

was also dispensable. I knew that, but there was so much I didn't
know—too much. I called Mac.

"Do you need an extra car?"

"No, but how much do you want for it?"

"I paid thirteen hundred."

"I'll give you thirteen hundred."

"Today?"

"Sure, if you need it . . . what's up?"

"I think I'll go East."

"What's East?"

"I don't know . . . I'll probably get a job selling heavy farm
equipment. I'll send you a card from Texas."

I spent the rest of the afternoon giving away the animals,
and somewhere around 1 A.M. I started to pack. I didn't take
much. My cleaning lady said she'd send the rest on when I got
settled, so I never saw those things again. I never even unmade
the bed. At seven the next morning I walked out the door and
took a taxi to the airport.

"Drive through Beverly Hills," I asked the driver.

"It's out of the way, ma'm."

"I have the time."

One last look at the wide, curving streets fanned and shaded
with palm, at the driveways strung with shiny cars sweeping up to
mansion after mansion, up to fantasies gone wild. Side by side
they stood, like the old back lot of Metro: the chalets and the ha-
ciendas, the Loire castles and the Tudor manor houses, the Cape
Cod cottages, and the Greek Revival temples, all in a row, separated by green satin, instead of a moat or a moor or a mountain.
All those empty streets, with never a passerby, a child on a lawn,
or a face at a window.

Like a wonderful, big pot of thick, rich soup the cast and the
stories on "Search," and the production in 1965 and 1966 all
blended together. The characters interacted, the stories interwove,
the people were interesting and sure of their craft and we were

having a good time. Terry O'Sullivan, who was just a handsome announcer when he joined us, had learned to let all his own strength and hopeless romanticism shine in Arthur Tate's eyes. Melissa Murphy was playing Patti, and I don't think I have ever worked with anyone more beautiful or sensitive. Carl Low came on to play Dr. Rogers, bringing his years of theatre experience, his taste, his timing, and his delicious sense of style. He knew how to polish a scene until it would shine.

Dino Narizzano played Dr. Whiting with his own thoughtful, haunting second thoughts, and Ken Kercheval burst upon us with a dynamic energy that could wire a room. Dr. Rogers' daughter, Emily, was played by Pamela Murphy, a lovely, feminine little brunette, and the Bergmans' daughter, Janet, returned from Chicago, played with delightful humor by Marian Hailey. For some reason, over the years, no matter who played Janet, she was always a foot taller than either of her parents. At least that has been true since she passed the age of twelve.

The family units were complete, the generations were defined but not separated, and between us we presented a reasonable cross section of white, upper-middle-class America. The fabric of the stories was deftly woven. Every time a thread was pulled it affected the whole pattern.

Gradually, we began to touch on the problems that had always been around but seemed more prevalent in the 1960s, maybe because they could be discussed. Dr. Rogers' daughter, Emily, became pregnant, and the subject of abortion was an issue that we talked openly about for weeks. When she decided to have the baby, the first illegitimate child was born. At almost any given moment since then, half the characters are of doubtful parentage. But to my recollection, that was our first.

We had a long story about drugs, and even the subject of impotence, although not actually discussed, was very clearly indicated and played. Arthur Tate had suffered physically, but the real damage had been done by Aunt Cornelia, and he never quite believed in himself as a man again. The arrival of handsome, mysterious Sam Reynolds was more competition than he was ready to handle, but before he died he had one great moment.

The scene was the Tate living room, and Jo had prepared ev-

erything for a lovely, romantic evening. The supper was cooked
and ready, the lights were turned low, and as a final touch she
put a record on the phonograph with soft, romantic dance music.
Now, in order to get the record player into the shot, the whole
unit, which was about four feet long and easily two feet across,
had to be put up on blocks. That way, the camera could shoot
across it to the couple dancing. It was a pretty scene as Jo and
Arthur turned slowly in the candlelight. However, just at the moment when desire closed the dancers in a kiss, the camera eased
in just a little too far and the whole record unit fell off its eight-
inch blocks! Now, rule one, when something goes wrong, is to ignore it and continue, but that was too much, even for seasoned
pros.

Our lips parted involuntarily. For an instant, we just stared
at each other before the irresistible urge took control and we both
turned to see what had happened. In the instant four stagehands
had already started crawling on their hands and knees into the set
to pick the damn thing up, so there was nothing for us to do but
go back into the kiss and try to keep it interesting until the stage
manager signaled the all clear. If Arthur's demise had not already
been predestined, that kiss alone might have proven what kind of
man he really was, but the moment came too late. Arthur Tate
died and, like all good actors, Terry was on his way to California.
The story of Sam Reynolds began.

It's hard to know who came first, the character of Sam or
Robert Mandan, but it was a combination that worked so well.
Sam was a wealthy, worldly, educated man. Bobby was handsome,
witty, and a wonderful actor. He was usually late for rehearsals,
and he didn't really believe in spending his evenings slaving over
a hot script. He could learn what he needed to know in the morning and read the rest off the furniture.

The story of Jo and Sam was never a simple love story.
When Sam arrived and bought a home in Henderson, the reason,
ostensibly, was business. He had taken over Tate Enterprises,
owned by Aunt Cornelia and inherited by her niece, Allison.
When the stories more and more centered around Henderson
Hospital, where Patti was nursing and Dr. Whiting was a resident
and Dr. Rogers chief of staff, Sam became involved and was later

Chairman of the Board. Still, there was always a faint aura of
mystery about him. He spent his evenings alone or playing chess
with Dr. Rogers. He had arrived too abruptly, and was more involved in the town than would be called for if his interest was
truly business. He was, also, just too attractive to be sitting
around every night playing chess.

After Arthur died, Jo went to work as the hospital librarian.
It was the first time she had worked outside her home in years
and she began, slowly, to respond to the outside world. She even
began to dress differently. The show still didn't have a clothes
budget, but we conned a better class of wholesale house into giving us samples in return for screen credit. Jo wore a lot of Italian
knits, and occasionally even a pantsuit, and began to take more
pains with her hair and her makeup. The relationship with Sam,
every time they met, was stormy, because she blamed him for
Arthur's death. However, everybody knew there was a lot more
going on. Even Jo began to suspect it, but she always managed to
subjugate her own feelings and think about somebody else's.

Patti was in love with Len Whiting, and that was stormy
enough to keep Jo too occupied to notice the long looks Sam gave
her every time he checked out a book. Then, just about the time
she was beginning to give him long looks back, who should arrive
from Puerto Rico, divorced and gorgeous, but her sister, Eunice.
Ann Williams was the new Eunice, and from the first few shows
was like a real sister. We began to notice after the first six
months that we even looked alike, except she was always truly
beautiful. She was not only beautiful, and younger, she made a
beeline for Sam, and since Jo had not responded even to a polite
good morning, and he had all those evenings, he began to see
Eunice.

It was a good situation, with all sorts of interesting side
effects. Jo, Patti, and Eunice all lived together—three women in
the same house, and two of them interested in the same man.
Every time he came by to pick Eunice up, or to have dinner,
there was tension. If Patti and her young man, Dr. Whiting, were
there the tension was heightened. It began to appear that Sam
was somehow involved with the young doctor. It was obvious that
he preferred the sister he was not going out with, and Jo was

becoming more and more dissatisfied with her life as a lonely widow. Life was slipping by, and as her friend Dr. Rogers kept telling her, she had to do something about it herself.

As has happened so many times, what was happening to Jo in an almost subliminal way must have affected my feeling about myself. Maybe it has always been the other way around. I'll probably never know. But certainly it makes sense that if you're spending your day playing a happy, busy person you carry over the mood, and the character was definitely more interesting than she had been in years. There were more stories in national magazines like *Woman's Day*, and I was even invited by my buddy George Ettinger on the big CBS junket to promote the fall season. I didn't even know there was such a junket, and, frankly, I was uninvited by a vice-president a few weeks later. By then I had gotten used to the idea and decided not to give up quite so easily. Our old friend, Arthur Tourtellot, was Mr. Paley's special adviser, so I called him. About two hours later I got a call from the vice-president telling me to be ready at five.

"Oh?" I said, truly surprised at that late date. "Am I going?"

"I had a call from Mr. Paley," he said, not sounding at all pleased. "I assumed you knew."

Well, I didn't, but I was glad, and I went. Nobody from daytime had ever had any kind of promotion of any kind from the network, and competition from ABC and NBC was growing. That trip, besides getting us a lot of publicity, was a lot of fun. I had a huge, glamorous suite in the hotel and, because the airlines were on strike, we were flown to Chicago in private Lear jets.

Coming back wasn't quite so grand, though it was certainly an adventure. Jack Whittaker and I were the only two who had to be in New York and they needed the planes for the folks from California, so we took the train. It was supposed to be in New York at 9 A.M. That gave me plenty of time to get across town and do the show, which, of course, was still live. But when I woke at seven-thirty and looked out the window, I noticed right away that we were not moving, and when I asked the porter where we were he said, "Buffalo."

There was absolutely nothing to do except sit there and run the lines. Actually, for a sports commentator with no acting expe-

rience, Jack played Patti very well. We finally pulled into Grand
Central at five after twelve. Richard was waiting with a taxi, and
I got to the studio in time to dab a little makeup while Dan gave
me the blocking for the scene, and without one rehearsal we did
it. Jack had run to a bar to watch, and when he called that evening he sounded just a little peeved when he said, "I thought I
was really better in the part."

That was the last summer of live. For fifteen years we had
gone on do or die, sick or well, prepared or not, and at last the
cavalry arrived!

There is just one little horror story that should be noted before it's lost forever. In one of our last live shows, Jo was at her
desk in the hospital library stapling yellow pages to pink pages.
The forms were actually from a defunct shoe store, but that probably isn't important. What matters is that Jo was busy! She was
so busy and so nervous she didn't notice that she had stapled her
thumb to the desk! Now, that is not a serious injury. It smarts a
little, but what is aggravating is that you can't move very far away
from your thumb. When you stand you have to lean slightly forward, because it is attached to the desk. When you answer the
phone you have to reach across with the other hand, in an X position, and when a young extra comes in and asks for a book, you
have to tell him to jolly well get it himself, you are staying with
your thumb and it is staying where it is. For fifteen years the
stage directions for the last shot read, "Fade out on Jo's stricken
face." That day, it was easier than usual.

In the fall of 1966, we finally were expanded to a half-hour
show, the very last one to make the move, and our live schedule
became impossible, so on the same day we began to do the show
live on tape. Actually, it did not change the show as much as we
had thought it would. Our workday went from eight in the morning till two, instead of twelve forty-five, and we ran a little faster,
but the work didn't bother anybody. Dan's precise, methodical
system of directing simplified the transition and kept the show on
time every day.

The biggest change I remember was being able to see ourselves occasionally. All those years we had been live we only saw
the Christmas shows, which we made kinescopes of. We couldn't

see it every day, because we were in dress rehearsal while the air show was on, but we could run into the control room and take a peek. Those peeks were a revelation, let me tell you, and I went directly to the nearest gym. Joel Mason had taken over as makeup artist when Maud left, and had been saying Jo should be a little more glamorous. Well, I saw what he meant and even began to try teasing that long, straight mop of hair. It also began to occur to me that there were certain angles to my face that were definitely not flattering, and Dan and I headed into deep water again. I had always objected to the design of the library set anyway, because it seemed dumb. My desk was directly downstage of the door and I sat with my back to it, unable to see who came and went. Also, I now discovered if I was talking to somebody at the desk the only possible shot of me was definitely the least flattering.

I suggested we move the desk to the other side of the room, facing the door, where the angles would be advantageous and the business simpler. I even agreed to stop fussing about going to the same shelf to pick out the latest treatise on brain surgery or a mystery novel. Dan would not budge and the old tension began to build again. Six months later I walked onto the set and demanded that the desk be moved before we began to rehearse and spent another morning with the old, sick feeling I got every time I won.

The next day I asked our lighting director, Frank Olson, to teach me about that. I learned words like cross light and top light. From then on, besides knowing where the cameras were when the scene was blocked, I knew where I could not be lit. Doris-do-it-all had at least two more notches in her belt, but she had passed thirty-five, and she had to know how to protect herself if she was going to survive.

After that blowup, Dan and I eased back into a Mexican standoff, but when the first really ugly article appeared, written about me, he sent a beautiful letter of rebuttal. Damn him! He could be so good! He even admired what I could do, but he seemed to despise me for doing it, and there was nothing either of us could do about that. At least the shows were good, and that was more important.

The shows were very good, the scenes were fun to play, the actors were fun to play with, and after nearly every show we would run across the street to have more fun at lunch. Frank and Ernesto came along most days, and at the big round "Search Table" there was always a lot of noise and a lot of laughter, and probably a lot of very silly jokes. I think it was at one of those lunches that Carl Low, who played Dr. Rogers, suggested it was time we did a play together. Larry Haines had opened on Broadway in *Generation*, with Henry Fonda. Kenny Kercheval was in *Apple-Tree*, and we all had the itch. Within a week, Carl came in with an offer from a theatre and a few days later he had a play. The next morning I showed all the signs of early pregnancy. Oh, not a baby, just sick with sheer, unadulterated terror.

The play Carl wanted to do was *Marriage-Go-Round*, and I had never in my life played comedy. Carl kept assuring me that I played it all the time with him and Larry, and if I could do it on television I could do it on a stage, especially if he was directing. There were only four characters in the play. Bobby and I would play the parts created by Charles Boyer and Claudette Colbert. Ann Williams was the sexy "other woman" and Carl would direct, besides playing two scenes as the "other man."

We rehearsed afternoons, either in my living room or Ann's, for three weeks. Carl, Ann, and Bobby had all done plays before, and I envied their confidence as they frolicked about what seemed to me to be enormous space, but they held me up all the way. Carl painstakingly taught me the basic rules. The flick of a gesture that pulls the eye to you before you say the line, the sets of three that set up a line, lay it in, then knock it down and, of course, the take, that exquisite moment when the ball lands in your court with a high bounce, and you have time to let the audience know you are going to slam it out of reach.

The night we opened I was so nervous I never actually felt I was on stage. I was still in the wings, watching somebody else who was a lot like me. By the middle of the week that had changed, and I couldn't wait for the curtain to go up. When we skated into the third act I could ride the laughter, and there were enough moments that were really good to give me confidence. I will admit I never found out what Carl was doing in our two little scenes that always brought down the house. The scenes weren't that funny, but the audience roared. When I asked him, he just looked innocent and vague. So I think maybe there are some things you can't teach, you just have to know.

It didn't matter. I had made it up onto that stage in a funny little town in Connecticut. Surely if I'd done it once I could do it again, and what is more exciting than finding out you can do something as wonderful as a play? The old fantasies began to flicker again. Maybe next time a musical!

The night the play opened, Richard was handsomer than I had ever seen him and sweeter than anyone in the world. He sent flowers, of course, but they weren't just flowers. He bought the little orange wooden wheelbarrow I had wanted for a year but wouldn't buy because it cost thirty dollars, and he filled it with orange and yellow chrysanthemums for my garden. He took everybody in the world out for drinks after the show, and when it was time to go home we went to our own little house, by ourselves. He had champagne in the refrigerator just for us. We built a fire, even though it was two o'clock in the morning, and found a station on the radio that played his kind of 1940s dance music.

We'd been married fifteen years, and many of them had been rocky. But there we were, in our own little house, away from our own little kids, with moonlight and champagne.

"Do you dip?" he whispered, and that was funny because it was the way he always established the perimeters of his dancing style with a new partner.

"I'll try." And we turned silently between the two old secondhand couches in the living room, with just the moon and the trees and the fire making patterns in the room. Then he said, so quietly I thought I hadn't heard him:

"Would you mind if I had an affair?"

"Don't make jokes. Not tonight. Let's open the champagne."

"No, I'm serious."

"You're drunk. Now don't make jokes."

"It's not a joke, but she's a friend of yours."

"Who is?"

"Maud."

"You're not having an affair with Maud!"

"I'd like to." It was a lie, and I knew it.

"Please, Richard, don't! Not tonight!"

"She's beautiful—she's alone now. She's always been attracted to me."

"You're making it up! Why now?"

"I've just been thinking about it, and it's the first time we've been alone and had a chance to talk."

It was gone. The feeling died and we never opened the champagne. I stayed in the country house by myself all that week. It seemed simpler. It was close to the theatre.

A fantasy, like your favorite pair of socks, can only be mended so many times. The patches give way more quickly, till there are no threads to catch. When Richard and I found we each had drawers full of threadbare fantasies the sense of waste and frustration began to smolder. Flashes of anger erupted more and more often. No one started the fire, and no one tried to put it out.

In May he said one night that he thought we could still make it if I would quit work and move to Scarsdale, but it was too late for that, years too late. It had probably always been.

In June I was invited to do *Life with Father*, in Ohio, and when I left we decided to call the trip a separation. He went to London and made the last trip back on the *Queen Elizabeth*. In August he went to Mexico to get the divorce and sent me a telegram:

"GOOD LUCK ON YOUR WESTERN ROAD TRIP."

In the summer of 1967 I was, for the first time in sixteen years, a woman alone and Fanny Fantasy was ready for love and romance! Somewhere, I knew, was the man of my dreams. He would, of course, be a sensitive intellectual with a delightful sense of humor who was also tall. We would work together, hand in hand, side by side, maintaining our independence and communicating constantly with a glance and a knowing smile. We would make love as no two lovers ever before us, and our soulful union would be complete and perfect. It would be nice, I thought, if he could play the piano.

Now that I was single, it was only a matter of time until our eyes met across that crowded room. There were, however, a few obstacles. I got on a train every morning at seven-ten and rode to New York. I went home every afternoon to a house occupied by an eleven-year-old daughter, a ten-year-old son, and my mother. Mother had been with us since 1965 on a week-to-week basis. After the divorce, she unpacked her bags and hung her clothes in the closet, Pearl's closet. After all, since Mother was there, we no longer needed Pearl to sleep in.

In between the two train trips, I did my show, stopped at the Goodwill and the supermarket. On Saturday, I went to the cleaners, the hardware store, the nursery, and, for a real rush, there were the misty wonders of the car wash. Not exactly romantic settings, any of them, and not places where eligible, single, wonderful men are apt to be hanging around looking for eligible, single, wonderful women.

"What," I asked myself early on, "is a single, eligible, wonderful woman to do?"

Early in July, my buddy Ann Williams, from "Search," did a very sisterly thing and introduced me to an old beau of hers. Ed was a doctor and interested in very little else, except food. He was not intellectual or witty, and he was quiet to the point of being taciturn, but he was tall and, after all, who's perfect? I invited him up for a weekend. Cynth was away for a month, at camp, so he could use her room.

All day Saturday I fried chicken while Ed played ball with Jeff. All evening Ed and Jeff ate fried chicken and watched television, while Mother and I did the dishes. Sunday morning Ed and Jeff went horseback riding, while I weeded the garden and set up the grill for lunch. I didn't mind! I was glad they were getting along so well. I had worried that Jeff would have a problem when I started going out on dates, and here he was, having a wonderful time with my first boyfriend. After all, there was the evening to look forward to.

Ed was going to drive me into New York late in the afternoon and take me out to dinner. I could foresee the evening and my little heart went pitter-patter. Obviously, after a weekend of domestic bliss, romance would bloom. That, however, was not the evening Destiny had in mind.

Jeff began to get very quiet soon after lunch. He didn't feel like playing ball and went up to his room with a book. I knew the signs. He was trying to be brave; he'd done the same thing when he was eight and we went to visit him at camp. He hated the place and wanted to go home with us, but he knew that was giving up and he couldn't let himself do it.

"Go right now," he'd insisted, "while I'm not crying. Go on, hurry up." I had left him then, crying so hard myself I couldn't see the road.

Mother was as helpful as she could be. "He'll be fine," she said. "I'll let him stay up and watch TV tonight." But then she got very busy digging ferns in the woods.

When it was time to go, I went to Jeff's room to tell him I'd be home Monday after the show. I was still okay and so was he. He even walked down to the driveway to wave, but that last moment was too much, and the dam gave way. When I looked back from the end of the road he was standing there sobbing.

We only drove about a mile, a very quiet mile. Ed was sweet. He didn't say anything, just patted my hand, turned the car around and drove me home.

Jeff was relieved and glad to see me, but the tension was still heavy. We had both given in to the situation, we were both wrong, and we both knew it. Our lives had changed and we had to find a way to handle it. Nobody had much to say at suppertime, and when I went to bed he was still glaring at the television set.

The problem of dating didn't arise again for quite a while. Ed was the only single man I knew. There were, however, other problems and the first serious practical one was living alone with a large white station wagon. I would have to learn to go farther than the train station. I decided to practice on the run to Barbara Carroll's house. Barbara had married again and lived with her husband Bert Block and little girl outside of Ridgefield. It was a tricky twenty-five miles that involved a short stretch of deserted highway, a strange town, several numbered signs that had to be read and followed, and a mountain road.

For most of that summer it was an overnight haul. I would arrive exhilarated but too exhausted to think of driving home. Perhaps I didn't really want to. As soon as we finished the supper dishes she would turn the lights low in the living room, sit down at the Steinway and play, just for me. Barbara had decided not to work until her little girl Susi was older, so she needed someone to play for as much as I needed the music. Sometimes she would play for two hours, filling the room, and my mind, with her fingers and her soul.

At some point in one of those evenings, I began to hear words. I had written lyrics to my own little tunes I could play on the guitar, but her music went so much further. I had to reach for images, and I began to write them down on yellow pads. She would play and I would scribble. We never talked much, we never needed to. It was understood she was my closest friend, and the yellow pads became a constant companion.

After camp, Cynthia stayed up in Vermont with Maud and her daughters for about a week before coming home. The minute she jumped off the train she called out, "Hi, Maud, I'm home!" We wrestled her duffel bag and suitcase into the wagon and she kept chattering, "Maud, I had the greatest time . . . Maud, you should see me water-ski! . . . Maud, I met the neatest boy . . . Oh, Maud, it's good to be home!" By then, dense as I am, I had gotten the idea that my beautiful, golden daughter was not calling me Mother anymore.

Before I started the car, I hugged her one more time and tried not to sound too sentimental. "You know, Maud, I've really missed you. It's good to have you home, Maud."

All the way out to the house she bubbled about her summer, but mostly she bubbled about my friend Maud's golden retriever. By the time we got home we had decided that what we needed more than anything in the world was a dog. That very afternoon we borrowed a copy of the AKA book, and all three of us pointed to a picture of a Shetland sheepdog. Before suppertime, we had a puppy that Mother named Bonnie.

"But I am not going to be the one who looks after this dog," she said, over and over while she mixed the baby food into the warm milk. "No, sir. I've raised too many dogs. You all want this puppy, you take care of it."

"Yes, Grandmother," we all promised, but she wouldn't let us feed Bonnie, even that night. It was Grandmother who sat on the kitchen floor, letting the puppy lick warm milk from her finger, and it was Grandmother's bed Bonnie slept in.

I'm sure I would have tried dating again that summer if the opportunity had presented itself, but it didn't. So, for some kind of social life I began to poke around the neighborhood. Many of the answers I was going to need were in one house down the hill and across the road. The family had moved in two years before, and the first time I stopped by that summer Betty had answered the door. She looked like she had seen a ghost.

"Oh, my God," she said, "you look just like . . ."

"That's who I am."

"You couldn't be! I watch you every day!"

"Well, I am."

"I even cut my hair!"

"You what?"

"I grew it long when you did, and I cut it short in front, just like yours."

"Oh . . . It looks very nice. I wish mine was curly."

"For goodness' sake. I can't believe it."

"I'm Jeff's mother. He's on your husband's Little League team."

"Oh . . . well, for Heaven's sake. Listen, come in, but please excuse the mess in my kitchen. The kids have been in and out all day."

I walked into the cleanest kitchen I had ever seen, with the whitest linoleum floor in the world, and wondered what her kids were like. There were five of them, I knew, who must have had between them fifty fingers that did not leave smudges. Amazing! As a matter of fact, they were amazing, all of them. Four sons, one little blond girl, and two wonderful parents lived in that absolutely spotless house, ate peanut butter sandwiches for lunch from a two-quart jar, and cooked hotdogs and hamburgers on a grill out behind the basement-level playroom surrounded by Betty's rock garden. Even the rock garden was amazing. It was built higher than my head, and Betty had carried every rock herself, tenderly filling the crevasses with soil and patting tiny plants into place. She also did five loads of wash a day, kept bathroom tissue in five bathrooms, and talked to all the birds who came to the feeder outside her kitchen window.

Paul took the seven-fifteen train to New York every morning and the five-thirty home. It was dark when he left in the summer, and in winter it was dark when he got home. He didn't think playing the guitar would get his oldest son anywhere, and I heard him say to his middle boy, "You'll never make it in Pro ball. You don't have a killer instinct." I'm sure he meant it kindly. He wore white socks and laughed a little too loudly, but no one could consider either a serious flaw in his character.

Richard and I had known them casually as a couple, and I thought it might be different after the divorce. I was wrong. They not only welcomed us, we wore a little path between the two houses. Betty and Paul would usually drive over in their big brown station wagon. The kids came and went on foot or bicycle. The two little girls played dolls together and Jeff played ball with their two younger boys.

About the middle of July, I happened to mention to the boys that I had always wanted a treehouse. We were out in the yard at the time, and I took them over to a dead apple tree that I thought would be just right. All we would have to do was saw the limbs evenly and put a platform across the top. That would require a chain saw, I knew, which was why I needed help, and in fairness I do remember saying, "I'll be glad to pay for whatever the lumber costs."

The next Saturday the big brown station wagon cruised down my road, and a lot of boys and one father got out. I was washing dishes by the kitchen window and I saw them walk over to my dead apple tree, pause briefly, and start down the hill into the woods. About fifteen minutes later they reappeared, got in the car, and drove off. Two hours later they returned, followed by a truck loaded with lumber, six hundred dollars' worth, and work began on the most fantastic treehouse even I could have imagined.

It was stretched between four trees on two-by-twelves and measured fourteen by seventeen feet. It was sixteen feet off the ground, and the sides that came up just waist high were of rough timber with the bark still on. It was truly wonderful!

While the men and boys were building, Betty and I spent a lot of time in her kitchen or mine, and I learned the names of all her plants and birds and a great deal about detergents. I also learned a great deal about a beautiful woman who lived almost her whole life for her family. Even her birds and her flowers were in the wall around them. There were many days she looked tired, with dark red rings inside her eyes, but I never heard her complain about anything except her own figure. If she got past a size eight she got cross with herself and went on a diet of one peanut butter sandwich instead of two.

I was never quite sure whether she was looking at Jo or me when she told stories about the town they used to live in and the births of her children, but she connected all of them to the story that had been running at that time on "Search." She was feeding her first boy when we went on the air in 1951, and the second one came along during the custody fight. Jo had always been in her kitchen when she ate her lunch or ironed the laundry. Jo had been her friend and now I was, but I don't know if we were ever quite the same woman. I know she fancied my private life as being far and away more glamorous than it was. When she looked inside my closet her face fell with dismay.

"It looks just like mine," she said. "All black and brown and good old navy blue."

I laughed. "You were expecting maybe feathers and glitz?"

She thought for a minute before she said, "I think that's what I wanted to see." I've wondered, since, who she was seeing in satin and shine, me or Jo or herself.

All in all, it was a gentle summer. The kids were reasonably calm. I had gained a friend and a treehouse. Bonnie was a fat, healthy puppy, and Sodie, our cat, had presented us with six kittens. Grandmother had moved every fern out of the woods and planted them on the far side of the brook. It even seemed that the pumpkins would ripen before Halloween. Sometimes the evenings were lonely, but the yellow pads helped. I was managing. I was making it alone.

One morning, on a day off, I was sitting at the kitchen table over a second cup of coffee, enjoying the view of my garden and feeling pretty good. I was at peace with the world when the phone rang.

"Hello?"

"Mary, where are you?" It was Mary Ellis, from "Search," and it was a silly question, since she had called me, so I just said, "Here."

"You're supposed to be on the show."

I was defiantly calm, but immediately on the defensive. "I didn't get a script."

"Well, you're on, and we're waiting." She hung up, and I began to realize what this meant. I was on and they were waiting. There was no train till noon, so it was zero hour for the final test. The trip into the city, by car! I had rehearsed all the exits and

routes in my mind so many times. I had been back and forth to
Barbara's all summer. I was as ready as I was going to be.

I picked up my purse and walked calmly toward the white
station wagon. I got in and fastened the seat belt. With hands
that trembled only slightly, I turned on the ignition and waited
until the engine warmed.

"Wait!" Cynthia ran out the back of the house toward the
car. She slid in beside me and started fastening her belt.

"Are you coming?"

The belt clicked and she nodded. "You'll never make it
alone, Maud." She was right, and I knew it.

The trip to the parkway was familiar and simple, since it was
also the way to the station, but my heart began to pound as I
turned up the long, curving ramp. I waited at the top until there
was no sign of a car in any direction, pressed the accelerator to
the floor and leaped onto the highway.

"Light me a cigarette, will you, Maud?"

"Sure, Maud." She got one out of the pack in my purse and
pressed the car lighter in, then held it while I dared take one
damp hand off the wheel. For fifteen minutes we sped along at
thirty-five miles an hour and let the traffic glide around us. Then
we began to gain on a truck that was only doing twenty-five.
Clearly, I would have to make a decision.

I had not, until that moment, ever passed a moving vehicle. I
checked the mirror. All clear. Cautiously, I pulled into the fast
lane, gunned the motor, and shot past him. A good safe mile
down the empty road I inched back to the right.

"Light me another cigarette, will you, Maud."

"Sure, Maud." She fished out another cigarette and found a
little bottle of Binaca in the bottom of the purse, which she tilted
to her mouth.

"You don't smoke, what's with the Binaca?"

"The label says it contains alcohol. I need a drink."

That was funny, and I took my eyes off the road for a second
to peek at her beautiful little face and laugh. "Thanks for coming, Maud."

"I didn't have anything else to do." She kicked off her sandals and pulled the long, tan legs up onto the seat and relaxed.

Somehow, that helped me relax a little, and for half an hour we moved along without incident. I even got the car up to the speed limit and spent some time in the fast lane. Too much time. Too late, I realized that everybody else was pulling off to the right. That was the exit, and I was in the wrong damn lane!

"Don't worry, Maud, there's another exit down here."

"How do you know?"

"We've been driving this road since I was four years old."

"That's true, but I was in the same car and it didn't help me! Where is that other exit?"

"I think you just passed it."

"Now what do I do?"

"We'll have to take the Cross-Bronx Expressway."

"How old are you?"

"Older than I was when we started." She had another little snort of Binaca.

"Okay, Maud, just follow that truck."

I obeyed and followed the big silver trailer onto the Cross-Bronx. There was no slow lane this time. Everybody was hurtling across the narrow span and the signs flashed by. Then, to my horror, I saw just ahead, "Next Exit, New Jersey."

"Maud, we've got to get off this thing."

"The exits are all on the other side."

"Then they'll just have to stop until I get over there. Hold out your hand and I'll put the blinker on."

She leaned out the window and waved to the truck behind us. At first, he just waved back at the pretty little girl, but then he caught on and signaled to the truck behind to stop. They all stopped, probably twelve trucks with angelic drivers, and let me drive straight across three lanes of traffic and down the ramp. For the next forty-five minutes we proceeded down Maurice Avenue from 225th Street to 110th, when it becomes Park Avenue, then over to the West Side. I had no idea how to park inside a garage, or out, so I took the car to the gas station and told the man to fill it up, change the oil, wash it, grease it, and put it somewhere until I got back. It cost twenty-seven dollars, and I thought it was a bargain. I had made it! I had driven to New York.

My maiden voyage was just in time. The Labor Day week-end was coming up. Tenants would be moving into the little house for the winter, and it was time to pack up everything and everybody. Everything was pretty straightaway. Everybody was more complicated. Six kittens, one cat who did not like cars and rode with her claws dug into my shoulder, one puppy who got car sick, ten or twelve boxes, one mother, and two kids to be transported. No problem! I had done it before, I could do it again! I got into the car, started the motor, pushed the little lever to "R" and backed straight to the door. On the way I did also manage, somehow, to dislodge the two posts supporting the back porch and flatten them against the house.

Jeff heard the racket and surveyed the pile of mangled wood. He knew I was about to cry, so right away he said helpfully, "Think of it this way, Mother, the car will be a lot easier to load. It's closer to the kitchen."

It was fall, and time for school to start. Jeff would be going back to Trinity, but Cynthia had moved the year before from Town to Dalton. It had been a big change from that gentle little group to the intense mixture of very bright, competitive, predominantly Jewish upper-class children. Her closest friend was Carla Javits, the senator's daughter. When she stayed at Carla's for Sunday dinner she couldn't help dropping names when she got home. She also began to work late into the night on her homework.

Jeff continued to stay in low gear, as far as his schoolwork went. At least twice a week he woke up with a sore throat or vague stomach complaint and stayed home, but he began to memorize whole books on his own time. Over and over he read stories about athletes or the Time Capsule History series. He learned by heart everything that happened to make news in one year and moved on to another. He'd stopped having tantrums, but he had retreated, spending most of his time alone in his room. In a way, I could understand. He lived in a house with three women who were a lot to contend with. He even wanted his supper back in his room, on a tray.

"All right," I told him. He could have his meals in his room when we were just the family. If we had company, I would expect him at the table. He agreed, but it was an uneasy truce that occasioned several battles.

There were arguments in the mornings, too, and thermometers broke at a truly unusual rate if I tried to check the seriousness of a sore throat.

"I feel terrible, Mom, really."

"I know you do, but you don't have a sore throat."

"I do too! You can't feel what I feel."

"Honey, I know you're going to stay home, just don't tell me you're sick."

"Grandmother will glare at me all day."

"I'll handle Grandmother, but if you tell me you're sick you'll start believing it, and then you will feel bad."

It was about that time I coined the phrase, "Guilt is bad for you." I was sure of that, if nothing else, and I wasn't sure of much.

He wanted to be alone that winter. His room was his fortress, and he lined the walls with books. I made an appointment with the headmaster of Jeff's school to tell him that the family situation had changed, and probably Jeff would need some special understanding from his teachers. His father was living in New York, but they didn't have daily contact. Male companionship would be more important, I thought. I assumed he had understood, but he called me in, several months later, to go over Jeff's grades and seemed genuinely surprised when I mentioned the divorce.

"I told you he might have a problem this year."

"But his grades are hardly passing, and you know as well as I do what his potential is."

"He's using his mind. He's memorizing everything he can lay his hands on. I'll bet he's read more than the other kids in his class combined."

"But he isn't making his grades."

"He's fighting his battles on two fronts, now. Perhaps he can't handle a third. I'm not going to push him until he feels he's ready." I was furious, and I stormed out, practically falling over the mother waiting for the next appointment. The minute I saw

the coat I remembered her. The lady in the brown coat, from
Town School! Here she was at Trinity. She was on her way into
the office and there was no time to chat, but she did say, "Please
bring Cynthia over to play with Fifi. They always had such a
good time together."

"I'll call you!" I said, and I made a mental note to do that.
Fifi was such a quiet, thoughtful child, like Cynth. She would be
a relief from the pressure of Dalton, for both of us!

It began that casually, one of the half-dozen close friendships
I have had in my life. Like the first moment of real contact with
Barbara years before on the beige couch, it was the first moment
of contact with Mary Ann. As with Barbara, we would not realize
it had happened until we looked back over the years of accumulated moments.

Getting settled back into the apartment and the kids into
school—with clothes and books and new friends—can occupy
your mind if you let it. I did. I realized in early November that I
was right back in a routine. I went to the show, ordered the groceries, came home, talked to Mother, talked to Pearl, saw the kids
briefly, depending on their moods, and ate dinner with Cynth,
Mother, and Walter Cronkite. After seven-thirty I was on my
own. I had a lot of time to fill.

There wasn't any deliberate splitting up of friends after the
divorce. As it turned out, most of the people we had seen socially,
like John and Jane, had known Richard all their lives and were
naturally loyal. It is also a known truth that single men are easier
to work into a group than single women. Add to that the fact
that Richard was charming and witty, while I tended toward
manic desperation, and the choice became even more obvious.

There were four couples who were very kind and invited me
to dinner parties a few times. I looked forward to the parties and
usually arrived early and breathless with expectation. There would
be somebody single for me, and it would be a pretty evening. It
did not occur to me for a long time that most men in my age
group, if they are still single, are not looking for the kind of close,
ultimate love that I was prepared to dispense on a moment's notice. What did become apparent was that I did not live the way
the other women did, with time to shop and have lunch. By

Christmas, only Marge and Bob were still hanging in. I spoke to
Mary Ann occasionally, but her life was so formal. Her days and
evenings were committed.

The one person I did see was Betty Rea. She and Oliver were
divorced too, and we were both sort of starting over. Betty was
handling it much better than I. She had always been social, and
she was still giving the same party. Her apartment at United Na-
tions Plaza was always full of fascinating people, and she was still
smiling and dancing. If she was hurt or disappointed she never let
it show. If she was frightened or lonely she called some friends
and ordered Chinese food; and she did it all with wonderful style.
Men flocked around her, and she kept nights alone mercifully
short.

"Let's talk about life," she would say at 2 A.M., curling into a
corner of the sofa with a brandy or a vodka. She was my friend
and she always included me. She gave me a beautiful robe for my
birthday and a gorgeous at-home gown for Christmas. She tried
to make me see how I should think of myself, but it didn't work.
The woman she saw was probably a lot like my fantasy of myself,
but the picture was too far out of focus. In an odd way, the gaiety
in Betty's apartment made me feel even more alone. More than
once I left abruptly and practically ran home.

One evening I asked Betty if she ever saw Bob Whitehead
and Virginia.

"Didn't you know?"

"What?"

"She's dying."

"Oh, my God! No, I didn't know."

"She has cancer. She didn't go to the doctor until it was too
late."

Pictures of the beautiful face with the gray eyes, of the
brown silk couches and pale yellow walls floated into my mind,
along with a vague, sick feeling of guilt.

"How did you feel about Virginia?"

Betty got up and moved to the bar to fill her glass. "She
nearly broke up our marriage. I told Oliver, finally, it was either
her or me."

"I said something like that to Lester, but it probably wouldn't have made any difference."

She had affected my life so much, in so many ways. I had spent so many hours thinking about her, and now she was dying. I'd heard she owned an antique shop and the next day I went by. I had never seen so many perfectly exquisite things together in one place. As I wandered through the shop, I realized that probably the first really fine things I had ever seen were hers. I was grateful to her, and I was sad. I wrote and told her so.

I gave one big party myself and invited everybody I knew, but even before people went home I felt ridiculous. I was tense and trying too hard. It was just like the parties I had given with Richard, and it didn't make sense anymore.

The yellow pads were the first and last resort. They were a godsend in more ways than one. As long as I had a pen in my hand, or a guitar in my lap, I was doing something. I could say to myself, "Oh, good! I don't have anything to do tonight, so I'm free to work." If I was putting something down on the pads, or practicing, I could call it work, and work is a very important word. It is also a great dodge, and a lie you can believe. Nothing was written of any lasting value that winter. Most of the songs were what I called the "question and traveling" songs. "What Am I Doing Here?" "Where Do I Go from Here?" Mercifully, "Why Was I Born?" had already been written.

By Christmas, Betty was in love with Pat, and Pat was in love with her, and they were very, very happy. Betty had always given a party Christmas night, so they came to my house Christmas Eve. Once the tree goes up, I always begin to feel festive, so I invited other people, all single people, I realized. It seemed like a good idea, and it was. Christmas was a warm, wonderful island.

Perhaps it was only the letdown after the holidays. Perhaps it was the long, dark days or simply the cold. January was like walking into a gray wall! I bought two tickets to a charity ball, but that wasn't until March. I had plenty of time to decide what to wear. Time was the problem: evening after evening, by myself, with my guitar and my cat. Sodie had become a great companion. The minute I sat down on the couch in the evening she would come trotting around the corner and jump up beside me, purring B flat and leaning against the guitar. It was a pretty picture, though twenty or thirty evenings like that in a row can get to you. Sometimes, it was just a simple case of "Mary feels sorry for herself." Frieda Face-Facts could handle that, but the doubts were growing. There were plenty of single men my age, but they were going out with much younger women. Socially, I had bombed all my life and nothing had happened to improve my personality, except that I was a little more eager and frantic. I had serious doubts about myself as an attractive woman, and every day the phone did not ring confirmed them.

Occasionally, rather than scream, or cry, or holler at the kids, I went to a movie. I would fix a drink in a little Thermos and catch the six o'clock show at the neighborhood playhouse. One night Jeff asked where I was going. "I'm running away from home," I joked as the elevator closed. Unfortunately, that night I saw *A Man and a Woman*, which is not a picture to see alone.

I was in a rotten mood anyway, and I walked in the door just in time to hear Jeff talking to somebody on the phone.

"No, Mother isn't here," he said, "she ran away from home."

"Jeff, who are you talking to?"

"Daddy."

"Oh, good grief! Give me that phone."

All that winter Richard was seeing a woman who had children about the same ages as ours, and about once a month the whole group would go away for a weekend together. The kids said she was very pretty, younger, and a wonderful skier. All sorts of uncomfortable feelings stirred up every time they went away. They had great times with Daddy, and Mother got all the fun of making Jeff go to school and yelling at Cynth to go to bed. The uncomfortable feelings were a mix of old anger, envy, and frustration. I was lonely and unhappy, and it was handy to blame Richard. I started "zinging" him in front of the children fairly regularly. I could tell a story about our life together, painting him Inadequate Al, uncaring and thoughtless. I did it so well I began to believe it myself, and added to my list of charms a jagged edge of spite.

In the spring, I decided I could show the kids a good time too! I took Jeff to Arizona, figuring it was time for him to learn to ride. That trip was not only unsuccessful, it was a minor disaster. My old trick of looking good in a saddle did me in once again. They gave a horse that was much too much for me and took me on a long, wild ride. For the rest of that week I was so sore I couldn't look at a horse, so I played Ping-Pong with a very bored son.

I took them both to Eleuthera and that worked out better; but then, almost anybody can have a good time on a hundred dollars a day. When we got back there was a note from Richard, enclosing Harry Kurnitz's obituary. He had died of a heart attack, alone, in a hotel in California.

In June the kids were going to camp and Grandmother was leaving for Oklahoma with Bonnie, so I rented the little house. There was no real point rattling around in two houses. The minute they were gone I panicked. I picked up my address book and practically ran for the phone, beginning with the A's and working all the way through. By the time I got to the Z's, I had had two drinks, my finger was sore from dialing, and my ear was ringing. I had learned that in the summer young single people shared beach houses, older single people belonged to golf clubs, and married people I knew went away to summer places the way I had. Obviously, I had not fitted myself into any of those groups. Somehow, I would have to find a group of my own. I had no idea how to begin.

Every evening I sat down at the typewriter, with a drink, and wrote the kids, between five and six o'clock. Then, I opened a can of tuna fish or put a TV dinner in the oven and had supper in front of the television. The rest of the evening was the guitar and my cat. The pile of yellow pads was growing, and so was the fear. It wasn't fear of the dark anymore, it was fear of spending the rest of my life alone. My chance was slipping by, and I didn't know how to get hold of it. I didn't know where to start. Like the loneliness, I put the fear into pretty words and hid it under the couch:

> I live my life in a moment, the moment
>   of my years,
> A grain of sand on a beach so wide;
> And ever the mighty ocean tide
> Sweeps away the footprints of each passerby.
> So very small am I.

I was lonely, I didn't fit in, and I zinged Richard, but all the time I knew it was really my own fault. I'd watched Betty make a whole new life for herself, so it wasn't age. What was it? I thought about Virginia and Harry. The last time I saw him he had come home from Switzerland for his mother's funeral. The kids were about three and four. He came by the apartment, but he didn't stay long, just watched the kids playing and pulled at the funny curl. Then he put his drink down and got up.

"What do you want me to say? That I made a mistake? I have everything I always said I wanted." He leaned down and stroked Cynthia's hair, and without looking at me he said, "Goodbye, Kitten."

Maybe he did have everything he wanted, but he died alone in a hotel room. Virginia was gone too. Virginia had had knowledge and taste, and finally power. Maybe that was what she wanted. Maybe they were both satisfied. To me it didn't seem like nearly enough! It was too lonely. An old sadness began to gather, the way mountains close in a circle when the sun goes down, and I thought about California. I hadn't been back in eighteen years. I wondered about the people who had seemed so important, and my tiny house.

Marge and Bob were renting a house in Beverly Hills for the summer. They had said, casually, that I should come out and spend a week. Lots of friends from "Search" were out there. It would be fun to see Ross Martin, and Hal Cooper, and Don Knotts. I wanted to talk to the people I had known before, in the old days. I wanted to talk about Harry, and I wanted to see my little house.

The first person I called was Lee Gershwin. Her voice was strange and distant.

"You've come back to bury ghosts? Is that why you're here?"

"No . . . not really. But I've thought about you so often. How's Ira?"

"We live very differently now," she said. "We hardly see anyone, but give me your number and I'll call you."

Helen O'Connell was on the road, Ross Martin was away on location for "The Wild, Wild West," Charlie Lederer's wife said he wasn't well enough to come to the phone. Hal Cooper was one of the busiest directors in town, but at least he took one Sunday afternoon off and drove me to all the old haunts.

My little house was still there, and a painter owned it. When she opened the door I said, "Excuse me, I built this house, and I just wanted to see it again."

The first thing I saw was the pink granite fireplace. Then she asked me, "Why does the roof leak in that corner?" Without thinking I turned toward the door. Sure enough, there was a dark stain on the ceiling and I laughed, "I don't know, but it always did."

The house was fine. It had survived. It could take care of itself. The little trees that were six inches tall when I planted them were thirty feet high.

For the rest of the week I sat by the pool by myself. When I couldn't stand it any longer I finally got up the nerve to call Mac. Nobody else had returned my calls. I knew he was married again, and busy, but I had to try. I felt more alone than I had in New York and I was desperate.

"I'm sorry, he's in a story conference and will be tied up for several hours." The secretary's voice was crisp, and it was a familiar litany. "But I'll give him the message."

In my mind I began to pack and get ready to go home. I had had enough. Two minutes later the phone rang.

"Mary! How are you and when can I see you?"

It was Mac, and he sounded just the same!

"Well, I'm pretty free. What's a good time for you? I'll be here for three more days."

"How about tonight?"

"Sure. Tonight would be fine."

I called Saks and made an appointment to have my hair

done and pressed my favorite dress. At Saks, an odd thing happened. I was looking through a movie magazine and the hairdresser pointed to a picture.

"That's who you remind me of. I've been trying to think since you walked in. You're just like her!"

It was a picture of Mac's wife.

He picked me up in a tiny red sports car and took me to a wonderful little restaurant in Beverly Hills.

"What do I want to drink?" he asked, and grinned at me.

"Dewar's."

"Yep."

Nothing had changed and everything was different, but he said some beautiful things to me.

"I'm married to the most wonderful woman in the whole world, and I fell in love with her from the back row of the balcony. She thinks you're great."

"How does she know me?"

"She met you for two minutes in San Francisco in 1961, and when she got home she said, 'I met the other woman in your life. I knew it the minute I saw her.'"

Of course I remembered meeting her, but I couldn't believe she noticed me. If I had been jealous the feeling dissolved. I had to love anyone who made him so happy. He talked and talked and talked.

"I wasn't sure where to take you tonight," he said, "after all, we used to be an item and I'm married. I started to call some quiet little place down by the beach, but then I thought, 'No, damn it! I don't have to worry about gossip and I'm proud of her. I want everybody to see us!'"

Driving me back to Marge and Bob's he was quiet for a long time. Then he said, "You know, I'm probably the luckiest man I know. I've had success doing what I want to do and three great women in my life. That's about all a man could ask for."

I closed the big iron gates across the driveway and watched the little red car zip down the long drive. I cried for quite a while.

I started a poem one afternoon, gazing up through the trees

down by the pool, and I called it "Southern California: It's Lonely There":

> Sweet it is to lie
> Upon a grassy hillside,
> Close my eyes and feel
> A sun that's shining everywhere.
> It warms a world that every blade of grass
>   can share.
> For a whistler on a windride,
> It is lonely, lonely there.

When I got back to New York I called Lester. I told him about the house, and he said he was busy with his school. He had three kids he loved, and his voice was very, very reassuring.

In August, I went up to Vermont to see the kids in camp. I flew to White River Junction, rented a car and called Maud.

"Stay where you are," she insisted over the phone, "you'll never find the house. I'll send somebody over to lead you."

I got into the little sports car Hertz had assigned me and headed into the night behind Maud's friend. The first mile or so was a brightly lit, two-lane highway and we just sailed along. Then he turned off onto a dark, curving mountain road and began to speed up. Maud had surely cautioned him that I preferred to drive slowly, but I don't suppose anybody believes there is a fast lane, a slow one, and, for me, there is also the grass. The other problem he did not seem to be aware of was how I felt about passing cars, and he kept zooming by anything and everything on the road. Now, it is hard to tell what color a car is at night—any car—so it was not really my fault that on one of his zooms I lost him completely and picked up another car to follow that also had a light top. I not only followed that car, I tailed it right into its garage. By then I was so rattled I stepped hard on what I thought was the emergency and bent the hand brake to the floor. I called Maud, of course, and her friend came all the way back to wherever I was and got me.

Morning does come, even on strange roads. I went to see the kids and drove just fine, once I could see where I was going. I drove that whole weekend, and I was so pleased that in a moment of wild, reckless enthusiasm I decided I could drive home and canceled my airplane ticket. Of course, the moment I hung up the phone I panicked. I went to the coffee shop to think it over and started to shake so violently I couldn't hold the cup. I had to put my face down to the rim and slurp. That is what made me angry. No! I decided. I would not have it. I would drive that damned car, and I would drive it that day! I got in and fastened the seat belt. The station attendant assured me that all I had to do was stay on 91, and it was six lanes wide, straight as an arrow. I turned on the radio and pulled onto the highway, breathing with some difficulty—but breathing. I found a music station and turned it up loud.

"The time is ten-o-four," the announcer said, and put on a Burt Bacharach record I hadn't heard.

"This guy's in love, this guy's in love with you . . ." I liked it, so I turned the radio louder and drove on for what seemed like an hour. I remember being so surprised when the announcer said, "And now, at ten-fifteen, the mellow sounds of . . ."

"My God!" I thought. "I've only been driving for eleven minutes! This will take forever!"

It did take forever, but I made it. I drove four hundred miles. Somewhere around noon I glanced at the speedometer and I was going eighty miles an hour with the top down and Burt Bacharach screaming in the wind. When I got home, I wrote the second verse to the new song about California:

> A thrill to fly
> Along a strange new highway.
> Birds are going my way,
> Wind fingers in my hair.
> I'm flying by.
> Music trails behind goes
> Blowing through my mind knows
> It's lonely, lonely there.

The kids came home, and Mother was back from Oklahoma with Bonnie. I was never so glad to see any three people in the world.

In November the doctor found another lump in my breast. It was the third one, and I wasn't very brave. I left his office and walked to the corner. I didn't hail a cab. I just leaned against the corner of the building and cried. It was benign, thank God, but it was a much bigger operation than either of the others, and I no longer had the proportions that attracted so much attention in Hollywood.

"Cut your hair!" Betty pleaded. "At least cut your hair! It will make you look ten years younger." She had said the magic word, and I agreed.

Betty's hairdresser at Bergdorf's pulled the hairpins as if he were activating a hand grenade.

"I'm not used to working with hair this long," he said cautiously.

"Nobody is. That's why I'm here. Cut it off."

He looked surprised and relieved. "All of it?"

"All of it."

"Shall I have it made into a braid?"

"Not unless you want a hair belt."

I think he thought that over, because he did pause before he said, "Exactly how short do you want it?"

I held up my index finger and mentally measured it, then I slid my thumb to the middle joint. "That short." It's the way I had measured when I cut my own hair before "Search" went on the air.

Before "Search" went on the air! My God! I had come full circle, only the circle was bigger now. There were circles within the circles, like rings around a tree. I was starting over; at least, I still had a chance to. As the hair slid from the pink cape to the floor, I caught glimpses of the girl who had crooned to a child so long ago, and it occurred to me, "We're both starting over. Jo is alone too, and now we'll both have short hair. Both of me!"

Within the circle on "Search," the family was close and complete. Frank and Ernesto produced it from a tiny, windowless office on the third floor of the production center. Ed Trach was the P&G representative and brought a new kind of sensitivity to our relationship with the company. He understood what the actors were trying to do, and his comments were supportive and helpful. For the first time, I became aware that the company took such an active and creative role in the story and the way it was presented, in the look and feel of the show. Ed was especially thoughtful and kind to me. He liked the Christmas shows when I sang. The first year I did my own "Bells of Christmas," he wrote a lovely note: "You should do more singing and writing," he said. That year "Green Coffee," an old Texas "play-party" song, became the love theme for Jo and Sam.

The love story of Jo and Sam was interesting, fun, and elegant. Sam was a man who had read and traveled. Dave and Julian wrote dialogue that was witty and articulate, and Bob Mandan made it sparkle. As the mystery of Sam unraveled, we discovered that Len Whiting was his son. The boy had been raised by his mother, Andrea, in Paris. He had never known why, and he would never forgive.

Sam was in love with Jo, and she was wonderfully, deliciously in love with him. They went to the theatre and concerts, or long walks by the river, and their favorite game was to finish a poem the other had begun to recite. Keats and Dickenson were often guest writers on the show. Only Sam's wife kept Jo and Sam from marrying. For years he had simply been separated from Andrea. When he finally asked her for a divorce, she flatly refused, and came flying back from Paris to find out why he wanted one.

Joan Copeland played Andrea when she returned from Paris, and she was stunning. Her flair and style alone would have been enough, but she also had the skill to make those choices that keep a character fascinating. Andrea plotted and schemed, Joan scintillated and smiled. She tried to get Sam back, and when that failed she tightened her hold on Len. She wouldn't let him be close to his father or the girl he loved. She would do anything to keep him to herself. Andrea was ruining her son's life, and Sam's.

Finally, Sam could stand it no longer. He told Jo why he had allowed her to take his son away from him. He told her about the night of the fire, the night Len's twin brother died. In telling the story, Sam described his life with Andrea, the courtship and marriage, and as he talked the audience saw the scenes that were pre-taped and edited on the air. Technically, the medium had come a long way, and Dan used it all beautifully.

We were turning corners. We were doing really good shows and having a fine time. The morning rehearsal was more like a party than work. Larry Haines always had a new joke, and if he didn't somebody would give him one just for the fun of hearing him tell it. Carl Low was excellent and elegant, Kenny was wild and obstreperous, Joan and Bobby were superb and late. They both always made entrances. Bobby, like the White Rabbit on his way to a very important date somewhere else, would dash in, tango with me across the rehearsal space, eat two apple turnovers, then give the script almost all of his attention. Joan's entrances varied with the hour. The later she was the better they got: "If you wanted perfect, you should have hired perfect."

Another face that was becoming increasingly important and evident was the beautiful young girl who had joined us straight out of high school as show secretary and was now our production assistant. Mary Ellis sat through rehearsals every morning, along with Dan, to time the show. She heard the fights and enjoyed the jokes, and she had gradually become, without knowing it, a kind of bellwether for me. I began to watch her face for reactions to what I was doing. You just can't tell, all by yourself, if what you're playing is working, and I never got to the point where I could really trust Dan. If Larry or Carl were on, they would watch a scene and tell me if I was wrong, but if they weren't I would look at Mary Ellis, or Tucker Ashworth.

Tucker was our young assistant director, and after the flash-back sequences it was announced that he would begin training as full director. Everybody was terribly pleased for Tucker, because everybody adored him. Tucker was a gentle, unassuming pixy, who knew everything there was to know. It was Tucker who chose the poetry Bobby and I used and Tucker who taught me how to read it. Carl and Bobby and I did a little musical as a benefit, and Tucker stole the show in a tiny part. He was articulate and thoughtful, with a sly wit. He was a gourmet cook. He was a generous, sensitive man, who took great delight in wonderful things and beautiful places, and obviously he was going to be a marvelous director. Dan loved him too, and took great pains helping him learn.

I had never socialized much with anybody on the show, but after the divorce I depended more and more on my buddies. Carl was my special friend. He came by the house early before the "Search" Christmas party to see if I needed any help. He let me talk about the kids when I was upset and gave me great advice. I depended on Carl for so much it went way past socializing. Tucker came by for supper occasionally, always with a book of poetry or a record he wanted me to hear of Bea Lillie or *Henry* V or something else wonderful. If I needed an escort, I called Ernesto. He hated big functions as much as I did, but he looked so handsome and was great with names. He was also the one we all went to if there was any kind of problem with a script or a schedule, or Dan. Frank was the producer, but Ernesto ran great interference for him.

Frank was so gentle, and he hated problems. He just loved his show and everybody on it, and everybody loved Frank. He appreciated what we all did and told us so. He loved to go out with us for lunch across the street, and every now and then he'd treat. Frank never had to throw his weight around to produce the show. His own kindness and occasional joy were reflected. He didn't have to tell the writers how to write, they knew that, just as we used to say to Dan, "Don't tell us how to act and we won't tell you how to direct!"

One morning he looked particularly pained and said, "But you do tell me. You tell me all the time!"

Dan could be so dear and so funny when he relaxed, just a little. He'd been through a bad time that year. A tumor developed behind one of his eyes. The tumor was malignant and the eye had to be removed. It was another thing that brought him closer to Tucker. Tucker had had the same operation when he was seventeen, but Dan was the only one who knew that then. We also didn't know that P&G had wanted to let Dan off the show just before he got sick. Frank had pleaded with them to keep him on, and after the operation nobody had the heart. So he stayed.

I still had little, unexpected flurries with Dan from time to time, but Frank and Ernesto were supportive and Ed Trach was appreciative. I could look around the makeup room in the morning and see the faces of half a dozen people I truly enjoyed and admired. I hadn't found anybody to love, but Jo had. So at least there was an outlet for all the emotion and lots of folks to hug.

Maybe it was doing the play or just the new material Dave and Julian wrote us, but acting was a lot more fun. New things were happening. The joke when we had a sad scene to play was "faster and funnier," and there was the edge of truth that made sense. I'd learned to string the moments more closely, letting the new thought begin to rise before the last one had run its course. I knew a scene was not right if there was one moment of dead air, and I had learned to feel the stillness.

Ross Martin once said, "An actor has two responsibilities to fulfill. One is the content of the script, and the other is the content of human behavior. Actors in daytime all have a unique opportunity to become masters at fulfilling human behavior. It is the nature and substance of our medium." I guess I've had as much a chance as anyone, if only because of the years, to do that. To quote another old friend: Peggy Cass said that on a soap there is a perpetrator, a victim, and a listener. Jo was the listener, and since I can't talk to my dogs without wondering how they feel, it probably came naturally to both of us.

Jo listened. She would always stop what she was doing to listen, but she was always doing something, and what she did was up to me. I created her human behavior. When she walked into a room she was always going someplace, with something on her mind. That gave her energy and purpose and, not incidentally, colored the scene she would play. I also gave her as much activity as the set allowed. Even in a house that stagehands vacuum, there is something to be done.

Probably the most important thing I gave Jo was my own insecurity. In the scripts, everyone came to Jo for advice. Her decisions were easy and she was always right. I added her hesitation, her doubt. It seemed to me that made her more real, more human and believable. Also, when things turned out for the best she could be relieved and excited, even surprised. It was probably a natural extension of a lady who rents out her country house because she can't find it. Still, the choices had to be made consciously and carefully.

Each character's relationship with other characters was so complex the continuity alone filled scenes with our very special reality. Jo thought before she spoke, and it was a rhythm that was hers. Larry Haines made large, all-encompassing statements and then panicked, peering into Marge's face to make sure it was all right, hoping he'd made sense and wishing he'd kept his mouth shut. None of that was in the script and nobody told us to do it. I remember Larry playing a scene with an actor who was famous on Broadway but new to daytime. The director wanted to get a shot of his face with Larry in the background, so he asked him to turn away on the line, but the actor hesitated.

"Why would I do that?" he asked. "What is my motivation?"

For five minutes the director floundered on about the man's doubt of himself in the situation, his need to hide his feelings, and his inability to lie convincingly. Finally, he looked to Larry for reassurance. "Do you know what I mean?"

Larry nodded. "Sure," he said, "you want him to play it to Camera Two."

The reality was never more evident or useful than the days when the show timed out short. If I was on, Dan would ask if I could fill anywhere from one to five minutes with a one-way phone, or business, or both; and there was always someone I wanted to talk to. With half a dozen words scribbled on the desk blotter, or on a card, I could ad-lib a whole scene, but Larry was the master. He would begin a conversation with an irate customer: "Look, uh, I know you ordered a blue car, but I thought the red was . . ." and then let the audience see the rest on his face as he repeated helplessly, "Yeah, but . . . yeah, but . . . yeah, but . . ." So all a director had to say was, "Larry, do two minutes of 'yeah, buts.'"

Only when you really know what you're doing can you afford to make jokes, and in the summer of 1968 the "intention" was to fill the time between commercials, the "action" was to find your key light, and the "obstacle" was the script.

On October 15, I didn't have a show to do, so I was home when Ed called to say he wanted to see me. He said he and Milton would be over after lunch. It seemed odd, and I was curious. I called the office to speak to Frank. He was out, and Ernesto picked up the phone.

"Do you know what Ed and Milton want to see me about? They're coming to my apartment."

"No, but something is going on," he said. "Bill McIlvaine called me a few minutes ago to say he's sending over my check, but I'm not to open it. He asked me to have a drink with him at five o'clock."

"Does Frank know what it's all about?"

"I haven't seen him all day. He's been at the agency and hasn't even called in. I told Bill I couldn't leave early. We have a taping tonight, and if Frank isn't there I have to cover it. He said to let somebody else do it and to be at the hotel bar at five."

When Ed and Milton walked in the door I knew immediately something was very wrong. Almost as soon as they sat down, Ed said, "We want you to know before you hear it from somebody else. We're letting Frank go."

"Frank Dodge?"

Ed looked so sad as he glanced at Milton. "There's been a lot happening on the show that you don't know about. The agency feels we have to make a change."

Then Milton said, "We'd appreciate it if you didn't say anything to anybody, especially at the show, until we've had a chance to make an announcement. We wanted you to know, because we know how fond you are of Frank."

I heard the words, but I couldn't believe what they were saying. "How long has he known?"

"He's being told now."

I stared down at the coffee table, trying to stay calm and rational and think of something to say. "The ratings are so good—he brought the show a long way."

"It has nothing to do with the ratings. We're fond of Frank too, but we need someone who can really run the show." There was absolute finality in his voice.

I knew Frank was weak sometimes, but who wasn't? He got

the show on. What was so terrible it couldn't be fixed or covered by somebody else? I could see his gentle face in my mind and the hands that never rested. Right now he was on his way to the executioner, and he would be totally unaware of his crimes. His own innocence had convicted him, but he would never understand that.

"I'll make some coffee," I said, and left the room.

Two hours later Ernesto walked into the hotel bar and sat down at the table where Bill was waiting.

"Open your check," Bill said almost immediately. It was a raise of three thousand dollars, but before Ernesto had a chance to ask why, he said, "We've fired Frank."

Ernesto looked down at the check and back at Bill. "And what does this check mean?"

"It's just to show our appreciation."

"Appreciation of what? Am I the new producer?"

Bill paused. "No. We're bringing in Bob Driscoll. But, of course, we want you to stay on as his associate."

In that instant, Bill stepped off his end of the seesaw and Ernesto hit the ground. He did not lose his balance. Very coolly he said, "Driscoll doesn't know the show."

"We've had him watching it for some time, but we'll need you. You know the cast and we know there will be trouble, especially with Mary. You're good at keeping things together. We need you."

Ernesto folded the check into his billfold and walked all the way back to the production center to catch the end of the taping. By the time he got there he had decided to leave the show. He would have left immediately, but he knew Bill was right. The show needed him. Bob Driscoll took over officially the following Monday, but nobody saw him for two weeks. He would arrive after the taping, when the cast had left the building, to go over his paper work. Ernesto ran the show, as he always had. Three months later, he walked out and drove up to the little garden house where he lived. The stock market had dropped, and his severance pay was about half what it would have been if he'd left when he wanted to, but he had some capital. He'd always been interested in real estate. So was his friend, Percival. Perhaps he would look around for a house to buy and restore. He was sick of television and agencies.

The winter of 1968–69 we followed the story of Andrea's disintegration. By late summer she had dissolved, completely and beautifully, and went off to a mental hospital. At last Sam and Jo were free to be together. There was only one little drawback. Bobby Mandan had been restless for over a year. We had written around him during tryouts for two Broadway shows and prerecorded his scenes, but that fall he decided he wanted to go to California. I'm not sure if money would have helped. He told me nobody offered him a raise and by October he was angry and insistent. I was frantic. The compromise the writers decided on was to write him out of the show for an extended period and let him see how he liked California. He would leave a week before Christmas.

About the same time, that October, Tucker asked me a strange question:

"Do you notice anything wrong with my speech?"

He had been speaking a little more slowly, and I assumed it was because he was nervous in his new job and was trying to make sure he was understood.

"What do you mean, wrong?"

"It feels slurred to me," he said. "Listen for a day or two and see if you can hear it."

For the rest of the week I listened. It was not so evident in the early morning rehearsal. He spoke slowly, by habit, slowly and deliberately, so careful not to mar an ego or disrupt the beginning of a performance, only to add to it. I could hear the effort, but no one else did. It was on the loudspeakers in the studio that the slur was evident. Several times we had to ask him to repeat. After the show we went out by ourselves for a drink, and the alcohol made the problem much more evident.

"Honey, it's got to be something psychological. I think you should see a shrink. But then, I've thought so for ages and you know it. This ridiculous life you lead has got to be doing damage. You disappear into that tiny box you live in and hole up until the next show. You probably drink too much, and I bet you never eat. Do you go anywhere besides my house?"

"Yes, I just don't like to talk about it. You know why."

"You hate being gay."

"I despise it."

"Then you should see a shrink."

He tilted his head to one side and grinned at me. "I'm having trouble talking. He'll never understand what I'm saying."

"Tucker, you have to. Whatever is bothering you is getting out of hand. It's even affecting your work, and you know that's more important than anything else to you. At least try. I have very selfish interests in you, and I need you doing your best." He grinned at me again, but the smile faded quickly, so I persisted. "Do you want the name of my doctor? He sure helped me."

"No, not yet . . . I bought a book of Keats for you, and I've marked the poems I want you to work on." He was tired, and the consonants were much softer, and blurry. "I'll come over one night this week."

"Which night?"

"I'll call you."

"You know you won't."

"When are you free?"

"I'm always free."

"We're a great pair."

"I think I've mentioned that."

"Mary, don't make me hate myself more . . ."

"Oh, honey, I didn't mean that! Tucker, please, see a doctor!"

Christmas has always meant too much to me. Every year the tree gets bigger, with more lights, more ornaments, and much more tinsel. There are always more presents and more people and more food. In 1968 the "Search" party had grown to include everybody who had ever appeared on the show, with special mystery guests from California. Actors from other shows would drop in after their official parties ended, and ours went on till two. I spent a week cooking.

After the "Search" party, there were preparations for Christmas Eve. We invited single people again, and so many people came we couldn't sit at the table. There were so many presents the wrapping filled the back hall, and there was still Christmas morning with the family. I always loved to buy presents for the kids. Any holiday was an excuse, but Christmas was the day I looked forward to all year. Their childhood is chronicled in my memory by the trains and bicycles and the dolls. I did love the dolls and they were almost worn out before Cynthia got them.

I love the toys and the tinsel, but I love the fables too, of love and peace and joy. I love the tradition, the music, and the smell of tangerines and ribbon candy. It is magic.

I guess both kids understood how important the day was to me, and long after they had outgrown Christmas stockings they went through the ritual because they knew I loved it. That year, Jeff went with me to buy the tree and when he saw me hesitate for a long time beside a skimpy one for fourteen dollars, he just took my hand and started down the street.

"Mom, once a year you deserve it. Buy the one you want."

I spent forty dollars and loved that tree. Then, Christmas morning, before anybody had opened their presents, Cynthia handed me a tiny square box. Without opening it, I knew. I had seen the little ring in the jewelry store up the street back in October. A carnelian seal in a beautiful shade of orange, and I had mentioned it to Cynth.

"Buy it, Maud. You've wanted a seal ring forever."

"Well, it costs a hundred dollars. That's a lot of money."

"Buy it! You never buy anything for yourself, and I know you want it."

"I don't want anything one hundred dollars' worth," but I couldn't stop thinking about it. The next afternoon, when I walked the dog, I stopped by the shop. She was right. I did want it. He was just closing. It was Saturday and he wanted to leave early.

"Sorry," he said through the crack in the door. "I sold that ring this morning. You should have told me to put it aside." For three months Cynth had been tutoring and baby-sitting, and spent every cent on the ring. She understood what Christmas meant to me.

I often thought she understood everything, or at least experienced the emotion, and when something happened to her it happened to me. I agonized with her when the dentist finally decided to put braces on her teeth. She was thirteen and it wasn't fair! All the other girls were taking theirs off and beginning to notice boys. It had to be done and each ugly wire was cemented into place. I had a nightmare that night about the man in the iron mask!

When we went to see the Beatles in *A Hard Day's Night*, we got a bag of popcorn after the first show and, without a word, went right back into the theatre. We eventually saw it five times.

I could have strangled her the day she picked up my guitar and the long, graceful fingers automatically grabbed chords that had taken me weeks to master. But extremes of emotion—like pride or anger or joy—all seem to churn my middle. It was probably a mix of all three. I understood her and I knew she understood me.

In the winter of 1969 she picked up one of the lyrics one day and read through it. "Maud," she said, "this is a poem about passion. That line isn't right." It was a little ray of wisdom and maturity I was not expecting, and she was absolutely right.

After a moment I asked her, "What is 'Back Against a Mountain'?" She said, "Oh, that's a song about awareness. I like that one."

I did not write another lyric or poem for a long time without asking for her comments. Then one day she noticed a little scrap of paper on the coffee table, about a yellow balloon that thinks it's the moon.

"That's nice, Maud," she said. "What's the rest of it going to be?"

"I don't know, but I'll show it to you when I get it."

Over the next couple of months I started the poem several times. Always she would shake her head. "No, Maud, that's not it." Finally I asked her what "The Yellow Balloon That Thinks It's the Moon" meant to her, and she said, "Well, Maud, everybody is the sun and the moon to themselves."

I was so startled by this revelation of insight I just stared at her. "You mean we're a bunch of yellow balloons bumping down the street?"

"No," she answered patiently. "When you mature, you realize you are not the center of the universe. You always feel like you are, but you know, intellectually, you aren't really."

I knew what the rest of the poem would be and I wrote it in an hour.

> Cynthia lives in a yellow balloon
>   full of sunlight, sunlight.
> She sees the world through a yellow balloon,
>   shining bright.
> In her yellow balloon, when it thinks it's
>   the moon, she goes flying by.
> You can't tell a balloon,
>   When it thinks it's the moon,
> You're too high.
>
> Cynthia lives in a yellow balloon
>   full of starlight, star bright.
> She says we all live in different balloons,
>   and she's right. Yes, she's right.
> When her yellow balloon is the sun and the moon,
>   she goes flying by.
> You can't tell a balloon
>   that's the sun and the moon
> You're too high . . . I wouldn't try.
> A gentle wind blows where my Cynthia glows
>   in the sky.

The other member of the family who cared about the lyrics was Grandmother. I call my mother Grandmother because that is what everybody else called her. Of course the kids called her Grandmother, but so did Henry, the superintendent of the building, the elevator men, all my friends, and Pearl. When some pipes broke in Pearl's apartment house uptown and threatened to flood the place she immediately called us. I was working, so Grandmother jumped in a cab and sped to the rescue. The firemen were about to hack away at everything in sight, but the one-hundred-and-ten-pound wonder took over. She was afraid that if there was too much excitement, Pearl would have a seizure.

"Now, look here!" she said firmly. "The water is coming from upstairs someplace. You just go up there and start chopping, and leave this place alone!"

The firemen looked at the tiny, gray-haired lady with the soft southern accent.

"Who are you?" And without a second's hesitation she said, "I'm Pearl's grandmother!"

Grandmother took care of Pearl and everybody else. She got up at four every morning and fixed breakfast for the night elevator man and the morning shift. Then she fixed something for the kids. Grandmother could cook breakfast and she could make wonderful egg custard or meatloaf. That was the extent of her repertoire. Nothing else was edible. She also could not make a cup of coffee without using every pan in sight. But she loved to cook and every night it was a race for the kitchen. The kids would watch the clock. If I hadn't started they would give me the high sign and I would begin to amble in that direction, trying to be as discreet as possible. God forbid I should make her think I was taking over! But it was tricky. I couldn't get down the hall going either direction without passing her room, and she had a short cut. She had Pearl's room, and it connected to the kitchen across the back hall. She could cut me off at the pass. Ten steps and she was there with a frying pan in her hand.

So, nearly every night she cooked, and whatever it was we ate. One night, Cynthia walked into the kitchen.

"Hi, Grandmother, what we having for dinner?"

Grandmother always got nervous when she had two or three pots on the stove at the same time, so she said a little shortly, "Chicken."

"Oh, good," Cynthia said amiably, then she added without malice and obviously without thought, "You going to fry it or burn it?"

What she meant was, are you going to fry it or broil it, but Grandmother never got the hang of the broiler, so it was usually charred.

Grandmother couldn't cook, but she could do anything else, and she did. She walked Bonnie every morning, and if it was raining or snowing she carried her to the park wrapped up in a shawl. She got up at four, and she fell asleep watching television every night. Cynthia or Jeff would tiptoe into her room and turn off the set and the light. She ran all day, but she had time to go to the library for the children, and if one of them had a paper to turn in for school she would be in the study at four-thirty, typing away. She read *Forbes* and *The Wall Street Journal,* and every history book she could get her hands on, and over and over she told the children how important their family was. They were the same stories I had heard as a child, and I enjoyed hearing them again.

The only home Grandmother remembered living in was Bon Aire, a big old house designed by Thomas Jefferson, that her folks bought about 1900. But she was born at Clover Creek in Highland County. That's where her family was from and that was the place she talked about.

The family dated back in that county to 1700, when Edward Usher and his wife, Lady Jane Perry, settled back up on Jack Mountain. She was a lady-in-waiting to the Queen of England, and he was a palace guard. Her father objected to the marriage, so they ran away. Their daughter, Margaret, married William Stuart, a Scotsman, who was shipwrecked in 1720, and they began our line of Stuarts. My generation was the first to be born outside that county.

Clover Creek was part of ten thousand acres my great grandfather owned. Two of his sons were killed in the Civil War, and he divided the land between the rest of his children. Mother's father got the homeplace because he was the youngest—only five years old at the time of the war. He was the youngest, and he was also going blind. Mother remembers being sent with him on the back of his horse wherever he went, to keep him from signing anything. People had taken advantage of his blindness. In the stories, I could see a lonely little girl who used to trudge five miles down a dusty path just to wave to a train, but I could hear pride, and a tradition of survival and strength. She was proud of the Stuarts and the Douglases and the Langhornes. They had pioneered that part of the country. They were men and women with vision and power.

I had been raised to believe that where you come from and your family make you what you are. I'd always figured, privately, there was a little more to it than that, but it was a fine heritage. Now, Grandmother was passing it on to my children, and I was grateful. I could put irritation in my pocket. How important is it who cooks the dinner when my own mother could give them so much?

"Write a song for me," Grandmother said one day. "I'll tell you what I want you to put in it, because I want it to tell about me when I was a little girl. I want it to be about the mountains in Virginia, and I want it to say, 'the mountains aren't blue when you get there.' I want a line about sailing in a cracker box in Katie's Creek, because I tried so many times to cross that little river. I want it to have a rainbow, because I used to run all day trying to find the end of the rainbow. I was so sure there would be a little three-legged pot full of gold. And I want it to say, 'I lost the magic of the mountains when I lost the magic of my love.'"

It took a long time, and I never managed to rhyme Katie's Creek, but I got her a box of wood on a river. I called it "When I Was Sure of You."

> I used to see a mountain, rising soft and blue,
> When everything was easy and all I had to do
> Was step across the shadowline
>   to make a soft blue mountain mine.
> And I was sure of you.
>
> I don't recall how many times we reached
>   to touch the sky.
> We ran to catch a rainbow, but we never could;
> No one told me why.
>
> I don't recall how many times
>   the two of us have tried
> To float across the river in a box of wood.
> But I know I cried, how many times I cried.

I still can see the mountain, rising soft and blue.
The climbing wasn't easy, but what I know is true;
That mountain rising far away is made of rock
    it's cold and gray,
And I'm not sure of you.
No, I'm not sure of you.

When the apartment closed in too much, I got on a bus and went up to see Ernesto. He and his friend Perc had bought a beautiful old Greek Revival house in Montgomery, and they were busy restoring it. Bedrooms were makeshift and the kitchen sink was in a shed, but it was fun to help with the plans and be there to discover what was under the paint.

I could take a bus to Ernesto's and I could take a train to Barbara's. There was more tension at Barbara's house. She was getting anxious to go back to work. It had been five years and Susi was old enough. I understood how important work was and I understood her. She was my friend. It had begun to occur to me that I had several friends! I had Ernesto and Barbara. I had Mary Ann and Betty, and I had Tucker. Though the relationships went back to before the divorce, the friendships were mine. They could not fill the time, but they took the edge off the loneliness.

Time was something I had to fill myself, and most evenings or weekends it was still the words and the music.

For two years I had written a lot of songs, as Cynthia said, about "passion and awareness." I had also written many, many songs about love and meaningful relationships. I rhymed "real" with "feel," and "share" with "care" too often. Song titles like "People in Love," or "I've Built Another Dream," are a definite clue to the state of mind I was in. True love, however, continued to elude me. I still had no idea how to start having a social life, let alone how to meet a single man. I went to a couple of parties at Mary Ann's, but they were elegant, formal evenings, and if anybody was eligible they were too polite to mention it. The most interesting man at those parties was Mary Ann's husband, Michel, a slim, gray-haired man who spoke softly with a French accent and had the kindest eyes I had ever seen. Perhaps it was the way he looked at me.

Finally, late in March, after almost two years, I met Ed and realized to my horror that, desperate as I was, he did not appeal to me or the kids. They promptly started calling him "Old Ed." They said it was because "Young Ed," the doctor, was still dropping in now and then for a free meal, and they didn't want to get confused. That wasn't the reason and I knew it. In a way they were right. He was a little stodgy and told me the first time we had dinner that he was glad I wasn't too fond of him, because he didn't want to get involved! At least that simplified matters. I didn't especially like him, and he didn't seem to care. We started going out together once every couple of weeks. That was a strict rule. He owned some movie theatres and managed some others, so we went to movies. He had a beautiful house in the Village and a wonderful collection of classical records, so we listened to music. We liked the same kind of food, and he was very tolerant if I wasn't hungry enough to order a whole dinner and just picked off his plate. Actually, for a couple of people who didn't care about each other, we got along pretty well, once every couple of weeks.

Spring came, and the kids and I went to Eleuthera again. Summer came, and the kids went to camp. Choosing a camp was always traumatic. They both changed every year, so obviously I never hit it right. Cynth had been to a fancy French camp with her friend Carla Javits. Then she and Jeff went to Brother and Sister camps in Vermont that were next to each other.

I waited with Cynth for her bus to leave. The group on her bus was older and oddly street-wise for my little girl. Jeff's group was a wiry bunch of athletes, and Jeff was still overweight. My heart sank. I'd have kept them both home, but it wasn't possible. I knew it and they knew it. At least I didn't cry until the bus was out of sight. It was another one of those sickening choices, and I never knew whether I was right or wrong. I would write them every day and, after all, they would learn to sail and water-ski and swim like fish, whether they enjoyed it or not!

Of course, I projected my own loneliness on top of theirs and I knew it, for all the good that did, so I would say to myself, "Go

home, Mary! So it's the wrong damn camp, they'll live through it!
I'll take them someplace fun when they get home and make it
up."

I did go home, and every day I wrote them and ate my can
of tuna fish. It was hot and muggy. There was nothing but reruns
on television. My hands left sweaty marks on the guitar. Still, I
sat there and wrote and petted my cat.

> Looking out my window, when the sun
>   is shining high,
> I can see a sparrow flying by; and a breeze,
> I can see it bend the trees.
> People come, people go,
> Some I've never seen before,
> But they live behind each door.
> They're part of me, my reality
> Is the place I see.
>
> Looking out my window, when the moon
>   is shining white,
> I can see the yellow squares of light.
> Dark and still, just beyond my window sill
> Shadows come, shadows go.
> Then my window, as I pass, has become
>   a looking-glass.
> My face I see; my reality
> Is inside of me.

In July, Ernesto said, "You've got to get out of that apartment! Let's go on a vacation."

"Okay," I said instantly. "Where?"

He thought for a few minutes. "Perc has a beach house on
the Gulf, in Texas."

"Texas in August!"

"Well, it's hot, but it's on the water."

"It's away from here! Let's go!"

Old Ed took me out a few nights before we left. We went
up to the Rainbow Grill, where Helen O'Connell was opening. It
was fun and pretty, and I hadn't seen Helen in years, so I was excited. Ed was attentive. He seemed really sorry I was going away.

He kept touching my hand, and there was a very tender look on his face I hadn't seen before. The kids were gone. So was Grandmother. Suddenly, after all the months, it was all right, and I wanted him to stay.

Freeport was fun, but not restful. Every evening half a dozen cars would cruise down our little road and we'd wind up with twelve for dinner. We laughed, we waltzed to a player piano in the ballroom of an empty plantation house. We bobbed across the gulf in a shrimp boat. We ate Mexican food and drank cold beer, and when a very young business associate of theirs showed up to stay with us for a couple of days he took me swimming in the middle of the night, and we kissed in the moonlight.

"The Burtons have nothing on us," he said, and I giggled.

Perc and Ernesto were waiting on the porch when we got back, not looking pleased at all, and I was delighted. I'd been kissed and somebody cared!

It was a real vacation and I had a lot to look forward to. The kids would be home soon, and I booked the three of us on a ten-day charter to London the second week in September. There was a new kind of relationship with Ed, and the very first evening I was home he said, "My house has gone on the market, but I told them no. You'd rather have a house with more sun, wouldn't you?" Something wonderful and warm gurgled in my middle. It was a proposal. It was more than that, it was an assumption, and I almost cried with joy. Yes, I did want a house with sunlight and a strong, quiet, thoughtful man. He took the kids and me out for dinner a couple of times before we left for England, and once we went with his two daughters, like a real family. I wanted a house with sunlight very much.

"When you get home from London," he said, "let's go away for a weekend."

The winter tenants had not moved into the little house yet, and it seemed like the perfect place to spend the first weekend alone with him. He took some scripts to read and a couple of books. We bought groceries and it was cool enough in the evening for a fire. I was so happy I was almost silly. I couldn't resist kissing the top of his head every now and then as I passed his chair, and I hummed while I cooked the dinner.

"Now, just leave me alone until I finish this," he said, and for an instant the little undertone of tolerance reminded me of Harry.

It was a lovely weekend. I'd always loved the way the moon traveled across the windows in that bedroom. Richard and I had never been happy there and now I was. Really happy. So happy I was still bubbling all the way back to New York.

When he stopped the car in front of our building he said, "I'm going to be out of town for a few days, but I'll call you when I get back. Maybe we can have dinner." The last phrase sounded oddly casual and distant.

"What do you mean, 'maybe'?" I said it lightly, but I watched his face.

"Well, you know how I am," he said. "Don't like to see anybody more than once every two weeks. Don't want to get too involved."

I couldn't believe he was saying that. He had proposed to me, and I had just spent the weekend with him, and I was standing there at the damn bus stop with tears about to roll down my cheeks. I picked up my suitcase and hurried into the building. I managed to get into the apartment without Mother or the kids noticing and went straight to my bathroom and closed the door. It's the place I had always gone to cry when I knew it was going to be bad. I could put a towel over my face to stifle the sound, so no one would hear me and be upset. I stayed in the bathroom a long time and Ed didn't call again for almost a year.

It was hard for me to understand what I had done wrong with Ed. I just automatically assumed I had done something. I had not fallen in love on the first date. It had been a long, slow progression toward what I thought was a lovely conclusion. Perhaps, I decided, I fell in love the way I drove a car—in the wrong lane.

I was sad, but the kids remained calm and philosophical.

Jeff said, "You'll probably get at least two lyrics out of it, Mom."

"And maybe an instrumental," Cynthia added.

"Two lyrics and an instrumental," Grandmother liked the

sound of that. "Two lyrics and an instrumental," she repeated cheerfully and headed for the kitchen to burn another chicken.

"He was too old for us anyway," she added, apropos of nothing, as she clicked on Walter Cronkite, and life was back to normal.

Normal, I finally decided, wasn't bad, either. The gynecologist gave me an "all clear." The show was a happy place to go to, and the kids were in great shape. Jeff began to take a different kind of interest in school. All the reading he had done on his own started to fit into his English classes and History courses. In his spare time, he tutored some children from the public high school near Trinity. For the first time he also began to take an interest in the school newspaper. His second grade teacher, Mrs. Riccardi, had set him on the right road when he was seven. Now Mr. Bundy, the faculty adviser for the paper, appeared at the right moment and took over.

Richard had moved to Maryland, and Jeff started visiting down there. One night, when I must have started to zing Richard, Jeff turned on me:

"Leave him alone! He's my father!"

There was no way to avoid the fact that I was wrong, and I'm sure I tried. At least I was getting smart enough to realize that.

Sometime that fall Pearl started managing the apartment house where she lived and decided that was all she could handle. It probably was, since she had also adopted seventeen stray cats. She still called if she had a problem, of course, and stopped in to fry chicken every now and then and see the kids. When Pearl left, Lucille took over. She never seemed to mind Grandmother's helpful advice and I don't remember a time when we didn't share the responsibility and the joy. It is our house.

I had my family and my apartment and my job. I was even beginning to feel pretty secure about money. I'd met a fancy stockbroker at one of the parties in my brief social season after the divorce, and he had run my savings up to a really respectable amount. Every time I saved a little money I'd send it down to him. Grandmother loved the stock market, and she kept track of the stocks he bought and sold, keeping a careful account in a black, loose-leaf book.

I was healthy, I had some money, my guitar, and the yellow pads. Love was still an elusive magic ring I could not seem to step inside of, but my fantasies were real to me. I kept imagining a kind of sensitivity and commitment, a depth of emotion I had never actually come across except with friends, or in music. It was there, in the chords that Barbara played, in the way she voiced them. Her music was satisfying in a way a conversation can never be. It was there, in the closeness with Perc and Ernesto when we drove through the country around their place and stopped to gaze at a street in the tiny town, or a farmhouse, or a tree. It was there in every moment with Tucker—in his face, in the poetry he collected for me, in the records he played, or the perfect Sundays he planned with brunch at the Plaza and a long walk through Central Park.

Perhaps, I thought, the kind of love I imagine does not exist with a man, at least not for me. Perhaps I passed the time when that was possible, when I was younger.

Late in October the very young man from the beach in Texas came to New York on business. I had forgotten how tall and handsome he was. We spent a lovely, late afternoon walking in the park, watching the trees turn and the lights of the city come to life. We stopped for dinner and walked home, talking all the time.

Toward the end of November he called long distance to say he would be in town Tuesday and Wednesday. We laughed over cocktails and talked seriously through dinner. We walked through the winter streets of the city, looking in the windows, and stopped for a nightcap in a silly, noisy bar when we got cold.

"I'm only staying a block away," he said, and there was an echo in his voice of the tenderness I spent so much time imagining. When we came out of the hotel it was after three and snow had blanketed the city. There was not a soul anywhere and not a sound. Neither of us had boots, and it was two miles to my apartment, but for some reason that just seemed funny, and we leaned against the building, laughing so hard the tears froze on our cheeks.

"Look," he said, taking my hand and pointing with the other. There were two headlights searching the darkness down

the middle of the deserted street and the glow of a tiny yellow
dome. A taxi! Probably the only empty taxi in New York, coming
right toward us.

"It's a sign," he said. "We're going to be good friends for a
long time." It wasn't love, but we were close and we accepted
each other. Acceptance was a dimension I hadn't thought of before.

By November, Tucker's speech problem had become so serious it was difficult to work and social life was a trial. His therapist
had sent him to see an internist, and the internist sent him to a
specialist. Two weeks before Christmas he was admitted to University Hospital for tests.

He missed the Christmas party for "Search," and on Christmas Eve he was still in the hospital. Everyone agreed we couldn't
have Christmas Eve without Tucker, so we packed up the champagne and the caviar and the presents and went to him. It was
snowing again, and the streets were still and white; still and white
as the tiny room with the snow outside the window and his face
against the pillow.

He didn't taste the caviar, but he took a sip of the champagne as we helped him open his presents. He had presents for
us, too; a book for Jeff, fur slippers for Cynth, and that year he
gave me a quilt his great-grandmother had made. None of us had
any idea that he had been through a spinal tap that afternoon
and must have been ready to scream with the pain.

Tucker was supposed to be released from the hospital two
days later, but there was no answer when I called. There was no
answer for three weeks. He had often refused to answer the
phone, but that was too long. When he finally answered he
sounded very far away, and his voice was so thick I had trouble
understanding him at all. It was two or three more weeks before
he finally let me come to see him. He would cook, he said.

As always, he tried to show me how he did it. He showed me
how to clarify the butter before he cooked the entrecôte, and how
to make the marinade for the mushrooms. I didn't care about preparing steak or mushrooms. I watched, and listened, and waited.

After dinner, he put on a record and after a long time he

said, "I'm sorry I ran away. You worried." He was tired and skipped words.

"Of course I worried. Are you all right now?"

He nodded, and the silence was suddenly threatening.

"Do they know what's the matter with you?"

He shrugged. "Long word."

"What's the long word?"

He picked up a pencil and wrote it on a piece of paper:

AMYOTROPHIC LATERAL SCLEROSIS

"What does that mean?"

"Going to get worse."

"How much worse?"

He cocked his head to one side and grinned. "Sign," he said, and made motions with his fingers. "Teach you."

"Sign language? You won't be able to talk at all?" He shook his head. "Tucker, there must be other doctors, other hospitals . . ."

He shook his head again. "No," he said, and for the first time that evening he looked straight into my face.

That's how he told me he was going to die. We never, ever said the word.

The next day I went to see my doctor, with the hideous words on the piece of paper, and he told me about Tucker's illness. He would lose his speech completely as the muscles in his throat and neck became paralyzed. He would have more and more trouble swallowing as the paralysis traveled down his body, and eventually he would have to be hospitalized.

"Two years," he said. Two years would be maximum.

Tucker was thirty-seven years old and he only had two years to live. He had a lot to do. There was his Commonplace book he kept with poems and clippings and notes each day. There was a director's manual of *Hamlet* that he had begun and must be finished. He had ongoing chess games with at least twenty people at any given moment. He had a running correspondence with Julia Child and William Buckley, and he was determined that I would learn to cook at least a few things perfectly. We spent an evening on omelets, and one on crepes suzette, and we began to work on French bread. There we ran into a snag, because you need a wet brick to make the oven steam. I never could find one that hadn't already been anointed by a New York dog, so after gassing the apartment a few times we gave that up.

Communication became more and more difficult. He was studying sign language, and I had learned the alphabet, but he usually resorted to large sheets of paper until his speech was totally gone. Then a major miracle occurred.

Tucker couldn't help noticing the young couple on the elevator and was surprised when they got off on his floor and walked to his end of the corridor. Finally he realized they were the new couple in the studio next to his. He smiled as they stopped by the door and he turned to his own. But his hands had weakened too much. He couldn't grasp the knob. He couldn't ask for help because, of course, he couldn't speak. Somehow, the young man felt the look. He held his hand out for the key and unlocked the door. Five minutes later a little three-by-five card was slipped under their door. It had a scribbled cartoon of Tucker and the words "I'm speechless."

By the time I met them, Den could understand almost everything Tucker said, and Cindy could translate almost as fast as he could sign. That was cause for celebration and certainly reason for a party. Tucker planned it and cooked everything, probably over the course of several days. Dinner for eight people, and everybody had a wonderful time. He told stories and laughed, and by the end of the evening it seemed natural that an idea could originate in one head and come out in another. We also established a pattern that night that continued through the rest of his illness. Each major change was a reason for a party. After that one there would only be four of us, but it was still a party.

Dear Mary—

Thank you for phoning to say all went well on Friday. I was quite nervous and uncertain about the whole thing; it was my first major hosting in a year, and I was worried that I'd invited too many people, that I was spreading myself too thin, that I was overworking poor Cindy, and so forth. Your nice words were just what the doctor ordered.

You are wise to see the rare fineness of the Murphys. They are good the way a rose is red or a lilac smells nice. And what I like most about what passes between us is that so much of it is unspoken, and need not be spoken . . .

Love to you and all your brood,

Tuck

Back in March an odd thing had happened. I got a call from Norwell's sister. A voice out of the past.

"Mary, dahling! How are you? This is Dana. Remember me?"

"Dana! For goodness' sake, of course! How in the world are you? Where in the world are you?"

"I'm here, in New York! Listen, I hear you're divorced."

"Yes, for three years now."

"Well, isn't that a coincidence! Norwell is getting divorced too. He doesn't know I know, but he is. So listen, I'm giving a little party for him. I think it would be very nice if you just happened to meet, and while he's in New York you could see each other. You know, the family always thought he should have married you."

Dana's rich voice, with the Gabor accent, had taken on a conspiratorial tone. I didn't have a lot of faith in matchmakers, but she did give good parties, and she knew a lot of interesting people.

Norwell was twenty years older, but the years suited him. I was twenty years older too. His face, which had never been handsome, was strong, and he walked like a man who is sure of himself.

We had dinner several times before he went back to London, and it was fun to talk about the past. We had been young together. It was pleasant to remember.

"I still have the ring," he said one night. "I've married two women since, but I still have your ring." Several times he asked why I had traveled so little in Europe.

"Come to London this summer," he said, "and I'll take you on the honeymoon you missed." By the time he left, a little of the old spark was glowing.

Dear Mary,

I've been invited out to Boonton for the rest of this week; a woody dell (which is what my friend's place is *in*) sounds like a fine perspective from which to view the young Spring. Santayana says somewhere that "though the world may lose its memory, it will never lose its youth"—and long about April I believe it!

Your pal,

Tucker

All through April, Grandmother worried about the stock market. She carried her copy of Standard & Poor's around the house, and every day she looked up my stocks in the morning paper.

"It looks bad," she kept saying, "but you are in good stocks. You can weather it, I think." Then one day she said, "I want you to call your broker and make sure your stocks are in your name. If you have a street account, he can do anything he wants."

"He can do anything he wants, anyway, Mother. It's a discretionary account. You know that."

"But if the company goes under and you don't have the stocks in your name, you'll lose everything."

Grandmother was the world's champion worrier, but to please her I called my fancy broker.

"Absolutely, everything is in your name," he assured me. "You have nothing to worry about, and if it really looks bad you know I'll get you out before you get hurt."

About the middle of May the stock market began to slide, but he had assured me and, as Grandmother kept saying, I was in good, solid stocks. Grandmother said it over and over, though when she left for Oklahoma in June she was still worried.

Dear Snick—

No, this is not a letter from your well-brought-up 6 year old nephew; it just happens to be a letter from one of the greatest minds of the Western World, whose Goddam son of a bitch of an electric typewriter tipped, teetered, tottered, fell, and "punished the parquet" (to borrow one of Cole Porter's happier phrases).

Well, it's already taken an entire "Search for Tomorrow" episode to get *this* far (and you know how long *they* are) so I'll sign off shortly—but—O Mother of God!—there's so much I want to *say* to you! Not in "answer" to your beautiful, beautiful letter, because it asked no questions: it just gave and gave and *gave,* teaching me, reteaching me—as have my glorious Murphys—that giving is the name of the game; and it's the only game in town.

Love now & ever,

Tuck

"No more camp!" Jeff had decreed, and I concurred with my whole heart. Even if he could have stood it, I couldn't. But I didn't have any bright ideas. It was Richard who came up with the solution. Friends of his had a ranch in Oregon, right next to an Indian reservation, and every summer they sponsored a kind of seminar with kids from the reservation and neighboring ranches and a sprinkling of urban youngsters. It was decided. The young man would go West. Cynthia had a new best friend, and she and Sally wanted to go to music camp in Maine. Everybody was going where they wanted to go, for once! I was free and clear. I would go where I wanted, too!

I wrote Norwell, giving him the dates of my vacation from the show. I tried to sound very casual, just in case he had changed his mind or had never been serious in the first place. Almost immediately I got a very formal itinerary, typed by a secretary, with a little personal note scribbled by him. We would go from London to Barcelona, to the Costa del Sol, to Rome, and back to London. I had never been to Spain or Italy. For him, it was a normal business trip, but for me it was a new and very exciting adventure. I began to shop for clothes. The trip was a whole month away, plenty of time to shop and, of course, daydream. After all, we had been sort of in love once. It could happen again. Anything could happen. He had said he would take me on a honeymoon, hadn't he?

I also began very casually to picture what it would be like married to a wealthy, sophisticated European. An apartment in London across from the Connaught and a place in Paris. A ski lodge in Austria and two little boys to raise. The fact that I lived and worked in New York muddied my picture only a little, like the fact that he wasn't quite divorced. Those were just details. The word I liked was "honeymoon," and by the time I got on the plane, Rhoda Romance was ready for one.

Actually, it was a beautiful trip, just not quite the one I had imagined. Most of the time I spent the days alone, sightseeing. When we met for cocktails and dinner, there were nearly always several other people with us, his business associates and friends, and they changed languages, it seemed to me, with each course. Not that it made any difference. I couldn't understand any of them, but I loved the way Norwell glided from one to the other. I also loved the way he ordered dinner and checked into a hotel, or told the limousine driver the shortest route.

There were no castles in Spain, at least not where we were. There were lots of trailer parks until we got to the hotel, which was almost like a castle. It was white and stood on top of the hill overlooking the sea, and that was as blue as the songs. I wanted to cry when I looked down from my window.

Barcelona was all brown, except for the geraniums in almost every window, and I met a beautiful old guitar maker. He was eighty-three and said he couldn't deliver a guitar for eight years, but he would take the order. I bought a guitar in a tiny street with laundry strung across it like flags. I found a whole Roman city down under the cathedral. I was the only tourist, and the guide held my hand and spent a whole afternoon showing me his treasures. The earth was yellow-brown, and tiny, flat-topped trees clung to the ridge of the mountains. The children had such serious faces.

It was difficult to talk to Norwell about things we hadn't seen together, and we spent almost no time alone. By the time we got to Rome I had already stored up too many images, too many feelings. If I had spent that first day in Rome by myself, I don't think I could have stood it. But I met two college boys on the American Express bus, and they saved the day. The tour covered the Forum and St. Peter's, and when it was over we took off in their Volkswagen. We climbed around the Colosseum and drove out the Via Appia Antica, then round and round the red and ocher streets of Trastevere. At five o'clock they drove me back to my hotel, and we sat out on the terrace, looking down on St. Peter's, passing my guitar back and forth.

One of them said, "This morning we were strangers, now we've been to Heaven and back together."

Very late that night, at a party with Norwell, I happened to see a little piece of ancient sculpture in a case. It was a cycladic face, a perfect, pure oval with a high, slanted forehead. Somehow, it struck a note that shattered the last defense, and the tears finally came. Norwell was moved, but he didn't understand.

We had a little time alone back in London.

"It's nice to come home and see you sitting there with the guitar," he said. His face was sad. He wanted his boys raised in the States, but there were those little facts in the picture, like divorces, and two thousand miles, and twenty years of very different lives.

"Do you have to do that show forever?" It was the one question I never asked myself. It was the final security, but in that moment I let go of a large corner.

"I think I could do it part-time."

When he drove me to the airport he was sure he would be in New York within a couple of months and I flew home, still imagining myself fitted into his life.

Cynth came home golden tan and humming, almost as tall as I am. Jeff came home a man. He was taller and slimmer, and a change was in his eyes. Richard's idea of letting him go to Oregon had obviously been wiser than we could have hoped. He didn't talk much about the summer. When I asked about it, he said, "Oh, we worked."

"Doing what?"

"Cutting hay, laying pipe, putting in fences."

The idea of Jeff doing any of the three was amazing enough. I'd never known him to make his bed. Then I picked up the manual he brought home, describing the seminar, and noticed his name listed as an instructor.

"Jeff, what did you teach?"

"Computer science."

"You what?"

"Well, the guy who was supposed to teach it left, and somebody had to. It's what the kids from the reservation wanted to learn."

"What do you know about computer science?"

"More than they did. It's really just the new math, Mom." He was beginning to sound patient. "It's pretty simple, and they were hooked up by phone to a computer in San Francisco. The people there helped me."

A few weeks later the family he'd been staying with told me another story. It seemed that all the kids slept outside on the ground while the seminar was in session. One evening, there were about twenty of them sitting around the open campfire when Jeff noticed that one of the older boys was squirting lighter fluid into the fire.

"Stop it!" he yelled, but the boy just smiled and sent a long stream toward the flames.

"Get away, everybody!" Jeff tackled the boy, wrestled the can out of his hand and threw it out of reach. The boy was older and stronger, and managed to get away, but at least he didn't have a live bomb in his hand. He ran off into the woods, and Jeff spent the whole night looking for him.

I don't believe Jeff thought the episode was important at all. It was just part of the first summer he could begin to be himself, not part of a family or a group, just himself.

Dear Snickelfritz—

. . . All jesting towards one side, do you want to know a very marvellous and true fact? You are one hell of an actress and

could doubtless play the hell [out] of the Bronx phone direc-
tory if they threw it at you (what am I *saying?* They have!
They have!) but you're *positively incandescent* when you are
playing (as now) a person *who is in love* . . . your scenes
with Tony are the *best work I have ever seen you do.*

There is a lightness, a sweetness, a dearness, a sense of a
slight-breeze-passing-thru-you. The unexpected. The under-
stated. The subliminal. The playful.

Mary, I hope you're free sometime tomorrow (Friday)—but
surely this weekend (for which I've made *no* engagements)
we will make it work. And work. And work.

1 tablespoon of love
after each meal,

Tucker
M.D.

Toward the end of August an unusually thick envelope arrived from the fancy broker. He always sent me "copies" of trans-
actions he made, and this one contained about twenty slips.

"That's what I was afraid of," Grandmother said as she
spread them out on the dining room table. She got out her little
black loose-leaf book and her copy of Standard & Poor's.

"He's churning your account," she said after a few minutes.
"There's three thousand dollars in brokerage this month alone,
and he's sold all your good stocks."

"What did he buy?"

"I don't know. I never heard of most of them."

I called him, and he assured me that he had sold the blue-
chip stocks because they had held their value, and he could get
more cash to buy stocks he felt had already bottomed out and
would be moving up. He reminded me that he had done well before, and was still doing right for me. The stock market was going
to hell and everybody was getting hurt, but he knew what he was
doing. When I asked him, point-blank, a second time, if the
stocks were in my name he said, "Absolutely, yes."

Three weeks later another envelope arrived, thicker than the
last, with over three thousand dollars in brokerage fees. That

night on the news there was a report that a major brokerage firm was in grave danger of going under. In *The Wall Street Journal* the next day the reports were confirmed, and it was the brokerage firm that handled my stocks. My fancy broker was taking no calls, but I left a message with his secretary that I would be down in an hour to pick up my stock certificates and put them in a safe-deposit box.

"I'm sorry, madam. No certificates can be removed from the office."

"They belong to me. They're in my name."

"Just a moment, madam."

"I'll wait."

"I'm sorry, madam, but according to our records those certificates are in the company name. They will be held until a decision is made about the future of the company."

I had trusted him and he had lied to me. He had used me.

A few days later another major brokerage firm bought the company, so there was no bankruptcy, but when Grandmother added up what I had left it was almost exactly the amount I had started with.

I remember looking at the figure in the book and thinking how odd it was I wasn't more upset. I went ahead and fixed supper. When I took Jeff's tray back to his room he was working on a short story and he let me read a couple of pages. Cynth had come back from music camp enthused about the piano again, and she was practicing. Actually, the money had only been numbers in a little black book. It was amazing! Our life hadn't changed at all.

Of course, Grandmother was upset. She was frightened and furious. She clucked around the house for weeks. "Well, I hope this is a lesson to you. You trust absolutely anyone! You might just as well throw the money out the window."

"Mother, he did well for me for a long time."

"He told you those stocks were in your name. He lied to you."

"Yes, he did. I know."

"Well, that's what I mean. You have to stop trusting people."

"No!" I said the word with too much feeling, and it startled her. "Mother, if I stopped trusting I wouldn't be able to act or write my songs, or . . . believe. If I stopped trusting I couldn't live. I've lost money, but it's only money. I can earn some more. If I stop trusting, I've lost everything."

I did try to write a song about it, about how I felt, but it wasn't important enough. There was no story, no real point of view. I couldn't stop trusting, but I did start waking up every morning between three and four in a cold sweat of terror. Sometimes I would just light a cigarette. Occasionally I would go to the kitchen for a glass of milk.

"What were you doing up in the middle of the night?" Cynthia asked one morning.

"Oh, the baddies came and got me," I said very casually.

She knew exactly what I meant, and Jeff said, "Oh, for God's sake!"

Dearest Mary—

You are something else . . . and then some. Awaiting me at my very doorstep were 24—count 'em—24 little loaves of bread—homemade white and glorious Jewish brown—wrapped for the freezer, thinly sliced and perfectly designed to save me countless long treks to the corner grocery from here to Thanksgiving! I have so much to thank you for that I wouldn't know where to begin—But I wouldn't *mind* beginning with the bread: "baskets covered with white towels swelling the house with their plenty." (I quote from Whitman: you deserve no less). And much more, more than I could ever itemize . . . You are beautiful. Love,

Tucker

In February, Norwell finally got to New York and I saw him every night for a week. As usual, there was a crowd everywhere we went. He had screenings to go to and distributors to meet. He did talk about my apartment. He was glad it had enough bedrooms for everybody, and we talked about money. His divorce wasn't final, but he was making progress. He talked a great deal about moving to New York. The taxes in London were taking too much and again he mentioned wanting the boys to be educated here. It was as though he assumed we would pick up where we left off twenty years before, and the idea was more and more appealing. He was strong and kind, and had made a place for himself. I liked his friends, even though I wished there weren't quite so many of them around all the time.

Once, when I was ordering food sent up to his suite at the hotel, I said, "This is his wife," but when I tried to stay over with him I got frightened and lonely and went home.

When he was getting ready to leave he said, "I'll meet you in California in June, and this summer we'll take a long trip together. Maybe spend a week on Capri or Malta."

It was easier to think about our life together after he was gone. Lord knows, I had plenty of time. The kids got very good at imitating his walk and his accent. Jeff had a name for him that bore a rude resemblance to his favorite drink, which was a Bull Shot, and Grandmother said, "His eyes are too small. Never trust a man who has small eyes."

Jeff stayed close to his room all winter, as he always had, but instead of reading he was hunting and pecking away on his typewriter. Over the winter vacation he took a crash course in touch typing. Cynth spent a lot of time in her room, too, studying, and talking on the phone. My Christmas present to myself was an extra line for the two of them. I was still writing most of the time, with weekends now and then at Indian Hill with Perc and Ernesto, and an occasional evening with Mary Ann and Michel. Those were very special evenings. The butler opened the door and immediately the big red retriever jumped all over me. He knew me, I belonged.

It was a beautiful house, full of beautiful things. I suppose the furniture and the paintings could have been in a museum, but with five kids and the dog running up and down the stairs it never seemed that way. It seemed quiet and gracious, like a house in another less hurried time, and as soon as I walked up the wide staircase I was part of it.

If there was a dinner party, Mary Ann usually put me on Michel's right and I always thought it was her way of saying I was a special friend and that Michel was fond of me. He let me know it, too. He was fond of me and interested in my life and the kids. He also let me know that no matter what I asked of him he would take time to give me an answer and, if possible, a solution.

The occasion was rare, but when Mary Ann and I did spend time alone everything simply fell into place. We never understood why. We really had almost nothing in common. Our backgrounds and our lives couldn't have been more different. We were simply friends, it was enough. Neither of us has ever been talkative, especially about problems, but somehow her presence gave me a different perspective on mine. Just the fact of her affection seemed to restore self-esteem and was a source of strength in itself. She said I did the same for her, but I could never imagine her needing anything I had to give. To me, she had it all. She ran her house and raised all those kids. In a room full of extraordinary people she was always the most beautiful and also the most unassuming. She could be enchanting and vivacious, but more often she sat listening, attentive, completely absorbed. Most amazing of all, it seemed to me, she handled a car like a racing driver, and I didn't find out for years that she hated driving almost as much as I do and couldn't park one bit better.

I just thought she was wonderful, but when I told her so she always demurred, "I never really did anything myself, and you've done it all—all by yourself."

One day I told her about the lady in brown and how I had watched her and envied her.

"They called me the Brown Mouse. For years I hid in brown coats and maternity clothes. Who could look up to a mouse?"

"Only another one, I guess. They called me Mary Mouse."

We still didn't talk about it, but we each understood where the other had been.

After an evening with Mary Ann and Michel I felt better about nearly everything.

The big event, however, was Barbara's opening at Shepheard's. She got wonderful reviews and did great business, and it was just like the good old days for her. She went to Chicago for a few weeks and bookings for the next season started coming in.

Tucker was weaker, but he was still managing. Cindy did his

shopping for him and put his laundry in with hers. He still worked on his *Hamlet,* kept up his correspondence, his chess games, and his wonderful letters to me. In the spring, Mr. Buckley wrote him a long letter asking him to come on his show. He had enjoyed the correspondence so much. Tucker had to decline. Of course, he had never mentioned that he was mute. He was beginning to fall occasionally, so even a trip to a neighborhood movie was a project. Den was always there to catch him, or lift him so quickly and gently no one else had time to notice. Tucker was spending more time in bed, and he decided that a waterbed would ease his body. That was, naturally, an occasion for a party. I took Chinese food up with me. It was the last time he could have that, it was too difficult to swallow. The waterbed, however, was a huge success.

It was time to make plans for the summer. Jeff would, of course, go back to Oregon, but that year he wanted even more adventure. He and his friend Bruce decided they wanted to get jobs working on a ranch. Cynthia would go adventuring too, all the way to France. It was time to use the language and perfect her accent, so she would spend the summer with a French family outside of Paris.

I kept saying I was going to meet Norwell in Europe, even though I hadn't heard from him for weeks. I had the month of August off the show, and I liked to say I was going to Capri or Malta. In the middle of June I got a letter. He was very sorry, he said. I was the last person in the world he wanted to hurt, but his life was too involved over the summer. It would be better if I didn't plan to come. Everybody in the family had seen the letter on the hall table, and they were waiting for me to read it. I didn't have to tell them what it said, they could see it in my face. For a little while, Grandmother looked very sad. She hated to see me cry. Finally, she stood her full five feet.

"Well, two lyrics and an instrumental," she said, with a finality that was oddly reassuring.

"Talk about last year's jelly beans," Jeff commented quietly from the next room, and Cynth put her arms around me.

"Maud, you knew it wasn't going to work. You were just making it up all the time. You know you're not too big on reality."

"I think you're right, Maud. I always could take it or leave it alone, now don't you worry. Grandmother's right, two lyrics and an instrumental."

Cynth didn't believe it would be that easy. "I'll sleep in your bed tonight, and you can wake me up when the baddies come and get you."

"Oh, for God's sake," Jeff said, and I thought he was beginning to sound very much like his father.

I did write a new song, but it wasn't about Norwell, it was about Old Ed! It occurred to me, fleetingly, that there were several similarities between my two rotten romances. The song was called "Done It Again."

Sometime that fall I heard that Norwell had a new son. Poor love, when he wrote that letter he was already married. I also heard she was very young.

Dear Robespierre:

My time is pressed: I have four hundred letters to answer: most of them demanding my body, poor dears.

But I always have time for you:

Do you know: extreme adversity is not a bad thing, not a bad thing at all. Because all of a sudden you see love blooming, blooming in all sorts of places. In a Mary Stuart whose loyalty is a benediction. In her mother, who gathers up her love and places it in a Pyrex dish. In a New York cabbie who leaves his front seat and rushes around to the other side to help me into his cab. In a Kelly Wood, who, timidly, graciously brings me a lovely gift. In an indescribably sweet and beautiful letter from a sweet and beautiful man—Ken Harvey. And a Billie Lou, who is a continuing grace to this earth.

So sure: it would be nice to be able to walk and talk. But I will borrow for a moment Miss Emily Dickinson (she won't mind) to say:

Behold the atom I preferred to all the lists of clay!

She was referring of course, to love. Which, when we poor, confused, silly, mistaken, proud, and weak human beings pull ourselves together long enough to realize it, is the very first priority.

If you had told me two years ago that I would be where I am today I would have said: Honey, you got rocks in your head: I'd kill myself first. Well, as you can see, I didn't; indeed, I have never felt less like killing myself. Human love is a flawed and often faithless commodity, but, it is well worth the hanging around, to see, catch, taste, and savor it.

You know you have mine,

Tucker

My birthday is the Fourth of July and Tucker's the sixteenth. In 1971 we decided to make a whole trip out of it. We rented a little cottage in Clinton, Connecticut, on the Sound, and the four of us took off in Den's purple Volkswagen. It did not occur to us until we got in the car that we looked to a casual passerby like a highly improbable group. Cindy was obviously pregnant, Den had grown hair to his shoulders on his head and face, Tucker was down to about eighty pounds and walked very unsteadily using a rose-thorn cane. I was my usual adorable self and would be more so in my pink bikini. We also realized on the way that the one thing we had each forgotten to bring was a hat. The only head covering we had between us was the tall, silk opera hat that Den had liberated from a movie he was working on. There was nothing to do but take turns wearing that. We remembered everything else we would need, all the birthday presents, the cassette machine and two large speakers, paper-thin bread with pâté that Tucker could swallow, and our kite.

It was a beautiful four days. We lugged the speakers to the beach in front of our cottage twice a day and played Tucker's potpourri of music and poetry. We passed the opera hat back and forth, and it looked just as bizarre with my pink bikini as it did on Cindy's round little body or Tucker's frail one. It looked fine on Den and even appropriate. He'd been a celebrity, anyway, since the day he decided to see what the kite could really do. There was a fine wind, and he had reeled out the first ball of twine and tied on our spare in the first half hour. We sent a kid to the store for another. When that was gone, another kid volunteered, and brought back two more balls, and then another. Six balls of twine he had let out, and the kite was a tiny black dot, barely visible. It took him four hours to haul it in.

That night at supper, Tucker said, with his tired fingers, "I think the kite touched heaven."

A week after we got back, Tucker went into the hospital for an operation. He was starving and they had to bypass his throat. When he came down from the operating room he was so weak he could hardly sign, but he still grinned at us. We couldn't find the hole! We thought it would be in his throat, like a tracheotomy.

"Joke!" he fingered, and pointed through the maze of tubes to his stomach. The hole went directly into his belly. "On you," he spelled slowly. "Now I can drink!"

From then on his food was prepared in the blender and dripped from an enema can Den rigged up on a pole, straight into his stomach. That was also the way he had his cocktails. He would order a case of Scotch, one bottle of something good for company, and eleven bottles of rotgut. He couldn't taste it, so what difference what went into the can. Den also put a device on his phone that triggered a cassette automatically. All he had to do was lift the receiver and touch a button. The voice would repeat, "Help! I'm a mute and I need an ambulance. My address is . . ." Den and Cindy hardly ever left the apartment, but the baby was coming, they might have to be gone.

Dear Snicklefritz—

(I know you're just raging with curiosity to learn how I found out your real name before you had it changed to Mary Stuart, but are just too damn proud to ask. That southern pride will be your undoing.)

Today was simply not my day. Your compassionate sympathy when I told you I wasn't feeling well was slightly misplaced: I felt rotten, all right, but it was my own damn fault: I had the granddaddy of all hangovers. On top of that—you won't believe this—my waterbed sprung a leak. Now wouldn't you think fate would just get tired of teasing me and go tease someone else for a change? The waterbed being essentially a product of the counter-culture, I am not too optimistic about the speed and skill of their repair service. Dependability is not one of your hippy's salient characteristics.

It wouldn't be proper for me to help your actor friend, but if I were to tell him anything, it would be what I tell all actors; what indeed I consider to be the "secret" of all good acting: i.e. find the leading trait of your character and play against it. (Which, in a way, may have a lot to do with the miraculous growth I've been seeing in you. What is Jo's leading trait? Why that's obvious—she is "good." And I think this incredible enlargement of your artistic palette I've been awesomely noting is that you are now playing *everything but* "good," and "everything but" is a hell of a lot richer than "only.")

I wish you could have seen me act in my heyday. I was a past master at the art of "everything but."

Basta!

Ever yours,
Tuck

No matter where the kids were, the habit of a drink and letters between five and six continued:

Tuesday evening

Maud,

At last, you are there and I guess you are fine. I could only read about a third of your letter, but that third sounded fine. Your father says, if I think I have trouble, his are illegible in French!

Lovely birthday with Tucker and celebrated his a week later. We made a special tape for him and I transferred it to cassette. Joanie and Vera did a scene from "Philadelphia Story." Vera was in the original cast and Joanie does Hepburn a little better than she does. Larry put on some old radio bits and we taped "Search" from the control room with all the racket, singing Happy Birthday at the end. Den gave him the silk opera hat, and now he won't take it off.

Had lots of conversations with your father. He is a lovely man. No wonder I married him. He is being a great friend and we are able to enjoy all the things we shared, like you. Poop I miss you but have fun . . . adventure . . . whatever. Tell me what you want to do, but for God's sake, print.

Your brother directed a production of "Life with Father." Where do you suppose he found seven red-headed Indians?

Love, Mom

Sweet Girl:

Good grief what a week! You are almost sixteen! How about that! We will celebrate when you come home, whenever that may be. Cabled you $300, which is kind of a present for now. Since I can't send you anything else.

Jeff is bouncing all over the place, too. Frantic calls in the middle of the damn night. Last night it was a panic about a hotel room in San Francisco. They've been working at the Huntleys' guest ranch but good old Brucie didn't like that, either. He's a hard fellow to please . . .

Thursday

Darling Heart,

Wrote a note to Mary Ann in Paris, saying you would call. She will worry if you don't, so do.

Lucille came in this morning with a check that bounced in 1969, so I guess I'll have a busy day tomorrow.

No, we can't change the ticket, but don't worry. You would eat more of the ninety-five bucks. STAY IF YOU WANT. I still don't have any plans, but if I decide to try a cruise, that might be fun together. So far, just on stand-by, but we'll see. You may have plans of your own . . . I know . . . I know! The new song title is, "A Place to Go!"

Love, Mom

It was the end of July. My vacation was perilously close, and I had no idea what to do with it. About six one evening, the phone rang. It was a young music producer named Chuck Glaser, calling from Nashville.

"You remember, I met you at Frank Music," he said, in a sweet, soft southern voice.

"Of course, I remember. I played some songs for you."

"That's right," he said, "and they gave me some tapes to bring back with me. I played them for my brothers and, if you're interested, I think we have a good idea."

"I'm interested." Truthfully, I was so interested my heart was beginning to pound.

"Well, we wondered if you'd like to come down and make some demos in our studio. We got a nice place here, and maybe we could put together enough for an album." He paused, and then he said, "Of course, I know you're busy."

"Well," I said, trying to sound busy, "how much time would it take?"

"We thought it would take about three weeks to get it together."

"Oh, well . . . uh . . . I think I could manage that. As it happens, I have a vacation coming up, and I hadn't really made any definite plans." I realized that sounded too eager, so I added, "I thought I might go to Europe, but it's not important."

"Well, then, you come on down," he said, and he was beginning to sound excited too. "I'll get you a hotel room, and we'll make us some music."

Ten days later, Chuck met me at the airport, picked up my suitcase and my guitar with hands that would wrap twice around the neck of a twelve-string, and drove me to The King of the Road. The girl behind the desk said, "Sure is nice to have you with us, Mary. My name's Louise." From then on, everybody in the hotel was another first name.

When I walked into my room, there were flowers from Tucker. The card read, "If music be the food of love, play on."

I had started falling in love with Tennessee from the airplane. It got greener and lusher close to Nashville, with all the lakes and rivers, and I picked out a beautiful piece of bottomland I knew Grandmother would love, before we landed. Maybe I was just ready to love Nashville, I'm not sure, but I do know it happened fast. Chuck drove me past the old Opry House in Printer's Alley, down the big, main street full of music stores and cowboy boots to Music City, and I felt as if I had come home. All those little houses—like the ones from my childhood, with alleys out behind, cluttered with junk.

"But where are the studios?"

"You're lookin' at 'em."

"Where?"

"Right there . . . see the sign?"

Behind a low wall was an old house that was all rebuilt, and, sure enough, the sign said RECORDING STUDIO, but right next door, the porch was falling down in the corner and an old lady was sitting in the swing in a cotton wrapper. The whole street was like that. The studios were in the houses, two or three on every block, but all the rest were just houses where folks lived, cutting the grass sometimes, sometimes not.

Chuck's studio was in an old, two-story apartment house. Just inside the door, there was a Coke machine and a pretty receptionist named Vicki. The walls were lined with record jackets and pictures of Tompall and the Glaser Brothers. Upstairs in Chuck's office was a shiny gold record: "Gentle on My Mind." That was their first big hit as publishers, and the money from that song had built the studio.

"This is Vicki's husband, Kyle Lenning," Chuck said, and I looked into a sweet young face with soft, blond hair. Actually, he was twenty-one, but he could have passed for seventeen.

"You'll be working with him for a few days, getting the songs together."

That night, Chuck's wife, Beverly, got a sitter for their kids and drove in to have dinner with us. No one, except Beverly, could look like that and have six children. She was a child herself; tiny and slim and beautiful. We had rib-eye steaks and hash browns, and salad. We talked about music and their kids, how they met, and building the studio.

"Every dime always went to the studio," Beverly said, without a trace of rancor or regret. "I didn't even have a washing machine until the sixth one was coming."

In the morning Kyle picked me up in his van and drove me to the studio. I had lead sheets on most of the songs I'd brought with me, and tapes of a few. The rest I played as best I could on my own guitar, and Kyle made a lead sheet himself. Then he set up a mike for me, sat down at the piano, and we started rehearsing and setting keys. I had more range than I realized and Chuck liked showing it off, so he put some songs lower and some higher than I had ever sung. I felt like I was squawking.

"You sound fine," came a voice over the loudspeaker, and the engineer played back what we had just done. Of course, he'd helped a lot with echo and heaven knows what else, but it did sound pretty good. So I kept on singing. For three days I sang three or four hours a day. Then Chuck picked out the ten songs he liked best and handed me four little sheets of paper off his note pad:

Tuesday, 7 to 10:	Listening Lord
	Don't Look Back
Wednesday, 4 to 7:	Sweet Side of Living
	When I Was Sure of You
Thursday, 10 to 1:	Hold Me
	Back Against a Mountain
Friday, 1 to 6:	Lonely There
	Around the Corner
	Over Dubs
Monday, 7 to 10:	Green Coffee
	Looking Out My Window

I wasn't sure what it was, he was so matter-of-fact, but it was our recording schedule. Tuesday at seven sharp I met the bass player, named Bobby Dyson, and guitar player Harold Bradley, and a drummer named Mark Morris. Kyle would play keyboards and the three of them, it turned out, would play everything else they could reach.

The first song was "Listening Lord." Kyle had given it a "rock" feel I wasn't used to singing. Of course, I wasn't used to singing anything. Except for a few little demos I hadn't worn earphones or thought about leaning into a mike since the first record in 1955. My hands and feet were like ice from nervousness, and the whole hour it took us to get a good track of that song I never took my eyes off the "N" in the signature on the microphone. I inhaled and sang automatically, and my pulse seemed to match the rhythm that was pounding in my ears.

"That's a good one," Chuck spoke over the system. "Come in and listen."

Everybody went into the control room and Claude, the engineer, rolled the tape back in a high-pitched electronic squeal of dots and dashes. Then, out of the giant speakers over our heads, came the song. I had heard them playing through the earphones, but I couldn't really listen, and I had not heard myself at all. For the first time I heard us all altogether; myself, the song, and the band. Then Claude turned up the volume, flooding the room with sound.

Cynthia had said it was a song about passion. Yes, I could hear the passion, but more important, oh! so much more important, I could feel it. All that passion I had put under the couch for so many years, pulsating in that room, and I was there, right there in the middle of it all. I was finally inside the music!

We had hours to go that night and long days ahead of us, beautiful hours and days. If it was an early session, Claude would bring a bag of sausage and biscuits. If it was late and we broke for dinner, we went together and took turns picking up the check. They brought something new and wonderful to each song that I hadn't imagined was there, but of course, it wasn't there until one of them heard it. Bobby Dyson played a long, solo intro into "Hold Me" and we had to do it over several times because there was a strange noise picking up. It was me. Listening to Bobby made me feel sexy, and I was rubbing my hands on my corduroy pants.

Harold Bradley brought seven or eight guitars to every session, and he would overdub two or three onto each song, but when we got to "Green Coffee" he used mine. We did it by ourselves, one voice, one guitar, just the way it had been written.

When they picked up the music to "Lonely There," somebody laughed and said, "Boy, she sure does write some strange chords."

Kyle said, "Wait till you hear the next one. She doesn't stay in the same key for two measures in a row."

The next song was "Looking Out My Window," and I had no idea it changed keys. I can't read music, and I learned jazz chords sort of by rote, or as part of a progression to a song. I learned them because I liked the more complicated combinations of sound. They all kidded me, but when we got to the song they understood what I meant.

Harold said, "Well, she's writing about light reflecting on a window. What she did makes sense even if she doesn't know it." He understood what I meant, he liked it, he made it sound wonderful, and he made me very, very happy. In one rehearsal of that song everybody broke into a spontaneous jazz break at the end, and that was the way we recorded it.

I learned to listen to myself on a playback with a little more critical objectivity, but each time the sound came pouring over me I still felt the joy. The joy and the thrill lasted long, long afterward. The joy was being part of the music. I was part of it because my music mattered to them, and that is what mattered to me.

The ten songs were finished and sweetened. Kyle had played every keyboard in the studio, trying to make four men sound like twenty. He finally decided that we had to have at least one horn. Chuck said the budget wouldn't allow, so he bought a flügelhorn with his own money, practiced for a few hours, and put it on himself. It was finished, but I think we all felt we were just beginning.

Two days before I was supposed to leave I got a message to call Richard in New York.

"I only seem to call you with rotten news," he said, "but you ought to know. Barbara's been in an accident."

"How bad is it?"

"I don't know, it's just a paragraph in *Variety*, and doesn't say which hospital . . ."

"I'll call the house and find out where she is."

There was no answer in the New York apartment, so I called the country. Susi answered.

"Susi, I just heard about Mother. What hospital is she in?"

"Oh, hi, Mary. She's home. I'll get her." I felt like a ton of bricks had just been lifted off my chest. She was home. It couldn't be so bad.

"Mary?"

"Hi, babe. How are you?"

"Awful."

"What is it—what happened?"

"It's my face . . ."

"Oh, my God. Honey—"

"It's bad, Mary, it's really bad."

"I'll be home in two days."

"Come up. I need to see you." It was the word that scared me: need. I had never heard her use it before.

I took a taxi from the train and Susi let me in. Barbara had her back to me when I walked into the living room. She was looking out the wall of windows toward the lake. When she turned, one whole side of her face was the color of a blood-red sun, her cheek bloated out above the long black crescent from her mouth to her eye. Her chin was a mass of bloody holes and cuts, where slivers of glass had been imbedded. I wanted, with all my heart and soul, to turn away, look anywhere else, but I couldn't do that to her.

After a while she said, "Thank God, it wasn't my hands."

"How did it happen?"

"The brakes failed."

"Were you driving?"

She tried to smile, but the corner of her mouth, where the gashes began, didn't move. "Of course not, I hired a driver. We felt it coming. I knew we were going to hit. If we hadn't already started to slow down for the toll booth we'd all be dead. Susi was in the back seat with Sylvia Simms, and I turned around to hold her back. That's why it's just one side. Sylvia threw herself on top of Susi, and she was fine—but Sylvia has a broken hip." She picked up an ice bag and held it to her face.

"I was lying on the highway waiting for the ambulance for a long time . . . they kept stuffing the clothes out of my suitcase into my face, and I could hear them talking, 'She's not making it,' they kept saying, 'she's losing too much blood,' and all I thought was, 'Die on the New York Thruway, in the middle of the afternoon, with the sun shining. That's just too dumb! I wouldn't dream of it.'"

"Have you seen a plastic surgeon?"

"I've got an appointment. There's still a lot of glass in there they couldn't get out, and, God knows, they tried. Four hours, Mary. They worked on me for four hours after it happened."

"You didn't pass out?"

"I don't think so, and they couldn't give me anything."

We talked all afternoon, until it was time for my train. I had to go back to the city. I had to work in the morning. When I left she had the ice bag in one hand and a dishrag in the other, wiping the kitchen table.

"You know, when you do die, you're going to rise one last time from your coffin to make sure it's dusted."

She laughed her crooked laugh and I left. I knew it wasn't the kitchen table she was thinking about. It was her hands. Keep the hands moving, keep doing something, anything, and don't think.

"Thank God, it wasn't my hands," she had said, and never once had she complained. She never did.

Dearest Mary—

Without doubt, the neighbors are complaining—but let them: a little excitement in their drab lives, that's what they need. Explanation is superfluous: I'm playing your tape. "Edge of Light" alone is worth my $5.98. It is good, Mary. It is better than good. It will fail, of course: how could anything *I* like succeed on the open market? Well that doesn't matter. What matters is the reward that lives and throbs in your heart. I was a creative artist once you know. I know that feeling. The feeling that you have done it *right*—there is no feeling on this earth, no, not even 12 Martinis, can touch it. Is the Duke of All Riverside Drive allowed to have a personal preference? It is, as if you didn't know—"Listening Lord". Which is as good as a prayer. (Which sounds like faint praise, 'til you realize that I was brought up on "The Book of Common Prayer.")

There is nothing worth the wear of winning but laughter and the love of friends. (Hilaire Belloc said that, and rather nicely, I think.)

Oh, Mary, life is short but art is long. Carry the flag for me, please, forever.

All love,

Tucker

Cynthia and Jeff had had eventful summers, and they both had hair to their shoulders. Cynthia insisted on wearing the high-heeled sandals she bought in Paris to school with her jeans, and Jeff began a campaign at Trinity to relax the hair and dress code. They both studied late into the night and spent hours on the phone with their doors closed. Cynthia even put a lock on hers. I lost track completely of what they were reading or studying. Cynthia, I knew, had enrolled in a course of French poetry and was taking advanced calculus. Jeff, simply, read everything, but I only got hints at the dinner table when we had company. If an author or a book was mentioned, he would fall automatically into conversation. Obviously he knew what he was talking about. He also seemed to have assimilated all sorts of information and background on the political scene, both national and local, in almost every area of the country. I wondered where he found the time, but then I remember walking into his room about ten-thirty one night to find him reading Shakespeare, listening to a Miles Davis record, and watching a ball game on TV.

"We use ten per cent of our brain in a lifetime," he said. "I'm trying to speed up the process."

Cynthia was becoming interested in politics too. She was assigned a research paper on the politics of the fifties. She had a choice of Alger Hiss or the Rosenbergs and chose the Rosenberg case. She read everything she could find in the library, and finally got hold of a transcript of the trial.

There were assorted long-legged, long-haired young people around the house at all hours, burrowed into either Cynth's or Jeff's bedroom. Obviously privacy was much more important than comfort. Grandmother squawked and flapped like a chicken who has hatched a brood of ducks, but to little avail. They were already out in the middle of the pond.

Dear Snick—

Your rather pointed silence aimed at the direction of my "Everything-else-but" theory of acting (admittedly a controversial, not to say, unique theory) suggests to me that perhaps it is one of those ideas for which the World Is Not Yet Ready. An even stronger suspicion: that I expressed myself very badly, expressing what is essentially an intuitive, poetic insight as if it were a logical syllogism. "Playing against" a trait by no means denies the trait: it supplements it—that is to say: we are *not* our traits: the human soul is not a croquet lawn, it is a battleground. If we can't laugh, we can't really cry; and if we can't cry, we will never truly laugh.

Mary: sudden decisionsville: I am moving to my brother's in Bronxville. The invitation has been long and generously extended. I will continue to maintain my New York apartment, and I hope to spend four to five days a month in it. (As long as I am here on this earth *it* will be here, and that's all there is to that.)

                                                              Tuck

After the car had taken Tucker to Westchester, Den and Cindy and I stayed to tidy up and found the letters. All the letters he had received were packaged with instructions to return them to the sender and stacked in shoe boxes. All the tapes were catalogued. Everything was in order. We went to visit several times that next month, but the snow in November made it difficult and we missed several weeks. We planned to go on a Wednesday, until his sister-in-law said he wasn't feeling well at all. Then she called and said we should come, it was important. He wanted to see us.

It was a bitter cold night and a long drive in a Volkswagen with no heater, but the house was warm and cheery. We stayed downstairs to chat with his mother and father. Tucker had asked them to move down from Connecticut to be near him for a while. Then we went up to see him. I didn't see the machines

until we reached the landing, a whole row of them, lining the upstairs hall: respirators, oxygen inhalators, resuscitators.

"Oh, my God," I thought, "they couldn't!" That was the
one thing he had dreaded, being kept alive like a vegetable.

His mother saw the look. "We have to have them," she said.
"It's the law. If we didn't, they'd make us put him in a hospital,
and he wants to be here."

Maybe it was the shock of the machines, and then the shock
of seeing Tucker. I wasn't ready. He had slipped so far in those
few weeks. He lay absolutely still, not even turning his head, too
weak to smile. Only his eyes moved, and the slim, white hand
limp on the sheet, with the fingers barely spelling. Cindy asked
him how he felt, and he said, "I'm ready."

We sat around the bed and made conversation, silly conversation. Cindy talked about the baby, I talked about the show, and
Den talked about the movie he was working on. It didn't matter
what we said, we couldn't stand the silence. We didn't stay long,
he was too tired and too weak. Cindy and Den went down first,
and Den asked if there was anything he wanted. He said,
"Peace."

When they were gone, I picked up his hand and kissed it. I
said, "You don't know how much I love you." His eyes darted to
my face, and the look was so intent I smiled. "Yes, you know," I
said.

I kissed his face and walked out of the room, down the hall
past the machines. I wanted with all my heart to stay and guard
him. They couldn't do it to him! Force those god-awful things
down his throat when he was so weak and so helpless. He had
been so brave, they couldn't make him suffer that final, hideous
indignity. But I couldn't stay. There was nothing I could do.

Two days later, on December 3, when I came out of the studio after the show, Mary Ellis was waiting for me.

"I didn't want to tell you before the show—Tucker died last
night."

I said, "Thank God."

I called his mother and we talked a long time. It was as if he
had planned it all, even the end. He had decided when he should
move, when his folks should come, and the morning after we saw

him he had asked for a nurse in the house. For the first time he didn't want to sleep in the room by himself. He knew he was going to die, and the nurse had let him go. They had never used the machines.

Tucker had done it! He'd gone the distance, with all flags flying! The last words I said to him were, "Yes, you know." He knew! He knew!

> "He knew it all, and only his kite swept the sky;
> If life has reason, it's to fly!"

Unfortunately, the principal reality of the 1960s did not cloud the skies over Henderson, U.S.A. during those years. The war in Vietnam wasn't even mentioned until Scott Phillips arrived in 1970, having served a tour of duty. He came to live with his Grandmother Ida and his Aunt Ellie in their big, old Victorian house, where he drank milk and ate cookies, and spoke briefly of his adventures around their kitchen table. He did not drink his first beer for over a year, and that was a major event in his life.

The part of Scott was played by Peter Simon, a thoughtful, sensitive young man with unruly straight hair, pink cheeks that made him look younger than his twenty-one years, and a wit that was just beginning to bud. Billie Lou Watt played Ellie Harper, and Vera Allen played Ida Weston. Billie Lou is like an ever-blooming rose, and Ida always reminded me of Ethel Barrymore. She was a lady of the theatre, accustomed to bright lights and deep cushions of knowledge and experience. They both knew how to make a simple scene important.

Scott became involved almost immediately with a girl who was definitely a new type, on our show. Laurie Lashinsky lived with her mother and her little boy in an apartment on the wrong side of Henderson—at least it was a side of Henderson we had never seen before. Kelly Wood played Laurie with haunting desperation, and a beautiful lady named Lilia Scala played her mother, spreading her talent before us like a thick, rich tapestry. Mrs. Lashinsky was a woman from the old country and never forgave her daughter's one great indiscretion. The little boy was named Eric, and was played by a little boy named Chris Lowe, aged four.

Ken Harvey was the other new, very important member of the permanent family, playing the part of Doug Martin. There was a mystery surrounding the character from the beginning, and a long history of mental illness. He had spent years in and out of institutions, and Ken Harvey's portrayal of that man as he returned to his profession and society was a beautiful experience for the show, and for us. Ken's own enormous humanity and warmth, his clear critical mind, his unending tenderness, filled the part he was playing and acted like a bond to meld the whole cast together. He touched everyone's life, and everyone was better for it. Those were the words he used to describe Tucker, but they were as true of him.

It would turn out that Doug was Scott's father, although he had never known the boy. When Scott's mother died in childbirth, Ida swore the man who had killed her would never know his son. One more happenstance completed the picture and managed at the same time to tie that entire family group together. Jo's sister, Eunice, bore a striking resemblance to Scott's mother, and Doug fell in love with her almost on sight.

By 1970 there were always at least two, and sometimes three, stories going simultaneously, moving up to a front burner as they grew more interesting or intense. So, while Doug was falling in love and trying to win his son's respect, Ida was hating him, and Ellie was the busiest peacemaker in history. Jo was missing Sam and worrying about Patti and Len.

The part of Patti was being played by Leigh Lassen, and had been since 1968, so we were beginning to accept the fact. Leigh was a beautiful young girl, and talented enough, but she liked to talk about her grandmother's escape during the Russian Revolution, or her diet of brown rice and nuts. Neither subject was fascinating to any of us. However, she was ours and she was sweet.

Patti and Len were married, but true love was not running smoothly at all. Since her very young days, when Lynn left, Patti had tended to be a whiny, neurotic girl only a mother could love, except for the years Gretchen Walther and Melissa Murphy played the part. I told myself that anybody who had been recast that many times is bound to have problems. Jo was patient and loving, and Len was patient and tense, until a new girl was admitted to Henderson General with a brain tumor. The new girl was suddenly very appealing.

The new actress was tall, with shoulder-length brown hair and a lush figure. Her face was not truly beautiful and her nose, like Ingrid Bergman's, was a little too large and just as unforgettable. She had an interesting range of qualities, from childlike vulnerability to absolute poise and assurance. Her name was Jill Clayburgh. The man in her private life was a young actor I had never heard of, named Al Pacino. But that same year, I appeared at a peace rally with Jon Voight, and when he told me he was an actor, I offered to help him get into the business. I've never been dependable when it comes to recognizing famous names and faces.

It's easy to say, in retrospect, that there was something special about an actress who has since become a star, but, quite honestly, I don't remembering thinking about Jill that way. I know I was fascinated by her. Actually, I think I was jealous. Her attitude was so positive and sure. She was from a wealthy family, but that was only part of it. She was the new generation of women, who automatically thought of themselves as important people. It gave her a wonderful sense of power and freedom. She was talented and intuitive, and she already had a lot of experience. Still she asked me, or Carl, for advice or help nearly every day. It was the combination: the inquisitive, little girl face, the quick turn of the head, and the long, sure strides that set her apart. Perhaps I did see how far she could go and just didn't want to admit it. She did one or two off-Broadway plays while she was with us, one with a little nudity, I was told, and I was impressed. She had talent and a tenderness I was drawn to. She had a lot of guts I admired. She had a whole life in front of her. I envied that most of all.

Jill played the part of Grace Boulton, and over the course of that year she and Len became more and more involved. When

Grace left town she was pregnant with his child. The character
died, off camera, but the baby lived and her cousin Harriet
brought it back to Henderson.

Jo had several scenes with Harriet and several scenes with
Len and Patti. The doctors told Patti she couldn't have children.
Harriet thought Patti and Len should adopt the baby, but Len
was almost unreasonably adamant against the suggestion. Late
one night, Jo was driving home after dinner with Dr. Rogers
when odd little bits of various conversations began to fit together
in her mind. Chance remarks by Len and Harriet, and finally
something Bob Rogers had said. Bob knew Grace was pregnant
when she left town but had no idea who the father was. In one
sickening moment the pieces fell into place. Len was the father of
Grace's child! In that same instant, the lights from an oncoming
car blazed in her face and she turned the wheel too sharply. Her
tires slid in the soft siding and the car spun out of control over
the embankment. The last shot in Friday's episode was the side
of a wrecked car with one wheel still spinning, and Jo's unconscious body on the ground.

There is an interesting little sidelight to that whole story. It
was designed and timed to coincide with a new show written by
Irna Phillips that was scheduled to appear opposite us on NBC.
The new show would air for the first time on Monday, and Jo
went off the cliff the Friday before. Irna sent our producer, Bob
Driscoll, a telegram. All she said was, "BRILLIANT."

It was a good idea. All Jo had done since 1954 was worry
about other people and give advice. Even while she was falling in
love with Sam, they were both fretting about the rotten kids all
the time. Finally, something had happened to her!

In 1970 the cast of characters was richer and more varied on
the screen and off. When Ernesto left the show as assistant
producer, a quiet, shy man named John Edwards came over from
Public Television to take his place. Oddly, the assistant producer
had always been closer to the company than the producer.
Ernesto had always been the one to drop by the dressing room
with a special note or a compliment and made it a point to appear on the set at least once a day. John didn't have Ernesto's elegance or assurance, but he was kind. He didn't have the authority

to do anything, but he listened to complaints and problems, and we knew he was a man we could trust. Though I knew I could trust John, it was our production assistant, Mary Ellis, I depended on. I made a joke to her one day as she was giving out notes after dress rehearsal:

"Why don't I ever get a note?"

And she said, "They assume if you do it, it's right."

That was a nice compliment, and absolutely terrifying. It is simply impossible for any actor to know for sure that what he is trying to do is working the way he wants it to. After Tucker left the show, I made it a point to lurk through the control room and catch Mary's eye after dress rehearsal every day. If she thought everything was okay she would nod, and if she didn't I would meet her in the ladies' room for a short conference. We also had two new directors. Bruce Minnix alternated with Dan, and after Tucker became ill Ned Stark began doing one show a week. One other very important person had appeared on the scene just after Thanksgiving of 1969. By 1970 he had changed everybody's attitude toward many things. Robert Anton was hired as a costume designer, and his vision of each character's wardrobe focused that personality so sharply it brought a whole new perspective. He would talk about the relationship of the characters to each other and to the story, and for me it was a totally new source of understanding. His curly black hair, his dark eyes, his chubby, graceful fingers belonged in a Renaissance painting. His sensitivity and his knowledge he handed me in shopping bags. He had, of course, studied with Lester.

When Jo finally regained consciousness after the accident, it was discovered that she had suffered a brain injury that left her blind. She would need an operation and the new brain surgeon in town was Tony Vincente, played by Anthony George. Tony had a long list of Hollywood credits, and he'd co-starred with Sebastian Cabot in a nighttime series called "Checkmate" for several years, but that was an action drama. A daytime drama is a whole different puddle of fish, and he swam out of his depth the first day. It had happened to nearly everyone from Hollywood. They simply weren't used to doing a whole show in one shot—a whole show with words and acting. It is hard, and everybody knows and everybody helps—especially when an actor is as personally charming and sweet as Tony. We were all crazy about him on sight, and he made no pretenses, which made everything easier. Carl worked with him between scenes, and I ran them an extra hundred times. Stanislavsky would have given some of those shows a two rating, but Tony's own appeal made up the difference.

For me, it was a new and exciting challenge to play a blind person. I decided that Jo would try to do as many things for herself as she could, be as independent as possible. Acting blind was not closing my eyes or wearing dark glasses or staring at the floor. It was simply not seeing. The pupils of my eyes never moved and did not quite focus. I would turn my head toward a sound or a voice, but never contact it with my eyes. In a two shot, where two faces are visible, it was obvious that I was looking toward the other person, but not directly at the face. I would go too far to the right, or perhaps slightly above. When I watched the show on the air, I realized that in a close-up the viewer could not make that distinction, so I asked Dan to experiment with the camera. I asked him to pull in closer, so I could play the wrong side of the lens, the way I would look at the wrong side of a face.

I also found a whole different level of concentration. The listening had to be so intense it was almost breathless to keep the contact alive and still isolate and negate one of the senses entirely. It worked whether you could see Jo's face or not. You could tell by the tilt of her head from the back that she could not see.

As Tucker said, "Play everything *but* blind," play touching, smelling, and listening. There were some lovely scenes in which to play it all. With Carl Low as Dr. Rogers, Jo would be eating lunch in her hospital bed. She never asked for help and he never offered any. When she spilled the soup or let the cottage cheese slip from her fork, he simply wiped it away without a hesitation in the dialogue or an inflection. With Dr. Vincente, whom she had never seen, and with her family, she listened to what they were not saying and reacted to the silence.

I suggested that Jo would ask for her guitar. She had time on her hands, and she didn't need her eyes to play. I wanted her to write a song around the little folk ditty Sam had loved, as a surprise for his homecoming. I wrote "Green Coffee" at home, of course, but when Ed Trach came by the house to hear it he insisted they write it in. Jo smiled as she sang it on the air. Everyone else cried. They knew Sam had disappeared. No body was found, but his personal effects had floated to shore and he was presumed dead.

Jo regained her sight, but for months she mourned Sam's death. Her friends tried in vain to kindle some interest in living. Finally, in desperation, her friend Dr. Rogers persuaded her at least to walk by the new recreation center he'd heard about from Dr. Vincente. It was such a good idea, that recreation center, a new and fresh one. If it had been handled a little bit more carefully it would have been great.

We'd never had a black actor in a real role, and all of a sudden we had Adam Wade and Al Fann in major running parts. Unfortunately, Dan cast all the small parts and the extras black too.

In the very first show, Jo dropped her reticence like a bath towel after a shower and joined in the activities. The first game was called "Trust," and she had to fall backward into a stranger's arms, trusting she would be caught.

The story only ran a couple of months. The mail was negative. There were still parts of the country where feelings were too close to the surface and, in fairness, the shows weren't all that good. The writing itself was self-conscious and stiff, though there were some beautiful moments. Adam and I sang together two or three times. He sang "I'd Rather Be a Hammer" while I played and sang the harmony, and that's what we wanted to say. I got to play a couple of scenes with Al Fann. The sheer power of that man was almost too much for me, let alone the little boxes we had to fit it in. A beautiful little girl, named Irene Cara, sang "Love Sweet Love" before the story shifted to a young white girl and her tragic death from an overdose. They were both good ideas, but we didn't throw the stones far enough, and they skipped along the surface.

Love Sweet Love was what we needed, and Jo was falling in love with Dr. Vincente, who was falling in love with her. Of course, there would be no story if it were that simple, so there was one small but very powerful roadblock. The small roadblock was his wife, Marcy, played by a small but brilliantly talented lady named Jeanne Carson.

Marcy was an invalid and had spent the last twenty years of their marriage in a wheelchair. She had power, because it was her money that sent Tony to medical school and set him up in practice. She used her power, and her nurse companion, played with smoldering intensity by Ann Revere, hovered like a malevolent shadow by her side through every spiteful move.

It was a dandy good situation. Those two ladies enriched the show and livened up rehearsals considerably. Ann told fascinating stories about theatre of the thirties and Hollywood in the early forties, and the long, hateful period of the blacklist. Jeanne could do every song and dance routine from the English music halls, where she grew up, and entertained us daily. In the scenes, she buzzed around her living room set with a huge, round, center fireplace in her motorized wheelchair, plotting evil, with relish and mustard. That story held through the fall of 1970 into the spring of 1971. That same spring, Ann Williams was pregnant, so Eunice was having a baby we would name Susi. Scott Phillips had married Laurie Lashinsky, and that marriage was already in serious trouble.

In April, the Bergmans' daughter, Janet, returned from her long sojourn in Chicago, but she had changed. She was no longer tall and blond, she was tall and brunette, and the part was being played by Millee Taggart. Janet was still married to Dr. Walton, but he had changed too. He looked remarkably like a young sailor appearing on Broadway in *On the Town*, named Ron Husmann. Along the way, their little boy, Chuck, had been forgotten or lost altogether, but then the Bergmans never did have much luck with small boys. Janet did have two children who managed to survive all the moves. Their names were Liza and Gary, and they arrived safely in Henderson, played by Kathy Beller and Tommy Norden. Kathy's career would take off when she left us. Tommy had already spent his teen years working with a porpoise named Flipper.

We would discover in the first month that Dr. Walton had brought his family back home because he knew he was dying of leukemia. We would also discover that Millee was pregnant, so that rather dominant feature of her anatomy was also written in and would eventually be named Danny. Babies were cropping up all over. Dino and his wife decided their two were not enough, so they adopted a Korean boy. Two years later they would add an Indian boy from Canada, and then a baby girl from the southern border of Texas. That year they moved to a huge, industrial space in downtown Manhattan, with room for a lot of kids and a hundred-seat theatre in the living room.

The story of Marcy came to an abrupt and unfortunately shaky halt. It turned out that she was not really paralyzed but merely faking, faking so well her doctor husband had never suspected, and her constant companion never guessed. It was the kind of dirty trick that could make a person hate writers! Jeanne and Ann had built such strong, believable characters, only to have new writers come on and make fools of them. Those writers only stayed a few months, and it served them right! We put our hearts and souls into each show, every character. We lay our talent and our intelligence on the line, so there are strong feelings when we are forced by a story to do or say something that seems ridiculous or inappropriate. Perhaps I take it all too personally. To protect Jo, I have so many times had to rephrase or rewrite to nudge a situation toward some reality I could feel comfortable with. There was nothing to do with that one, except trust Jeanne to play it and make it work.

Once Tony learned her secret, the divorce was quick and Marcy went with her nurse to live out West. Jeanne left, with her beautiful husband, Biff McGuire, for a season of Shakespeare at Stratford. They are actors in the true tradition. They are transients, traveling to where the work is. The tools of their trade are their minds and their bodies and their talent.

Jo and Tony were free, at last, to plan their life together, and play the love scenes Tucker loved so.

Sometime over the summer, Tony operated on a young boy who had been injured playing baseball. Tony grew fond of him, and when he learned the boy's father was dead he paid more attention than usual to him. Jo spent time with him too, and while he was in the hospital his mother was killed in an automobile accident. That did it! Jo and Tony would not only get married, they would adopt Bruce and start life as a real family. Tony had never had children, and he wanted a son.

Bruce was played by Robby Benson. Robby was not quite fourteen when he came on the show. He was shy and awkward and looked almost exactly the way he looks now. If the extraordinary gifts he has since displayed were churning, he gave no hint in those years. He was just a tender, gawky young man with a large mouth and grave, expressive eyes, who delivered his lines with a thoughtful hesitancy. I would say now that he was probably listening.

Eunice and Doug were expecting a baby and moving into a new apartment. Scott was separated from Laurie and enrolled in law school. Dr. Dan Walton was making many—too many—trips out of town, and Marge and Stu Bergman began to suspect he was seeing another woman. It was true, but the other woman was a doctor. Everybody was busy and involved in the story, and the new writers had a knack with dialogue that was fresh and inspiring. I loved Ralph and Jean Ellis from the first script. They wrote lines the way people talk, with thoughts that don't necessarily follow each other. It was harder to memorize but fun to play. The shows were good, the cast was fun, and we looked sensational! Bobby Anton had spent fifty thousand dollars in Bonwit's alone.

Until Bobby came on our show, I had never even been on the floor where they sell designer dresses. He says I taught him to look at a profile and the back of a dress almost before you look at the front, to see yourself the way other people or cameras see you. He taught me to think of myself as someone who is important enough to wear silk. Once you know how it feels, I'm not sure it's that important. You've already changed inside and that's all that matters.

Jo and Tony were a good-looking couple on the porch of Jo's house, in June 1971, planning their wedding, but at the end of that show the scene shifted. The camera dollied past deep foliage and a high paling fence, to the corner of a hut lit only by a kerosene lamp. In the distance were the sounds of jungle drums. Two men, in rumpled fatigues, lounged on cots, and one of them held a faded photograph in his hand. Even in the dim light we knew it was a picture of Jo. The actor was not Bobby Mandan, it was George Gaynes, but the character's name was Sam. Sam was alive. By September he had made his way back to Henderson.

Ken Harvey was one of the people I cared for most, and admired, on the show. Luckily, he played Doug Martin, who was Jo's brother-in-law, and also her close, dear friend. He and Sam had been close too, so he was the one who was contacted by whatever vague, international agency about Sam. He was the one to tell Jo that Sam was alive. The Ellises wrote a beautiful script, and almost all of it was Doug and Jo. There was room for the shock, all the joy and anguish his news would have to cause. The emotions came in waves, overlapping, peaking, receding, and rising again.

There was too much to accomplish in one morning, so it was one of the rare occasions when we asked Bruce Minnix, the director, to work the afternoon before. We trimmed the script and set the camera shots for every move, so they would be part of the scene as we memorized it. So much of the drama had to be unspoken, but remembered and seen. Memories of Sam had to fill the silence, awakening old dreams that were not ended, only put away. Pictures crowding pictures—of Tony, then of Sam, again of Tony. Finally the last shot, alone on the porch, with "Green Coffee" in the background.

Oh, God, it feels good to act! To choose the pictures and paste them in your mind, then play the scene with another human being. Just using those emotions, letting them free, sends a rush of adrenalin, stimulating your mind to another level of awareness. You hear the other voice, see the face, and with every sentence new pictures flash. You turn away, toward the reassurance of a little red camera light, or the warm, gold beam of a key light. You have prepared so carefully, and you think you know exactly what will happen—but there is always more, something unexpected from your partner, from the music, or yourself—when it all comes together. In that circle of absolute trust and commitment, your mind is like a great, dark stage, with one pin spot on the moment, and it is magic.

I said, when it all comes together! Of course! The magic is what happens in between. The same magic that had happened in Nashville, when I heard the music. Tucker said it too: "The best work I've seen you do—maybe it's the joy in your music." Maybe joy is like the silk dress. Once you know the feeling, it's yours.

On September 3, 1971, we celebrated our twentieth anniversary! It was a gorgeous party in the penthouse of the Hilton. Bobby had bought me a beige sequined evening dress that spring, and he told me I should take it home from the show, for the party. He bought Melba a beautiful apricot chiffon, and Joel made everybody up so we'd look pretty for the publicity pictures. I had ordered a limousine to take us from my apartment, and a few people were coming for a drink first. Peysa, our wardrobe mistress, and Joel, of course, and Peter, my lawyer.

At five o'clock the phone rang, and a vaguely familiar voice said, "Are you by any chance free for dinner?"

"Who is this?"

"Jesus Christ! Have you forgotten me, too?"

"Charlie!"

"Yeh, I just got in. I probably should have called you, but I thought I'd take a chance."

"Do you, by any chance, have a dinner jacket with you?"

"I got a dark suit, why?"

"There's a big party tonight. They should have invited you, so if you want to go you're the mystery guest."

I've never been absolutely sure it was really coincidence, but he did say, "What's the party?"

"It's the anniversary of the show, a big one, Charlie, twenty years."

"My God! Has it been that long?" Then he paused before he said, "Yeh, I'd like to go, if you're sure it's all right."

"Where are you staying? We'll pick you up in forty-five minutes."

"I'm at the Plaza. I'll be ready."

There was some confusion when the elevator stopped at the penthouse floor with all of us. Milt Slater said Cynthia and Jeff and Peysa should get out, then he pushed the button for the next floor up. He was gracious when I introduced him to Charles, but he had a lot else on his mind. I was, apparently, later than they had expected, but what I was late for I didn't know.

On the top floor we got out, and there were more people and

a couple of photographers. Then somebody handed me a huge bouquet of yellow roses and steered me toward the head of a long, circular flight of stairs. Oh, good grief! The whole cast, the ad agency, and Procter & Gamble were all gathered at the foot of the stairs, and there were photographers all over the place. The first faces I looked for were the kids', and they were by the door, looking so pleased I almost cried. I just stood there for a couple of minutes, I guess. For one thing, I was so startled I couldn't move, and for another I was afraid I would do something tacky, like fall down the stairs.

"Start now!" Milt urged firmly from behind, and with one hand clutching the rail I did.

The flashbulbs started popping. Golly, that was a fantastic feeling! It's one of the few fantasies that's just like the fantasy, maybe because there are so many lights going off in your face you can't see, but I did feel loved! I felt loved by all the people I cared for so much, from the company and the show I had grown up with. Bob Short, Milton, Melba, and Larry cut the cake with me. It was beautiful, with our logo and our clouds. It was a beautiful evening. We were all really together. There were speeches, and toward the end of the evening they played the first episode of the show, with Jo crooning "Hush Little Baby" to Patti. At the end there was Charlie's name, and I reached for his hand. I was so glad he was there! Some time around eleven they started turning off the lights and putting the food away, but nobody wanted the evening to end.

"Let's all go to my house!" I said. "Larry, you stop by a deli and get some cold cuts. I have plenty of booze. All we need is ice."

"I'll take care of that," Jeff said, and in one motion he pulled a five-dollar bill out of his pocket, handed it to a waiter, and picked up a huge, plastic hamper full of ice cubes. It all happened that fast and we crowded into one of the elevators to go down.

We were almost to the street floor when Jeff suddenly looked strange. "Where's Cynthia?" he asked.

"Oh, she's in the other elevator. She'll come with somebody else."

We'd been at the apartment for about fifteen minutes when the phone rang.

"Maud?"

"Maud! Where are you?"

"Well, I'm at the hotel with Peter, but we figured when we came down from the terrace and everybody was gone you'd all be at the house. We'll be right there."

Jeff had taken over the situation at the hotel and Cynth was out on the terrace with my handsome young lawyer. They were growing up, and they had shared my big night. They had made it even more important.

By the middle of September, Sam was home. Jo had said "I love you" to two men, and she did not know herself how she felt. Tucker put the dilemma succinctly: "Will Jo marry Tony? Will she marry Sam? Will they quite sensibly set up a ménage à trois? Alas, people in soap land rarely act sensibly." There would be weeks of scenes, I knew, before a decision was made. It occurred to me that since the music always helped me, perhaps it helped everybody else. Sam had his theme, so I wrote one for Tony. I suggested the organist play "Green Coffee" when I was with Tony, and "Tony" when I played a scene with Sam, so the audience would feel Jo thinking about the other man. John Edwards especially liked the idea, and by September he had more to say about everything. By November he would replace Bob Driscoll as producer. I was glad. John had so many qualities that brought out the best in other people.

It was a period on the show when ideas flourished. The scripts were good, the directors were innovative, and every actor on the show brought something thoughtful and unique, especially Tony. He had blossomed into a wonderful leading man. Just a little too late. By October a decision was made. Jo would marry Sam after all, and she believed she loved him. Tony was strong and helpful, and only in scenes with young Bruce, in the apartment they shared, did he admit his desolation.

A wedding date was set for Christmas time, and Sam began to plan the honeymoon. I knew that working with any new actor takes time, and George was a wonderfully intelligent, handsome man. For a month I didn't worry, but by November I began to get edgy. It was the chemistry. The chemistry simply was not there. By the end of November I began to panic, and I said something about it to Bruce Minnix.

"I think you're right," he said, "but you better do something quick. The announcements are being printed and the wedding set has been ordered."

I went to see John Edwards after the show that day and told him how I felt. He asked me what I thought we should do, and I said, "I don't know, but give me an hour." I went across the street to the little bar where we had lunch and had a Bloody Mary and thought. When I got back to the office I said, "I think Jo should retreat from the whole situation, emotionally. I think she knows she is making a mistake. Sam is not the man she loved, he has changed too much. She is in love with Tony."

"What do you mean, retreat emotionally?"

"Well, she could retreat completely—turn off her mind and go into a kind of catatonic state. But I think she should retreat back to where she was when she learned that Sam was dead, back to the safety of that reality. She was blind then. I think she should retreat into hysterical blindness."

After I left, John called up Ed Trach at P&G, and the Ellises. Apparently, everybody liked the idea, and agreed it was the direction we should go. Within a week Jo's vision was beginning to blur and just after Christmas, on the night before the wedding, she turned to look at the tree in the Bergmans' living room, and the lights went out. Jo was blind for a second time.

A few days after Christmas, Mary Ellis called me at home, in the morning.

"Melba is ill."

"What's the matter?"

"We don't know, but she's in the hospital. We rewrote today's script and Millee is playing the scene. I think it's bad, Mary. I knew you'd want to know."

At four o'clock she called again.

"I think you'd better go to the hospital. It doesn't look like she's going to live."

Melba died four days later of a cerebral hemorrhage. She was buried in the apricot chiffon. Larry and Melba and I had been together for twenty years. Marge will always be part of the show.

On Christmas Eve, 1971, quite late in the evening, after nearly everyone except Peter had gone, Elliot called. Mary Ann had introduced him to me a couple of months before, and the four of us had dinner. I hadn't seen him since, but he had been in California on business, he said, and skiing in Aspen.

The fire in the fireplace had burned low, Christmas presents and paper were strewn around the room, and the tree glowed in the corner behind the piano. He didn't care for a drink, he said, and settled himself cross-legged on the floor. I remembered he was handsome, with thick, white hair and a young face for a man of forty-seven, and I remembered saying to Mary Ann when she asked me what I thought of him, "He's so full of himself he'll never be able to see anyone else."

That night he seemed different. He was quiet and thoughtful, the blue eyes so very intent.

"Let's go to the midnight service at St. James," he said.

"It's almost twelve now and we'll never get in."

"Sure we will." He rose in one graceful move. "Are you coming, Peter?"

Peter shook his head. "I have to get home. Early morning with my girl tomorrow."

Elliot went into the hall to get his coat, and Peter winked at me and made an okay sign with his fingers.

We sat in the last row of the church, way to the side, and Elliot reached for my hand. It was strange, holding hands in a church, but it was also very easy, very natural. He was an Episcopalian too. We both knew the service by heart and most of the hymns. As we walked home, it started to snow. He sat with me in the living room until the fire was cold. The kids came home from their parties and he talked to them awhile. He was on the Board of Directors at Trinity School, so he and Jeff knew the same people. He asked me to go out Christmas night, but I had told

Melba I would come by her house. I didn't know it was the last time I would see her.

I had never been to Melba's apartment before. I'm glad I have it to remember, it was so like her. French furniture, with apricot silk and velvet. Her bedroom was soft blue and white, with brass headboards. It was elegant and feminine, as she was in everything she did, but what many people didn't know: Melba was a brilliant woman. She read and studied all her life. Her son, Eric, knew, and he had the same kind of mind. I could see it in his face that night, and the same sensitivity. I knew what he meant to her and so did he. At the end of the week, there would be great solace in that.

"How about driving up to New England with me and my kids for New Year's?" It was Elliot calling from his office.

"I'm not sure. Let me see what Cynth and Jeff have planned. It gets to be kind of a lot for Grandmother if there are too many extras floating around here. I'll let you know tonight."

We went out to dinner a couple of times that week, and a couple of times I cooked dinner at his house for him and his son, John, who was about to graduate from Trinity. After dinner, John would abruptly wheel his bicycle out into the hall for a speed run, he said. I knew he was leaving so we could be alone. It was too cold to be bicycling at night. Elliot didn't smoke or drink, but after a search they did find one ashtray for me and half a bottle of Almadén.

It was an attractive apartment, with blueprint-blue walls and a big, L-shaped sofa upholstered in brown. There were a couple of very good modern chairs and a big glass coffee table. It all looked like Elliot, and he was a strikingly handsome man. He was tall, strong, and athletic. He walked with long, enthusiastic strides in heavy climbing boots. He took beautiful photographs and loved to show them on the wall over the couch. After his divorce his son had stayed with him, and his youngest daughter was there every weekend. The oldest girl was away at college. He looked wonderful in navy blue turtlenecks with the collar of his sheepskin turned up against his tanned face.

Cynth and Jeff were both going to parties, so I figured it was all right to go away for the New Year's weekend, and I did look forward to it. New Year's in a little town on the New England seacoast with Elliot was about as romantic as anything I could think of. I knew John, of course, and I met Elliot's daughter Ann when they picked me up. She was twelve that winter, and very beautiful, with long, curly red hair and a sweet, if reticent, expression on her little face.

We sang songs in the car and they made a big fuss over the way I sang the harmony. Ann especially liked that. We played some games, but the favorite with Elliot's family was "count Mary's cigarettes." I only smoked one every hour and everybody applauded. I had planned to sneak an extra one in the ladies' room when we stopped for gas, but Ann went with me so that was out.

It was a long day, and we didn't stop for dinner until almost eight o'clock. The three of them disappeared into restrooms immediately, so I lit a cigarette and beckoned to the waitress.

"Could I please have a vodka martini on the rocks. I'm kind of in a hurry . . ." Unfortunately, she chose that moment to recognize me.

"Say, you know who you look like?"

"Yes, as a matter of fact, I do. Thank you. That's who—"

"You look just like—uh—what's-her-name. You know, twelve-thirty to one . . ."

"Yes, I know. That's who I am, but could you bring me a vodka—"

"Jo! That's her name! Boy, she's been on a long time."

"I know. I am Jo. Now, could you just bring me—"

"You're on TV!" Her shriek of laughter was a mixture of delight and disbelief. "No!" She put her hands on her hips and bent down to peer into my face.

"No," she decided definitely, "No, you're not."

"Okay," I agreed, "I'm not. But could you please . . ." It was too late. Elliot and John and Ann were on their way back to the table. I threw the cigarette on the floor under the table and stepped on it.

"Do you know who this is?" the waitress demanded as soon as they sat down.

"Of course I do," Elliot said quickly, completely misunderstanding the situation. "It's all right. We came in together."

"Well, she's not!"

"She's not what?" Elliot seemed confused. I shrugged, and the waitress kept right on talking.

"Pat, who is she?" She snagged another waitress passing by with her arms loaded, and if John hadn't been quick we'd have been buried alive in meatloaf and mashed potatoes.

"Who?"

"Her."

Pat put her tray down on our table and stared hard for a full minute before the light dawned. "Sure! She's on that show—what is it? Oh, yeah! 'Love of Life'!" Then she leaned in for a closer look. "Say, are you really blind?"

"It's Jo! I said it the minute she walked in." Our waitress reversed her field without hesitation. "Wait till I tell Martha, out in the kitchen, who's here!"

John smiled. "Hey, you're really a big shot!" He looked pleased, even a little impressed, and Ann giggled.

"Well, in a place like this they probably don't have anything to do but watch television," Elliot said. I glanced at him, and a tiny defensive spark went off, but our waitress was back before I had a chance to answer.

"Hey, would you come out in the kitchen and meet Martha? She can't believe you're really here."

"Sure," I said, and as I rose from the table I noticed a pack of cigarettes in the pocket of her uniform.

As soon as we were out of earshot she whispered, "I ordered you that martini. It's on the house. I guess you don't like to drink in front of your kids, huh?"

I just nodded and decided Martha and I would probably have a nice, long chat.

Elliot's mother, Connie, was a gentle old lady who did not see well and walked painfully. She served canned macaroni and cheese with the Sunday ham, but she got out her wedding china.

The ferns that cascaded to the floor in that sunny dining room had belonged to her grandmother. She said the secret was to cut them all the way back every ten or fifteen years and soak them with rainwater. The childhoods of her three sons were recorded in a book of poetry she let me read, and she had the tallest pussy-willow tree I have ever seen.

One day she said, "You're important, Mary. How does it feel to matter to someone else?"

I slept in a big, four-poster bed with Ann, in a room choked with furniture. There were harpoons and maps on the walls and framed photographs everywhere.

When we went out for dinner Elliot ordered a martini for me, and everybody waited patiently while I drank it.

It was a long, beautiful drive back, and I only smoked five cigarettes. After I got into my apartment there was a major battle to settle about some friends of Cynthia's who had stayed later than Jeff thought they should, and I smoked a whole pack, but I didn't mention it to Elliot.

A week later he said, "I think I'm falling in love with you," and two weeks later he said very casually, "I have to go to California next week. Want to come with me?"

"To California?"

"I have to be in San Francisco for a day, and then down to Esalen and Santa Barbara. It's a beautiful drive . . . Have you ever been down that highway?"

"No, but I always wanted to."

"Good! We'll spend a day or two at Esalen, do some hiking."

"Well, I'm not so good at that . . . What's Esalen?"

"It's a beautiful place up on a bluff, overlooking the water. You'll love it—everybody is really themselves."

"Well, I'll ask tomorrow at the show, and see if I have the time."

Mary Ellis checked through the scripts the next morning, and by a wild stroke of luck I had those days off. She was as pleased as I was.

"Where are you going?"

"San Francisco, and down the coast to a place called Esalen that he says is gorgeous, and on to . . ."

"Esalen?" Her face clouded just a bit.

"Yeah, have you ever heard of it?"

"I've been there." She hesitated for a moment and then she said, "Look, it is beautiful . . . You know what it is, don't you?"

"No."

"Well, it's a sort of an encounter place—a kind of group therapy."

"Oh, good grief!"

"Well, you probably won't get into any of that if you're only there a day, but just look out for one thing . . ." She paused, choosing the words. "Just don't go down the hill," she said. "There's a sort of blockhouse down there, and don't go."

"Why? What's down there?"

"Well, I'm not sure, but I think it's some kind of bath, and whatever it is, I know you wouldn't like it."

"Okay, that should be simple. Any other advice, buddy?"

"Just have a good time. He sounds wonderful." She hugged me, and I went home to face the real test. The kids, I figured, would agree, but Grandmother would go through the roof. I was right.

"Why, you hardly know that man! You can't go all the way across the country with him!"

"Mother, times have changed. Everybody does it!"

"Well, you don't. You're a lady!" I was suddenly feeling twelve years old, and that made me so angry I would have gone whether I wanted to or not.

Elliot seemed to know every inch of San Francisco, and we covered most of it on foot. It was fun, it was exciting. He was like a kid in a candy store, running down the streets and up the hills, while I panted along behind. In the morning we bought a loaf of French bread, a chunk of Monterey Jack, and a huge, hard-shell crab. The man on the wharf cracked the shell, we picked up paper napkins and cups, a bottle of wine, and started our adventure.

I knew it was going to be a beautiful drive, but I never could have imagined how powerful, how breathtakingly beautiful it would be. The Pacific Ocean was molten silver when I first caught sight of it. The mountains rose straight up on our left, deep and wild and mysterious, with gigantic feet in the water. All day long they grew higher and higher, while the breakers slithered and crashed, licking caverns into the rocks below. Every little while, Elliot pulled off the road to grab his camera when something caught his eye. It could be a wild flower or a hawk wheeling above a burned-out tree, or a distant, misty shadow between the breasts of the mountains.

I smoked only two cigarettes all day. Elliot felt sure that the next day I would not smoke any. There would be no need to. He did not like to kiss me if I smelled of tobacco, he said.

At noon we stopped for a picnic in a sandy cove that reminded me of a scene from a movie with Elizabeth Taylor and Richard Burton—*The Sandpiper*, that was it. I think I saw it three times. We drove out of the way so he could show me a beautiful old adobe mission, and we stopped for tea high up on top of a mountain. It was a perfect day.

We arrived at Esalen about dusk, and it was not what I had expected. There was a kind of compound with a big, common building and long rows of tiny, cell-like rooms with two iron beds, a prefab shower, and a bureau. The sheets and blankets were folded on the beds, so clearly you made your own, and there was a broom in the corner. I did my chores and we went to supper in the big common room. It was served, cafeteria style, with whatever they had, mostly vegetables and homemade bread. I think the meatloaf was made of something besides meat, and there was no catsup on the long table we shared with half a dozen strangers. I bummed a cigarette.

After dinner we went for a walk around the compound, and he was right, that was unbelievably beautiful. The moon rose, shining a path across the dark water, and the waves curled in, a hundred feet below.

"Come on," he said, "I'll show you the rest."

We walked along the precipice with a high, ornamental iron grating.

"They put that in after a couple of people jumped," he said

matter-of-factly, and I shuddered. I looked at the faces more carefully after that.

We walked to the other side of the common, and suddenly I
realized we were going downhill. I stopped dead and peered into
the darkness. Sure enough, down below, clearly visible in the
moonlight, was a small white stone building. "Don't go downhill," Mary Ellis had warned, and I froze.

"What's the matter? Can't you see? Here, I'll help you." He
stepped ahead of me and took my hand.

"Uh . . . I'm tired . . . I think it's time to go to bed."

"Not yet. There's something I want you to see."

"I'll see it tomorrow . . . uh . . . I'm really tired."

"Don't be silly, come on. If you're tired, this is just what you
need."

"No! I . . . well, I think I'll pass."

"Nope, you have to at least see it." He was pulling me down
the hill, gently, but definitely. "Why are you walking so funny?"
he teased over his shoulder. "Like your knees are locked together."

"Oh, it's my shoes," I said. "It's hard to walk downhill in
heels. Listen, why don't I just wait for you?"

"Because you have to see it."

We had arrived at the bottom of the hill and walked into
what looked like a public bathhouse at any municipal pool. The
sign straight ahead said WOMEN, with an arrow pointing left, and
MEN, with an arrow pointing right. I breathed a great sigh of relief and turned left. He roared with laughter and grabbed my
hand again.

"Nobody's been in there for years. They don't even fill the
tubs," and he hauled me around the corner to the right.

Now, to be honest, it was beautiful, absolutely beautiful. The
room was open toward the sea along one whole side, with the
moon on the water. Inside, there was a candle burning in an
amber glass, and somebody was playing a recorder. It was dark,
but when my eyes adjusted I could see that there were two huge
stone tubs and, to my astonishment, there were people in one of
them talking slowly and softly. The murmur of the voices, the
whisper of the waves, the glow of the moonlight and the glow of

the candle with the haunting song of the recorder—yes, he was right. It was incredibly beautiful. But I had seen it, and I automatically turned to leave.

"Nonsense." He pulled me away from the door. "You've come this far, now you have to try it." With that he pulled off his sweatshirt, stepped out of his jeans, and stretched out on the ledge along the window, letting the chill night wind blow across him, and I just stood there in my silk Halston pantsuit, feeling the water that had sloshed out of those damn tubs seep through my shoes, not knowing where to go, or even where to look.

When nobody else has clothes on you begin to feel obscene if you do. Two more very young people came in, dropping their T-shirts and jeans as they passed through the door, and stepped into one of the tubs. Okay. Either I had to walk up that dark hill by myself, or I had to get wet. It was obviously easy for him, and if we were going to get along, maybe he was right, I should at least try it. I unbuttoned the jacket to my suit and took it off before I realized the whole business was going to be a lot more complicated than I had anticipated. Deciding to take off my clothes was step one, but getting them off and finding a place to put them was something else altogether.

I was still dressed for a plane trip, with a suit, blouse, a scarf, shoes, and panty hose, which were, by then, soaking wet. I felt around in the darkness and finally found a nail. All the time I fumbled with buttons and wet stockings a nursery rhyme from my childhood kept running through my mind: "Hang your clothes on a hickory limb, but don't go near the water." Nancy Neat squeezed the water out of the toes of her panty hose, folded them, and tucked them carefully into her shoes before she approached the tub.

It's hard to know what the social amenities are supposed to be when you're about to get into a bathtub with half a dozen strangers. Is it a carefree, "Hi, guys, how's the water?" or a more formal "Good evening"? Actually, all I managed was a smile. Nobody noticed me or my smile anyway. What they did notice was the yelp of pain when my bottom hit the water. Even the recorder stopped, and several heads turned my way.

"Uh . . . it's, uh . . . hot!" I explained hurriedly, trying to maintain my dignity and extricate myself as rapidly as possible from that steaming caldron. I climbed out and, again, I wondered about the social amenities. Having shared the intimacy of their tub, however briefly, should I excuse myself and explain my abrupt departure, or would a simple, casual wave suffice? Again, nobody gave a damn. They turned back to their murmuring, not seeming to care a whit that they were being boiled alive.

After a moment of indecision, I couldn't help noticing that the stone floor was freezing my bare wet feet, and the cold night wind on the bare rest of me was making my teeth chatter. I decided it was better to boil than to freeze and stepped into the other tub. That one was, mercifully, unoccupied, so I spent the next ten minutes alone in a kind of squaw dance, squatting in the water as long as I could stand it, then hopping up to freeze again. Ten minutes was enough to decide the baths were not for me. Besides, I still had the problem of getting my wet self dressed, because, of course, I had no towel. I knew it was not going to be easy to stand in the dark on one foot and yank wet panty hose onto a wet leg. It wasn't, and I felt ridiculous, just as ridiculous as I looked.

Elliot said I was wonderful as I squooshed up that hill in my soggy shoes. He said I was well on my way to becoming really free and in touch with myself, the kind of woman he could truly love.

In the morning we had breakfast in the big common room. Elliot had oatmeal with raisins, wheat germ, honey, eggs, and milk poured over it. I looked the other way while he ate it and thought about smoking a cigarette with my coffee. After breakfast we went for a walk. He had his camera, and for an hour he photographed a hummingbird hovering in a flowering vine. I looked down the cliff at a tiny beach house in the cove. It was very like the house Elizabeth Taylor had in the picture. I looked at Elliot, so tall and strong, so intent with his camera. "Yes," I thought, "we're like the Burtons in that picture, almost."

We walked across the road and he showed me a mountain he had climbed.

"Come down here," he said, "and I'll show you where we started from."

Completely unsuspecting, I followed him down the embankment from the road to the edge of a rushing stream.

"Just follow me," he called as he stepped lightly and gracefully along the slippery bank, and follow him I did. For two hours we walked straight back into that canyon. Twice we had to cross the stream, which had widened into a small river. He ran across a rotting log and beckoned for me to follow.

"Come on, don't give up on me now! You can do it!"

Sick with fear, I inched my way across. The second time, he crossed on the stones, dancing from one to another. He held his hand out to me, but it was too late. My foot had slipped and I had fallen into the water.

Every little while something caught his eye and he stopped: a drop of dew on a leaf, a spider in her web, a shaft of light filtering through the age-old redwoods or the pebbles at the bottom of the stream. We could have been at the end of the world and the beginning of time. The graveyard of a million seasons was beneath our feet, and he was joy itself, enraptured by his world. I watched him and marveled, but while he ran down the hillside I clung to the brambles to keep myself from sliding helplessly after him. It was almost suppertime when we walked back into the light of the outside world and looked down on the tiny house. In the movie he had loved her, and she was free.

"You did very well," he said, and I thought for one awful moment he was going to pat me on the back. "We'll get you some hiking shoes next time."

"Well, I'm glad I did it, but I'm not sure I really want to try it again."

"Nonsense! You'll love it! You'll just have to build up your confidence a little, and build up those muscles."

I smoked my last cigarette and drank the last of the Almadén while he was in the shower.

Santa Barbara was beautiful, the hotel was beautiful, and we had a beautiful suite with yellow sheets. Several women made a fuss over Elliot and seemed quite envious of me. When we left his friends' house he grabbed my hand and we ran to the car. I felt like Elizabeth Taylor again.

When I got back to New York there was a call from Chuck Glaser. He was in town from Nashville for a week trying to place the songs. He still hadn't put strings or back-up voices on yet. It turned out that was difficult if you haven't worked from arrangements in the first place. Of course, I don't think he had meant to. Those tapes were to be the demos for an album, but his brothers were pressuring him to sell them as they were. I went with him once, to a big meeting at Columbia.

"You sound like you're eighteen," one of the young executives said, turning his gaze from the speaker to me, and I suddenly felt even older than I was. I was embarrassed.

"I clammed in that phrase." They laughed.

"It's interesting," somebody ventured. "Good songs, but I don't know what to do with them."

"Chuck, this isn't country, it's not rock, and it's not really pop."

"She's personal, though. Doesn't sound like anybody else." It was the man who said the songs were good, and I started to watch his face.

Chuck stood up and turned off the machine before he began his pitch. He looked as out of place as I felt, in his brown polyester pants with the wide belt and big silver buckle. His boyish gestures were awkward and his hands were too large. The wide Indian bracelet was too much in that room full of expensive flannel. He needed more space.

I knew when we left they were going to pass, but I don't think he did. I don't think he allowed the word into his mind.

Barbara called to say the second operation was over and she was feeling better. She never let me know before she went into the hospital. She didn't want me to worry.

The first of February, somebody named Audrey Eisman called me about doing "The David Frost Show." She asked me to meet her at Sardi's for a drink after my show. Sardi's at three in the afternoon is deserted, so I assumed the very beautiful, slightly overweight young brunette was waiting for me. She described the show we would be doing. It would be all people from daytime, and it had been her idea. That was what she did for David. She booked his guests and interviewed them in advance so he would know what to talk about. She obviously already knew a great deal about me and my show, so the interview was simple, but we talked for almost two hours, and I began to realize that Audrey, like my neighbor in the country, had spent long hours with Jo.

I was nervous about doing the show, and when Audrey called and asked me to bring my guitar, I was much more nervous. I had never played and sung, except on "Search."

"Oh, you don't have to sing," she assured me. "We just want the guitar as a prop."

Joel came to the studio to make me up, and I wore a simple brown velvet jumper Bobby had designed. At least I felt pretty. Elliot and John went with me and sat in the front row where I could see every move they made.

During the first half hour I didn't say very much, but everybody else was up and on. They told plenty of stories. Elliot looked at me and shook his head sadly. During the second half hour a couple of people sang with the band, and there were more stories. David had laughed the two or three times I managed to get my mouth open the first third, and he began to look at me for a signal. If I had something to say, I nodded.

In the third half hour he stopped whoever was talking and turned to me. "Mary, sing something."

My heart went into my throat. "I don't even know where my guitar is."

"I do. I had them bring it from the dressing room. It's right behind the set." He reached back and handed it to me, and I looked around for a place to sit. We had not planned anything. Actually, I sat down on the steps to the stage, because my knees were beginning to shake so violently that was as far as I figured I could go. I looked up to make sure there was a microphone over me and started to play "Green Coffee." My hands were so numb I couldn't do the arpeggio all the way. I could arpeggio up, but I couldn't get down. I decided after three verses it was the longest song anybody had ever written, and I was so lucky I hadn't dropped the guitar up to that point I should quit while I was ahead. I skipped the last verse altogether.

After the show, Elliot said the song had gone very well but that I should have been more aggressive in the talking segments. Two weeks later, Audrey called and said David wanted me to come back and do a whole show by myself with him. I had a lovely evening, and before I knew it Audrey had become part of the family. Grandmother called her "Little Audrey," but not to her face.

Elliot and I saw each other constantly all through February, with and without families. If he worked late I would buy groceries for two houses, fix dinner at home, and run up to his apartment to start dinner for him and John. I hadn't practiced my guitar or written any words since I met him, but that would wait. It was very time-consuming, being in love.

Once, Cynth and Jeff went up to his house for dinner with his family. They were quieter than usual, but perhaps I was too, in his house. They both looked a little startled when he started the applause for my cooking. I was careful not to catch their eyes. He didn't like having dinner in our house. He just didn't like the place.

"I like my mother, but I would never live with her," he said one night, "and I just don't like all those musty old antiques around. This is a modern age, everything should be new and clean and modern."

He was probably right, I thought. I'd had fun collecting the stuff, but maybe it was musty and old-fashioned. I hadn't really looked at the house for ages. It was just there. A vague dissatisfaction grew and erupted into cross words at home.

The end of February we were invited away for a weekend to the ski lodge of some friends of his. I'd met them, they were lovely, and they thought it was delightful to have a guest who didn't know how to ski and didn't want to. I was going to take my guitar and have a whole weekend with the days to myself to practice and write. I really looked forward to it. At the last minute, Elliot announced that Ann would be going with us. He assured me it would be all right. Ann was behind in her schoolwork, so she would be studying while I practiced. It wasn't as good as being alone, but there was nothing to be done.

Saturday morning started just fine. Everybody got up early, had a big breakfast, and left for the slopes. I volunteered to do the dishes and that got them out even earlier. I got out my pads and my guitar, put a log on the fire, and settled in for the day. The quiet lasted until about nine o'clock, when Ann appeared in the doorway.

"I'm bored, let's do something."

"I'm doing something, and you have studying to do."

"I can't study until I have some air."

"Go for a walk."

"Let's both go for a walk! We could go snowshoeing!"

"I have no idea how to snowshoe."

"It's easy, and there are lots of them downstairs."

"Ann, I don't want to snowshoe . . . You have to study, and I want to practice." I was firm, but she was persistent. About ten o'clock I gave up, or in, or both.

"We'll go out on the snowshoes for fifteen minutes, and then you will leave me alone for the rest of the day, is that agreed?"

It was agreed. I put on my jacket and pulled a pair of snowshoes off a peg in the back room. I wasn't sure how to put them on, so I sat on the end of the bed fiddling with the laces for quite a while, getting hotter and crosser by the minute. When they seemed secure I clomped over to the door and encountered a new problem—how to get out and still reach the doorknob. My solution was to back out, pulling the door after me. It closed and the automatic lock snapped. Only then did I turn and assess the next hurdle, because that is exactly what it was. Right outside that door was a fence!

"Don't worry!" Ann called gaily as she skimmed over the snow, held the wires down and stepped over.

I took one step, however, and sank to my knees in soft powder. Eventually I crawled on my belly under the fence. Outside, I found, was no better. If possible, it was worse and it certainly was farther. The only place to go was down and, before I gave up, I dragged myself probably fifty yards, lured on by the sight of Ann sliding effortlessly across the top of the snow. Of course, I was forty pounds heavier and had no idea that snowshoes come in sizes determined by your weight. When I sank all the way to my waist I knew I was in serious trouble. I scratched the snow away and took the stupid things off, and finally got up the hill on my hands and knees. I wanted very much to hit that kid, only because I was so frustrated and frightened and tired, but I didn't. I found our host's liquor cabinet instead, and had two sherries. Then, I picked up my guitar and tried to make my hands stop shaking. I had certainly learned my lesson, and I assumed she had learned hers. I was wrong. At exactly two she began to whimper again.

"I want to go skiing."

"Go with your father tomorrow."

"No, today."

"Well, I can't, so you can't."

"We could go cross-country! I saw a place just the other side of town that rents—"

"No!"

"Please!"

"No!" And I still find it hard to believe that the little girl who ratted on me every time I smoked a cigarette in the room I shared with her actually talked me into driving somebody else's station wagon twenty miles to a shack where they rented cross-country ski equipment.

"But, you understand I'm not going with you."

"Of course."

"And you understand we are only going to stay for one hour. Those clouds look very heavy, and I don't want to get caught in a snowstorm."

"One hour. I promise."

The man in the shack was very nice but also firm. "I'm sorry, she's a minor, and we can't let her go alone."

"Then send somebody with her."

"There's nobody here."

"Daddy would love it if I learned to ski cross-country, and he'd be so proud of you."

"That's blackmail."

"Please!"

"*One hour!*"

The man who owned the shack shook his head, "Sorry, madam, we don't have the right size for you in right now. A lot of ladies are out on the trails."

"Good—"

"But we could give you some shorter ones if you don't go out on the trails. You'll have to stay on the parking lot."

"Ski on the parking lot?"

"It's a big parking lot."

"Please!"

"One hour!"

For exactly an hour I did sort of ski around a parking lot. He was right, it was a big parking lot. He was also right about the skis. They were not the right length, because I sank into the snow, just as I had sunk on the snowshoes. I also fell, and it was very, very difficult I discovered to get up with long sticks bolted to your feet.

At about four-thirty I paid the man in the shack and we got into the station wagon. Just as I turned the key in the ignition, it started to snow. It did not scatter a few pretty flakes, it started to snow so hard I could hardly see the road. I drove the last ten miles in low gear. The engine smelled of fire and smoke when we got back to the lodge and I did not care.

Elliot came back all rosy and smiling. "Did you two girls have a nice day?"

"I don't really like baby-sitting."

"I'm surprised to hear you talk that way about Ann . . . you two have always gotten along so well."

"Let's just say it wasn't a good day."

"Well, tomorrow I'll take her with me. She studied today, so she deserves to go skiing."

"Good."

The snow had stopped falling in the morning. The day was crisp and bright. It was my day and privately, at the breakfast table, I thought I might even venture out for a little walk after they had all gone. I would not, however, wear snowshoes and I would stay on the road.

I could hear Elliot on the phone, arranging for Ann's ski lesson, and with the prospect of a whole day to myself I even forgave her the day before. Then, something Elliot was saying caught my attention.

"That's right. Ski lesson at ten o'clock, for two."

He came back to the table beaming.

"Two what?" I asked, just a little sharply.

"Two people. I booked a lesson for you too."

It was a split second before I managed to stammer, "No." In that split second he had started to applaud and everyone at the table joined in, so nobody heard me. I do not know why I went, why I let him back me into that corner.

The rented boots felt like steel teeth in my ankles, and I have not been able to wear fur since. I know how a trapped animal feels. I sidestepped up a hill, until I thought my legs would give in beneath me. When they pushed me out of the chair lift at the top of the hill, I managed to get all the way down in wide zigs and zags, falling face down into a snowbank because it was the only way I knew to stop. Still, I did not say anything. I packed up my clothes and said goodbye to our hosts and got into the car. I sat very quietly for probably an hour, listening to Elliot extol my virtues. He had never been so pleased and proud of me. I really had a natural knack for skiing and would probably be very good. I had tried, and that was what really pleased him. I had the guts to go up that mountain and ski down it. All I needed was a little more practice, to build up my stamina and my muscles, and . . .

It was about there, at the word "muscles," that I went completely, totally, wholly, wildly insane. Two entire days of rage exploded in about ten minutes. Their jaws dropped in amazement! I was even surprised myself. When I had finished, Ann leaned over to turn the radio on and I snapped it off so hard I broke the knob.

"*And*, I will not sit in this car and listen to rock and roll!" Not another word was spoken until we got to a Howard Johnson's, at about six in the evening. They turned right to the soda fountain and ordered ice cream. I turned left to the bar.

When I got home, the kids took one look at me and Cynth ran to get a cigarette while Jeff made me a drink.

"I'll get the ice." Grandmother hurried to the kitchen, and she didn't really approve of anybody having a drink, ever.

I told Mary Ellis about my adventures and she laughed for the rest of the day every time she looked at me. The next morning she brought me some long underwear with little pink rosebuds all over it.

My scene in the car had frozen my relationship with Elliot pretty solid. He felt nothing for me physically, and was very sorry I had upset his daughter so much. I was sorry too. I liked Ann. I just didn't like skiing. For two weeks we spent evenings together, but I went home earlier and earlier. Spring vacation was coming, and he suggested both families go to Aspen together. The way he said it made it clear. This was my way to make amends.

He made all the reservations for hotels and planes, but about the first week in March the three of us began to experience little second thoughts. For one thing, the accommodations were far from ideal. The thought of sharing dormitory space with no privacy to read was appalling to Jeff. Cynthia announced, simply, that skiing was a sport for masochists. They were willing to go through with it, but we agreed that what the three of us really wanted to do for the spring holiday was rent a nice, big cottage in Antigua, pack a lot of books and my guitar, and lie on a beach for two weeks. If that was what we wanted to do, why in the world were we going to drag ourselves to Aspen and be miserable. I called Elliot to talk about this new possibility, but he wasn't home and John answered.

Something in John's voice, for some reason, opened floodgates I didn't even know were there. I suddenly heard myself saying things I would never have mentioned to Elliot. I was talking to John as if he were the adult, and he answered as if he understood that and accepted it. I didn't want to live my whole life on Elliot's terms, according to what he called his "life-style," and even if I wanted to, I couldn't. I didn't know how. Finally I said, "John, I'm not going to Aspen."

"Dad's going to assume that's the end of the relationship."

"I guess it is."

I called my travel agent at home and asked her to make arrangements. I told the kids the plans were officially changed. I learned my script and played the guitar for a little while, and about ten I went to bed.

It was turning off the light, I guess, that started it. Lying alone, in the dark, I began to realize what I had done. I sat up, fumbled for the light. I would call him. I would talk to Elliot. We would work it out between us, but I put down the phone and went out into the living room. Almost as soon as I closed the doors the dam gave way and the water rose out of control. I had thrown away my last chance, and I was sick with terror and regret. Suddenly, like convulsions, the tears exploded. I could not sit, I could not stand. I prowled back and forth across the rug, holding on to the furniture, moaning and sobbing. I could not think—I could not stop thinking. The sobs shuddered through my body. As if I had been poisoned, the retching would not stop.

Once or twice it seemed to quiet and I tried to go to bed. I found a tranquilizer left from the old days. I made myself a drink, I took two aspirins. I did everything I could think of, but as soon as I turned out the light the retching would begin again. All night it went on. From sheer exhaustion, I fell asleep close to morning. When I woke the storm had passed, the passion was spent.

The pain was still vivid, but so were flashes of insight. I walked around the house, touching my musty antiques, looking at my pictures and my windows with the sun streaming in. There are no mirrors, but I could see myself and my years. Perhaps there were too many, and too much. There was no room for all of me in Elliot's life, and what he could not accept I could not leave behind. For a little while I had really thought I could. No, I had not thought. I had reacted, pretended, played the part, been the person I assumed he wanted me to be. Like a shadow, I had attached myself to him and followed.

Three times since the divorce I had built a life around a man. The first two walked away from me, so I had never had to face it. I had only known the feeling of failure and rejection. This time, if we were going to stay together, it would have to be different somehow. I wasn't sure, exactly, but I knew something was missing. It didn't matter that Elliot didn't like antiques or cats, or my mother—even cigarettes and an occasional martini. It did matter that he did not seem to care how I felt.

We had dinner together a few days later. I had calmed down. He didn't even know I had exploded in the first place, only that I didn't want to go skiing. He was cool but pleasant as I tried to explain that I needed to feel it was all right to tell him when I was uncomfortable or unhappy. The blue eyes were wide with astonishment, and the tan face was bland and smiling.

"Naturally," he agreed. He was a sensitive man, and I could tell him anything.

I said, perhaps hesitantly, that I didn't think it had worked out quite that way, and he answered quickly that he was sorry, but that was my problem. I tried to explain again, but the harder I tried, the farther away he seemed to be. I began to feel foolish, defensive, and even apologetic until I finally, finally realized that he didn't have the foggiest notion what I was talking about, and he never would. In that instant, I saw him, really saw him, for the first time. He knew it, too, and it was over.

I would never, I promised myself, go through that ritual again. I would live my life and if it was lonely, then perhaps that was of my own choosing. I liked my house. I loved and admired my children and my mother, and my cat. About that time I had a dream that recurred several times. I dreamed about the little house in California that Lester and I had built, but it wasn't on a hillside. It was a tree house, a wondrous tree house with several rooms on different levels, and I lived there by myself. Somehow, that house in the dream reminded me of the one Elizabeth Taylor had in *The Sandpiper*, and I was that woman she played who was, so completely, herself.

Cynthia went with me to Antigua, but Jeff decided to spend the vacation with his father. They spent a lot of time together that winter. Richard had moved to Washington, D.C., and had lots of friends, as always, in broadcasting, politics, and newspapers. It was a stimulating life. Jeff enjoyed it, and he enjoyed his father. He had a chance to talk about things that interested him, the books he had read, local and national politics, and Johnny Carson. Jeff had memorized more routines than we cared to hear. His father was a fresh audience, and a good one. Jeff was proud of his father, and his father was proud of him. Richard introduced him to his friends, took him to the parties, and gave him a chance to swim in a very big pond.

It was during that trip that Richard suggested he apply for a job as a page at the conventions. As he had been wise in suggesting that Jeff go out West, he understood Jeff's potential and knew where to lead it.

In Antigua, Cynth and I bought some fabric for Elliot's daughter, Ann, and she made herself a lovely dress. She wore it over to show me, and we spent the whole day together. I got a beautiful letter from his mother Connie. She told me about her pussy-willow tree, her cat, and she said she missed me.

There are some scraps of poetry among my notes, entitled simply "Antigua":

> It seems I am so often at the ending
>   and relieved.
> Why do beginnings hold so little fear?
> How can I plunge headlong and drunk
>   with expectation, into hope?
>
> She is a cat who rubbed against your happiness
> And wandered off, tail high, alone.
> She'll find a fire of her own.

Cynthia finished her junior year of high school with almost straight A's, and plenty of time to hang around with her friends. It seemed to me they picked very odd hours to come and go, and the destination was always vague. She spent some weekends on Long Island with her friend Emily Friedan. Emily's mother, Betty Friedan, was deeply involved in the women's movement, and it must have been much like the house my mother grew up in a few miles away sixty years before. Her friend Oliver had already appeared in two movies, *Summer of '42* and *Class of '44*, so he had enough money to spend on dinners and taxis. That winter, he was in a play on Broadway, besides school, so he not only had money, he had late hours. Both kids had curfew, and Jeff kept saying I wasn't strict enough enforcing it, but only once did she really frighten me.

I had asked her to call when she was leaving her friend's house, because I didn't like her in cabs alone at night. She called at twelve and said she was leaving. She didn't arrive. At two, I called the police and they alerted all the patrol cars on the Upper East Side. When she walked in at five-thirty in the morning with two friends, there were three patrolmen in the kitchen. I didn't have to say anything. I had to leave for work in two hours, I had not been to bed, and she had been very thoughtless. She did just forget. I could believe that. I had been sixteen, and I had forgotten about my mother, too.

"Okay, guilt is bad for you . . . just don't do it again!"

She was sixteen and sometimes thoughtless, but she was sensitive and wise in so many other ways. She was tender and aesthetic, almost to the point of pain. She read Kafka. She loved T. S. Eliot. Her big campaign was to convince her English teacher that Bob Dylan was a true poet and a major one. She read Camus in French. She spent hours looking at Art Nouveau in the shops along the avenue and arranged the food on her plate for a still life. When I asked her one day what it felt like inside a theorem she said, "The same way it feels to you when you find the right chord for a song. The tension is perfect." I understood what she meant. She wanted a Klimt poster for her birthday, and to me she looked like the women he painted.

In June, Jeff got word that he had been hired as a page by NBC for the Democratic and Republican conventions. He still planned to go West, so he would leave New York for Miami, go from there to Oregon, and straight back to Miami. He would be traveling twenty thousand miles by himself, earning his own money as he went. My only contribution was a suit.

He was so tall and slim, Brooks Brothers didn't make one in his size. So, Bobby Anton said, "Take him to Meledandri." The only suit young enough for him was a pale taupe cotton suede, that cost two hundred and twenty-five dollars, but it was worth every penny just to see his face as he looked at himself. He was fifteen years old. He was off to see the Wizard, and he was ready!

The kids and Mother had gone. Mother took Bonnie with

her, so it was just my, cat and me. That summer, for the first
time, there was no frantic rush for the telephone. I spent evenings alone with my guitar and my yellow pads, because, by golly!
that is what I wanted to do. I still put the lyrics under the couch,
but I had had the fun of doing them, the joy and the satisfaction!
I loved to run my fingers along the neck of the guitar, pressing
down at random just to hear a different combination, find a new
direction. I loved the words that seemed to come from nowhere
into my head and the hours I could spend finishing the pattern,
telling the story, sanding the rhyme.

The very young man was in town occasionally. He had never
forgotten a birthday or a holiday call. We were friends. I remembered, again, acceptance, and just plain fun. We rented a car and
drove through New England. We had no plan, no destination, no
reservations, just a little time. I love to ride in a car. You can look
back and see where you have been, you can see ahead, and you
are not in a place, you are detached, in motion. There is something to look forward to around every curve.

I spent some weekends at Indian Hill with Perc and Ernesto.
The house was finished and beautiful. I had my own little suite
upstairs in the oldest section of the house, but on my birthday
Perc insisted I sleep in his room, the big square one in the front
of the house facing the river. I climbed into the high four-poster
and lay for a long time with the breeze across my body and the
song of the river. I ran my hand along the cool sheets and almost
automatically thought, "What a waste. I should be with a man
on such a perfect night, someone I love." I even tried to picture
him, but no face that I could conjure seemed to fit. I had not
known a love I would go back to. Love had always been a test,
and I had failed. Love had been a giant bowl I had poured myself
into and could never fill. It had drained my energy and left me
empty.

Only my imagined love was constant, strong, a place to lean
against and trust, with deep pockets for my love, a smile of welcome. So intimate, my naked morning friend, when passion
throws the sheets aside, my ageless child, my lover and companion.

He was not there. Perhaps he would never be, but I had the

feelings just the same. I could hear the river rushing, feel the wind billowing white curtains. So it would be for me.

In September, the show insisted, as always, that I take a damn vacation. In a swivet of indecision I booked passage on a ship touring the Greek Isles. Cynthia panicked for me.

"Take the guitar," she kept insisting. "Maud, you'll die if you don't."

I didn't, but I took the five hundred balloons Betty Tour-tellot gave me, and as I was walking out the door Jeff handed me a brand-new Dartmouth jacket his father had given him, a light little nylon shell with the school letters on the back.

"I just have the feeling you'll need it."

He was right. Everywhere I went, students talked to me. If it hadn't been for them, nobody would have. Too late, I discovered that my inside cabin was somewhere in the hold, and not one soul spoke English. Even solitary confinement, however, cannot spoil the glories of ancient Greece, or the mysterious wonders surrounding the blue sea.

The first three days alone in Venice were a little too much, but later, with a glass of wine, in Crete or Mykonos, or sitting on the steps in Santorini, I would blow up a balloon and the children came. One after the other they appeared, until the white square was filled with long black dresses and dancing colored lights.

I had time to look and read, and plenty of time to observe the other people from a stool at the end of the bar every evening:

> This is just a movie show
> In a language I don't know.
> The titles would explain, no doubt,
> But I'm on the inside looking out.
> All I packed was fantasy.
> Dreams are not a place to be.
>
> Magic circles every where,
> Husbands, lovers, wives all there.
> Each family gathered close around
> Its circus ring,
> And I'm the only clown.

BOTH OF ME 359

In their faces I can see
My own reflection mocking me.

Now and ever chasing rainbows.
Never waiting till the rain goes,
I'll stand outside the candy store.
Someday I'll find what I was looking for.

On a tombstone in Crete, marking the grave of their most famous poet, the inscription was translated, and I wrote it down because it disturbed me so:

I have no fear
I have no hope
I am free.

Months later, I learned that in Greek the word for hope and
the word for expectation are the same. I think he meant, I have
no expectation, I am free.

Sometime in the summer of 1972 I happened to mention to
Ken Harvey that I would love to find someone to handle the
music and the next day he had come up with a name and a
phone number.

Nat Shapiro's outer room was papered with album covers,
and if you looked closely most of them were from *Hair*, or had
music by Michel Legrand. The inner office was crowded and
dingy, with records and books stacked everywhere, a coffeepot on
a hot plate, and behind the desk in the corner a tall man with a
round belly, named Nat Shapiro. He had straight, black hair that
tended to fall into his eyes and small, delicate hands. When he
listened he held his head high, cocked a little to one side, almost
like a bird.

"Play for me," he said, ever so gently, and for the first time I
was not nervous playing for someone new.

While I played he got out his camera and took a picture of
me. "I like to record the beginning," he said.

I stayed quite a long time, playing other songs and talking, and when I left he asked me to make a tape of everything in my catalog. He said there was someone else he wanted to hear the songs, but he was very explicit, "Just play them yourself and sing. I don't want any fancy production."

The next time I saw him, there was a young black man in the office.

"I'd like you to meet Harold Wheeler," Nat said, and the young man rose to shake hands with me. He was about my height, but his body was slimmer. He wore dark glasses, and he had a scraggly little beard on the tip of his chin.

I suppose it was agreed that day that the three of us would become partners, because that is what happened. I don't remember another moment when it was not taken for granted. We simply began. Harold made an appointment to come by my house, and begin putting the music down. For the first and last time he arrived at the appointed hour. I played a song for him on the guitar, and he made a few notes on a scrap of paper. Then he went to the piano and began to play. He was working with the melody, moving the bass line, inverting the chords, adding others, and he was not aware of anything else. He did not notice when Grandmother came to stand in the doorway, and when I looked at her we both had tears in our eyes.

If the music has done nothing else for me, it has brought me into the company of genius. When great musicians are performing, they are great. A great musician's working, experimenting, listening, is a kind of revelation nothing else I've ever experienced can touch. It is a glimpse inside a complex mind allowing sensitivity to control the moment.

Over the next two years I would share hundreds, thousands of moments with Harold. There was always something new, something unexpected, something wonderful.

The task before us was clear-cut and monumental. I was to continue writing, but with guidance from Nat and Harold. Nat would arrange for publishing and, if possible, get us a record deal. Harold would set and arrange the music and, if possible, teach me to sing. We always worked at my house. Harold would arrive between one and two hours late, put down the black attaché case and take out the folder marked "Mary's Demo Music." At some point he drew a heart in red pencil around the words. Usually, he would have something to drink, but he rarely wanted dinner. When he left, he disappeared like a will-o'-the-wisp. The timing was erratic, but he was around enough to seem like part of the family. The kids were used to coming home from school and waving hello from the hall, so as not to interrupt, and Mother usually managed to station herself where she could hear every note.

"Tell him not to play so jazzy, and not quite so loud," she said. "You write simple songs, and they sound better played simply."

Her favorites were "Hold Me" and "Cherry Blossom Spring." When I wrote a new lyric she was always the first to hear it, listening so intently, then the wordless little nod and always the same sigh of approval. With one finger she would draw a line of tears down her cheek.

Usually, we just worked on the music. Sometimes, if it was late, we would talk, and Harold told stories about himself. He didn't have a piano until he was nine years old, and he played his first concert when he was twelve. At fourteen he was scheduled to play a concert somewhere in Texas. If he was slight of build at thirty, he must have been tiny as a boy. At least, that is the way I saw him in my mind when he told the story about going into a diner to get his supper. Two men chased him out and he hid in an alley until it was time to go on stage.

One night, after we had worked for six or eight months, he said, "I think this is the one place I feel completely at ease. If I needed a place to stay, and it was three in the morning, I think I'd probably come here and lie down on a couch, knowing it was all right."

It was the way I felt too. I had discovered a kind of circle in myself, and the house had become a circle around the circle. I think it was Harold who started to call the apartment "Mary's Mountain." Only once, after almost a year, was the spell broken. He walked in for rehearsal, and I knew instantly something had happened, but it was half an hour before he would tell me what it was. He kept saying it was just a mistake and wasn't important.

"The elevator man stopped on two instead of bringing me all the way up," and he said finally, "I hadn't said where I wanted to go. I never do."

"Of course not, he knows you."

"He said, 'Oh, I thought you were the colored boy who fixes the machines on two.' I said, 'No, I'm going up to Mary's,' and he said, 'Oh, you're the boy who tunes the piano.'" Harold grinned. "I told you, it wasn't important," and went to make himself a drink.

Not important! Tears were streaming down my face as I rang for the elevator. Al was so upset and startled he started to cry too.

"But I did think he was the colored boy who—"

"Don't use that word!"

"What word? I thought he was the boy who tunes—"

"Don't use that word! He is a man!"

When I walked back into the living room, Harold was already at the piano, his beautiful, beautiful hands on the white keys, and I said, "We're safe inside the music."

Without looking up he said, "You talk in song titles. Did you write the rest of the words for 'Lonely There'?" I nodded, and as he played the ride-out he had added to the song, I sang him the new words:

> "Winter wind blow gentle now my willow's bare.
> Sunlight walked across the sky and down
>   the stair.
> Darkness close my eyes, it is too lonely,
>   lonely there."

For me, the winter of 1972–73 was the music and the mountain. There was hardly ever a reason to go out, because everyone I wanted to see came here. We didn't even close the door until we went to bed, so friends and kids streamed in and out, and I cooked dinner for whoever was around at mealtime. I met Michel Legrand in Nat's office one afternoon, and he sent me some tunes to write lyrics for. He or Nat always invited me if Michel was recording or playing jazz in a club. Like Harold, he had been a child prodigy, and any man who can hear every instrument in the orchestra all the time must live too close to heaven and too close to hell.

One night after a recording session we all walked in the rain to a bar for a drink, and he asked me if I'd ever written a song about death. I asked him why, and he said, "I carry death in my pocket."

Another night he had recorded with sixty-three musicians and singers, live, and I knew he had written the arrangements the night before. He said, "I write a page of music, and I turn to the next. I never see it again until I walk in the studio. If I did, if I looked back once, I would be on that page for the rest of my life."

During most of that session his little girl was wheeling her baby carriage back and forth across the control room, murmuring to her doll in French. All the songs that night had featured the alto sax, and Phil Woods could do no wrong. At one o'clock the musicians filed out and Michel turned the faders up till the room screamed. He let me touch heaven with him.

It was Jeff's junior year. If possible, his momentum seemed to build, and he had begun to make some valuable personal contacts of his own. At school he worked with the channeled energy and concentrated direction of an already mature man, but occasionally I still saw the flicker in his eyes of the boy. One day I noticed the bottle of Jack Daniel's was missing from the bar and a funny, sweet odor coming from his room just before he dashed by me, his face ashen to green, and threw up his toes. I was greatly relieved.

Most nights he still worked until three or four. He was maintaining a straight A average in school and spending hours on the newspaper as the editorial editor. He felt enormous pressure to bring up his grade average that still included his slower years, and his one big goal was to be named editor-in-chief of the *Trinity Times* for the next year. In May I got a call from school. The lady said I would probably want to be there for the graduation ceremony. I knew he had won something, but I also knew nothing was as important to him as the paper. "Search" rehearsed the afternoon before, so I would have the morning off, and I took a cab to the school.

I always feel a little uncomfortable going to parent functions by myself, so I had gone in a side door that opened into the hallway instead of the lobby. I stood around for a few minutes, actually not sure if it was time to go and sit down, when I heard voices coming from around the corner, and someone saying Jeff's name. A whole group appeared and after a moment he saw me and sauntered over.

"Hi, Mom. You're early."

"I'm always early . . . So, uh—what's new?"

"Oh, yeah," he said, and turned the newspaper in his hand, so I could see. There it was! A banner headline, naming Jeff editor-in-chief. That was the tradition, to name the new editor with the last edition.

"Don't you dare cry."

"I promise! I won't even kiss you. But I don't think I'll take off my dark glasses."

He left with the gaggle of friends and I was glad of the chance to swallow the lump in my throat. Twenty minutes later, I did not even try to remain cool. I had assumed the surprise was his being named editor. When the headmaster announced that, for the first time, a junior had won the award for outstanding citizenship, and Jeff trotted down the aisle, the tears ran down my face and dripped freely from my chin. I kept thinking, "His father should be here to see."

Cynthia's senior year was intensely social and casually academic. She had already finished most of the work required and the curriculum was designed to give students the choice of where best to spend their time. A lot of time was spent discussing colleges. I had, quietly, hoped she would go to Radcliffe and was not aware that at the last minute she withdrew her application. Everyone else, including Jimmy on the elevator, had much more influence on her decision. The person who seemed to have the most was her old friend, Carla Javits. Carla had graduated a year early and gone to the University of Michigan. Perhaps there was something appealing about having a friend already established, perhaps it was the anonymity of a large university. There was, too, a small inner circle for students who were academically advanced. She was accepted into Residential College and the deed was done. She would go to the University of Michigan.

Cynthia's graduating class had distinguished itself. More of them had been accepted at Harvard and Yale than any class before them, but at the last moment a serious cloud fell over them all. A joke had appeared in the yearbook, in the form of a Double-Crostic. The joke was on the headmaster, and he was furious, so furious he decided to expel the perpetrators and withhold the diplomas of everyone even vaguely connected with the foul deed. The seniors were called in one by one and asked—with the promise of immunity—to name names. The whole ritual smacked of McCarthy and they refused, but they had no recourse. Four of the outstanding students might be restrained from going to college. The one way to get even, they decided, was for the rest of the students to refuse to shake his hand when he gave them their diplomas.

Cynth looked more beautiful than I had ever seen her. She wore a little brown sleeveless shirt and a long white pleated skirt. I sat between Richard and Jeff in the auditorium and listened to Nat Hentoff's speech. It was the time of Watergate, and Mr. Hentoff talked about "Auto Anesthesia," about people who see and hear and know what is wrong, but remain silent.

The headmaster took his place at the podium, and the class of 1973 began to file by. Two thirds of them had taken the hand he extended, when he called Cynthia's name. She walked down the steps, across the stage, and stopped. He handed her the little white scroll, and as he held out his hand she whirled, the white skirt fanning out around her feet. The audience caught its breath in one gasp.

Richard said, "My God, what did she do?" and Jeff said, "My God, she did it!"

Two more rows shook his hand, and her little friend Sally's name was called. Even in her platform shoes she was short, and her steps resounded across the stage. She was the only other one who refused his hand.

A few minutes later we walked into the reception on the top

floor of the school, and as Cynthia appeared in the door they started to applaud.

She stopped and turned. "Let's go," she said. "They don't understand. That's not what it was about."

That same month, Harold and Nat and I went to Bell Records to meet a man named Dave Carrico. We met in a room that reminded me of the first-class lounge on a 747. There was a piano and a few chairs in the long narrow space, and some windows that let in the soot and the noise of Broadway and Fifty-seventh Street.

We did about four songs, and he said, "I like you, because you're singing to me. Let me talk to some people and I'll get back to you."

A week later he came to the house with Gordon Bossum, who was in charge of sales, and Irv Biegel, who was head of A&R, which stood for Artists and Records. That night we did half a dozen songs. Then Irv asked if I could do a standard. We had never even tried a song I hadn't written, but I said, "How about 'Little Girl Blue'?" It was a song I always did with Barbara, at a party, so at least I knew the words and I assumed Harold knew the tune. I didn't even look at him, I just listened and floated into the song. He could make magic, that man. He could weave a carpet for me to fly on.

When we had finished, Irv said, "Let's make a record."

After they left, I started clearing away the glasses. Grandmother was in the kitchen.

"I heard! I heard!" She tried to smile, but she was too happy so she ran her finger down her cheek. "We did it, sister! We did it!"

That was the first of June. They wanted the record for release in September, and Harold would be in Vegas with Petula Clark for the month of June. Since I had made my first album in one day, that seemed like all the time in the world. I didn't know most people spend from six months to a year. Actually, we spent six days from the first day of recording to the final mix and mastering, and three of those Harold stayed up all night doing demos for somebody else for quick cash. I was a little cross, especially the night I knew he still had to write the string parts. It never entered my head he might need the money. Harold always insisted on paying for the cabs and drinks. Money was a subject that had never come up.

The company had decided that an album of completely unknown songs was chancy, so they asked me to find some familiar material. Frank, my hairdresser suggested I sing "Peaceful" by Kenny Rankin, and "Let Me Be the One" by Paul Williams. I had loved John Denver's "Take Me Home, Country Roads" since the first time I heard it in Nashville. It reminded me of Daddy and the last trip to see him, when I was afraid I wouldn't get there in time, that one line: "I should have been home yesterday." Harold hated the song, until I suggested putting that part first. He heard the urgency in the words and put it into the rhythm track.

The record company wanted me to sing "And I Love You So" by Don McLean, and the theme from *The Poseidon Adventure*, "The Morning After." That was the list, along with six I had written myself and one with Michel Legrand.

It was a long way from the little demo records, the beautiful week of music with sausage and biscuits, to the huge recording studio on Fifty-seventh Street in New York. We were in Studio A, at Media Sound, with an enormous console, ten feet by four feet of dancing lights and knobs and a thoughtful young engineer named Alan Varner, who seemed to know what it all meant. There was a couch in the control room, just behind the glass, where you could sit and listen to a playback, and there was a bench at the back that wasn't as comfortable, but the sound was better. To the right of the control room was a small isolation booth for a singer, with glass on two sides, looking out into the studio or the control room. The first three days were spent putting down the rhythm tracks. I met the musicians: Dave Dutemble on electric bass, Robert Thomas on drums, and the two guitarists. George Davis I already knew—he played with Michel—but the young man was new to me. Actually, even Harold had not met Brian Koonin until that day. The man he had asked for first was busy.

"I want a very sensitive player," he told the contractor.

"Well, I've heard the boy, and he is sensitive, but he's not experienced."

"I'll go with sensitivity."

It was the first professional date Brian had ever played. He hadn't even finished school, and his twentieth birthday happened to be the week we recorded.

Of course, Harold played all the keyboards himself.

In the taxi on the way to the studio the first day, I said to him, "I'm not ready, Harold. I'm not a real singer."

"You're real," he said, "that's what's good about what you do, and you'll never feel you're ready. Probably in a year, maybe in a month, you'll sing better. When the record is finished you'll want to start all over. You'll hear the mistakes, and you'll hate it. But you can't do that. All you can ever do is your best this day, this minute. It's honest . . . it's all you can ask of yourself."

An hour later I was standing in the middle of the studio, running the song, while the musicians played through their parts. Harold nodded to me, and I went into the little booth and clamped the phones on my head. We ran through the song a couple of times. Alan made adjustments on the mike, and it was time to begin. My knees were like water and my mouth was dry. My breath came in little gasps, automatically, and my mind was like cotton candy. I think it was the sight of Harold's hand, stroking the air on the downbeat, that made it possible. His hands were always graceful, expressive, but when he played or conducted they were music themselves. I would do the best I could that minute. It was all I could ask.

The promotion tour was to begin September 9. I would travel over a two-month period to about fifteen different cities, appearing on the local television and radio shows and signing album covers in department stores and record shops. The first major appearance was on Jerry Lewis' telethon, Labor Day weekend. Harold didn't want to take the time, and for me it was another first that I dreaded so much I couldn't make myself think about it. Nat was firm. It was important and we should go. Another singer he managed was appearing too, and Harold would conduct for both of us. I had no idea, then, how many hours he would have to spend writing parts for horns and reeds for my two songs. I thought we had arrangements from the album. I was wrong.

Joel gave me lessons in putting on my makeup, Bobby bought me a black mat jersey pantsuit and high-heeled sling pumps, and I figured I was as ready as I was going to be. I did love the idea of appearing on such a big show and going to Vegas. Only my knees and my stomach refused to react with enthusiasm. It was too important, and without Harold encouraging me and supporting me, no way could I make it. Always, the burden fell to him and he accepted it.

They called our flight and we threaded down the tube to the door of the plane. The hostess took the boarding passes from Nat and said, "You've given me four boarding passes. I see only three people."

She couldn't see Harold, but I could. For a split second, the lips pressed slightly, the anger and hurt hidden behind dark glasses. Nat hardly noticed, and the other singer didn't at all, only Harold and I. We didn't say anything, we just walked to the back of the plane and took two single seats by the window. On the back of a vomit bag I started to write "Safe Inside the Music," while he made notes for the next album on another.

That night I borrowed a guitar and began the music:

> Unspoken words are like a pistol in your hand.
> They may go off when someone cannot understand.
> Words are gentle spoke in rhyme.
> No words at all are best sometime.
> You and I are safe inside the music.
>
> PLAY YOUR SONG AND I WILL SING MY SONG FOR YOU.

The night before the show I had a nightmare that I had fallen off my high-heeled shoes, and I spent two hours trying to figure out a way to dye my sneakers black. Ink! That would do it!

But I didn't know how to shorten the pants, and by then it was time to get ready to go. Harold and I held hands on the way to the entrance, and his were as cold as mine.

"Don't you ever get over it?" He shook his head.

"No, you just get used to it."

The show was fine. Harold's piano and his arrangement were behind me, and out front somewhere there was an audience, but up close, where I could see, were my own familiar little red camera lights, like friends from home.

Before I got ready to go on tour there were a number of things to get ready for around the house. One was Cynthia's move to Michigan. She had been home all summer and we'd had fun, but all in all it had been a disappointment. Expectation hung in the air and clouded conversations about everything. Plans with her boyfriend, Danny, hadn't jelled. Buddies were away, and somewhere in her middle she must have been edgy about college and the rest of her life. She was edgy, and I was too busy. I let the days slip by without paying attention to the dates until it was almost time for her birthday, and I had found no present that really pleased me. I had thought to give her money to buy clothes for school, or fix up her room. Too late, I realized that was not what she wanted. She had hinted about a piece of jewelry in an antique shop, but it was too late to run and get that. The shop had closed and somewhere I knew it wasn't really the necklace we were talking about. I remember the remorse and guilt and regret, but I had forgotten the letter. She found it recently among the papers she had saved. It is dated July 28, 3:30 A.M.:

It is almost your birthday. You are almost a woman hovering before you fly. There is no thing that I can put into a box and wrap that says what it means to me. You have been my joy since the day you were born. I will not be lost when you leave, but you know, and only you, how I will miss you.

I seem to have failed you today . . . Because I did not treat you like a child . . . the appropriate surprise. Perhaps that is my gift. I did not intend it, but each thing that occurred to me bore the mark of my taste, or standards, or money, which you

36. Queen Mary.

37.   On the street where I live.

38.   Twentieth Anniversary. Larry Haines, Melba Rae, Charlie Irving, Mary, Chris Lowe, and Dan Levin.

39. On "The David Frost Show," 1972.

40. Tony George, when Jo was blind.

41. Jo with Linda Bove from the theater of the deaf.

42. Mary and Brian Koonin.

44. Listening to a playback with Michel Legrand and Nat Shapiro.

43. Harold Wheeler and friend.

45. With Ross Martin in Vegas, 1973.

46. The concert that didn't happen.

47. The "Search" cast of 1976.

48. With Ernesto at Woodville.

49. On location for NBC, 1975.

50. Twenty-fifth Anniversary, September 3, 1976. Mary, Cynthia, and Jeff.

stand away from and so do I. You have succeeded in being yourself, finding your own way.

I did not want to go to the jewelry store on an errand anymore than you wanted me to. My only true gift is the way I feel about you, as a daughter, whatever that means. You came by magic to stay awhile a few years ago. We have become very good friends and we are very lucky. You have not been Mary's daughter. I have been Cynthia's mother.

No thing seemed appropriate today, unless it is something you have never had before . . . a car. Yes, that is a symbol of independence. Okay, learn to drive and this is your IOU for one car. It just has to be something you want, not something to wear, or play with, or lose. You are almost ready, almost.

Go to Michigan my love and enjoy! Enjoy your mind and your sweet self, your face and your body. Get back in the habit of using that mind. It's too good to waste, and too much fun. Take care of yourself, and you'll have more fun.

Mail the attached coupon when you are ready and . . .

love, Mom

It was the wrong school. I knew it! Too big, too impersonal. I hoped and prayed one professor would catch her interest, fan the spark. "Please, God," I prayed every night, and the special prayer I always say when a plane is taking off or landing, "Please, God, take care of them for me."

There was a lot going on at home and there were strange vibrations around the record company. For three months we had all had such a good time together. Irv loved my stories about getting lost and made me tell them over and over. Beverley Weinstein liked to tell about the day we took the pictures for the album cover, and I walked everybody to death trying to find the right spot. Melissa Manchester and Barry Manilow were the young big acts on the label, and they just said, "Hi," when I saw them, as if I really belonged—whether I was rock and roll or not. It had been an easy, comfortable place and one evening Larry Uttal said, "Mary, we don't expect you to make it with this album—it may take three or four—but we believe in you."

Suddenly it all felt different. Of course, Paranoid Polly thought it was personal, until Beverley told me over lunch that the company was probably being sold. That's what was wrong. Nobody dared make a move.

Probably it was not the best time and the best way to start out across country. I had no idea what to expect and no idea what I was supposed to do, and the trip was a lot like a roller coaster ride. At least I started at the top. The first morning, I stood in the middle of a very pretty suite in Phoenix, Arizona, all by myself, and listened to the album with the kind of joy I had first experienced in Nashville. All that music, and I was right smack in the middle of it! I cried real tears of joy. Then I had brunch with a television writer, and from one to two I signed albums for fifty ladies who made me feel so good I wanted to kiss them. I spent the afternoon in a booth at a fair, supposedly signing autographs, and nobody told me until five o'clock that the fair was only open that day to children with emotional or mental handicaps. I had cocktails with a wonderfully thoughtful man from a local newspaper, dinner with a music reviewer, and at nine I got on a plane for Seattle.

In Seattle a record promoter named Jerry Morris was in charge, and we charged. There were two or three television interviews and a couple of disc jockeys, but brunch was the main event, with writers from the two big papers and several small ones. It took time to meet each one individually, lunchtime, and I still hadn't talked to everybody, so I wrote a speech on my napkin. It was Jerry who started calling me "Mother," and the name stuck through the tour. Well, let's face it!—there weren't any other ladies over forty peddling their first record albums that year.

At seven that night I was scheduled for the last album signing. Only half a dozen ladies showed up. One sweet young mother with a child in a stroller stayed until everyone was gone. Her dress was shabby, and the baby shouldn't have been out so late. She had come to see Jo, I knew that. She bought an album, and she shouldn't have spent the money.

I wanted to give her one, but I didn't know how. I thought of her so many times in the next few weeks, and I remember her now. One of the beautiful people who touched my life and helped me, and I didn't know how to thank her. I had to go. I had to catch a plane for Dallas, because some maniac had put the trip together without a map, or maybe somebody like me had gone to work for an airline.

In every city there was at least one disaster and something wonderful. If the ads had been placed on the Want Ad page, very few people showed up, but then, some sweet disc jockey would like one song and I'd sell a few albums. In Cleveland, five hundred people were jammed into a discount house called Bill's, and I wanted to hug everybody, so I did, and the promoter said, "Jesus! There goes Mother! We're gonna lose her altogether this time!"

In St. Louis, a young announcer on the evening news, who didn't approve of Soap Opera, was so rude the switchboard was swamped, and the next afternoon the store was jammed. I never knew what to expect, still I couldn't stop hoping. I so often felt I had failed, but if there were only five ladies waiting they were upset too, and they were so dear to me they made up for it. In between appearances, I ran back to New York and did the show once or twice a week.

Harold and I were scheduled to go to an affiliate meeting in October. I had done "Search," and he had a recording session. We managed to fall into the plane with our bags in our hands as the door was closing. We hadn't seen each other for weeks, and we hadn't even planned what we would do. The plane landed at five. We had a rehearsal at five-thirty, and we both already had done a day's work. But there was one lovely moment. A beautiful woman in the front seat stood up and came back to us.

"Mr. Wheeler, I never had a chance to thank you. You ran out after the concert, but I wanted to tell you, you were magnificent."

Harold was standing in the aisle, pleased, but a little embarrassed, too. He thanked her, and then he said, "I'd like you to meet a friend of mine. This is Mary Stuart . . . Mary, this is Miss Leontyne Price."

I guess I knew he performed serious classical music, I just didn't think about it, and of course he hadn't said anything. I can't even say I was prouder, after that, to be his friend. I don't think that could have been possible.

When we got to the hotel Harold had to borrow a piano from an upstairs room and revoice the chords around the keys that wouldn't move.

Again, the show was fine. It was another in a growing list of firsts. That night, I could see the audience. I sang for half an hour and even talked a little. I took a plate of cold meatballs from the hors d'oeuvre table after the show. There was some bread on one of the tables pushed out into the hall on my floor when I went up to bed, and that was dinner. I had an eight o'clock flight in the morning to someplace else. Harold had taken the night flight back to New York. He had an early morning jingle. He was so busy he was living on a diet of Tootsie Rolls and brandy. Still, he took time to promote the music and help me.

Two weeks later a young college student from North Carolina called to ask if I would like to do a concert. I automatically said no, because the idea of doing a whole concert was preposterous. But when I mentioned it to Harold he said, "Do it! We'll be fine." The concert was scheduled for January 8.

I was in town to do my shows for "Search" two or three times a week during October and November, and every now and then I went by the record company. The faces were still noncommittal, and folks were beginning to talk about going to work someplace else. The promotion director had already left and nobody was hired to take his place, so there wasn't any promotion except what Janet Storm and Enid Moore, my buddies at CBS, could drum up.

The last appearance was on "The Mike Douglas Show," December 8. Nat and Harold, Joel Mason and I all piled into a limousine and drove to Philadelphia. I had to go to Dayton that night to sign albums in a big department store, but then it was really over, and I could go home and start getting ready for Christmas.

The "Search" party was the biggest ever—Lucille counted over two hundred and fifty people—and I think it was the happiest. As always, any actor who had ever been on the show who was in town came by. Our camera crew and stagehands all brought their wives. Bob Short and Stan Potter, and John Potter, our new P&G representative, saved our party for last, and everybody from the record company came. Several times I noticed John Potter talking to Irv Biegel, and I overheard the word "premium" as I passed them. I heard John Potter say, "We would want more than one album if we were to get involved." I wasn't sure what the situation was at the record company. I had a feeling it wasn't good, but it was Christmas. I would worry about that after New Year's.

After New Year's there was one other little thing to worry about. I had promised Jerry, from North Carolina, I would do a concert at his college. I had not seen Harold since the trip to Cleveland, and the eighth of January was beginning to feel very close. I suppose if I had had the time, I'd have worried myself sick. I didn't know how to put a concert together! I'd never even seen one! I did make a list of songs, and began to put them in some kind of order. Then I started making notes of witty sayings and clever remarks. After a couple of days I threw those away and started making notes about the songs and why they'd been written in the first place, and finally, just after Christmas, I managed to get hold of Harold.

He came by for an hour one evening and rearranged the songs, and then he said, "Run the rap."

"What's the rap?"

"You're an actress," he said, "and you have something to say to the audience."

I said, "Oh," and thought for a few minutes.

I started to talk "to the audience," and he clicked his stopwatch. After a few minutes he shook his head.

"No," he said. "You're rambling all over the place. Shorten it down to four minutes, and we'll run the show in one piece. Let's see . . ." He got out his appointment book, picked a day just before New Year's, and as he was leaving he said, "Oh, call Brian Koonin. He already knows the songs, so he'd be good to take along."

I called Brian and told him about the show. He said fine, and when I mentioned that Harold and I were going to do a runthrough, he said he'd probably be there. Everybody, you may notice, was being very, very casual about the whole thing, behaving as though standing up on a stage and doing a two-hour show was something they did everyday. Well, maybe they did, but I didn't, and I was beginning to feel the clutch. By New Year's I was running lyrics and running that damn rap all day and all night.

We did have our run-through, and it went amazingly well. It had occurred to me that we should put in some Carolina songs, and that they would be pretty sung in harmony. Harold turned to Brian. "You're the youngest, you're it. You sing with her."

Brian just smiled. "Okay," he said. "And maybe I ought to bring my banjo."

Jerry called to say that everything was arranged down there, and that he even had a group of students all rehearsed to do backup vocals. What had started out to be a quiet little trip to a tiny town to try out some material and learn how to do a concert, began to get out of hand, I thought. Nat was going, the record company was sending down at least one person, and everybody was still being cool as a cucumber except me. I was mostly nauseous.

At least twice every day I ran the whole show, all two hours, by myself, once out loud in the afternoon, with a little cassette of Harold and Brian playing the songs. Then, at night, after I went to bed, I ran it all again in my mind. Harold and Brian were to go down the afternoon of the sixth for rehearsal with the backup vocals and promotion. On the fifth, Harold called to say he couldn't be there until the afternoon of the seventh, so Brian and I went alone.

There was a lot to do. We had interviews all day in Greensboro, and a lunch for the press. Brian drove the big Cadillac they loaned us and we rehearsed our harmony in the car. He got sick, so I found out what he doesn't eat and that we could talk easily about almost anything, like fear and oddball sensitivity. Brian is small, about my height, but under 120 pounds, with thick, wavy brown hair. His eyes are even bigger seen through his glasses, and his face is almost too handsome. He was also very, very young. It occurred to me that we were going to look pretty odd sitting on stools together down front. But our voices blended, and the banjo sounded so sweet. He even made it seem easy, and I know he was almost as nervous as I was. Harold arrived about five in the afternoon, and we sat up until one, writing the show. I wrote a list of cues for each song and he did a sound and light plot for the men mixing the mikes and running the spotlights and dimmers.

The instruments, mikes, and amplifiers we had rented arrived at the theatre in the morning, and Harold showed the stagehands where to put them. The band arrived about noon the day of the show. About two, we had a sound check.

"I want you to at least hear the new things you've never done with a band," he said to me.

That lasted about two hours, and a lot of that time was spent adjusting sound levels and mikes. Except for the run-through in my living room, and a couple of hours with Brian in the car, it was all the rehearsal we had.

At five I did an interview for the local TV station, and at six I went with Harold and Brian to have supper and get ready. I think by then I had gone past nervousness into shock. My hands didn't shake while I put my makeup on, and I could eat, but the tension felt like the high E string on a guitar. It was a totally new situation. I had no idea how the body and the mind would react.

"Hey, Harold, what's the band doing for the opening number?"

"I'll let you know. I have to go to the john."

"Come on, Harold, we only have five minutes."

"I know. That's why I have to go to the john."

"Jesus, Harold, we got to play something!"

"Great idea! We'll do 'Something.' Now I'm going to the john."

Five minutes! I peeked out from behind the curtain. The theatre wasn't full, but there were about a thousand people there. The house lights were still on and I could see faces, all kinds of faces, and I remember thinking, "They won't hurt me!"

The band played "Something." Harold introduced me, the audience applauded, the long, yellow finger of light swept across the stage, and that was it! The first number was another Beatles tune, "A Little Help from My Friends," with the kids from the school, then a new one I had just written, called "Piece of a Dream." It seemed to fit, because it talked about new towns and new faces, and it had a nice "up" tempo. My heart was pounding and my knees felt weak, but they held me up. Three songs, four, five, and then the scary part—the rap.

I had written some key words on the floor, in case I forgot, just the way I did at home on "Search." They were laughing! I talked about Grandmother, and told a story about the kids, and they laughed! I relaxed a little and looked into the faces. Six songs, seven—too many ballads, I thought to myself—but the last song in the first act went well, a good solid rock gospel called "Show Me the Way." The kids sounded wonderful, and they were marching around with tambourines, having a great time. I was feeling better.

The second act started with "Take Me Home, Country Roads," and I heard the applause as soon as I left the wings. The second act was mostly country songs. Grandmother's song, with the story about writing it for her, and "Don't Look Back." They applauded again! They recognized it! Then Cynthia's song, "Yellow Balloon," by myself on a stool, with Brian playing. Suddenly I heard my voice filling the darkness, and then I heard the silence. One voice, one guitar, and the silence. There was closeness, acceptance in that silence. Acceptance of me and my little song about my daughter, and it was as if the audience had opened a door for me to pass through. A door through the barrier of fear and reserve. The reserve that hides behind the fear, the fear that what is not perfect will not be accepted.

I was far from perfect. Still, I was welcome. I don't suppose anyone in the theatre knew what a gift they gave to me that night.

Brian came down front with his banjo, and we sang our Carolina songs. They applauded and sang with us. We did the rest of the show and I could feel it moving faster. Harold held it all in his hands and let the music build around me. I was standing in a spotlight, in a little theatre, in a tiny college town, not feeling like myself at all—or maybe feeling completely like myself.

There was a standing ovation and an encore, and another standing ovation, but it's the faces I remember, and the silence. When I walked off, I was writing a new song.

There was a big party after the show that I don't remember

at all, except for some wonderful ham biscuits in the kitchen. I do remember there were still people in my room when I went to sleep. I was tired. I was at peace.

Harold had done it all, and the next day when Brian still didn't feel well and there was no one to drive the Cadillac to the airport, he did that, too.

On the plane he said to Brian, "That song you do alone with Mary is the showstopper," and Brian said, "I think it's because we're not ashamed to show how we feel about each other."

Brian went back to school in Boston, and a month later I sent him up a lyric:

> I can walk across the ceiling,
> or ribbon underneath my door.
> Never had much middle ground,
> never could just hang around.
> Haven't got a lot of time left anymore.
>
> He's the only other person, who knows the way
>   it is.
> But he's all I'm gonna need, so that's OK.
> We have so many ways to say,
> Baby lean on me we'll make it
> through the day.

He wrote a tune and sent it back on a cassette. We've been on so many planes to so many cities. So much has changed in both our lives, but we've been writing together ever since.

Meanwhile, back at the record company, the news was terrible. The company had not been sold, but nobody was moving in any direction. The sales reports were in, and I had only sold about fifty-five thousand records. It was respectable for a first album, but not enough to get picked up if there was new management. Irv Biegel was very nice about it.

"Mary, you can't sell records one at a time in every record store in the country. You have to have air play."

"How do you get air play?"

"You have to hire your own promotion."

"Okay. Who?"

"It's expensive."

"How much?"

"A thousand a month, plus expenses."

"Yipes!"

"And, you really should have a guy in some major cities just pushing the single."

"How much is that?"

"A hundred a week for each guy, plus expenses, and they spend a lot."

"I can't manage that, but maybe I can handle one promotion manager."

"Then get Bernie Ilson."

It was a big decision, and of course I talked to Nat about it. He didn't say much at the time, just looked very sad. I got a letter a few days later. He was terribly sorry, he said, but he simply couldn't be involved with a high pressure campaign. It was not his style. He wished to end his relationship as manager, and hoped we would remain friends. I was frantic, but nothing I could say made him change his mind. If the record was going to be saved, I had to do it myself.

Harold had been right, I did hate it. I had been singing in front of audiences for six months and was sort of learning how to do it. The record was old-fashioned and dated to me. There were clams, and the levels wavered. The phrasing was awkward in places, and square, but it was all I had. If I didn't sell that one, there would never be another. So, I went out on the road again. Bernie set up interviews with the press and got me coverage in every newspaper in the country. I called up local shows and said I was Miss Stuart's manager, and I knew she would be in that area and available for the show. There were small, local shows and more important ones like Phil Donahue, in Dayton. Sometimes the show paid my plane fare, sometimes I paid it myself. Toward the end of March I had just about worn myself out and made myself sick. One week, I was on "Search" on Wednesday, flew to Boston in the afternoon, did an interview and a talk show Wednesday night, and went to bed at one. I got up for an 8 A.M. talk show in the morning and put on my makeup sitting on the side of the bed, because the light in the bathroom was behind me on the ceiling, and it was pitch dark outside at six.

I had lunch with Brian before I took the shuttle home, already feeling ill. By the time the taxi got to Manhattan I couldn't make it. I asked the driver to stop and then I threw up right in front of Mary Ann's house. I was sick all night, but I had "Search" in the morning and Friday night I had to fly to Louisville for a telethon. Phil Woods' band was there, and they held me up when we had to do our long walks around the stage. Sunday night I went back to New York to do "Search" Monday morning. Then I flew to Pittsburgh for a TV show on Monday night and a late radio interview. At eight o'clock Tuesday morning I flew back to do "Search," a little late for rehearsal. Tuesday night I went to bed and slept for the first time in a week.

I had sold fifteen thousand records, but I still hadn't gotten any air play, and the numbers just weren't high enough. Two weeks later, the company was sold. Clive Davis would be taking over and I knew he would pass. At least I had tried, and I had been there. I had felt the music and heard the silence. No one could take that away.

The traveling and anxiety on the road were too much, and too much was going on at home. Jeff was in the middle of choosing a college, and in April I began to feel uneasy about Cynthia. She didn't want to come home for spring vacation, so I went to see her. It was raw and cold in Ann Arbor, with snow on the ground and an icy mist in the air. We were the only two people in the dormitory except for one boy who played *Tommy* on his hi-fi out the window over the deserted quadrangle.

When I had spoken to her over the phone, and when she was home for Christmas, she had talked about New Morning and the bookshop where Carla worked. While I was there, she spent two of our three evenings working for a film society. I met her after one of the films and gathered that what she did was collect the money and also pass out pamphlets spread on a table outside the auditorium. A small man with long, curly hair pulled back into a kind of ponytail was just collecting the last of them as I arrived. I didn't get a good look at him. He seemed to be in a hurry. His name, she said, was Glen.

We had a good time together when she was free. She had fixed up her room and it looked just like her. The walls were painted dark blue, with dark blue sheets and a blue and white quilt I'd sent her. Her Klimt hung on the wall at the end of her bed. There was a Matisse print and a tiny Picasso with just three lines on another wall. Little things that she enjoyed were scattered around. A beautiful brass teapot and two cups from the Craft Fair, a scarf she spread on her trunk that doubled as a table. There were candles in shades of purple and blue, in beautiful little candle holders, and of course her record player, with a stack of Dylan records.

"When I got here," she said, "I'd walked up three flights with all my bags. I opened the door, and the room was hospital green with dirty black linoleum. I cried for two hours."

She could laugh then, but she had cried when her bicycle and the new white rug were stolen.

We had one nice dinner and went to see *Paper Moon,* because she knew I would love it. I had some lyrics along to work on. I finally wrote a chorus to the song about the cruise ship, and she particularly liked that:

> Tell me what I'm doing here,
> I can't remember very clearly
> What I thought I'd find.
> I've lost my only mind.
> Started going nowhere,
> Now I think that I have gotten there
> Don't talk to me, you'd better shout.
> How do I get out.

We talked about the courses she was taking and obviously none of them really interested her or was much of a challenge. She had finished a lot of the required work in high school, so she was sliding through and making straight A's. One course on film drama and one on China were all she talked about. She was obviously restless and dissatisfied. She saw a lot of Carla, and weekends I gathered they both worked as volunteers at the film society.

"You know, I'm not one for beer parties or the dorm scene, Maud. So at least I get out of here on Friday and Saturday nights and see some neat films, for free."

"Okay, that's fine, but college comes first."

"I'm not sure . . . All I've done all my life is study. I've been in school since I was three years old. All that education, and I've never actually produced anything. At least at the film society I feel I'm doing something. I feel useful."

The three days were strained. I sat around her room waiting, for hours at a time. She was upset about it, but she had promised to work through the vacation. I left Sunday afternoon for New York. When I got into the bus for the drive to the Detroit airport she had already gone to a film showing.

Jeff had sent his applications in to the colleges of his choice. Harvard was first, and he desperately wanted to be accepted. His grades were straight A's, and when his SAT scores came back they were phenomenal. He had a perfect score of 800 in history. Still, the early, slower years brought the average down enough to make a problem for him. For weeks, his temper was short. He was disappointed in school, in himself, and he found fault with every move I made. Little misjudgments over the years, that had always occasioned a "dumb mother" joke, were suddenly major issues.

"Well, you blew milk and cookies, Mom!"

"I what?"

"Other peoples' mothers got out the milk and cookies after school. At our house there was a goddamned band in the living room!"

"Hey, come on . . . !"

"And men! What do you think it feels like, to have your mother out with guys all the time doing God knows what!"

"Look, damn it, guilt is bad for me too! Lay off!"

Arguments grew uglier. He was apparently even having problems at school, and his great friend, Mr. Bundy, was on sabbatical in England. One day he informed me that he had checked in with the school psychiatrist and I would be getting some bills. I didn't mind that, but I was terribly upset that he would check in with a doctor whose name I didn't even know. I'd had enough therapy to understand how important the right doctor is.

In a way, I thought, I understood what was going on. Like Cynth, he was about to start out on his own in the world. He didn't feel ready, but then nobody ever feels ready. At least I knew that. I also knew that the natural person to blame, if he wasn't ready, was me. Of course, I blamed myself, too. I knew I had made a lot of mistakes, and probably the list was a lot longer than I realized. Cynth was standing on the edge of something dark, and frightening, and I could not reach her. Jeff was not slamming doors—they were closed and locked.

The letters came from the colleges. He had been rejected at Harvard and accepted at Dartmouth. I knew his father wanted him to go there, so did John and Jane, his godparents, and privately I thought it was a much better school for him. He had spent his life in a big city. Four years in a quiet little New England community seemed a far better choice. I also thought his decision to see a therapist, whoever he was, had been wise. I was proud of him for being able to admit he had a problem, but, God knows, I couldn't say it to him.

One argument must have gotten out of hand, with old stored-up anger and resentments surfacing through the years. I don't remember what was said, but I remember, very clearly, walking around the house most of the night, and finally sitting down at the typewriter. It's interesting to me that neither of the kids ever acknowledged any of the letters I wrote them, but they both saved every one.

My Dearest Son,

The baddies are really here tonight . . . can usually fight it out in bed . . . but not this time. And for the first time in weeks . . . you are not up . . . wouldn't you know.

I can remember the years very clearly too. No, not just cozy house. I remember the anger . . . the war games and the pictures. I remember the fear. But as you say, it doesn't help that I remember, only what you remember. When we talk about it it comes out in pieces . . . and each piece gets distorted because it is not a picture itself . . . but it has all the colors of the rest of the puzzle. The fear which held you to me . . . and me to you . . . which made your father angry . . . which brought on the tantrums . . . and more anger . . .

and more fear. It was a difficult time for me, too. I am so sorry I was not wiser.

However . . . since I go through this every night, in some form or another . . . I've learned to work my way back . . . and the only way is to start thinking something positive.

My thoughts tonight are for you . . . the positive ones. I know how you feel . . . and I only wish I could have been where you are now when I was your age, because your doors are open. You have a marvelous mind . . . which you have disciplined yourself. You are aware of your weaknesses . . . and you even know what to do about them. I pretended (damn well too) that I was somebody else until quite recently . . . and that is a terrible waste of time. The hardest part of therapy is recognizing that you need it. That is a step so few people make . . . really make. You seem to have a sense of yourself that can handle it . . . accept a real picture. I'm not sure you know how important . . . how difficult . . . how great that is. By the time you are ready, by God, you will even be able to accept the imperfections in your perfect wife . . . your perfect children and your ideal community. You are able to question . . . wow.

Your father always said I loved you too much . . . and Cynth and him. He said once it was like a wall of emotion he couldn't see over . . . maybe that's what you meant when you said you had always known how much I needed from you. Again, you see very clearly. Maybe it's just as well I write feelings down, or spread them over the whole audience.

I think you are doing what is best. The choices are an ego trip . . . and nobody gets enough of those. You worked damn hard to earn them . . . As I said, you learned the discipline . . . you are learning to write, you are really awfully good . . . and if you can settle for a while in a place where you know it is alright to be. Where you do not have to be perfect and suave and forty . . . just plain Jeff, off guard, at ease . . . is enough for anybody!

love . . . Mom

It was decided he would go to Dartmouth, and he left after graduation to work on a newspaper in Amherst, Massachusetts, for his father's friends, the De Sherbinins. His graduation, however, like his sister's, was not uneventful. His final editorial was a blast at the headmaster when he discovered that Mr. Bundy had been undermined and dismissed in absentia. The speeches he and his friend Stephen Crist made during the ceremony blasted the whole system and forced the school to look for a new headmaster.

I was relieved not to have any more kids to get into a private school, and we all went to the Plaza for lunch—his father, his grandmother, and his favorite teacher since the second grade, Mrs. Riccardi.

That summer Jeff wrote three articles I still treasure. He covered a Little League game with language that gave it the drama and importance of a Major League play-off. He did a beautiful review of Bo Diddley and a nice, chatty piece about the governor's surprise visit to a town meeting, which pictured concisely the posture of politics amid the staunch wisdom of everyday folks.

In August we did the concert again, at the Guthrie Theatre that Oliver Rea had built in Minneapolis. The CBS affiliate sponsored it as a benefit for the local Cancer Society. I guess it went all right. Harold was brilliant, as always, but I was beginning to feel a distance, and without his support there was no way to make it. I was so lonesome the night before, I sat in my room and cried until I was afraid my eyes would be swollen. I called Brian in his room down the hall. He brought his guitar and played awhile, then held my hand till I felt sleepy.

At the end of August, Cynthia decided not to go back to school. She assured me she was only taking off one year. I pleaded with her to come home and talk about it, let me come out, or even change schools, but she wouldn't—or couldn't—listen. She had turned her face in another direction.

The following are excerpts from a taped conversation with Cynthia in August 1979:

"All that summer I had worked around the bookstore, doing mimeograph work and anything else that was menial. There was a lot going on that I didn't understand, but I figured I could sort of skate by that. Mostly, it seemed we were working very hard, doing something not for our own personal good, and that was a very gratifying feeling. Instant meaning to my life!

Then we started to have a lot of meetings, self-criticism meetings. The first one was about me, and everybody said some pretty terrible things. They said I was useless, that I didn't understand, and I didn't know what it was to work. Around August it got worse. They said I wasn't serious. They were right, I wasn't serious, but I was damned if that group of obviously very bright people was going to tell me I couldn't handle it. It was a kind of challenge, a challenge to my spirit, and I took the dare. I was not going to fail!"

In September she moved into the house shared by the members of the New Morning media cooperative. There were ten adults and one little girl, age four. A baby boy was born that fall. The cooperative ran the film society, owned the bookstore, and produced a weekly radical newspaper called *The Michigan Free Press*. Between them, they also took care of the children. The little girl was named after a leader in the Weather Underground.

A few weeks later, I was shopping with Barbara Carroll on Saturday afternoon. She was getting ready to open again, and she looked gorgeous! I was happy for her, it was fun, and we giggled through Bloomingdale's for three hours. When I got home, the elevator man hurried up to the corner to meet me.

"Bonnie's been run over."

"How's Grandmother?"

He didn't have to say anything, I knew. Her dog Bonnie was the love of her life. Her baby, the only baby left.

Mother was sitting on the floor in the front hall, hugging her knees, rocking back and forth.

"My Bonnie, my Bonnie, my Bonnie . . ." she said it over and over.

Carl drove us up to the little house, and we buried her. All the way up, Mother sat with the stiff little bundle in her lap wrapped in the yellow cashmere nap blanket she always left at the foot of her bed for Bonnie to sleep on. For days she could not eat or sleep. For hours she stood looking out the window. The sight of a toy, or the shadow of a memory, brought on the tears.

It was not just losing her dog, I knew that. It was Cynthia out of reach, Jeff leaving, and now her baby was gone. She felt her job was done, and for her that meant her life was finished. She had never been able to live just for herself.

One day she said, "When Daddy died, I remember thinking, 'My phone will never ring again. There will be no one to say good morning to.'"

"You still have me, Mother."

"No, I don't. Your children are grown, you have your own life to live."

"Well, it's a big one, plenty of room for both of us. Always has been."

"No. I'm always on the edge of it. That's not enough."

"Well, before you make any large decisions, let's fix this place up. It looks worse than that apartment on North Cheyenne."

She smiled a little. "You wouldn't let Daddy get out of the chair. Made him sit there and hide the holes in the slipcovers."

"Well, we don't have to live like Okies, you know."

We ordered new slipcovers and new rugs for the living room and dining room. Grandmother still liked to answer fan mail on the dining room table, and Sodie still liked to sleep right beside the typewriter. Sodie was getting old, so Grandmother had to help her up and keep a chair close so she could get down. With a typewriter and a cat on the dining table, obviously the house still wasn't exactly elegant, but it was certainly an improvement and Grandmother was busy. The only room I did not touch was my bedroom. I had divided that years before, and added space to Cynthia's room. I would leave that as it was. She might still be coming home.

Harold went out on the road as arranger/conductor for *The Wiz*, and I had a feeling I would not be seeing him for a long time. I met a new arranger named R. Bell who wanted to work with me and seemed very interested in the music. He charged one hundred dollars for each three-hour session. In a way, it was a relief to know where I stood with him, but it also made me think about the hundreds and hundreds of hours Harold had given me for nothing. How many hours, how much talent, how much love.

One afternoon the butcher in the store across the street called to say someone had abandoned a little dog, and would I come pick it up and take it to the ASPCA. Of course, that meant we had another dog. Grandmother held him for three days, until he stopped shaking, and named him Tiger. I didn't notice until after Christmas that there were yellow stains on the new white rug and outlining every new slipcover. That Christmas was so different. Christmas of 1974 was different in every way.

Melba's death in January 1971 had stunned and saddened the whole company. The decision not to even try replacing her was unanimous, but the idea of writing her death into the script was unthinkable. None of us could have played it. The Ellises wrote around the character for weeks and then began to refer to her death, as though it had happened some time before. It was actually months before Larry and I had a scene in which we talked about it, and we barely made it through that one. She had been so much a part of the life of the show for so long. We all had shared so much. Her good luck was always last, and every day for weeks I felt the tears burn and missed her, just before we went on the air.

Millee had her baby in December, but Janet was still pregnant. So Millee was padded for several months, and Danny was born just before his father died. Jo was still blind, and those months were some of my favorite times on the show. Her relationship with every character on the show grew warmer, closer. There was a tenderness in a touch, an awareness, a sympathetic strength all around her, especially from Tony. He had turned out to be everything I could ask for as an actor and a friend, and it glowed through every scene. Jo had always been the strong one in the story. She was the one other people turned to for an answer. Suddenly, she had none. She was dependent on her friends and her family for little things like a trip to the grocery store, and even her mind had turned on her.

There were many scenes with a new actor on the show

named John Cunningham. John played Wade Collins, the psychiatrist, and those scenes were an actor's dream. They were static and wordy by necessity, but the idea itself was the essence of method acting. To quote my friend Ross Martin again: "You realize how complicated human emotion is when you find out how difficult it is to hide that emotion." Jo's problem was the emotion she was trying to hide even from herself. She was in love with one man and trying to convince herself that she loved another. Tiny fragments of that truth had to shine through the cracks and be visible before she fumbled the lid back on and shut it out again.

The story itself brought us all closer, I suppose, but I think it was just one of those magic times when the company fit perfectly together. The story was spread smoothly and evenly over all the characters, and each had a special flavor to add. Perhaps the simple fact that everybody was happy on the show and very busy outside had something to do with it. After *Generation*, Larry Haines appeared on Broadway in *Promises, Promises*, and was nominated for a Tony Award. Somewhere along the line he also took up needlepoint, which he added to our rehearsals. Ann Williams played one of the leading roles in *Applause*. John Cunningham had a long list of Broadway credits and came to us fresh from the leading role in *Company*. Ken Harvey was becoming more and more involved with the management of our union, and would eventually serve as local president of AFTRA and then president of the national. Joan Copeland stood by for Katharine Hepburn in *Coco*, and Peter Simon's first play was produced.

Of course, we still had babies, lots of babies—on and off the show. Ann Williams had her third, and Carl had his first grandchild. When Ann was pregnant, Eunice conveniently gave birth to Suzi; but when the baby was scheduled to appear on-camera Ann's daughter was still too young, so Carl's grandson played the part. When the next baby boy was born on the show, Ann's daughter was just right and she played him. It didn't matter, really. They had plenty of time to find out about sex.

Through it all, probably the busiest person on the show, and drawing least attention to herself, was always Billie Lou Watt. She very deftly fashioned a character out of the glue that was supposed to hold other stories together when no one was really looking. If they were watching, she was sitting quietly in a corner of the studio with her needlework. All that time she was also writing beautiful poetry, learning the names of every tree in Central Park, and keeping up with a professional tap class. She cooked, she sewed, she raised three children and kept her soul alive. As Tucker said in a letter, "Billie Lou is a continuing grace to this earth."

The family was close, and rehearsals in the mornings were quietly riotous and exquisitely productive. Larry's needlepoint of a bowl of flowers progressed nicely, but he was color-blind, so somebody else had to pick out each new thread. Color-blind, maybe, but Larry always had an eye for a pretty girl, and one day there was a particularly beautiful one on the set as an extra. She had a sweet face and long, blond hair and could not have been more demure in pale gray silk and dark gray velvet. Of course, we didn't tell Larry that Mary Ellis had hired her as a special present for him, or that she was the reigning queen of porno movies. So it was much funnier every time he sidled up to her.

"Uh . . . haven't we worked together?" he would ask, and she would shake her head sadly.

"No, Mr. Haines, I don't think so. I would remember you."

Our important new pretty girl in 1971 was Courtney Sherman, who came to play Kathy, a young law student. Scott's marriage to Laurie was breaking up and he had gone back to law school. Kathy was the first person he met. Kathy was, from the beginning, a new kind of character for us. She was bent on a career, was not at all interested in a home or a family. If the part had been played by almost anyone else, she would never have been sympathetic or even interesting. She was the voice of reason, with cold, analytical opinions.

Courtney was young and inexperienced. She was shy and soft-spoken, and it was difficult to believe the hard line of Women's Lib coming from behind that sweet, very beautiful face. For months she got critical notes from the director and producers every day, but on a show that has to be done so fast, they are all too often "result" notes. They tell you what they want to see, not how to do it. If you don't know how, they can be very destructive. One day I watched her face during the note session after dress rehearsal. It's not wise to offer suggestions unless you're asked, but it seemed important. She was so good, and so close to being right.

"Courtney, honey, it's your voice . . . You're still talking like a little girl. The voice doesn't fit the rest of you. Get it down where it belongs."

"You're right," she said. "I know it. I've just been avoiding facing up to it." She didn't smile, but she had a lot on her mind. It's hard to be a young actor. It's a lot harder if you're talented. Talented, sensitive actors know where a scene should go, and the skills to get it there take time. Just the sound of a voice is so important. The sound itself can lead your ear to an important word, or expose an unspoken thought. What is even more important, using the voice properly brings the whole person to the listener. A breath, a few pounds of air pressure, can strum a set of vocal cords and the bones of the face will amplify the sound enough to make it audible, but it takes a whole body to make it ring and rumble. The orchestra needs a timpani. An actor needs every bone in his whole body, connected, in touch with his mind and his idea. Courtney learned, she learned it all and she was wonderful.

The story of Jo and Sam and Tony was coming to a climax by January 1972. Sam's personality had gone through radical changes, and after George Gaynes left and Roy Snyder took over the part, he changed even more. Jo was still blind, and still unsure of her real feelings. Tony was still strong and devoted, and Sam was slowly but surely going around the bend. Sam demanded a wedding date be set. He refused to wait for Jo's therapy to show results. He would take her to see specialists in Europe, but they must be married immediately!

He made an appointment with a justice of the peace, but in the middle of the ceremony Jo could not, or would not, repeat the vows. Nothing he could say moved her. Sam bustled her down the hall and out into his car. He would take her home, he said, but the drive was too long and slowly Jo began to realize he was taking her, against her will, to some other place. She didn't know where, because she was blind. Sam had gone crazy and kidnapped her.

Stories like the kidnapping, told in a paragraph, can sound overmelodramatic and ridiculous. Indeed, over the years the press has constantly reduced our stories to a level of dimestore pap. Occasionally, yes, we have gone too far, or, caught between writers, a good story was mishandled. But for the most part the characters, the behavior, and the stories have been genuine and real, and occasionally great. Of course, they were dramatic. They would be impossibly dull if they weren't. They also used the people playing the parts much more than any other dramatic medium. Sam had changed, because Bob Mandan was not playing the part, but also, Sam had been through a year of prison camp and come home to find his lady love about to marry someone else. He had, when you think about it, a lot more reason to get into a paranoid huff than Othello! We never had the language that let us soar, but we had very real people to portray.

Sam kidnapped Jo and took her to Doug and Eunice's cabin on the lake and "Search," for the first time, went on location. We went with a camera truck and a crew, and in two days we shot all the exteriors for three weeks of shows. There was, in two days, no time for rehearsals, and I was very glad I had grown up in low-budget westerns, and that Stan Gould was handling the minicamera. It was a wonderful chance for Bruce Minnix, too. It is hard to shoot scenes that will be edited into a show you haven't even read. It is also hard to play them, incidentally. The last scene was described simply: "Jo realizes Sam is dead and leaves the cabin." The only line of dialogue was "Help!" We made up the rest.

There were a couple of interesting young actors with us on that trip and the girl joined the long list of stars that began to blossom on our show. Susan Sarandon was one of the few I would have picked out. Like Jill Clayburgh, she had a sense of herself. Her quality, of course, was totally different. Personally, I always felt she was thinking, "I don't give a damn what you think of me, this is the way I am and I like it!" She was talented, with a great sense of offbeat timing. She had a darling face and a cute little body that she draped all over the place. I hadn't seen anything quite like that up close, and she made a big impression. She should have, she was adorable, and half of everything she did was attitude.

Susan played a young hippy hitchhiking with her boyfriend. He was the one who killed Sam. Tony came to rescue Jo, and the shock of Sam's death brought back her sight. Jo and Tony were married at last, and actually lived happily for a while.

After Eunice had her baby, she decided motherhood was not quite as fulfilling as she had hoped and went to work for John Wyatt, played by Val Dufour. John was a lawyer, but he also happened to own a magazine. Eunice suddenly developed a talent for writing and investigative reporting, while John Wyatt developed an eye for Eunice.

Women all over the country were asserting themselves, and so were we. Unfortunately, Doug Martin was suddenly, wildly chauvinistic, but Ken Harvey did his best to take the curse off, and his best was usually enough.

Eunice's investigations led her, of course, to the underworld, so we had another private detective. This time, he was a lot more fun. Tom Ewell played the part, and his preparation and range were a lesson to us all. So was the result. He was Columbo long before anyone else ever thought of it. Kathryn Walker joined the show as Bob Rogers' terribly neurotic daughter, Emily, and spent months plaguing Patti. After an absence of a year, Chris Lowe came back to play Eric, a wise old man of eight. Chris has spent his whole career, and much of his life so far, on "Search," and has certainly been through more than anybody else. He has been traded back and forth between various sets of parents seven or eight times, lived in fourteen different houses, had both legs broken, and nearly died of pneumonia. As a person, he is a quiet, thoughtful, thoroughly delightful young man who commented one day: "Eric takes everything so seriously . . . he just doesn't know how to have fun!"

Sometime in 1972, Dan became unhappy about some ideas that had been suggested to the directors and wrote a letter of resignation. I don't know if he was sorry or glad when it was accepted. It had been a long run and—in spite of the fights—he had done some beautiful work. So much emotion had passed be-

tween us, so much pride and so much anger. We had brought
out the best in each other, and the worst. The words he said
before every show for fifteen years still ring in my ears: "Play
with love."

The news ideas had probably come from either our new P&G
representative, John Potter, or our new associate producer, Ben
Saffron. They both had ideas and offered them. The director who
was hired to replace Dan was Nick Havinga. He had ideas too,
and a long list of prestigious credits. CBS was still far and away
the leader in daytime: sixteen per cent higher than NBC and
thirty-nine per cent higher than ABC. Whatever we were doing,
Fred Silverman's team was still doing it right and we were having
a wonderful time.

In May 1973 we began the story of Melissa, and if I had one
favorite I think it might be that one. Melissa could not speak or
hear, and the part was played by Linda Bove, who had been deaf
since birth. In the story she fell in love, but she could not think
of marriage until she had worked out her feelings about herself.
Her parents had always treated her as someone to be protected
and sheltered, because she was different. She had to find her own
independence.

For six months we played scenes in sign. I would interrupt
her dialogue so the audience knew what she was saying with lines
like, "No, I didn't say you shouldn't go," or "What do you mean
you want to leave?" then go right on with my own line, which
meant I had to know her part as well as I knew mine. It all had
to happen so fast it was like dribbling a ball down a basketball
court. We would both be dripping wet and exhausted after the
show.

Someone asked Linda how we worked together, and she said,
"I read Mary's lips and she reads my mind."

Linda was a beautiful actress, but again, it was the personal
relationship that made the shows truly important. We cared for
each other and we depended on one another so much. The dialogue was scripted every day in a way we knew would not work
for us. Jo simply repeated every word. It would have been slow
and clumsy. Each morning the big, brown eyes would look at me
to see if I had fixed it. Then came the smile as she looked over

my script. She especially loved it when I interrupted her with, "Hush, now," or "Will you be quiet for a minute!" She helped me, too, going over and over the signs so I knew exactly where she was each second. I knew some signs from Tucker, but it was like doing a simultaneous translation of *Tartuffe* with high school French. She taught me the signs, but it was the face and the big brown eyes that guided me.

When I brought in record albums for the cast she said, "I'll never hear it, but I can see the music in your face." She was a beautiful, beautiful person!

I have been so fortunate! I have had the privilege of sharing so many exquisitely intimate moments with so many extraordinary people! Some of the moments have happened on camera, all of them have been reflected at one time or another, become part of the programming. I choose the word, because a soul, a mind, must be something like a computer, with the years and moments constantly fed it. My brother turned out to be a geophysical engineer and one of the leading experts in oil exploration computer technology. He designed the system used by the huge company he works for. One day he showed me pictures that he studies. The pictures done by the computer talking to a seismograph. Yards and yards of unbelievable lines and slashes, peaks and waves give him information, and give me goose bumps.

I am fortunate to get goose bumps, and I have been fortunate enough to be around some wonderful, talented people for a long time. People whose minds are accustomed to the discipline of memorizing scripts automatically apply that discipline to everything else. They see, they listen, they absorb, storing experience and nuance. They are people who are unashamed of sentimentality, who give with overwhelming generosity. Sandy Duncan may need wires to fly Peter Pan across the stage, but she flings herself into the audience with every gesture. She is only one of the hundreds of beautiful young people who came through our doors to speak one line, or fill the background, and learn.

Think of the wonderful character actors who have come in to stay a week or two: incredible people who have made the great literature of the English-speaking world part of their vocabulary, whose voices ring with range and power, whose minds leap toward ideas, a word or a phrase recalling another, and another. Actors are people who often live more than one life at a time with grace. I think immediately of Frances Sternhagen, Roy Scheider, Robert Burr, Mal Throne, and Ben Hammer, but the list is long and longer. They are actors who commit every ounce of themselves to every acting moment. Never have I heard one of them say, "This material is beneath me." They play it and make it play. And they tell stories: " . . . Did you hear about Barbara Harris auditioning for a commercial? She read the material for the casting director. He nodded and said, 'Miss Harris, that was beautiful! Can you read it faster?' She nodded and said, 'Of course I can.' Then she got up and left" . . . laugh.

Good actors give themselves, they use themselves, and they constantly try to improve. They take singing lessons, dance classes, work with experimental theatres, and all the time they listen and they see. They see the world around them, and they see themselves, with a third eye that notes and puts away. No matter what the circumstances, good actors do their best, and any group of actors who have come together for the purpose of putting on a show refer to themselves as "the Company." Well, I'll tell you, it is still one of the most satisfying feelings of my life to be part of a company. Every time I walk on a stage at CBS, or pull open that door with the flashing sign, ON AIR, it is new and deeply gratifying. I belong. I am part of the family, a member of the company.

In the fall and winter of 1973 and 1974 it was like coming home, and I needed it more than ever. I remember walking out of the studio one day during rehearsal at the same time Tony came in and hugging him just for joy, and appreciation, and all the sweet things we shared. I said, "I just love working with you!" and he hugged me back. "Me, too."

By 1973 there were too many stories going to recount them all. Scott and Kathy were married, and Laurie had died. Scott insisted that her son, Eric, live with them, whether Kathy felt motherly or not. A beautiful relationship developed between Kathy and Eric, and Mom and Dad got up every morning to face the world on opposing sides of a lawsuit. Kathy went to work for

Doug Martin, and poor Kenny had to treat lady lawyers as badly as he treated wives. The women's movement was young. A lot of people weren't used to all the new rules.

Janet married Wade and moved into the Collinses' mansion with her three children, and promptly started trying to persuade Stu that he and Tom would be better off living with them. Patti and Len had adopted Grace's child, but Patti decided that she still wanted to try and have a baby of her own. In January she discovered a clinic, where difficult pregnancies were a specialty. Byron Sanders was the famous obstetrician who ran this very posh establishment, and a fascinating woman with a trace of Texas in her speech, named Marie Cheatham, came from California to play his head nurse.

Marie is very beautiful, with skin like cream. The first few months she came to work wearing everything she owned, because she was not used to the cold and only had light, California clothes. I remember watching her walk down the hall in a sort of draped skirt, an Indian blouse, heavy socks, and large fur slippers in a hideous shade of magenta.

"Marie, if you're going to be our sex symbol you better shape up," I called from the door to my dressing room, and she grinned back over her shoulder.

When she had been on the show a few months her mother was killed in an automobile accident. She got back from the funeral and came straight to work, as actresses do. They come straight from the hospital, or wherever, and do their job. That day, I asked her who she was having dinner with.

"I guess I'll just go home."

"No, you better come to my house. Not a good night to be alone."

When she walked into my door she started to cry and we talked until almost midnight. We've been friends ever since.

"Somebody told me I should dress funny and look awful when I came on the show," she said, "because you get jealous of other women."

We laughed at the time, but I couldn't stop thinking about it. Jealous? Of course I'm jealous. I envy women who are beautiful, who are sure of themselves and thin. That just has nothing to do with liking them, and women on the show are on my team. They are pros who show up on time and know their lines, and nearly everybody is good-looking anyway. It's a good-looking business and I'm proud of that. Sometimes an actress comes on who is so beautiful and so good she breaks my heart. Playing a scene with somebody like that is what it's all about and I don't care what they look like. I just think they're wonderful.

Oh, occasionally we get pretty faces who arrive "batteries not included." They have no craft and no spark and assume that beauty is enough. It's funny. Wonderful actors so often doubt themselves and dull ones almost never do. No, I don't like them, but I don't envy them either.

Marie is beautiful. She's good, and her character, Stephanie, dominated Jo's life for several months. She came to Henderson, ostensibly, to be near Patti until the baby was born, but it was obviously Tony who interested her. She had had an affair with him years before and was still in love with him.

Sometime that spring Tony started to get restless. He said he was unhappy about the story, but it seemed to be more serious. He wanted to leave the show. No one was able to talk him out of it, and his contract was up, so the character had a heart attack, and Tony was promised his days would be numbered.

Our makeup artist, Joel Mason, was unhappy too. He had a raise coming, but no one in the office would authorize it. Of course everybody at CBS knows how good he is, and other shows were trying to hire him away. That was unthinkable, so I made up the difference myself.

"Mary, I can't take money from you."

"Well, we can't do the show without you."

"I've been with this show for twelve years. They owe me."

"They don't always know who's really important. Or maybe they know and don't want to admit it, but I know and so do the other actors."

Then we began to run into even more trouble. The television writers went on strike, and our scripts deteriorated noticeably. I have no idea who was writing them. I often suspected no one was. We also changed producers. John Edwards left, but to our enormous relief, Ben was put in his place. He called all the actors into a meeting and thanked us for helping so much with the scripts and asked us to keep up the good work until the writing situation could be straightened out. We weren't really worried about that. As long as we worked together we could always come up with something. The important decision as far as I was concerned was the new associate producer. Mary Ellis and I both thought she was the logical choice. There were several hurried meetings in the ladies' room or my dressing room, with the door closed, and a couple of calls to Cincinnati before the decision was announced. She got it!

One day in the first few weeks Ben took me to lunch, and after some warm chitchat he said, "Mary, I need a story. I know you've come up with some good ones in the past, when there was a problem. If you have any ideas I could use them."

"Well, I know it has to be a mystery," I said, "and I think it should be one that the audience can't figure out, a real who-done-it." I also thought a good mystery would interest Tony enough to want to stay.

What I came up with was a very good rip-off of the movie *Rebecca*. I had always thought Marcy was gotten rid of too easily. She could be brought back and used by Stephanie. She would die, and even Tony would believe he had done it. Ben and I also talked about new music for the show. I had been pushing for a new sound for almost a year. Other shows were giving up the organ for recorded orchestrations. We were one of the few left with our old sound.

Harold and I had even gone into the studio and put down a new theme and some incidental music, to give them an idea of what we meant. Mary Ellis went with us the day we recorded and she said, "Yep, that's the sound." Ben said he would listen to the tapes and let me know.

In June, John Potter noticed that our ratings had improved considerably during my promotion tour and asked me if I would keep Bernie on a few more months, till he could fit it into the show budget. A thousand dollars a month was a lot of money for me, but I said I would.

When the writers' strike was settled, we found ourselves written into a very large hole which somebody decided to fill in one very long day, and dumping is certainly a fast way to fill a hole. To catch you up and set the scene: While Patti was waiting for the baby, Eunice was getting in over her head with the underworld. She was last seen wearing an orange hat in a boat on the lake outside their cabin. Doug heard a gunshot, saw a person wearing an orange hat fall into the water, and the hat floated to shore. Eunice had been missing for three days. Doug was out looking for her killers, and Suzi was staying with Jo and Tony. The day began just before dawn. Jo was restless and worried and woke early. Tony had to get up anyway because he had an operation to perform.

The mood was somber as Jo and Tony decided that if, indeed, Eunice was dead they should offer to raise little Suzi. Tony left for the hospital and Jo drove over to Eunice's apartment to pick up some clothes for the child. When she walked in, she noticed right away that a man she knew casually as a business associate of Eunice's was standing in the middle of the living room with a gun in his hand pointed at Eunice. Jo's first line of dialogue as scripted was: "Karl, what are you doing with that gun?" (PAUSE) "Eunice, you're alive!"

For the next five episodes he held both Eunice and Jo at gunpoint, trying to decide what to do. He finally made up his mind to leave town and take both of us with him, but Eunice managed to stall for one entire day because her feet hurt. Then, as luck would have it, the phone rang, and Jo convinced Karl that if she didn't answer her husband would be suspicious, because he knew she was there. Jo very cleverly managed to mention the tape recorder in her office at the hospital library, which had clues on it. Poor Karl mulled that over for the rest of that episode, and finally they were on their way out the door when the elevator opened and Tony came to the rescue with two policemen.

Cornered, the desperate Karl climbed out the window and edged along the parapet, prepared to end it all. For three days he tottered between life and certain death while Tony tried to talk the poor man into giving himself up and going off to a nice, safe prison. Finally, it was the old "Hey, fella, don't you want a cigarette?" trick that brought him in. Tony crawled out on the ledge, endangering himself, and managed to grab him. No sooner was the man safely handcuffed when the phone rang again. It was the hospital emergency room. Doug Martin had been shot and Tony rushed to save him.

So far, the day had lasted two weeks and it was only four in the afternoon, Henderson time.

We have played so many hospital waiting room scenes over the years they do tend to blend. Nurses pass through from time to time, looking anxious and busy, and have no information to impart. The principals sit around and look worried. They move to the window and look worried. They talk about things they should have done, and cry. They say things like, "You have to get some rest," and "Drink some coffee, it'll make you feel better." At least once in every waiting room scene somebody says, "The doctors are doing everything they can," and, "You have to be strong, he's going to need you."

When the doctor finally appears, the nearest of kin invariably says, "Is he . . . ?"

The scenes are fun to rehearse, because they are not treated with very much reverence. Usually, the doctor shrugs and says something like, "There's nothing we could do, his contract was up." Personally, I have ended all such scenes for years with my impression of Jack Benny thinking, "Well, mercy! Think of that!" On the air, however, everybody manages the tears and the sorrow.

The day was close to the end of its third week when Tony brought the dreadful news that Doug would be paralyzed, but we still couldn't go home. After a four-hour operation, Doug miraculously regained consciousness, noticed that he couldn't move, sent for his wife, and informed her that he wanted a divorce. He wouldn't let her waste her life with a paralyzed man. We had certainly established a record for something, though it's not one of the ones we're proud of.

In July, Stephanie's little girl came to live in Henderson, and Stephanie began to hint that Tony was her father. She was a pretty little girl, and more of a professional child than the ones we had raised ourselves. Her name was Andrea McArdle.

Doug was confined to a wheelchair, but could still handle his law practice. He moved to Washington, insisting that the divorce go through, and happened to meet Mr. Pace. Mr. Pace's daughter, Jennifer, had come on the show about the same time Marie did, played by a beautiful girl named Morgan Fairchild, also from Texas. At first, I suppose nobody took her seriously. She was twenty-two or -three, had a lovely, slim figure, and changed her very expensive clothes every twenty minutes. She had a lovely face, to which she applied four separate layers of makeup every morning. She had long, blond hair that stayed exactly where she put it. Her name was always in the papers, linked with Baryshnikov or Telly Savalas, or somebody else, and we thought she had no sense at all. She came to work one morning on the subway, dressed in short shorts, high-heeled sandals, and a strapless blouse and was amazed that men had noticed her.

With all that, she was very, very sweet, and it was all genuine. While she was watching us and learning how to act, we were watching her and learning a few tricks ourselves. I still put some white on my cheekbones, under the base, because she told me to. Morgan was fascinating, and Jennifer made a beeline for Scott.

Patti had her baby, but Len was drinking too much, so they still weren't happy. Dino had left the show, and Len was being played by Jeff Pomerantz.

The summer and fall of 1974 should have been a good time for everyone. Everybody was crazy about Ben. He and Mary Ellis and John Potter were enthusiastic about the new head writer they hired in California. Ann Marcus had a lot of nighttime credits, and we actually got the scripts on time. Still, there was a vague feeling of unrest, mistrust. More than once, Ben called me into the office to ask about the feeling among the cast about the show and the production staff, and asked me to do what I could to smooth any ruffled feathers. One day he mentioned that he had heard several music tapes and ours was far and away the best. I asked him to please let me know as soon as they could make a decision. There was a lot of work to do and Harold had other commitments.

During the summer Bruce Minnix was let go from the show quite abruptly, so we only had two directors, Nick Havinga and Ned Stark, and the tension began to grow. It's hard to put all the events into exact order now. They are blurred in my memory. I suppose I want to forget. The first one had to have been in the summer, because I remember the scene we were playing. It was outside the nursery, looking at Patti's new baby. I walked into the rehearsal in the morning, and Tony was already upset about the script.

"I know what you mean, love. I'll fix it," I said, and was just reaching into my purse to get my glasses and a pencil when he threw his script at me and flew into a rage. It lasted ten or fifteen minutes. We could not even rehearse, and I was so upset I cried all morning. He called me an ugly name as we were walking into the scene on the air, and apparently it was all because I had said I would fix the scene. I had fixed a thousand scenes. I didn't know what he was talking about. Fixing a scene doesn't mean changing it, necessarily. Usually, it is simply sparing it out, editing. A writer may get repetitive trying to make sure his point is made. If he saw it in rehearsal he would edit it himself. Sometimes, words seem right on paper but are clumsy spoken out loud. In scenes with Tony, a few cuts would shift emphasis, making him the strong one, and it worked for both of us.

After the show, I went to the office and Ben was very sympathetic. Tony was just upset about something else, and it would blow over, he said. He asked me to write Tony a letter and try and make up.

A few weeks later I asked about the music, and on Friday morning Ben said he was sorry it was taking so long, that they just hadn't decided on the specific sound they wanted. He would let me know. Half an hour later I was walking through the control room and I heard someone tell Dwight Weist, our announcer, to stay late and rehearse the new music.

"What new music?" I asked the sound man.

"Oh, the new opening of the show, with the new theme, is going in on Monday."

I was furious, but I was more hurt than angry. He had lied to me and I couldn't understand why. On Monday he came down to the set to talk to me about it, but talking made me cry and I had a show to do.

A chill, like the one years before, had spread to the hall outside the dressing rooms. Tony and I had no more cross words, but the old magic was gone. He was still not happy with the show and wanted to leave. Then, out of nowhere, one morning Nick Havinga blew up at me. We had a simple scene to play, between Jo and Eunice, in Jo's living room, that involved the morning newspaper and the phone. He had blocked it with the newspaper preset in the window seat behind the couch, and both of us on our feet through most of the scene. I suggested we put the newspaper on the desk, where it would be handy for Ann to see when she went to the phone. I also thought the two sisters would be relaxed enough to sit comfortably and talk to each other. It was a scene where the intimacy between them was more important than the words. Ann agreed, and even went a little further.

"I think Eunice would kick off her shoes and put her feet on the coffee table." It was the kind of suggestion we made every morning of the world, the kind of suggestion directors depended on us to make. We knew our characters so well, and we knew how women behave. Of course, sometimes suggestions didn't work or were impossible to shoot, but Nick wasn't talking about that. He was screaming at me on a very personal level.

"I've told Frank Olson you would be standing behind the couch, and if you're someplace else he'll have to relight, and the show will run late."

"All he has to do is tilt the light. The same key covers both areas."

"All he does all day is light you! You take so much time he can't bother with the rest of the show!"

"That isn't true!" It wasn't true, but Nick wasn't listening. He screamed at me for ten minutes. I was not only impossible to light, I was impossible to work with. I changed the script, I wasn't satisfied with the blocking.

I stood there and took it, because there was no place to go and we had to rehearse the scene. I had been through so many days like that with Dan, when all the energy went to keep from going to pieces. No, not all the energy. There was still the show to do and the decision to make. I was right, I was sure of that. When you make that kind of decision you have to be right, but just being right wasn't important. Being good was the only thing that mattered, and we couldn't be as good if we wandered around the room. It would look staged and it would feel staged. It was only one out of thousands of episodes, but to me it was still important. Every show was important. I stood my ground.

He reblocked, and in his heart I think he knew I was right. Frank tilted the light and we didn't run one second late. After the morning rehearsal I went down to the set, because I couldn't hold back the tears and I wanted to be alone. He had said I needed special light, and that was telling me I was old. He had said it in front of the whole cast. Frank did take special pains with my key light. He did with everybody. He cared about the show.

So many times since he'd come on the show, Nick had asked me to help if a show was long and we needed a cut, if he needed business to fill or blocking untangled. He was used to working in the nighttime, on a long schedule. Probably I was abrasive sometimes, but there wasn't always time to worry about that. There was barely time to do the show. To me, ultimately, pussyfooting around was condescending. I respected Nick too much for that and he knew it. That was not the problem, just as the light was not the problem. It had to be something else.

Peter Simon was the first one to tell me that Ben had called one meeting I had not known about. "Mary has to be disciplined," he told the cast and directors. She must be "de-starrified." Then Tony called, and I had a long evening with Nick.

He was under pressure, he told me. Then he said, "But you always were the one who saved us. You saved me a hundred times."

At least I understood what was happening, but I still did not know why. I called John Potter in Cincinnati. I didn't say anything specific over the phone. Mostly, I think, I just wanted to talk to a friend. He suggested we all have dinner together. We would go to "21" on Thursday.

I remembered the dinner at the Tower Suite, and I was already sick at my stomach getting dressed. At the last moment I said, "Jeff, put on your suit and come with me. I need you."

Like the night back in the sixties, nothing was said over dinner, and like that night John and Bob and Ben were there. I ordered chicken hash and had eaten about three bites. Jeff carried the conversation, and every now and then I heard him mention ratings and relevance, or talk about marketing and other subjects that no kid on his way to his freshman year at college is supposed to know about, and he had ordered a martini, which at "21" is murder. It was over coffee and a brandy I distinctly heard Jeff say, "Gentlemen, you must understand. Mother is a star."

Nothing else about that evening was important then or now. I never mentioned any of the silliness in the show. It didn't matter anymore.

Jeff picked out a cigar on his way out of "21" and put me in a taxi. "I'll be home later," he said, and he knew exactly what he had done for me.

I hadn't said anything, but I did write Ben a letter:

My Dearest Ben,

I have cried too many useless tears in the last few weeks . . . I am weary of it. I feel like a blind woman who has been stumbling around looking for a light switch . . . and all the time my friend had his hand over it.

The problem seems to be basically one of trust. You and Mary Ellis have been aware for weeks of the strong anti-management feeling among the cast . . . you kept asking me to help. Since apparently almost everybody was aware of how you felt about me they must have thought I was a goddamned fool. Oddly . . . I don't.

Trust is a marvelous elastic thing. It also is a necessity . . . on many levels. As far as the show is concerned, it is the only thing that makes it possible to do the best show possible. That one idea is what brings us all together in the first place.

Your words . . . "Mary must be disciplined . . . destarrified," make little sense to me. Being a star is a quality . . . not an attitude . . . a parent disciplines a child . . . we are all adults. Certainly it does not take four or five grown men to handle me. I barely make it through the day with everybody helping a lot. So bringing me down is not hard . . . but then, what good am I to you?

I am difficult to work with . . . you bet I am! I demand everything of myself . . . and that is catching. It is a fantastic medium . . . one chance to be part of something wonderful . . . human beings caring, relating . . . TRUSTING. That is all we are about . . . just people . . . trying their best to communicate with other people. Communicate is another word we should get back to . . . it's another part of the problem.

Credit is a tricky wicket, too. Who gets the credit . . . who gets the applesauce. I can tell you from many years of listening . . . it is a sound that is gone before you start the next one . . . it is no ride.

I know I am the star . . . so I don't have to do anything about it . . . except try to be excellent every day.

So what is left? . . . Only the pleasure of doing it, and doing it well . . . doing it together. I guess that is the other word that needs thinking about, talking about . . .

I wrote the letter, but it stayed around the house for a few days and by then I had decided not to mail it. There wasn't any point, really. What had been happening, I finally realized, was a kind of power struggle, and that was the last thing in the world I wanted to win. I didn't want power, I was terrified of power, but I was obviously doing something that made Ben feel he had to fight me. I made decisions he felt should be left to him. I had made decisions for so many years I did it automatically, and the funny part was I hated making decisions so much half the time I would make one and then pretend it was someone else's. Like a long distance runner I had obviously built up muscles that took long strides, without realizing. Of course, I still paid Bernie and Joel. The show needed them and nobody seemed to mind.

All was quiet, if cool, for the next few months. It was time for Christmas. I called the office in November to get a date for the Christmas party, but the answer was vague. I called several more times and it was getting late. I had to arrange with caterers and hire bartenders. In December, Ben said it would be impossible for me to give the party because I had five shows that week, and I assured him that had happened before. Something was wrong, so again I called John Potter in Cincinnati. He said Ben didn't want me to give the party anymore, he wanted to give it himself.

"Why didn't he just say that?"

"We told him not to hurt your feelings."

I didn't have five shows that week, I only had one, and I'm delighted to report it was an awful party. We had half of the cocktail lounge on top of the Pan Am Building, from seven until ten. For the first time in fifteen years there was no room for the camera crew, or the stagehands and their wives. Jeff said he heard an actor ask why the party wasn't at Mary's, and somebody answered, "She's redecorating her apartment and doesn't want it messed up."

I met our writer, Ann Marcus, for the first time. She was a small, handsome woman, athletic and tan. She came toward me and sat down across the table.

"I want to get to know you," she said, smiling, but her gaze was, somehow, too direct, too thorough. Perhaps I was too aware of the power writers had over my life, and looked too hard for a spark of reassurance.

A few minutes later, someone mentioned Mac's wife and Ann talked enthusiastically about her.

"Then you must know Mac," I said, and Ann looked puzzled.

"I knew him . . ." She paused. I guess she saw the look on my face. "Oh . . . I'm sorry. I thought everybody knew . . . he died a little over a year ago."

Mac was gone. What had he said?: ". . . I've had success doing exactly what I want to do and three great women in my life! I'm the luckiest man who ever lived."

Yes, dear friend. We'll go to Mexico another time.

It was a strange Christmas in 1974. Carl gave me a doll that looked just like him, and I put it next to the one Cynth had given me the year she heard me say I was sad because there would be no Christmas doll. She was a funny cloth doll with splayed toes and a silly, smug grin that seemed to say she'd had a few toddies.

"What'll we call her?" Cynth had asked, and with one voice we both said, "Maud!"

My little girl was gone and I was haunted by images of her. I had been out to see her after she moved into the house and it was a terrible trip. She had almost no time to see me, and I spent hours in the hotel, waiting. The people she worked with walked past us on the street without speaking. I might have been a shadow, and they were shadows to me. I hardly ever saw a face. I went to the house where she lived. There were old, broken sofas and chairs, with dirty blankets thrown over them, and grease on the kitchen counter you could scrape off with a knife. It was Cynthia's turn to wash dishes, so we did it together. No one had taken the trash out for three days, and the basement smelled of garbage.

Only the little girl spoke to me. She brought me a book and climbed into my lap, so I read to her. When she went to bed she called down and asked me to read a little more. Upstairs I saw

the room where Cynth lived with two other women. Her little
corner had her blue sheets, her Klimt, and a candlestick.

They'd had a bad time. They had to cancel the film society
and bankrupt the bookstore. Their newspaper, *The Michigan
Free Press*, was all they had left and they were concentrating on
that.

We had one lunch, and she arranged the fruit and the cheese
on her plate as she always had and sipped the wine.

"How do you manage, Maud?"

"The less you have," she said, "the more important each
thing is." She smiled, and the mouth was still the soft, sensitive
one of a child. "You know, being really poor is amazing. It's not
just being cold or even hungry, it's sort of being outside the system . . . You go to the store and you can't buy the large, economy size because you only have enough money for one meal. You
can't buy stuff on sale, because you never have enough money
ahead, and the stores that will give you credit charge you double."

"I know," I said. "When I was little, I went to the store
with thirty cents to buy dinner. We lived on a dollar a day."

"Yeah, you knew about all that, and I used to hear you talk
about it, but I never really believed it. I always thought you were
sort of making it up. I'm beginning to understand."

When I got into the bus to leave we both cried, and after we
had turned the corner I saw her running across the street. She
had an appointment to sell an ad two miles away, and she had to
go on foot. It was snowing and she had no hat or gloves. I bought
her knitted gloves and two darling hats for Christmas, and I sent
along my sheepskin coat. I tried to think about how beautiful she
would be. She always looked wonderful in hats, and she loved the
coat. It made me cry.

We talked on the phone fairly regularly. Then, in January
she called and said she would like me to release the money in her
trust fund. I said no. Not that there was all that much money in
it. Richard and I and the barber had lucked into the only mutual
fund on the market that didn't quite double in fourteen years,
but it was enough to see her through a couple of years of college.

I wasn't on the show very often, so I had more free time
than I wanted, and considerably less security. As always, music

filled the space. R. Bell's attitude and style were totally different from Harold's, and it was almost like learning to sing all over. He was still musical director for Judy Collins. He had been "piano man" with Janis Joplin, and the hole in his bathroom window was a reminder of a drunken game of darts with Bob Dylan. He was more folk and rock and roll, but, like Harold, his soul was in the piano. If he worked late and didn't get home he slept under it, a man and his ax.

We were always working on a new song, and it seemed we were forever making demos. There was no more room under the couch, so we piled them up on chairs or in the corner. Grandmother began buying *Billboard* and listening to the radio to see what was being played, and she had lots of suggestions. She also commented freely on the demos we made, and she especially disliked a heavy rhythm sound.

"What's that racket?" she asked when we brought home a new demo of "12-String Baby."

"That's a rimshot."

"Sounds like somebody dragging a stick along a picket fence," she said, and, as far as she was concerned, that was the end of the rimshots.

If I was so upset even music wouldn't help, I cooked. I bought a huge, red pot, and every time I felt an anxiety attack coming on, I filled it with something comforting, like pea soup with peperoni, or stew. I enjoyed quiet, uncomplicated chores like chopping and rolling pasta dough. The kitchen was peaceful and, of course, once I'd filled up the pot I could call someone to come over and eat it.

Actually, most of the time I didn't have to call anybody. They were already here. Friends from out of town and kids of friends seemed always to be around, and with my kids gone there was plenty of room. Audrey came, and Joy's daughter, Wendy, and a young guitar player who got stranded when his band folded. They all stayed for weeks or months and Jimmy, the elevator man, started calling my apartment "the hotel."

I did love my apartment. All the curtains and the drapes were finally gone. Summer sun or soft gray winter light filled the rooms. There were plants and trees in every room, and they were like friends. Always, there was a tune or an idea running through my mind, or an idea swelling into words. The couches in the living room were strewn with instruments, and there were so many cases under the piano somebody said it looked like a mother hen trying to hatch guitars. I loved the music and I loved home. At night I lit candles and put a log in the fireplace, even if I was alone.

"It's just like burning money," Grandmother fussed, "and we're not even having company."

"It's for me, Mother. For me."

Grandmother was restless. The kids were gone, she didn't have enough to do, and she needed more from me than I had to give. She started going off on sudden, unexpected little jaunts. Very sudden, unexpected little jaunts. I thought she had gone to Macy's the afternoon she called from Toronto.

"Toronto!"

"I just felt like getting away."

"You might have told me."

"You don't have to know everything I do. I called you, so don't worry."

"When are you coming home?"

"I haven't decided, but I'll keep in touch. I may go someplace else from here. I love to ride the bus."

"Do you have any baggage?"

"No, and it's a lot easier that way"—she laughed—"except they look at me funny when I check into a hotel."

"Mother, for God's sake! Let's talk about this. After all, we're both adults."

"I'm not, and I never have been!" That was the end of that discussion and the beginning of Grandmother's roaming.

Sodie was getting too old to jump up on the couch and I had to help her. I also had to cut up her chicken livers in tiny pieces she didn't need to chew. She'd been my friend for seventeen years, it was the least I could do.

In one conversation Cynthia mentioned that she no longer slept in the room on the second floor of the house. She had been moved to the basement. When I woke in the middle of the night I smelled the garbage.

Still, she was determined, and if she wasn't too tired she was enthusiastic. She had begun to write for the paper occasionally besides selling ads. They were planning a special edition for the Art Fair, a sort of Art Fair Guide, and every time I talked to her she asked me for recipes, anything that fed a lot of people for very little money.

It was a long, cold winter. Barb was booked to play a solo concert in April out in California. The middle of February she slipped stepping out the front door of her house to pick up the paper and broke her right arm.

"If you say one word about being accident prone, I'm going to hang up."

"Will you be able to play the gig?"

"The cast doesn't quite cover my fingers, so I'm practicing. It's supposed to be off in four weeks. I'll have three weeks to build up strength."

I had dinner with my lawyer, Peter, and he told me Chuck Glaser had had a stroke. Thirty-nine years old with six children, and the whole side of his body was paralyzed.

Perc and Ernesto had spent most of the time in Mississippi for a couple of years, restoring the home of Jefferson Davis in Woodville. In February they sold Indian Hill and I went up for our last weekend. Grandmother was away, so I hired someone to stay with Sodie. When I got home she could barely walk, but she had waited up for me. I wouldn't get up in the morning until I heard Lucille come in. I knew my cat was dead, and I spent a totally hysterical day and eighty dollars on 270th Street and Broadway at the only pet crematorium in Manhattan. I would take her ashes and sprinkle them under the trees at the little house, in the spring. Sometimes it seems that spring will never come, but it always does.

The night before Barbara was to leave for California to play the concert, we went to Carnegie to hear Michel Legrand. During the second set, she got up and practically ran out of the theatre.

When I called she just said, "Had a little anxiety attack, I guess."

"But you're going . . . ?"

"With my Jacuzzi and my orchestra."

"A Jacuzzi? . . . They'll think you're really kinky. Good luck, love."

She told me later she thought she was going to faint during the first fifteen minutes of the concert, but then the music took over and she forgot everything else. While she was in California, she signed a recording contract with Blue Note. The siege was over. Barbara Carroll was back!

Sometime in early spring I went down to Philadelphia to do "The Mike Douglas Show." I was probably feeling good. Mike is just as relaxed as he looks, and he makes everybody feel good. He also has a great band. I was sitting by myself on the train when a strikingly handsome woman walked up the aisle and spoke to me.

"I know who you are," she said. "Would you mind if I sat down for a few minutes?"

She said her name was Dicky and she was on her way from the family's summer place in Hyannisport to their farm in Maryland. She looked like that was exactly what she should be doing. She had four children who were all grown, now, and she had just started her own business, which was going very well. She had watched "Search" for twenty years.

"My friends have always kidded me about it, and I only watched because of you. I always thought you were very special."

I told her about my two kids, and she told me about her four. "David plays the guitar, and writes songs," she said, "but now I'm worried about him. He wants to go to New York and see if his music's any good."

"Well, don't worry . . . He could stay at my house, and I know all the people he should play for."

"You've known me for about twenty minutes, and you're inviting my son to stay at your house . . . Do you always invite strangers to live with you?"

I only had to think about that a minute. "Yes, I think I probably do."

When I got up to leave the train in Philadelphia she said, "You're everything I always thought you would be." It was one of the nicest things anybody ever said to me. It meant more than she could have imagined.

Her son, David, did come to New York, and he did stay with me. R. Bell and I both liked his songs a lot. He was a senior at Dartmouth, and when he left he said, "I'll see you freshman weekend. Save some time for me."

Freshman weekend was complicated. I had to go out to California to do Dinah Shore's show the Thursday before, and it's hard to get to Hanover from L.A. It had been a busy Thursday, too. Dinah Shore is probably the most gracious woman in television. She is totally unselfish. When the wardrobe lady checks to see what color clothes you have brought, and you ask what Dinah is wearing to make sure you don't clash, she says, "Miss Shore will change, she doesn't mind."

When you stand at the mike with her, she asks if you have a profile preference, and she listens when you talk to her. She does, however, have folks on her show, occasionally, who are not so giving and charming, and if you're not very careful you can get pushed right off the end of that couch.

That was a nice day, though. I was singing a song I wrote with Brian, and when I introduced it I said, "Brian, this is your graduation present. Now you're in ASCAP." ASCAP is the American Society of Composers and Publishers. You have to have a song published in sheet music or played on a network to get in, and that show was all he needed. I knew he'd be as proud of that little button as I am. I was also relieved the kid was finally out of school. Long distance collaboration is a pain!

When I got off the plane in New Hampshire, a handsome young man in a raincoat got out of a Volkswagen and trotted toward me. It was my son.

We had a beer with his roommates, checked me into my room, and went to dinner. David found us in the restaurant, and by the time we made the rounds of the beer halls, late that night, there were ten of us. One very pretty student named Barbara leaned over and said, "I know you're a famous actress, but if you don't mind, I like it best when you sing." I don't think Jeff had arranged that, but he arranged everything else. The other parents all went to a big dinner dance, and the kids thought I should at least see it, so we watched from the fire escape and I taught them how to lindy.

After the party at his fraternity house, the two of us sat over a nightcap for an hour and talked. He was planning to go to Washington as soon as school let out. He'd met Mr. Rockefeller at a party, and he was going to ask him for a summer job as an intern at the White House.

Jeff had some work to do the next afternoon, so David drove me out, through the New Hampshire spring, to his house. We both played his guitars, and he had some poetry he wanted me to read.

"You got anything new?" he asked.

"As a matter of fact, there's one you might like . . ."

> I feel quite certain I'm a fraud
> Who chose the company of poets.
> In words that don't belong to me,
> Arranged by wind, mysteriously,
> I've borrowed my identity.
> You are right who turn away,
> I don't belong.
> I will not pay the price of living life.
> I've bartered for my moment
> On the needle pointed spire
> Of childish hope and fierce desire.
> My house a bending, swaying tree,
> If that's pretending, let it be.

When I got on the little puddle jumper to fly to New York, I sat next to the only man who smiled and we introduced ourselves.

"You up for freshman weekend?"

"Yep."

"Have a good time?"

"The best time I've ever had in my life. Only one regret."

"What's that?"

"I never met his faculty adviser, so I didn't get marked present."

"That's no problem at all. I happen to be Jeff's adviser, and we have two whole hours to talk about him. He's quite a man."

"Yes. Yes, he is . . ."

It had truly been the best weekend of my life. I felt close to Jeff, and on his own territory everything was easy. He was thoughtful, sensitive, and even quite fond of me. My new friend, David, had shared his private thoughts and ambitions, and all the young people had let me into their lives—not just as Jeff's mother, but as a person who acted and wrote, and sang a little, and said something they wanted to hear. If being alone meant sharing that kind of time with people like that, it was a whole lot better than sharing with any one person, at least anyone I had ever known . . . except, perhaps, one.

"Lester? This is Mary. I was just thinking about you."

"Oh?" I could hear the little self-conscious laugh. "Well, how are you?"

"Oh, I'm okay . . . I'd like to see you sometime, if you have a minute."

"I'll give you a call and come by for some coffee. I'd like to see you, too."

When he came into the apartment I was a little upset that he'd gotten older and his belly was round, but the expression on his face was just exactly the same: tender, attentive, expectant, without ever pressing. The gestures were the same too, the fingers straight and close together. I was not so calm, and proceeded to audition for probably an hour. I showed him poetry, sang him songs, bombarded him with stories about the kids and finally, for a big finish, burst into tears. At least he finally had a chance to talk. For two hours he told stories about old friends and all the places he had been. He'd had a beautiful life. He and his wife had traveled everywhere, his school was the best of its kind in the country, and he had three daughters he adored. He enjoyed his classes, and there was always one gray-eyed girl in at least one of them.

After a while, he noticed some yellow sheets on the coffee table.

"New poetry?"

"No, that's a speech for the graduating class of a high school out in New Jersey."

"What are you going to talk about?"

"They asked me to talk about success, whatever that is."

"Well, it's something different for everybody."

"I guess. It's power, or it's money . . . It's the power money buys, or the things."

"What is it to you?"

"I think it's time, time and choice. Success has bought me that. I can choose how I want to spend my time, now."

Lester listened and thought for a moment. "Just remember never to confuse success with achievement," he said carefully. "Success is an artificial measure. You can have success without achieving anything. Of course, an achievement can succeed, but it doesn't have to. It is its own reward."

As always, he had a way of setting the pieces straight, recognizing the truth of the picture and helping me see it.

In Henderson, U.S.A. the winter and spring of 1974 and 1975 had been filled with violence and intrigue. Stephanie convinced Tony that he was the father of her daughter, Wendy, and he and Jo separated. While Doug Martin was driving his car from Washington to Henderson he had a flat tire. Being partially paralyzed, he was unable to change the tire and was trying to flag down a passing motorist when he was hit by a car driven by Len Whiting. The injury was almost worse than fatal, since he was paralyzed from the neck down and only kept alive by respirators. The plug was pulled by a stealthy shadow and one of our most valuable characters was gone. Len confessed that he had been the driver of the car. He was found guilty of manslaughter, as well as leaving the scene of an accident. He was put on probation and sent to work in Appalachia. Patti was sent away with him and has not been heard of since.

Jo and Stu decided that Stephanie was lying about Tony's fatherhood and, in the most bizarre script ever handed to either of us, they attempted to persuade the real father to admit the truth by bribing him. The dialogue had been written for two hardened cons, and the situation was ludicrous, but weeks of plot were built on it. So, the five thousand dollars had to be handed to the man. At least we did it our way. We tiptoed around Stu's office, closing doors and pulling shades, saying all the words, but never speaking above a whisper. We only made one major change in the concept. Instead of Stu saying, "We gotta get the cash to him in small bills," we decided to pay by check. Well, after all, we wanted some kind of record, didn't we? We also reasoned that people who accept bribes probably don't give receipts.

In April a young character named Robin was admitted to the hospital. She had been beaten up but refused to tell who had attacked her. I was told that Jo would befriend her, and Robin would be a kind of surrogate daughter. Things, however, did not turn out that way.

Tony was still determined to leave, and in June Dr. Tony Vincente had a fatal heart attack trying to save Robin from another attack. Two weeks later, Robin was killed on a bus and the story shifted to Scott, who just happened to be in the seat behind her. I missed Tony, but, in a way, it was a relief. He had been so unhappy for a long time, and his dissatisfaction had spread through the company. Perhaps the feeling was there before and he had caught it from someone else.

I hoped there would be a story line dealing with Jo's loneliness. For the first time in her life on the show, there was no man in love with her. From my own experience, I knew that is what most women left alone in middle age have to face, and what many women fear. However, the subject was dismissed in one or two episodes. The story centered around Scott and Kathy, and a new murder mystery involving the Collins family. It had been a whole year of violence and five major characters were dead or gone. The ratings were high, but I do remember wondering at the cost.

In early summer, quite abruptly, we changed producers. Ben had been with us just a little over a year, and Mary Ellis had been the associate producer all that time. It was the moment for her to take the final step. She had been with the show all her working life, since she was nineteen years old. She had been in on all the fights and seen the characters develop. She had production experience in every area. She was the obvious choice. My only fear was that it was too obvious, like Ernesto, but I need not have worried. The changeover was fast and smooth, and I was very happy for her. I was happy for Ben, too, in a different way. He moved on to a big network position, and he was obviously highly qualified. I would never feel quite the same way about the show, but I would not need to. I will always be grateful to him for making me see that. The show had changed, and so had I.

In June, Jeff went to work at the White House as an intern, assisting Mr. Rockefeller. At the end of July I went out to Ann Arbor to spend Cynthia's twentieth birthday with her. It was hot and muggy, and almost every minute we spent together we had the children with us. I had presents for her, but she asked me if I would buy something for the kids, too. The little girl needed a dress to start school in, and we bought toys for the baby. We went to one movie, but I spent most of the time in the ladies' room with the little girl, trying to pin her underpants together so the pin didn't show.

The children were precious. I understood why Cynth loved them. I saw more of the people she lived with, and I was beginning to get their names straight. George and Barbara were the parents of the children, and George headed the group.

She took me to the building where they worked. There were a couple of desks, a table or two they had obviously found on the street, and a few chairs. There was a coffee machine, posters tacked to the walls, records stacked on the floor, and piles of returned papers against the back wall.

She showed me several issues of the paper, and I was impressed. They had redesigned it, the logo was in color, and it was hard to believe that ten people could have done it all. The physical input alone was staggering. I didn't understand what they were saying, but I have trouble with the New York *Times*, so I am no judge.

"What's the Indo-China Peace Campaign?"

"That's Jane Fonda and Tom Hayden's piece. We've been working with them."

"What do they do?" Her answer was simple, because she knew I really had no idea, but it wasn't condescending.

"Well, after we signed the Paris Peace Accords, you know, the war didn't stop. We also promised a lot of reparations, which the Vietnamese never got. There's still a lot of land that won't grow anything. We're trying to get people to care about that."

"I see."

"But don't read the international section. It's kind of silly. We get a lot of it off the television, and George hypes it up." She smiled and showed me a copy of the Art Fair Guide. "This is what we're really proud of, and it was a huge success. The Chamber of Commerce was tickled pink."

On a blackboard there was a schedule in chalk, with everyone's name, and what they were to do at an appointed hour; writing, selling ads, paste-up, returns, and always, day and night, the children, everyone took care of the children.

George and Barbara both came in while I was there, and they spoke to me, though from a distance. Glen was the only other one I recognized. He didn't speak at all, but I got a better look at his face. It was sort of funny-looking, but tender, and so sensitive he seemed always to be asking a question.

"Every day Glen gets angrier," Cynthia said. "We're becoming more and more of a business, and that's not how he wants to spend his life. His father had brown lung; he knows what it means, because he's lived through it. He wants to organize people."

Sometime in the fall she told me Glen had walked over to her desk late one night, slammed his fist down, and walked out. They didn't know at the time he'd broken his hand.

In September, Mr. Rockefeller asked Jeff to take the fall semester off from school and join his staff. Jeff was nineteen years old and had his own office in the White House. I was amazed but somehow I wasn't surprised. I don't know what I had expected either of the children to do. Expectation for them had always seemed presumptuous. It was like a label that implied limitations, and fulfillment is such an unending possibility. There is always something more to do, more to feel, more to experience, to change. Better try to give them a firm place to take off from than a finite place to go.

Jeff was incredibly well informed and articulate, at ease in any company. Cynthia had gone a different direction, but she asked as much of herself. She could write a story for the paper, lay out the page and paste it up. She could sell the advertisement and design the copy. She could cook dinner for twelve people and take care of the kids at the same time. There were many nights I woke up and walked the floor, worrying, but somewhere, somehow, I understood why she had to do it:

> "It had all been so easy all my life. I had to find out where my strength was. I had to find out if I could survive."

In September I went to Europe to narrate a film for NBC's Public Affairs. I wasn't needed on "Search" and it was good to get away. I spent a whole month looking out of the window of a Mercedes bus at the countryside of France and England—the spires of Chartres reminding me that the human spirit has always reached far beyond itself, flags fluttering from a white castle in southern France rekindling fantasy, the lace of Canterbury restoring peace and humility. In Brittany there were geraniums in the windows of long stone barns. South of Paris the sun glistened through the mist—mile after mile of Monet. In England cows grazed, and smoke rose from the chimneys of cottages already four hundred years old.

In London I walked into a restaurant one night and two very beautiful girls came over to me. The Nashville accent came as a surprise.

"Aren't you Jo? . . . You look just like her."

"I sure am."

"Are you, really?"

"Really."

"Well, would you sign this menu? I just can't believe it."

"Glad to . . . What's your name?"

"Linda. We're here with George Jones's band. You ever hear of him? He sings Country."

When I got on the plane a week later, the same girl came over to my seat.

"You remember me?"

That day she'd had a lot to drink and she was talkative. She told me about her life and her two boys. Sometimes the words were harsh, even shocking, but there was a sweetness about her. There was innocence in her honesty, and she was beautiful, the way Marilyn Monroe was beautiful, and always a child.

"My husband was shot and killed, and his parents said they was gonna take the baby away from me, so I rented a room and just stayed there. If I hadn't had the stories on TV I'd have gone crazy . . . I was only seventeen and scared all the time. I used to think if I just had a friend like Jo I could make it."

"Well, now you do . . . at least we look a lot alike."

"Listen, I want you to meet George and Shug. Shug is his manager, and maybe you could write a song for George. He sells a lot of records."

Before the lunch was served, Shug and George had invited me to Nashville for Music Week in October, and I said I'd love to write a song for George and Tammy Wynette. I was excited. If they liked it, Brian and I would finally get started. When we landed in New York, I had a good start on "Golden Rings."

Brian wrote a tune and we made a little demo on a four-track machine in R. Bell's living room. Just before I left for Nashville, I called Chuck Glaser to tell him I would be there. I dreaded it, but I had to see him.

When I played the song for Shug, he said, "You sure sing pretty and it's a good song . . . maybe too good for George, but Tammy's gonna love it." We went into another room and he played it for three men who were sitting there with hats on.

"They're gonna rip off your song," Shug said, joking, but I didn't laugh.

That night I went to George's nightclub, Possum Hollow. He introduced me to the crowd and told them I'd written a song for him, and everybody made a big fuss over me.

Linda, from the airplane, was there that night and she'd brought a friend along, a pretty, well-dressed woman in her early thirties with a soft, southern accent.

"She didn't believe I knew you, but I told her you'd probably sit at our table." Linda was even more beautiful than I remembered her and she seemed calmer, more sure of herself.

Her friend looked at me a long time before she said, "I'm in Nashville with my husband and my two little boys. My husband is attending a conference. Linda and I knew each other when we were little, so I called her." As she talked her accent got softer, moved further back into the hills.

"It seems strange to talk to you. I feel I've known you all my life. When I was little, we lived in the country and we were dirt poor. We didn't have no car, we didn't have no money—we didn't have nothin' but that box, and I used to watch you." She toyed with her drink for a moment and her face relaxed into a self-conscious little smile.

"I think you helped me see myself somewhere else. I think you gave me . . . Hope . . . At least I know you're the one got me out of there."

Linda reached across the table and took my hand, "And she's my friend," she said. I nodded, but I thought to myself, "No, little one. You're my friend. I'm the one who needs you." On my napkin I scribbled, "You gotta make it, baby—there's a little bit of you in all of us."

After that night, I never heard another word from Shug or George. They sent people to pick me up when there was a party, and during Music Week there were lots of parties. Each time it was a different person and the Cadillac was a different color, but nobody said another word about the song.

The last day I had a date to have dinner with Chuck and Beverly. I assumed Chuck would be in a wheelchair, so I offered to meet them.

"Hell, no," he said. "I'll pick you up."

When I got off the elevator in the lobby he was coming toward me, taking one long step with the good leg and swinging the other on ahead of it. He didn't even use a cane. We walked out to his car, where Beverly was waiting, and he swung himself into the driver's seat.

Over dinner he told me he'd had the first stroke an hour after they sold the music catalog. He had three more after that.

"I heard them say, 'He's dead,' and I figured in a way they were right—but I guess it just wasn't my time. You'll see, in six years I'll be back where I was." I believed it, and Beverly would be right beside him.

There was a big Columbia Records party that night, but Shug had forgotten to leave any tickets for me. When we got to the door, Chuck was going to explain that there was a mix-up and that I was a star at CBS, but all he had a chance to say was, "I'm Chuck Glaser . . ." and the door swung open.

"Mr. Glaser! You come right on in! It's a pleasure to have you here."

I paid my hotel bill and took a cab to the airport. I tried several times to call Shug. He was never in. A couple of months later, George and Tammy released a song called "Golden Ring." It wasn't like our song, but we couldn't use our title after that. It got up to number one on the Country charts and was nominated for a Grammy. I felt bad, so did Brian, and the worst part was, I don't think Tammy ever even got to hear ours. At least I had a new friend, and a friend like Linda lasts a long time.

When Mary Ellis took over the show she began, almost immediately, to make changes. The biggest, most apparent change, was in the casting, and she hired some beautiful people. Almost everybody got a new set of kids. Stu got a new son, Janet got a new son and a new daughter, and I got a new Bruce named Joel Higgins. They were all delightful. Meg Benet was unbelievably beautiful and as sweet and talented as she was lovely, Rick Loman was strong and thoughtful. John James was the tallest of them all, and if Larry stood upstage of him he disappeared entirely; but Higgins was, for me, the joy of those days.

The character of Bruce, since Robby Benson left, had been played by several young men and never really had an impact. Joel Higgins and I were soul buddies, and that was that. He picked up somebody's guitar the first week, and that deep, mellow voice of his rolled straight through the studio. Somehow, it was always just at the right pitch, the right timbre. I could slide my harmonies in and ride so close we were like one voice. He'd look at me and grin, "Boy, Mom, you sure hear funny . . . Show me those chords of yours again." Our scenes were good. We cared about each other, and Joel wanted to learn everything I had to offer. That's gratifying, but mostly it is just plain fun. It is such fun to give a talented young person an idea and watch what they do with it. His own intuition and his own exuberance took each suggestion and ran with it, sometimes in the other direction, but always it made the scene and the relationship better. When Mary Ellis mentioned that he was doing very good work, she told me he said, "Yep! The longer I work with Mary, the better I get."

How could you not be crazy about a man who said things like that?

All the daytime shows by the middle of the seventies were moving pretty much in one direction. They were getting younger and more restless. Also, anyone casually flipping a dial around the middle of the day was bound to hear a lot of music being played, picked, and sung. From the early, gentle sounds of Jo's guitar and "Green Coffee," daytime had gone a long way. "Search's" answer was a tall, curly-headed rock singer named Steve Kaslo, played by a tall, curly-headed man named Michael Nouri—who also happened to play absolutely beautiful guitar.

There were other changes. Ann Marcus left our show as head writer to do "Mary Hartman, Mary Hartman," and we moved. The studios in the production center were crowded so we moved, temporarily, down to a little studio on Twenty-sixth Street. It was an inconvenient neighborhood, and the studios were old-fashioned. The makeup rooms and the dressing rooms were small and dirty, but, in a way, it was a blessing. Actors have, since they were allowed to sleep within the walls of the city, survived on a diet of coffee and sticky buns. They have walked onto cold, drafty stages in winter, inhaling generations of dust and perspiration. They have rehearsed in buildings long ago condemned for any other use. They have showered with cold water and dried with paper towels, and have been grateful for toilet facilities that should be considered hazardous to one's health.

Conditions were not that bad on Twenty-sixth Street, but they were far from grand, and we were cut off from the rest of the television world. That was the saving grace, I think, because we turned more to each other. For the first time, we had a Green Room so we spent time together. We ate our lunches there, which varied from a cold grilled sandwich to a dishpan full of salad to be shared. Billie Lou would work on a patchwork quilt, and occasionally I'd catch her humming to herself, running through a tap routine. Marie did beautiful embroidery, answered her mail, and did her accounts all at the same time. Larry puzzled through the directions for a macrame purse, with a huge pile of wool on the table in front of him, his glasses sliding off his nose.

"I got such a long nose I keep working it into the pattern! Listen, it says I gotta use brown now, somebody find me some brown."

There was one phone and it was our only contact to the outside world. If anybody had a guitar, everybody played it. Somebody was always running lines or touching up their makeup, and Morgan usually managed to change clothes at least once a day. We watched the show with scant reverence most days, but if anybody had a really good scene it was genuinely appreciated. If anybody was manic, everybody caught it.

"Did you hear about the Hollywood agent who found his wife in bed with an actor? He said, 'What are you doing?' The actor sat up. 'Oh, well, right now I'm doing "Kojak," but next week I'm doing "Hawaii Five-O," and then I'm doing . . .'" . . . Laugh.

"How many times a week do you make love, Larry?"

"How many times a week is semi-annually?"

"Millee, I can't rub your back one more minute. My thumbs are numb."

"Don't stop now, I think I'm in love."

"But I'm gay."

"Well . . . I'm cheerful."

Courtney, eight months pregnant and totally unself-conscious, doing her impression of Raquel Welch singing "Get Up and Boogie" was one of the fine moments, and one of the newly married men said very quietly, "What is the number for planned parenthood?" Two years before, Courtney and Peter had married.

They were our only True Love story. They had also developed into the two best young actors we ever had on the show.

The children played their own games through it all. Like children brought up in a big family, they were accustomed to mayhem. Neil Billingsly, who played Janet's youngest son, was fond of skate-boarding through the halls.

Millee decorated every inch of her own dressing room, then started on all the others and brought posters for the makeup room. Actually, the move was probably hardest for Joel Mason. He is a Virgo who wants everything neat and tidy, and there wasn't even a cabinet to put away the makeup in the tiny room he shared with Frank Bianco, our hairdresser. But then he discovered all the beautiful fresh vegetable markets in the neighborhood, and he decided that if he became a vegetarian it would improve his love life. We thought that was funny, because the one thing on our show that has never needed improvement is Joel's love life.

By the time we moved to Twenty-sixth Street, Steve Kaslo's sister, Amy, played by Ann Windham, a tall, fascinating blond girl with a mercurial personality and great talent, had joined the cast. She and Bruce had a child, and little Bethany was practically born in our Green Room. She was nursed there, she learned to walk, toddling across the room to her favorite big people, letting them hold her doll and saying her first words, "TV Daddy."

It was a big family, as it had always been, and the cycle had come around again, all the way around. The new story for Jo was the inn she would buy with her friend, Stu. They were going to restore an old mansion and build the Hartford House. It's where we had begun, the two of us, in the old Motor Haven. For the first time, really, since we went on the air, I started to work regularly with Larry, and it has been one of the supreme pleasures of my career. Perhaps it is good that I had to wait. I may not have really been ready before, not really free. The show in Carolina had made more of a difference than I could have expected. That edge of nervousness that dulled the senses, however slightly, was finally gone. I was free to hear our silence, too, free to pause, free to catch his gesture and make a comic moment by simply imitating, free to enjoy!

During the fall Cynthia called often. She mentioned the money in her trust fund once or twice, but I wasn't about to release that. Then, after a while, the conversations shifted to the promise I had made to buy her a car. She was ready, she said, but she didn't want a plain car. She wanted a van.

"But Maud, you still can't drive. What are you going to do with a van?"

"I'm not going to stay here all that long, and when I leave I'll live in it." The whole idea was preposterous, and I am ashamed to admit I called to price vans.

As Christmas got nearer, the talk from Ann Arbor shifted again. They were going to incorporate, she said. If I would release the money in her trust fund, she would use it to buy stock. The Art Fair Guide had gone so well they were planning to put out a special Christmas edition. She was already selling ads for it, and it promised to be a financial success. Suddenly, just before Christmas, she called to say they were all coming to New York and they wanted me to give a party for them. It was to be a quiet evening. They wanted to talk to some potential investors. Jeffrey called to say that Mr. Rockefeller had asked him to take the whole year off and join his speech-writing staff, but he would be home for Christmas.

I got out my big red pot, and every other pan in the kitchen, and started to cook everything in sight. When there was no more room in the refrigerator, I put pots in the windowsills, every windowsill in the house. I also cooked hams and turkeys. Desserts are too hard, so I bought a dozen. Cynthia's group was not staying here, and they announced that she had to stay with them. I announced that if she didn't stay here, there would be no dinner party for them, and she stayed.

There was a lot of tension around the house if Cynth and Jeff were both here, and if Richard was around little wisps of smoke would rise. Christmas Eve, it got to be too much and I called Mary Ann. I had a little present for them, but mostly, I wanted to be there and not here.

Both kids went with me, and even walking a few blocks calmed everybody down.

All five of their kids were home and it was the first time in years we had all been in the same room. The young people talked about school and work and friends. They had known each other nearly all their lives. Now they were handsome, graceful young adults, but I remembered them all in that room as children. That was what I wanted, that feeling of continuity. There was strength in continuity, in family and friendship. There was reaffirmation in just being together. I had run to that house that day because I needed it, and it was there. Both kids must have felt it too. By the time we walked home our own tension had eased and we were closer.

The party for The Michigan Free Press was to be Christmas night, and finally I got to know the rest of the group, at least the ones who had come. George and Barbara, an intense young woman named Lisa, a tall, gentle boy named Guerin, and a black man named Booker, who was their lawyer and business manager. Guerin's mother and stepfather came, and George's mother, then Lisa's mother and father. Lisa had been with the group for three years, and her father had already put in twenty-five thousand dollars. That seemed like a monstrous amount of money to me, representing years of savings. Obviously, no one was wealthy. They were just people, very pleasant people, but there was nothing extraordinary about anybody.

After dinner we all sat in a kind of circle and George explained their proposal. He had printed copies to pass around. Basically, it was a simple stock offering. The preferred stock would remain in the hands of the officers of the cooperative. Cynthia would be an officer, and they wanted ten thousand dollars. They wanted six thousand from her, and four thousand dollars from me, which was about as much as what the van would cost. They wanted twenty thousand dollars from the others. George's voice was low and sincere. He was thoughtful and articulate. At least I assumed he was. I only understood about half of what he was saying. He used a great many long words and spoke in a kind of political jargon that was unfamiliar.

I talked to Richard and Jeff about the money and they were both adamant. We had several bitter arguments and Nat, my business manager, was simply furious. I wasn't sure, myself, how to even begin thinking about it, or reason, except that I felt the money itself should not be the most important consideration. It was, after all, only money. I was more frightened that I might support Cynthia in something that would do her harm, and I had no real way to gauge that. I just didn't know, and somewhere I felt she had the strength and instincts herself to do what she believed was right, or at least what she had to do.

They went back to Michigan, and for days I thought of little else. She seemed very sure that this was what she wanted and, after all, the money would be hers in a year anyway. She seemed sure, but she was only twenty years old, with no experience in the world at all, except for two semesters living alone in college. She had gone from one family to another. That was the part that frightened me the most. They seemed so close, so interdependent, like people who have fought a war or survived a catastrophe together. They were a kind of family, and perhaps she needed that, because I had failed her. I had given her everything else under the sun, blanketed her with gifts and love . . . and guilt.

". . . No, not guilt, really. I grew up on Madison Avenue, in a society where nothing means very much and everybody's terribly blase and terribly cynical and the game is to see who can be more blase and who can be more cynical. The buck is almighty . . . Your mind is pelted with the media, your classmates are erudite and ho-hum about everything. You read a lot of Kafka, you read a lot of Camus and really get in touch with the Science of Meaninglessness . . . But at some point you have to have something that is important to you, that you are in touch with and that you are making grow. The Free Press was that and much more. Just the fact that there was a paper and I participated in that paper was always there. It gave me an enormous feeling of pride."

Richard went through the roof, Jeff went with him, and Nat had a fit, but I sent the money. She had gone so far in search of something. I would go with her as far as I could.

Sometime after Christmas the phone rang. It was Jerry, the boy from North Carolina, where we did the first concert. He wanted to come to New York and look for a job, but he didn't have a place to stay. I said, sure, he could stay here. Everybody else did, why not? Besides, he could play the piano a little, and he was interested in music. It would be fun.

He'd only been around for a few weeks when he started talking about putting on another show. I said absolutely no. I had been through that, the weeks of being sick at my stomach getting it together, and for what? I had found out, even in my brief attempts, that audiences were not beating down my door demanding that I perform.

"They just don't know what you can do," Jerry kept insisting.

"Then the people of the world will just have to live with that huge hole in their lives."

"You know how well the show went in North Carolina, even with no rehearsal at all."

"That was a tiny town, and I had Harold then."

I knew very well it was not a good idea, but Jerry had one more way to get to me. He knew where the soft spot was.

"It's the only way to get the music going, to get it heard. If you do a show and it's successful, you'll get a record deal. How many years are you going to keep putting it under the couch?"

A few months later Jerry went to work for a company that booked road tours and bus and truck shows. Around April, on his own, he began to sound out theatre managers in Florida and Ohio. He got two firm offers and began to put together a budget. His plan was to do three shows in one area on a weekend, flying to, say, Cincinnati, hiring a bus to take us to Cleveland and Columbus.

"But, Jerry, those theatres are enormous, what would I do, sweep up?"

"They are all on subscription, you don't have to sell tickets, that's all done." He kept talking to theatre managers and I can only assume he is the world's greatest salesman. He put together a three-month tour, three shows every weekend. I still hadn't signed anything, but as long as I wasn't committed, it was all right to think about how much fun it could be. After all, there was no harm in that.

All that spring Cynth seemed fairly up when she called. They had moved into another house and she had a real room to sleep in. She still worked sixteen or seventeen hours, seven days a week, but she was reasonably healthy.

". . . I was getting really good at selling advertising, and I was putting out the best calendar in all of Michigan. I still meet people who say they bought the paper for that calendar."

Her calendar was two full pages of information and capsule reviews. The movie and the time for every theatre, every concert or gallery was listed, and every cabaret and restaurant. It was a staggering amount of work, and she was right. It was a thing of pride!

In March, a book came out about soap operas and Cynth decided to do the review herself. In a way, she came out of the closet. She had never publicly been my daughter before. She said some beautiful things about me, and when we talked about it she said, "I never really appreciated what you did or what you went through all those years until I had responsibility myself. You know, Maud, for a woman programmed in your time, you've done damn well."

As she had all her life, she zeroed in on a truth I had never recognized. It had never occurred to me that I was programmed, but of course I must have been. Every woman in my generation was. We grew up expecting to live our lives as wives and mothers. I had always wanted to be an actress, but somewhere underneath it all, the foundation, the bedrock of security and acceptance, probably even identity, had been marriage, and I had failed at that. All the years of the baddies, the whispering campaign in my head, the song with the words "you're inadequate," repeated over and over. All my lists of little daily failures that never seemed to account for the panic or the anguish. All those years, the buttons had been pushed. The elevator automatically stopped and made me view the ruin or the empty floor. It would probably always stop, maybe for the rest of my life, but the images evoked would never again fill me with fear and regret. What a gift, my little Maud, what a gift!

In May, Jeff invited me for a weekend in Washington. He gave me his room in the house he shared with four young people and whirled me through his city in his zippy red car. My son, my little boy, the baby I had held in my arms, walked me through the White House, opening every door with a wave and a casual, "Hi, just want to show Mom the Oval Office." My heart stopped only once, when someone said, "Don't open the drawer, Jeff, it's on red."

He was not a page or an intern, he had a terribly responsible job on Mr. Rockefeller's staff. He handled correspondence, explaining policy or the Vice-President's views on current topics. He prepared briefs for the Vice-President on documents ranging from congressional reports to newspaper and magazine articles, or books on current topics. He had also prepared, edited, produced, and distributed the Office Procedures and Correspondence Manuals, all by himself. For two days I listened and marveled. My father always said my brother and I could do anything, and I had always believed my kids could. It was almost as if a wind had begun way back on Jack Mountain in Virginia and was still blowing. I don't think I am one who moves. I have always been a stayer, but the wind went through. At least, I didn't hinder its passage. It was behind Jeff now. He would sail on and on.

In June, Jerry said I had to make up my mind about the tour. He pointed out that it was a good time if I was ever going to do it. "Search's" twenty-fifth anniversary was coming up in the fall, and there would be a lot of publicity. A number of people had said our songs were really closer to show tunes than popular music, maybe they would go over better presented in a show situation. One minute I was tempted, the next minute I was terrified, and all the time I knew I couldn't possibly do it. R. Bell would be out with Judy Collins and Brian's father was seriously ill. Without either of them the whole idea was silly.

Then I went to a Spinners concert and met a man named Frank Owens. I'd heard about him before. I knew he conducted for Petula Clark. Since I wasn't really serious, it was all right to sort of talk about the show, and he wasn't really interested. He said he never went out on the road, but he did say he'd like to hear some of the music. He listened for about an hour and said he would make an exception and go out of town. I was flattered, though not really optimistic. There was still too much to be done. I didn't even have backup singers. Then he just happened to mention that his wife, Beverly Henshaw, might do it, and she had a friend she always worked with, named Linda. I knew it was a wild idea and, really, just for fun, we all got together one night in my living room, the girls, Frank, Jerry, and I, to go over the music.

I should have known better. It had happened before. That magic, the first time I hear what other people bring, when all of us fit inside the music. It is absolutely irresistible. Even when I don't want to do it, I can't stop. You can say I go bananas, you can say I'm not rowing with both oars, you can say anything you like, and you would be right. I get hooked, I get carried away, and it's just like Mickey Rooney in all the old forties movies, shouting, "Hey, kids, I know where there's a barn! Let's put on a show!" Jerry brought over the little pile of contracts and I signed them.

There was still an awful lot to do, like writing the show, and the arrangements, and learning how to sing them. Jerry thought we should have a choreographer, and we would need someone for sound and lights. We needed gowns and costumes. Mickey Rooney always did it in a week, but we didn't have to worry about that—we had all summer. We wouldn't open until the first week in October.

When I spoke to Cynth during the summer, she often sounded tense, but I assumed that was because she was just too tired all the time. They still lived on practically no money, and for almost three years she had worked all the time, morning and night, day in and day out. Sometime in the summer she mentioned that she'd had a tooth filled without Novocain, because she had an ad appointment right afterward. She also started to talk more and more about Guerin, the tall, soft-spoken boy I had met at Christmas.

> "We were putting out the new Art Fair Guide, and I had to spend most of my time selling advertising. I just couldn't do the calendar by myself. Guerin started helping me on that. Also, Guerin and I were the only ones who felt strongly that we should make some changes in the paper. We'd made some, we had more local news, but George and Barbara wouldn't let us make that final step. We still had a huge international section. We knew that if we were going to make the paper go, we had to make it a more open and accessible organization. We had become a community newspaper."

She was tired and she was tense, but she was still determined. She believed the paper could be successful if they could just hang on. She was twenty-one that summer, and most of her friends were going into their senior year at college and thinking about graduate school. I know it was on her mind, but it was one of the few things we didn't talk about. She had chosen a different path, and she would walk it all the way. At least I would get to see her in September. She and Jeff would both be home for the big anniversary party.

On September 3, 1976, "Search for Tomorrow" celebrated its Twenty-fifth Anniversary, and Mary Ellis did it right. They hired the ballroom at the Plaza, and it was a black tie dinner dance to remember. Actually, I remember very little of it, because I spent most of the evening being interviewed for papers and magazines, but I have pictures to prove I had a wonderful time. Jeff came down from New Hampshire and Cynth flew in from Ann Arbor. I made my entrance between the two of them, and I walked down the grand staircase with Larry Haines.

It had been a long day, the kind that I take an hour at a

time. I had a difficult show, a couple of interviews, and in between I was trying to memorize my speech and arrange for the cocktail party at my house before the dinner. On those days I just say to myself, "Okay, this is right now, and then we'll think about that." Somehow it always gets done. There had been twenty-five years of those days, and too many of them had made me ill with fatigue and nervousness. This was the celebration, for survival, and for excellence, I suppose. There was certainly enough excellence to celebrate. Everybody connected with the show, even the ones I fought with, had done their best, what they thought was right. Perhaps they were right, at least we had made it, and we'd done it together. The show had been on the air longer than any show in television. We had the all-time record. That is something to be very proud of, and that is sort of what I said that night:

"Twenty-five years and a big party usually mean somebody is retiring. I feel I am just beginning and if that is the way I feel, then that is what is real for me.

"Twenty-five years! We talk about the years as though time has a reality of its own. Oh, I suppose it's a fact, or a lot of facts. It's also one hundred 13-week cycles. Funny, in all the years I have never been aware of when one began or ended. It's also a lot of shows, and I've never kept track of them, either. The only reality that had any meaning at all was what happened between the people, and there were so many wonderful people, so many millions of moments. I know the moments happened because I felt them. I felt that kiss of time as it passed.

"Twenty-five years is Korea, Kent State, Vietnam, Freedom Riders, Women's Rights and nude beaches. Twenty-five years is a lot of children born to us who have grown to be men and women. But when I look into these adult, thoughtful faces, it is the flicker of childish expression or gesture that recalls a moment from the reels of memory stored. It is not the birthdays counted or the year of graduation.

"Everyone, in the course of a lifetime, has choices to make and corners to turn. Corners must be turned blindly and some people settle along the block before they get there, never make the choice. Some people keep zigzagging through their lives. I wonder if they know what they are looking for, if they would recognize it, and how many times they pass it by unknowing.

"I am a very fortunate woman. Twenty-five years ago I turned a corner and came upon an empty space. It was not a plain or a meadow, not a field or a mountain. It was just a space. Three wise men, Charles Irving and Roy Winsor and Bill Craig, coming from three separate directions, turned corners in their own lives at almost that same moment, and came upon that same space, and they had an idea. Where there had been nothing, we built a town. People came to live there, they married and had children. They built businesses, kids went to school and grew up. People moved there from other towns, and it grew into a city.

"Oh, you can't find it on a map, and at night the houses and the shops come apart and are stored in scenery docks, but it is all real. If you don't believe me, ask millions of people all over the country and they will tell you it is real. Maybe a special kind of real that is a little gentler. It is a place to share a fantasy, an idea, a friend, or an emotion. The emotions are not play-pretend, we all know that and so do they. If that is not reality, I don't know what is.

"Many beautiful people have passed through our town. Some, like ornamental trees, have blossomed for a season and gone on to bloom again, or fade. A very special few have stayed and grown to giant, shady trees. Yes, we have roots and a history. We have a present and a past. Melba Rae and Bill Craig are forever part of that; and we have a future, for we continue. We are a happy never-ending. We are a lovely place to go, and where I want to be. Thank you, for making that possible."

Cynthia hugged me afterward and said, "Maud, I've never been so proud of anybody in the whole world." She went back to Michigan and Jeff went up to Dartmouth. He had taken one year off, but he decided that if he worked straight through the next two years he would graduate with his class.

After the anniversary party we had exactly a month to finish rehearsing the show. It was pretty much all written, except that we knew it would have to be trimmed here and there. My own music told stories about me, so we had used them as a kind of red line and filled in with all kinds of wonderful songs. We started with Beatles music and went all the way back to barbershop and the big band songs of the forties, and around again to disco music that the kids did by themselves, and Broadway show tunes. It had turned out to be more expensive than we had planned. The bills came in for rehearsals and Nat began to scream. The bills came in for costumes and gowns, and he screamed louder, but Nat always screams. It's his way of telling me he loves me. Of course, he also knew that the other shows had lost money. He didn't want that to happen again.

"Nat, we have contracts."

"I don't trust anybody."

"They are signed contracts, and the theatres are all on subscription. We can't lose. All we have to worry about is putting on a good show."

The closer we got to opening, the tenser I got, but the show itself had sort of taken over. There was music piled all over the house, and costumes filled one whole closet. There were also four thousand yellow balloons and two thousand posters. We rehearsed the dance numbers in a studio, and every night we ran musical numbers in my living room. Every afternoon when I got home from work I ran the whole show by myself with a cassette machine, and after I went to bed I went over all the rap.

The last week before we opened on Friday we were to have band rehearsals and run the whole show. We had rented the instruments and the equipment we would need. We had hired a sound man, and Jerry was going to double as lighting man and road manager.

The first booking was in Kentucky. We would do four shows there in a tiny theatre, and it had been set up as our tryout. We were doing it for almost no money to break in the show. I had "Search" that day, so I was a little late, but there was a lot to be done. They could start rehearsal without me. I got to Bill's rehearsal space, took the elevator to two, and had started back to studio A when Jerry stopped me. He looked upset, and I knew something was wrong.

"We've been canceled," he said. "I didn't want to tell you in front of everybody." Luckily there was a bench because I sat down suddenly.

"How can we be canceled?"

"They didn't sell enough tickets."

"I thought they didn't have to sell tickets. I thought it was all subscription."

"Well, in Kentucky it was different."

"I see . . . Well, that's a bummer."

"What do you want to do?"

"Cry."

"I mean about the rehearsal."

"I have to pay everybody anyway. Let's rehearse."

That rehearsal, I have to admit, was not easy. I had to go through it with energy and enthusiasm, and I still felt like crying. When I got home I did. I cried that night, and over the next couple of weeks I cried a lot more.

I started checking around the other theatres and discovered that there were no absolute assurances anywhere. The theatres were on subscription, but we weren't necessarily part of it. We were also not selling very many tickets. I went out to a couple of cities to try and get last-minute interest, but it was too late. Three more theatres canceled, which meant we would be working at a loss, and I couldn't afford it. Three weeks later, it was all over, except for one show in Roanoke, Virginia, and, truthfully, we should have been put out of our misery before that one. It was our dress rehearsal, our opening, and our closing. It could probably have been worse, though it is hard to imagine how. At the last minute, Linda couldn't go with us, so we had a new girl who had never sung the music and had never even heard of a big band. Jerry went ahead and hung all the lights, but he made one little error. He thought amber was the same as straw. What he wanted was a bright, sunny stage. What he got was pea soup. I couldn't see the faces in the audience, I couldn't even see the band, and what I did see of the dance number looked like a band of gypsies that had lost their wagon.

Sometime in that last month I got so tired and anxious I started to moan funny little involuntary sighs when I least expected it. The show had meant much more to me than I was willing to admit, and the sadness when it ended was long and deep. There was something I had finally gotten up the nerve to say that was never going to be heard, something that mattered enormously. For weeks when I woke in the night it was with a little cry, a moan.

After Roanoke, I walked into the apartment and hung the gowns on the back of a door. I put the guitar back under the piano and sat down to have a long think. It had been a failure, I knew that. I knew what was wrong with the show and I knew how to fix it, but it was too late and the disappointment made me feel sick. I sat there, going over and over the mistakes, for a long time. Then, out of nowhere, a word sort of clicked into my mind. Irrevocable. It was not irrevocable! It was not as though someone had been hurt, or real damage was done. Nothing had actually happened, except that I lost a few thousand dollars and my ego was battered around. I didn't stop crying for quite a while, but I knew I would in time, and I knew where to file the disappointment. It even fit alphabetically, right before expectation! The only thing I couldn't file were the moans. I still have them.

I called Cynth, mostly for selfish reasons. She always found the right things to say to make me feel better. I'm sure she tried, but I could tell she had things on her mind, too.

"We had expanded too fast and we were spending too much money. We were putting out an edition of the paper in Lansing, and that was costing us. We had salaries to pay and George kept insisting on equipment he said we couldn't do without. Booker was our business manager, and a good one, but even he couldn't stop George's spending. George kept saying, 'You never get big if you don't think big.' Guerin and I were the only ones against the Lansing edition. George called me a fiscal conservative . . . I worried about money all the time."

In November, I went out to visit Cynth and I was treated royally. There was a special dinner at the house for me, and George told glowing stories about their impending success. After

Christmas, it would be smooth sailing. They were putting out a big Christmas special and that one push was all they needed. Cynth told me privately that it was going well. She was in charge of advertising and it looked as if every page would be sold. The last night I was there she said George wanted to have dinner with us. He asked me to loan them five thousand dollars. I saw the look on Cynth's face, and I could tell she didn't know he was going to do that. It was only for two months, he said, just until all the revenue was in from the Christmas special. It was simply a matter of cash flow.

> "After Christmas it became apparent that there had been some misunderstandings about the money. We sold a ton of advertising, but George had spent the money on equipment and trade-outs, and there wasn't even enough to pay the printer, so we couldn't deliver what we had promised. There were some serious fights. By then, I had pretty much lost faith in everybody except Guerin. He was a close friend, always. Sometime before New Year's I said to Barbara that I thought I was falling in love with him, and everything began to change."

During January I knew something was wrong. When I called she was always out, and she rarely called me. When I finally did talk to her I said I was coming out, but she said not to. She said everybody in the house had the flu and there was no reason for me to catch it. I knew she was sick, I could hear it in her voice. Every morning I watched "The Today Show" to see what the temperature was in Michigan, and all that month it stayed below zero, with snow and ice.

> "During January they really closed in. It was like that first summer. I couldn't do anything right. I couldn't sell advertising and I was the reason we were in financial trouble. They came down on me, and they came down on Guerin. Maybe because I was sick anyway, I took it personally, and began to fall apart. I started shaking all the time, I couldn't think straight . . ."

In February I got a call from Cynth that she was coming home, maybe for good. I left a prepaid ticket at the airline, but two days later she called to say she had changed her mind.

"They told me to get out until I could get my act together, and I was about to do it, just walk away. Then, at the last minute I couldn't. I knew that if I didn't get it together there, I never would. I had to stay. But I made up my mind to do it on my own terms. I moved even closer to Guerin, to where he was emotionally. We had both seen the top of the mountain and decided not to climb, but there was still the paper. The paper was always there . . . just that fact was so important. We went to work on the Spring Special. It was harder. The paper had lost credibility, and we had to go to advertisers and say, 'The money you gave us is gone, now how would you like to invest in another project?' . . . That was the hardest part, but by then Guerin and I were both pretty much removed, no longer involved with the decisions."

She had almost come home, and I had a feeling that before too long she would, but it would only be when she was ready. I still watched for the weather reports, I still worried, and as I pieced together a picture of George, I found I was frightened of him. He was a selfish man with a single-minded purpose. He used people. He let no one get in his way.

At home all that spring there was a stillness. Brian's father died. They had been close all his life, and it was a terrible loss for him. It was his father who had bought the first guitar when Brian was five, and when he couldn't find a footrest small enough for such a little boy he made one himself. Brian didn't feel like making music for a long time.

R. Bell left Judy Collins' tour abruptly just before Christmas and had been in bad shape since. He was drinking too much, and despondent. When he came over he would stay too late, and very often he'd be sleeping on the couch in the morning. At least he was writing, and his music had plenty of room for feelings.

Grandmother was still on the road a good deal of the time, showing up sometime the first week of the month when her social security check came in. At least she called regularly, and wherever she was she listened to the radio. Anne Murray and Linda Ron-

stadt were her favorites. She appeared one afternoon with her little dark-blue coat and blue knitted hat, while R. Bell was playing.
She stood in the door for a few minutes before she said, "I like
that. Sing me that one." She sat down, but she didn't take off her
hat or her coat.

She was right, it was her kind of song; slow, easy country.
When Grandmother listens to a poem or a song she sits so still.
She folds her hands in her lap, like a good little girl in church,
and there is never a trace of an expression on her face.

> She would wait at night for his footsteps in the hall
> Supper filled the silence and the time.
> In his chair by the light,
> Like his shadow on the wall.
> Feelings filled the room without a sign.
>
> What he meant to say only echoes in his mind,
> Like a song but he's forgotten how it goes.
> Words all gone astray
> With the years he left behind.
> The distance cross the room is all that grows.
>
> He wonders why, he wonders why.
> Years go by, makes you wonder why.
>
> Then late one night slipping quiet from her dream
> Into moonlight shining cold across the room.
> In her gown of white,
> Humming softly till she seemed
> A young bride waltzing slowly with her groom.
>
> Round and round she turned holding memory in her hand
> Like flowers dry and withered with the years.
> And his body yearned for the day his life began
> While words of love were drowning in his tears.
>
> He wonders why, he wonders why,
> Years go by, makes you wonder why.

Grandmother nodded and drew the tear with her finger, then
unconsciously she turned the worn gold band, and I could tell her
arthritis was bothering her.

In June, Cynth called to say she was coming to New York

for a few days. I could feel her tension the minute she walked in the house and we spent the worst three days of our lives.

"They want to borrow ten thousand dollars."

"I haven't got it and I wouldn't lend it to them if I did."

"It's only for thirty days."

"That's what George said last November."

"It's safe this time, Maud. I told them I wasn't going to ask you unless it was guaranteed. They'll give you a lien on all the equipment as security, and God knows George has bought enough to secure the national debt."

"Little Maud, I just don't have it."

"Well, could you borrow it? . . . Really, it's only for thirty days."

"How do you know that?"

"We just have to rest our loan at the bank. George borrowed fifteen thousand dollars to tide us over the spring. Now Booker says all we have to do is show the bank we have the money and they'll renew the loan and give us another five."

"Do you trust Booker?"

"He said he'd quit if anybody defaulted on a loan from you."

"That wouldn't get my money back."

"I think it shows he's sincere . . . Maud, if you don't get the money back I'll leave the Free Press."

"Oh, no you don't! If you leave, it's because you want to. I'm not going to have that stand between us for the rest of our lives."

"If we don't get it, we're going to fold. That's the last thing George said before I left. He said, 'Don't come back without it.'"

"I don't give a damn about George."

"Neither do I, but I care about the paper."

"I know you do, love. I do know that." We both cried, and Nat was furious with me when I asked for the money. I didn't have it. I had to borrow, but I did insist they sign the papers, giving me a lien on the equipment. They sent the papers, I sent the money, and we entered phase two.

The minute they got the money they started pressuring Cynth again. George said they couldn't register the lien because the bank would find out they had borrowed money from someone else, and that would lessen their standing. He kept insisting it was just a formality anyway. Nat said the lien wasn't legal unless it was filed. I agreed to wait thirty days. If they hadn't paid the money I would not only register the lien, I would sue.

The first of July, Cynth called. She said, "I can't talk now. Are you going to be home tonight?"

"I am now, why?"

"I can't tell you now, but if you're out leave word on the service where I can reach you. It may be late."

It was after one when she called me from a pay phone on the street.

"Maud? . . . A funny thing happened today. I went to George and I said, 'What about my mother's money?' and he said there had been a little misunderstanding with the bank . . . It turned out that we owed the IRS fourteen thousand dollars, and the minute the money went into the bank they grabbed it. I asked him what he planned to do now, and he said he wants to come back up there and beg for mercy."

"I want you to come back up here, and stay!"

"I will, but not yet . . . It seems there is one more little misunderstanding. They didn't want you to register that lien because there were already two liens outstanding."

"That's fraud."

"I think that's what they call it . . . They lied, Maud."

"They fooled me too . . . Just get out of there. I'll leave a ticket."

"No, not yet. Call Nat, and tell him to wait a few more days, then file the lien. I'm sorry about the money, Maud."

"We'll worry about that tomorrow. I just want you out of there. Once I file that lien they know I can close them down, and God knows what they'll do."

"They don't know it yet. I'll be all right, but don't call me. Just leave a ticket and I'll see you soon."

I didn't hear another word for almost ten days. Then, about eleven o'clock one night, she walked into the kitchen. She was wearing jeans and an old tweed jacket. She had no luggage, just a big leather purse I'd given her years before. She hugged me, and I held on for a long time. Then she put the purse down on the washing machine and pulled out a dirty white envelope and started counting money into stacks. There was five thousand dollars in small bills.

"That's what took so long," she said. "I knew they had some money someplace, and they owe you too much. I wasn't going to leave without it."

"If I'd known you were taking that kind of a chance . . ."

"It's okay, Maud, it's okay. I'm home . . ."

". . . What they didn't realize, is that I would never not have a place to go to, and what I didn't realize for a long time, is that I would never not want to go there."

Guerin called the next morning to make sure she was all right, and then he started hitchhiking east to join her. He left the note saying they would not be coming back.

The two of them stayed around for about a month. Guerin fixed the hi-fi, rewired the lamps, and Cynth helped with the mail that had piled up all summer. Then they called a company that arranges to have cars driven to other cities. They would drive one to California, they said. They'd always wanted to see San Francisco. They would get jobs, maybe go back to school. They would see.

"We'd learned there was absolutely nothing we could not do. If there was something needed doing, we did it. It's quite a freeing experience. You find out that all those limitations you always thought were there aren't there at all. If you have to, you do it."

I did not need to worry ever again. The wind from Jack Mountain was behind her too.

In the fall, Barbara had put out one album of her own music and backed Rita Coolidge on one of hers. She toured with Rita and Kris Kristofferson for a while, and then settled into the Carlyle, in New York, playing the most elegant piano in town. Perc and Ernesto opened Rosemont Plantation in Woodville to the public, but there is one tiny tenant house with the big, old four-poster bed anytime I get to Mississippi.

I hadn't seen Betty Rea in a long time, probably because she is the busiest casting director in town. Awhile back, though, I had heard rumors that after Oliver divorced his third wife, he and Betty were back together. I talked to Didi, their oldest girl, when she got married, and she told me a kind of nice story. She and Betty had gone to Tiffany's to order the wedding announcements, and the saleslady was very upset about the wording of the parents' names. They were listed separately, but gave the same address. There was a lot of embarrassed hemming and hawing, until Didi got bored and cut it short.

"Look," she said, "print it and face it. They're living together."

Everybody's kids were grown, and like Lester's doodle for *No Exit*, the circles kept getting smaller, coming in on themselves. I decided it was probably time to get out the big red pot and do some serious thinking about what was probably the rest of my life.

I was often content
When my children were young
All the love that I craved
From small arms around my neck.
My days so full of their lives
And they gave me so much.
I was almost at peace
When I put them to bed.
All I needed was sleep
And the nights spent half listening
Were not quite alone.

Now my children are grown
And I have myself
Just myself as a reason for everything.
The small arms are graceful and long
Reaching out for a life of their own.
They are witty and kind when they tease,
And remember mistakes I have made.
I remember them too,
And the list is long as the hall to my
    bedroom at night
Past the rooms where they slept.

Sometime that summer, my little friend Audrey Eisman mentioned ever so casually she thought it was time I started writing a book.

"Search's" twenty-sixth year on the air! We had sweet writers, a pretty, feminine woman named Peggy O'Shea and an ex-actor named Jimmy Lipton, who wrote elegantly articulate words for us. The Hartford House was beautiful and I was so proud of it, you'd have thought it was real and we truly owned it. Ned Stark was still directing us and doing some of the most beautiful camera work we had ever had on the show. So many of the big, complicated shows fell to him because he knew how to handle them, and the results were stunning.

We had a new director named Bob Schwartz, who liked to experiment and had enormous regard for actors. Nothing was indelible until the show was finally taped, and he carried an eraser on a long string around his neck to prove it. He also spoke excellent Yiddish and told great jokes in a gentle, offhand manner every morning before rehearsal began.

"Did you hear about the two girls from the Salvation Army who were taking a shower after a long parade? One of them said, 'Excuse me, but you have the biggest navel I think I've ever seen,' and the other one said, 'Okay, tomorrow you carry the flag.'"

Bob Getz was still associate producer and had turned out to be one of the nicest, and certainly the handsomest, ever. The biggest change came from Cincinnati. We had the first woman representative from the company. Gail Kobe is a petite, stylish young woman with a background in acting. She cared about the show and was deeply involved. Mary Ellis was, of course, the producer, and the best we had ever had. She seemed to enjoy the new position, and God knows she had earned it, but I know she was bothered by the distance that grew, by necessity, between her and the cast. She had spent her whole career with us and would never get over, or forget, our family feeling, our history. She made the decision, but she broke down and cried when she told me Carl would no longer be on contract.

Peter and Courtney were both restless and talking about

leaving the show. Chris Lowe thought he would take a leave of absence if they went. He was going into high school and it was more important than doing a show. He would leave, but two more teenagers had joined us. Andrea McArdle was starring on Broadway in *Annie* and Lisa Peluso took her place. Lisa is a beautiful girl with astonishing emotional power. That year, she was twelve and just beginning to giggle, and I called her Kate. The other new addition was Stacy Moran, who came in to play Suzi when Suzi suddenly aged a few years. Stacy is beautiful in another way, and right now swimming is more important than show business. She is my pet and I call her Tallulah.

We still carried within the family our own continuity. Our stage manager, Peter Brinkerhoff, and our assistant director, Charles Dyer, were both preparing to direct. In the office, Gail Starkey seemed to move up every week and Bonnie Bogard reminded me very much of Mary Ellis a few years ago.

We'd moved back to the production center, and while some things were the same, others seemed very different. The makeup room was the same but there were twice as many actors in the cast.

Joel was overworked and cross enough to quit every couple of weeks. Thank God, he didn't, and a beautiful girl named Fran Paris was fixing our hair. We were in the same studio, but the sets were so big, and there were so many of them, the cameras could barely move.

One day, the big terrace behind the Collins' mansion was set up for breakfast, and the crew was stapling smilax to the plastic brick walls made in the shop downstairs. The shop had also stamped out the paneling in the lawyers' office and the rough, gray stone of the prison cell. Just behind the cell a tree was growing out of a grass mat, and there was another terrace with bright awnings and gay tablecloths. If you turned right, there was a small hospital office and a large intensive care unit.

That morning in the early rehearsal, Millee was upset. Her car went out of control and she nearly had an accident. It hadn't been her year. Her house burned down, her husband had a heart attack, and she was seriously ill herself a couple of times. She was late once or twice, and we taped early for her a couple of times, but she never missed a show and as long as she could talk she did lovely scenes and she was funny.

"Millee, what are you giving the kids for Christmas?"

"Baltimore." She even saw the bright side of losing her home. She could start decorating again.

Marie had been on the road with a play and was flying in for the show. She was tired and cross, and Val ran out of patience. They had a blowup in rehearsal and Val stomped out of the room, straight into a closet. No one else would have had the guts to come out, but by then it was over. Val is the dearest man on the show, and a wonderful actor who cares more about each performance and everybody than is probably possible.

After rehearsal, there was a brief meeting of the cast to elect Louis Arlt as our AFTRA representative. The business had changed. Hours were longer, shows were being done in segments, and negotiations with the network were coming. Louis played David Sutton, with a strength and sensitivity reminiscent of Ken Harvey.

At the production center there are miles of hallways to pass through, no matter where you are going. They are all immaculate, cream-colored paint with modern prints hung every now and then. There are also back halls, lined with the paraphernalia of our weekday lives; there are trees and shrubs and potted plants, furniture in huge cages marked with the show and the family names. There are hundreds of yards of carpets and drapes, and flats stacked and ready. Outside the rehearsal halls, little knots of actors always run lines and you can overhear some bizarre conversations.

"Do you think she's really insane?"

"I'm not sure, but I know she shot Sally."

The newsmen pass through the halls, producers, directors, stagehands, technicians, production staff, security guards, writers, secretaries, and actors. You can't walk twenty feet without seeing somebody, and for me, I will admit, there is always enormous pleasure in the sound of "Hi, Mary!"

I don't count them, but no matter what else has been going on, I can walk through the halls and feel a lot better. Sometimes, somebody says something nice about a show we've done together over the years. Sometimes it's something they've seen me do, but usually it's simply, "Hi, Mary." It's enough. I belong. CBS has never put a picture of me in the catalogue of their shows, and I was not included in the Fiftieth Anniversary show, or even the photograph. I've been nominated five or six times for Emmys by the membership, but I can't seem to get past that magic panel of ten at the Academy, so I don't have a doorstop. It doesn't matter as much as I thought it would. Twenty-seven years of, "Hi, Mary," makes up for a lot.

Saying goodbye is always the hardest kind of show to do. Lord only knows how many funerals we have had over the years, and they are painful because somebody we have worked with is not going to be around. Funerals are also difficult for the directors, because there are a lot of people and they are boring because nobody has much to do except sit around and heckle the bereaved.

Far and away the finest funeral we ever had was Steve Kaslo's. Joel Higgins was to deliver the eulogy, and everybody knew he was appearing off-Broadway playing a preacher man, so, in dress rehearsal, as he walked down the aisle to the front of the chapel somebody called out, "Give us the word, Brother, give us the word."

Higgins hesitated for one split second, then he stepped up to the podium, wheeled around to the assembled mourners, spread his arms wide, shot his cuffs, and let it all hang out.

"Brothers and Sisters! . . . Do you hear me?"

"We hear you, Brother."

"Do you know why we are here?"

"Tell us, Brother."

"We're here to celebrate! Celebrate, Lord Jesus! This boy has gone to heaven!"

"Amen."

For fully five minutes, Higgins let his voice roll and thunder out across that studio, extolling the virtues of that dear, dead boy, "called away in his prime, O Lord! to his reward in Hollywood!" and the chorus responded, "Amen, Brother, amen."

It was a good day. It was a fine, fine day, and we ended that rehearsal in a rousing chorus of "Lord Won't You Buy Me a Mercedes-Benz."

All goodbyes are difficult, and when somebody leaves the show there is a party and nobody wants to go. When it's somebody's last show, I pick up a script and read through it the night before, and I know if it's going to be really bad. I knew it was one of those days when Higgins left. I cried when I read it. Higgins was my boy. We had worked together for almost four years, we had sung together every Christmas, and I just plain loved him. I knew that. I also knew he had to leave and we had to play the scene. I would be sad and the tears would flow on the air, but up to then we would make a lot of jokes and pretend it wasn't happening. At least that is what I figured until we sat down in our folding chairs in the rehearsal hall in the morning and started to run the lines and I couldn't do it. I couldn't get the words out. I couldn't even see the script.

"I liked you better when you were Robby Benson," I tried to make jokes and it didn't help, I just couldn't do it. He was really leaving, it wasn't play-pretend, and I was going to miss him terribly. He was sad too, and he hugged me and that made it a whole lot worse, and we actually gave up. Somebody else read the words and timed it.

When I talked about the real emotion that has gone into all those shows, I guess that is what I meant. The tenderness and the love, that is real, that is all real. Oh, we did the show, and I managed to control, and that's what the scene was about anyway. Jo didn't want Bruce to see how sad she was. Only one place in the scene nearly finished me even on the air. I had to look at the picture he'd brought me of his baby girl and say, "Someday she'll grow up and you'll have to say goodbye to her, then you'll know how it feels."

A couple of days later, Keith Charles, who happens to be one of the actors I greatly admire, stopped me in the hall.

"Mary, you did a beautiful scene with Higgins I just happened to catch. I love to watch you work."

I told him how difficult the scene had been, and by then I could sort of laugh about it, but just the fact that he bothered to mention it mattered so much. The emotion, the love shared with my buddy, and the admiration of a peer. Mix that in with a few "Hi, Marys," and it's not a bad life, not a bad life at all.

"Hi, Mary! My God, don't you ever change?"

"Haven't got time. Besides, my contract forbids it."

"Hi, Mary, how are the kids? I remember when they were a belly we had to shoot over."

"Careful, you'll give your age away—or, worse yet, mine."

"Hi, Mary. Worked your show last week, but you weren't on."

"As long as you call it my show, I'm there somewhere."

"Hi, Mary, saw you on the news last night, and I told my wife, 'Now that's Mary!'"

"Yeah, that's Mary, hanging in."

"Hi, Mary. It makes me feel good just to see you."

"Then give me a hug, Lonnie. Give me a big hug."

"Hi, Mary! Hey, it's good news, guys, Mary has inserts, we'll be out in half an hour."

"Hi, Mary. Say, remember the good old days?"

"When we felt like we were putting on a show?"

"This isn't show business."

"No, but it sure beats working."

"Hi, Mary! Lookin' good."

"God knows, I try. So do Frank and Joel!"

"Hi, Mary! You never come up to the office anymore."

"Well, I just wanted to ask you something, Mary Ellis. We've worked together for a long time, and you've seen me at my worst and my best. From the inside, it's hard to tell what that's like to other people. Tell me honestly."

"Quite honestly, friend, I've seen you in too many situations I didn't think anybody could manage . . . all the anger . . . the years of pressure . . . the petty jealousy. But I don't recall a single day you didn't handle—with grace."

"Thank you, buddy. I needed to know."

My bedroom faces east and north, and in the morning from my bed I can see the sun drawing pink outlines around the buildings just before it climbs straight up out of the Long Island

Sound and begins its daily run down the East River, around the Battery, and its long, fiery descent into New Jersey. Jeff says, "How else would you go to Jersey."

It is probably a New Yorker's view of the world, and I think I'm finally one of them. It is where I always wanted to be, and it's everything I had hoped.

So many years ago I started out looking for a fantasy, looking for a feeling, and it's all here, everything is here. There is privacy and anonymity, but any time of day or night there are other people somewhere near. It is lonely, there is anger and desolation and fear, but there is power and energy, too, and if there was not human kindness like a huge rubber band around us all this city would not be possible. It is filthy, but it is grand and proud. It is hopeless, but around the corner there is a possibility. You only have to stand for an hour, watching people go by, to realize, whether you like it or not, every single soul in the world is an individual.

I'm one of the luckiest, and I know it well. I live in a neighborhood, as everyone does in the city. I am simply Mary to all the shopkeepers, and I do not shop with cash. I buy everything within a few blocks of my door, so if a check bounces now, I don't have far to go. If I like something, I tend to buy more than one. I don't know whether that is a sign of laziness or lingering insecurity. It certainly isn't affluence. I guess I just wasn't meant to be rich. I tried the stock market a few more times but the results were so disastrous I began to worry about the companies I had invested in. My last major move was into New York City bonds two days before the papers announced that the city was probably bankrupt. Now I'm afraid to buy U.S. savings bonds for fear of taking the whole economy down with me. I do, however, have enough to take taxis without thinking twice. I have a dozen silk dresses and I can run up the street in my sneakers and get a hair cut without once looking in the mirror. That may be the greatest luxury of all.

Somewhere along the line, I guess I acquired some charm, or what passes for it. At least, I feel fairly comfortable in most groups. That does not, however, include cocktail parties. I feel about them the way Grandpa felt about beans. He said, "I don't

like beans and I'm glad I don't like beans, because if I liked them
I'd eat them, and I don't like them."

On June 1, 1978, I woke early, made coffee, and packed my
bag. Cynth had come in from California the night before, and
the two of us were flying to Hanover for Jeff's graduation. I was
in the shower when I heard Lucille's voice.

"There's a suitcase out there. You coming or going?"

That was a question she always asked since the day she very
carefully put everything away just before I was to leave. It was
the only mistake in our ten years together, and I daily look forward to the sound of her quick little footsteps in the hall and her
constant admonition, "I'll do that!" She is a beautiful woman
and a wonderful friend. She feels her only failure in life was not
making a lady out of me. Anything else she knows she can do, so
she does it.

Cynth took a shower and washed her hair. That had been
the only shock. It was curly. I was sure she thought it made her
look older, but to me she looked eighteen again and so beautiful
she almost made me cry.

We were to stay at Maud's house. It was either that or the
dormitory, and the choice was obvious, though I hadn't realized
her girls would have to sleep on the floor to make room. Six
women in one house, and if anyone called Maud we all answered,
but it was a good time to be together and close.

Everybody was together and close. It was like a replay of my
life with Richard, before the kids were born. John and Jane were
there, as Jeff's godparents, and his very close friends. When he
started moving out on his own, they were one of the first directions he went, and as Jeff said, "There was nothing personal, all
those years. They just don't like little kids."

Joan and Tom Braden were there because one of the eight
they wrote the book about was graduating too. So many people I
hadn't seen in years. There were parties and lunches and dinners,
and Jeff had arranged a schedule for every waking moment.

The first night was a party at the McLanes. The first weekend Richard and I spent away was at their house twenty-five years
before. Charlie McLane, who went up the ski slope like a Christmas tree. The tender man who sat one night with two children

on his lap and another peeking over the arm of the couch. I had asked how old the little boy was, and Charlie looked at him for a puzzled moment and said, "He's not very old." The boy was grown now, but Charlie and Carol were just the same. A little older, but not all that much, and still reaching out in all directions. The Bradens were just as I remembered, too. Joan talked with the same brisk intensity, and Tom was still the boy with a cold smile. John and Jane were the real pleasure, and one I had missed.

"You're really writing a book, Mary?"

"Really going to try, John."

"Well, it better be truthful, you know how you are."

"It'll be the truth according to Mary."

"I'm glad for you, and impressed. Writing is hard."

"If I get in trouble will you help?"

"You won't get in trouble. You've come a long way."

There was a time I would have thought it condescending, but that's not the way he meant it. It was just the truth according to John. The truth according to Jane was, as always, a revelation. Jane had done so much and was still having a wonderful time! She had gone into real estate, I'm sure, because she was really good at arranging other people's lives. She knew where they should live. She also knew that somebody had to save the beautiful, old houses and restore them. She knew somebody had to fight the power company so the cables would not be strung across the most beautiful sections of the county, and she got a bullhorn for Christmas so she could personally chase hunters away from the wild ducks that came for the winter.

I watched her talk with Cynth and old memories came back. She didn't seem to make statements, she asked questions, but the answer was hidden somewhere inside. It was good to see John again. It was good to see Jane.

Saturday afternoon, Jeff and his girl gave a party for thirty or forty people, and Saturday night Richard took everybody to dinner and gave Jeff the watch his father had given him. Richard often covered emotion with a joke, but no man ever cared more for a son and a daughter, and they both knew that.

The circle kept coming around. Sunday morning Richard

and I stood together on the sunny field with all the other proud parents.

"Richard, maybe it's not the time to ask, but how do you feel about the book?"

"It's one of the more anxiously awaited publications."

"Do you want to read it before I send it in?"

"No, it's your story, you tell it."

"There will be a lot of anger."

"I suppose so. There were a lot of disappointments."

"It went both ways. I'll be telling my side."

"That figures."

"Of course, someday you'll probably write a book too, and—"

"Mary Stuart! For the last time! I do not want to write a book! I never wanted to write a book! I just want to enjoy my life!"

He said the words so patiently, with only an edge of exasperated tenderness, of quiet desperation. We laughed and he hugged me.

The speeches were over and the honor students marched by. Jeff had distinguished himself scholastically, and as the senior editor for *The Dartmouth*. He graduated with honors in a double major, and his columns for the paper covered everything from college drinking to Kissinger as a network newscaster. He waved to us once or twice. Then we lost him again in the sea of black. At least we heard them call his name.

"We must have done something right, old friend."

"Either that or we got awful lucky."

"Both, I think, a little of both. He did the rest."

Richard held my hand and loaned me his handkerchief. We had a drink together and it was all over. Jane and John offered to drive Cynth and me to the airport, and Richard would stay to help Jeff get his stuff together. Jeff had the diploma, but all the way home I kept feeling like I had graduated.

I was always taught not to speak to strangers, and it is a rule I have never followed. However, the rail of a man who wandered unsteadily through the delicatessen leaning on a gold-handled cane, wearing the latest thing from the dustbins and smelling strongly of alcohol, gave me pause to wonder if perhaps there was not some truth in Mother's words. He said, "Who are you, pretty lady?" and Joe answered for me. After all, it was his deli.

"Don't you know her, Gardner? She's on television."

"Oh? . . . And what do you do?"

"I act."

"Well, I'm very sorry, but I've never seen you."

"That's okay. Watch tomorrow, I'm going to sing."

"What time should I do that? I'll have to make arrangements. I don't have a television."

"Oh, about twelve-thirty."

I assumed he would not remember the show or the conversation and went home to cook my supper. The next day flowers and a note arrived and a friendship began with Gardner Brown. He taped the song I sang that day, and over the next few weeks he taped everything I had written. When he heard I was writing a book he took his tapes down to Doubleday and gave them to his friend Sandy Richardson. Then, he brought Sandy to my house and stayed sober almost all evening while Sandy and I talked. Sandy already knew me. His daughter Wendy had seen me on television when she was about fourteen.

"I want you to watch somebody I like," she had said, and for four or five years he had noticed me. He liked what he had seen me do, he liked the little poems and he was interested in publishing my book.

Audrey had said it was time for a book. Sandy said, "Write one for me." But there was still one person whose opinion mattered more than all the rest.

Dear Jeff,

Tried to call but the phone in your dorm is obviously used only for outgoing calls since it is either busy or ignored. Perhaps a letter is best, since the question is serious and I may need proof of reply in years to come. How would you feel about your mother writing a book? It would be about me and you and Cynth and Dad and invade a lot of privacy, so think about it.

Would you mind? Is it a terrible idea altogether? SERI-OUSLY, do you think I can do it?

While setting down your answer, bear in mind that I have given you my all these many years and have not paid the tuition for your senior year.

Love, Mom

Dear Mother,

Of course I think you can—and should—do a book. Yours is a great story, and who better to tell it?

I know you are worried about making our private lives the stuff of public consumption. But it strikes me that what you've been doing all your professional life is sharing your private, original person with countless audiences. As long as you are willing to give and share more of yourself, we are certainly willing to stand beside you.

I admit I used to resent that you were such a public person. I used to wonder if we were as important to you as we would be if you had no public to care for.

But I have changed the way I feel. I've certainly basked in more than my share of true motherly love and affection and worry and care. In fact, we are all better off that you had other outlets for your energy, or you would have driven us crazy long ago.

I respect what you are, admire what you've done and, unashamedly, love you very much. So go to it.

Assuming I have taken the whole matter seriously enough and will be continuing my education, one note of caution: Mother, for God's sake, get a good editor. Whatever else you may be, you are the world's worst at spelling, grammar and punctuation. Whatever fears I might have about exposing our lives to public view, the thought of a whole book without a comma or a capital letter is the most chilling of all.

Cheers, Jeff

About a week later, Sandy took me to lunch at "21" with Carolyn Blakemore. She is a senior editor at Doubleday and a wise, wonderful woman, so it is probably not important that she is not a perfect speller. She is nowhere perfect, and we get along fine.

That was the winter of 1977. It's been two years and the pile of pages is very high. Grandmother is fine, but if you ask me where she is I will ask you what time it is. Both kids are great. Jeff is assistant to a vice-president at Time, Inc. He has a sense of history and will probably spend his life where decisions and policy are made. Cynth is more concerned with people individually. She worked as a waitress so she could intern at a public television station out west. She was hired as a reporter but wound up doing a little of everything. Two of the shows she produced were about children who had been abused or violated and children who had been abandoned. She did the research herself, wrote them, did the on-camera interview and the editing. They are both being used as training films now, to help other children talk about their problems.

I'm still Hannah Homemaker and Nancy Neat. I'll probably always be Rhoda Romance, and Agatha Author has been around a lot lately. None of them will ever be perfect, they're all just me, but I'm not being one at a time anymore. Isn't that amazing!

I'm still not sure I can write a book and I'll never feel it's finished, but it is time now. I've done my best and that is all I can ask. Jack Mountain is very far away, but of course I always leave the windows wide, and every now and then I think I feel a breeze.

TO BE CONTINUED

V2